WOODROW WILSON

and the Progressive Era

1910–1917

The

New American Nation Series

EDITED BY

HENRY STEELE COMMAGER

AND

RICHARD B. MORRIS

Please renew/return this item by the last date shown.

So that your telephone call is charged at local rate,
please call the numbers as set out below:

	From Area codes 01923 or 0208:	From the rest of Herts:
Renewals:	01923 471373	01438 737373
Enquiries:	01923 471333	01438 737333
Minicom:	01923 471599	01438 737599

L32b

WOODROW WILSON

AND THE
PROGRESSIVE ERA
1910-1917

BY

ARTHUR S. LINK

ILLUSTRATED

HAMISH HAMILTON

LONDON

First published in Great Britain, 1954

by Hamish Hamilton Ltd.

90 *Great Russell St., London, W.C.*1

Printed in the United States of America

For My Mother and Father

Contents

EDITOR'S INTRODUCTION   xi

PREFACE   xv

1. THE NEW NATIONALISM VERSUS THE NEW FREEDOM   1

2. THE NEW FREEDOM   25

3. THE NEW FREEDOM AND THE PROGRESSIVE MOVEMENT, 1913–16   54

4. MISSIONARY DIPLOMACY   81

5. MEXICO: INTERFERENCE AND DEFEAT, 1913–17   107

6. AMERICAN NEUTRALITY, 1914–15   145

7. THE PREPAREDNESS CONTROVERSY, 1914–16   174

8. DEVIOUS DIPLOMACY, 1915–16   197

9. PROGRESSIVISM AND PEACE: THE CAMPAIGN OF 1916   223

10. FROM PEACE WITHOUT VICTORY TO WAR   252

ESSAY ON SOURCES   283

INDEX   315

Illustrations and Maps

These photographs, grouped in a separate section,
will be found following page 140

1. WOODROW WILSON
2. WILLIAM HOWARD TAFT
3. THEODORE ROOSEVELT
4. GIFFORD PINCHOT
5. SENATOR JONATHAN P. DOLLIVER
6. SENATOR WILLIAM E. BORAH
7. Wilson Being Inaugurated by Chief Justice Edward D. White, March 4, 1913.
8. Wilson and His Cabinet, 1913
9. LOUIS D. BRANDEIS
10. OSCAR W. UNDERWOOD
11. CHAMP CLARK
12. CARTER GLASS
13. WILLIAM J. BRYAN
14. ROBERT LANSING
15. EDWARD M. HOUSE
16. FRANCISCO VILLA
17. VICTORIANO HUERTA
18. GENERAL VENUSTIANO CARRANZA with His Staff
19. BRIGADIER GENERAL JOHN J. PERSHING
20. "Horse Marines" in Vera Cruz
21. Pershing and the Staff of the Punitive Expedition

22. Sir Edward Grey, British Foreign Secretary
23. Theobald von Bethmann-Hollweg, Imperial German Chancellor
24. The Great Preparedness Parade, May 13, 1916
25. Charles Evans Hughes in 1916
26. Governor Hiram Johnson
27. Wilson on Campaign Tour, 1916
28. Wilson Reads His War Message to Congress, April 2, 1917

Maps

The United States and the Caribbean, 1913–1917   95
The United States and Mexico, 1913–1916   110
The Submarine Enters Modern War   158

Editors' Introduction

A HALF century ago the House of Harper launched the American Nation series under the editorship of the distinguished historian, Albert Bushnell Hart. There had been earlier co-operative works of this kind—Justin Winsor's *Narrative and Critical History of America* comes to mind—but none on the scale of the American Nation series, none as comprehensive, none as effectively designed for scholar and layman. The principle behind the original American Nation series, which is now out of print, was simple enough: that the history of America was too large and complex for any one scholar to master and present, and that its adequate presentation must be, therefore, of necessity, a co-operative enterprise.

The American Nation series, ultimately completed in twenty-seven volumes, established itself at once as an authoritative synthesis of the historical scholarship of that day. Affectionately known to two generations of American students and scholars, it exercised a pervasive influence on the study and teaching of American history. Some volumes, by virtue of scholarly originality, philosophical insight, or literary charm, quickly became classics; others pioneered along new paths of historical discovery, stimulated new investigations, inspired new points of view.

It is no criticism of the American Nation series to observe that it represented the scholarship and the point of view of the turn of the century rather than of the mid-twentieth century. The discovery and exploitation of new and rich mines of source material, the deepening and broadening of historical investigations, the importunate advance of new points of view, all these have operated to make most of the volumes of the older series inadequate to the needs of our generation. It is for this reason that the House of Harper is once again launching a comprehensive co-operative survey of the history of the area now known as the United States from the days of discovery to the mid-twentieth century. It is hoped that this new series will perform for our generation the service that the original American Nation series performed for two earlier generations.

When, back in the days of Jackson, George Bancroft inaugurated his massive *History of the United States,* he could look forward with some confidence to mastering the events and the problems he planned to describe and explain. Yet even in his own lifetime, and before he had completed his Author's Last Revision, readers found his range of interest too narrow, his interpretation too partisan, his philosophizing too simple, for the illumination of the past. Already before the turn of the century the age of specialization had set in, and with it the fragmentation of the past, chronologically and topically. In recent years, as we have come to see not only how complex are the threads that make up the tapestry of the past, but how dependent each is on the others in making a recognizable pattern, there has developed a determined effort to overcome the evils of excessive specialization and fragmentation. Our own generation has not only broadened the scope of history to embrace such interests as science, technology, public administration, religion, economics, and similar subjects, but has developed a new inter-disciplinary approach to the problems of historical interpretation and presentation. The time has now come for a judicious appraisal of the findings of the new history, a cautious application of the new techniques of investigation and presentation, and a large-scale effort to achieve a synthesis of the new findings with the traditional facts, and to present the whole in attractive literary form.

To this task the New American Nation Series is dedicated. Each volume is part of a carefully planned whole, and co-ordinated with other volumes in the series; at the same time each volume is designed to be complete in itself. Some overlapping is doubtless inevitable, but it has seemed to the editors that overlapping is less regrettable than omissions, and from time to time the same series of events and the same actors will be seen from different points of view. While for the most part the series follows a chronological organization, separate volumes or groups of volumes will be devoted to cultural history, constitutional history, and foreign affairs.

It is in many ways appropriate that this first volume to appear in the new series should address itself to a period which was in part the subject of the final volume of the original American Nation series: Frederick Austin Ogg's *National Progress, 1907–1917.* The difference in scope and even in title suggests something of the change in perspective and in approach that the new series reflects. Professor Link devotes half again as much space to roughly half the period of years covered by Professor Ogg's book, and he is by no means as confident as was his predecessor that these years spell progress. An immense body of new evidence, and perhaps a more critical attitude toward that evidence, has enabled Professor Link to tell a more complete and better balanced story than it was possible to tell a generation ago. Into this volume Professor Link has distilled the results of years of research in the career of Woodrow Wilson and the prodigious events which make that career so significant. Based upon an impressive body of documentation, this volume considers the dilemma which confronted progressives in the first Wilson administration, and appraises the President's plans and achievements on both the domestic and the international scene. Professor Link's volume will be preceded in the series by a study of Rooseveltian progressivism and the challenge which it evoked, and followed by a volume on the First World War and the collapse of Wilsonian idealism and internationalism in the twenties, while other volumes will tell the story of cultural and constitutional developments during these crucial years when the United States was emerging into world power.

HENRY STEELE COMMAGER
RICHARD BRANDON MORRIS

Preface

THIS book represents an attempt to comprehend and re-create the political and diplomatic history of the United States from the beginning of the disruption of the Republican party in 1910 to the entrance of the United States into the First World War in 1917. Every scholar thinks the period he is studying is the most important interval in history, and I perhaps have an exaggerated notion of the significance of the events I relate. Even so, none can doubt that these were momentous and terrible years, not only for the American people, but for all mankind. In this country the great progressive movement found its first culmination in the formation of the Progressive party, the election of Woodrow Wilson to the presidency, and, above all, the enactment by Congress from 1913 to 1917 of a comprehensive reform program. How this came about and how progressives found an answer to the great dilemma that had divided their ranks and confounded some of their leaders—this constitutes my first theme. At the same time Europeans attempted to solve the dilemmas created by rival imperialisms and nationalisms by appealing to the God of battles. How the American people and government were eventually drawn into the vortex of this awful struggle is my second theme.

In this volume I have attempted to synthesize the results of five years of research that I made for the next three volumes of my biography of Woodrow Wilson, which will cover Wilson's first administration. The present book is, therefore, in the nature of an outline of my larger, more detailed, and more copiously documented study. As this volume is based almost exclusively upon research in the sources, I have included secondary works in my footnotes only when I was specifically indebted to them. The literature on this period, none the less, is already varied and rewarding; and in the bibliographical essay I have tried to present and describe it in a way that will prove useful to students and scholars.

It is now my pleasant duty to acknowledge my deep obligation to the institutions whose financial assistance made it possible for me to do the research for this volume. The Princeton University Research Committee extended several grants during the period 1946–49. From 1950 to 1951 the John Simon Guggenheim Memorial Foundation, the College of Liberal Arts of Northwestern University, and the Northwestern University Research Committee all co-operated to enable me to leave Evanston for fifteen months of sustained research. I can never fully express my gratitude to Mr. Henry Allen Moe of the Guggenheim Foundation, to Dean Simeon E. Leland of the College of Liberal Arts, and to Professor Gray C. Boyce, chairman of my Department, for their indispensable help and encouragement.

In writing this book, moreover, I have leaned so heavily upon the counsel of my friends that I like to think it is a co-operative undertaking. From the beginning of my research Professor Edward Mead Earle of the Institute for Advanced Study has sustained my determination. Moreover, he read the manuscript and made many suggestions. I am indebted to the editors of this series, Professors Henry Steele Commager and Richard B. Morris, for their help and suggestions. Every page of this book bears testimony to their contribution. Professor Morris also assumed the onerous tasks of cutting my overly copious footnotes and seeing the manuscript through the last stages before publication. My colleagues, Professors Richard W. Leopold and Ray A. Billington, both read the manuscript and saved me from many errors, as did Professor Charles Seymour, President Emeritus of Yale University, Professor George E. Mowry of the University of California, Los Angeles, Professor Edward H. Buehrig of Indiana University, and Mr. John W. Davidson of the Manuscripts Division, Library of Congress. In addition, my former colleague and now head of the Hispanic-American Division of the Library of Congress, Dr. Howard F. Cline, read Chapters 4 and 5 with care and discrimination. He helped me find my way through the maze of Mexican politics and revolutions.

I gratefully acknowledge the permission granted by the Yale University Library and Mr. Charles Seymour to use quotations from the

diary and letters of Edward M. House and Frank L. Polk; by Mr.
Allen W. Dulles to use quotations from the diary and letters of Robert
Lansing and by the Yale University Library and Professor Sherman
Kent to use quotations from the papers of William Kent.

I must also thank Mr. Konrad C. Mueller, formerly of Harvard
University, for his help in translating German documents and news-
papers; three of my graduate students at Northwestern, Messrs. Edward
Lurie, David W. Hirst, and Gerald N. Grob for their assistance in
checking proof, footnotes, and bibliography; as well as Dr. Marion
McKenna of Hunter College and Mr. Cass Canfield and Mrs. Beulah
W. Hagen of Harper & Brothers for their aid in preparing the manu-
script for publication.

Finally, to my wife, Margaret Douglas Link, I owe a debt I can
never describe or repay. She has not only inspired my work at every
stage but has also been my best collaborator.

A. S. L.

Evanston, Illinois
February 22, 1953

WOODROW WILSON

and the Progressive Era

1910–1917

CHAPTER 1

The New Nationalism
Versus the New Freedom

THE ELECTION of 1912 marked the culmination of more than twenty years of popular revolt against a state of affairs that seemed to guarantee perpetual political and economic control to the privileged few in city, state, and nation. The uprising that came so spectacularly to a head in the first years of the twentieth century—the progressive movement—was the natural consummation of historical processes long in the making.

To begin with, the philosophy of *laissez-faire* individualism, upon which the exploitative and competitive system depended for ideological justification, had suffered steady erosion by the writings of neo-democrats like Henry George, Lester F. Ward, and Henry Demarest Lloyd. By 1900 the ideal of an individualistic society had given way, at least in the minds of many intellectuals and political leaders, to the concept of a society organized for collective action in the public interest. Moreover, under the spur of economic adversity of the eighties and nineties, a large segment of the farmers had abandoned their traditional individualism and had organized politically to implement a comprehensive program for the control of the railroads, the large corporations, and the money supply. Finally, there were numerous evidences during these years that the old impulse to doing good, which had been the wellspring of American humanitarianism, was not entirely dead. This spirit manifested itself in an organized way mainly in the cities—in efforts to make the churches more responsive to social and economic needs, in campaigns to clean up the slums and protect the weak and helpless, and in spasmodic drives to wrest control of city governments from grafters often allied with vested economic interests.

Thus the progressive movement of the first part of the twentieth century was an outgrowth and a fulfillment, rather than a beginning. All during the years from 1900 to 1917 the reform crusade was in motion on various levels and was moving in different directions. But there was some unity and a general chronological development in it. The first reform wave came in the cities, with a great drive to overturn the politicians allied with corporations, railroads, and utilities. Considerable success in this endeavor led next to campaigns to capture the state governments, as the city crusaders invariably found that the city machines were either adjuncts of or else the main cogs in the state machines.

Inevitably, the reform impulse also affected the two great national parties and their leaders. By 1908 William Jennings Bryan of Nebraska and his progressive followers again dominated the Democratic party. The Democrats, however, were still a minority and were so badly rent by internal dissensions that they offered little immediate hope of effective leadership for the liberal element of the country. Much more important a development before 1912 was the steady infiltration of progressive ideas among the Republican leadership and rank and file, especially in the Middle West. The leader of that party from 1901 to 1909, Theodore Roosevelt, never managed and rarely attempted to dislodge the remarkable combination of conservatives who dominated it and determined its policies. Even so, Roosevelt held office during a time of transition, and there is no doubt that the service he rendered the reform movement was substantial. He was a shrewd opportunist with an eye on the main political chance, it is true, and the sum of his legislative accomplishments was small. Yet his constant sermonizing about the malpractices of big business and high finance, and his successful and important struggle for the conservation of natural resources, stirred millions of citizens into a high state of righteous indignation. In brief, his chief contribution to the reform cause was the publicity he gave to it.[1]

Roosevelt, therefore, appreciated the meaning and significance of the progressive movement and dealt carefully with the rising Republi-

[1] As George E. Mowry has pointed out in *Theodore Roosevelt and the Progressive Movement* (Madison, Wis., 1946), pp. 15–16.

can insurgents. The fact that he succeeded in keeping them in good humor while he worked closely with the Old Guard in Congress is testimony to his superb astuteness. His one great mistake, and it was an error of personal judgment, was in choosing William Howard Taft to succeed him. If Roosevelt had selected Charles Evans Hughes, the brilliant, crusading, and independent Governor of New York, the future history of the United States might have been considerably different.

But it was Taft whom Roosevelt put into the White House in 1909; and for all his superficial joviality and apparent progressivism, his intelligence and integrity, Taft was ill equipped to play the role the political exigencies demanded. The job ahead would have taxed the resources of a Roosevelt, but Taft possessed neither Roosevelt's astuteness nor his energy. In order to prevent the disruption of the Republican party, Taft had to facilitate the shift in party control from the Old Guard to the insurgents. Instead of boldly doing this, he vacillated at first, finally aligned himself with the reactionaries, and so completely alienated the progressives that a rupture was inevitable.

A few examples will suffice to illustrate Taft's bungling leadership and to set the stage for the opening event in the election of 1912, the Democratic landslide in the Congressional and gubernatorial elections of November, 1910.

When, at the beginning of the Taft administration in 1909, the insurgents in the House of Representatives maneuvered to unhorse the reactionary Speaker, Joseph G. Cannon, Taft was forced to choose between the rival factions. He supported Cannon, and the insurgents came out of the fight wondering how deep the President's progressivism went. Soon afterward occurred the revolt of the insurgent Republicans in the Senate against the Aldrich amendments to the Payne tariff bill, which the House had just adopted. Taft at first encouraged, then deserted the insurgents, and made one move after another that quickened their disaffection. First he made a thirteen-thousand-mile speaking tour of the Middle West in September, 1909, which, instead of assuaging the insurgent temper, further inflamed it. Then during the following autumn and winter he supported his Secretary of the Interior, Richard A. Ballinger, in a long and bitter controversy with Gifford Pinchot and other conservationists. Ballinger was officially exonerated by the Republican majority of a Congressional committee; but in the eyes of the country he stood convicted as a foe of conservation, and Taft was discredited.[2]

Finally, in the spring of 1910 the President took the last step in his devolution from progressivism to conservatism. He joined the Old

Herbert Johnson in the Philadelphia *North American*

The tariff issue: Taft pleads with Aldrich, who rejoins: "Aw, hang the consumer!" T. R.'s big stick gathers cobwebs.

Guard in a well-planned and generously financed campaign to root insurgency out of the party, by defeating progressive Republicans for

[2] *Ibid.*, pp. 73–87. Alpheus T. Mason, *Bureaucracy Convicts Itself* (Princeton, 1941), is a definitive study of the Ballinger affair. For a defense of Taft and Ballinger see Henry F. Pringle, *The Life and Times of William Howard Taft* (2 vols., New York, 1939).

renomination in the coming primaries in the Middle West. The insurgents, in turn, were goaded by the administration's attacks into virtually declaring their independence from the party dominated by Aldrich, Cannon, and Taft. The flames of Midwestern progressivism had now indeed become the raging prairie fire of insurgency, and the battle for the control of the G.O.P. that transpired during the spring of 1910 promised to decide the fate of Republicanism in the nation as well as in the great Mississippi Valley.

In spite of the ruthless use of the federal patronage, the sending of the best stand-pat orators into the Midwest, and the widespread use of money, Taft's campaign against the insurgents failed completely. In state after state—Indiana, Wisconsin, Minnesota, the Dakotas, Kansas —the progressives triumphed. Nothing was more suggestive of the administration's impending doom than the refusal of the Midwestern rank and file to turn against their local leaders. Already by the summer of 1910 there was considerable talk of organizing a third party in 1912 should Taft be renominated. Already progressives were turning to Roosevelt as their messiah.

The estrangement between Roosevelt and Taft was one of the most important by-products of these two years of bitter party strife. Soon after Taft's inauguration, Roosevelt had obligingly gone off to Africa to hunt big game. By the time he returned to New York in June, 1910, he was definitely alienated from his one-time friend. What had happened meantime to bring this about?

The coolness that Roosevelt now felt toward Taft was born of a series of incidents, many of them petty and personal. The event which, more than any other, convinced Roosevelt that Taft had betrayed his policies was the Ballinger affair. A few months before his return to the United States, Roosevelt had a long conference in Europe with Gifford Pinchot, leader of the anti-Ballinger group. We do not know what the two men said to each other, but we do know that Roosevelt never felt the same about Taft after that meeting. Pinchot, moreover, had taken with him a sheaf of letters to Roosevelt from Senator Jonathan P. Dolliver of Iowa, Senator Albert J. Beveridge of Indiana, William Allen White of Kansas, and other Midwestern progressive Republican leaders, all presenting full bills of particulars against the President. From that day on, Roosevelt was convinced Taft had permitted the

Old Guard to maneuver him into a position that made the revolt of the insurgents inevitable.[3]

Meanwhile, after Roosevelt's return to America the war within the Republican party increased in bitterness and intensity. In one Midwestern state convention after another, the Republicans greeted Taft's name with boos and catcalls and refused to endorse his administration. Important, also, was the fact that the revolt was spreading to all sections of the country except the rotten boroughs of the South. In June, for example, Hiram W. Johnson and the progressives in California smashed the old ring that had long been dominated by the Southern Pacific Railroad and captured the Republican party lock, stock, and barrel. In New Hampshire, in Washington, and in numerous other states the insurgents were also triumphant.

Although by this time Roosevelt had committed himself to the progressive cause, he tried hard to maintain an air of impartiality, and he labored sincerely during the fall of 1910 to bring the warring factions together. He knew the outcome of the disruption of his party would be to present the presidency and control of Congress to the Democrats in 1913, and he was still enough of a conventional Republican to believe this was about the worst thing that could happen to the country. But when he tried to take a hand in organizing the state convention in New York, as a means of strengthening the national administration, Roosevelt found that Taft had come out against him and had aligned himself with the reactionary bosses in the state. Rebuffed and resentful, Roosevelt set out upon a great tour of the West where, amid wildly cheering crowds, he enunciated the advanced political and economic philosophy that he called the New Nationalism.

The Democratic party, like its ancient rival, was at a critical juncture in its career in 1910. It had been fourteen years since Bryan had captured leadership of the party, fourteen years without patronage or national office, without real unity or effective purpose. Bryan had never been unfaithful to the progressive cause, had broadened his program since 1896, and still commanded the devotion of many of the rural Democrats of the South and West. Yet even Bryan's own spokesmen knew the party must have a new leader if it was ever to win a national election again. This was the conviction particularly of the

[3] Mowry, *Roosevelt,* pp. 125–126.

leaders of urban, middle-class progressive Democrats and was shared by The Commoner himself.[4]

Democratic hopes of profiting from the division in the Republican party were realized beyond the wildest expectations in the Congressional and gubernatorial elections in November, 1910. It was a virtual Democratic landslide throughout all sections except the Pacific Coast. The House of Representatives went Democratic for the first time since 1892, by a large margin,[5] while enough new Democratic senators were elected to enable them and the insurgent Republicans to control the upper house. In addition, Democratic governors were elected in many traditionally Republican states: Massachusetts, Connecticut, New York, New Jersey, Ohio, Indiana, Nebraska, and Colorado, among others. So sweeping was the victory that the party was at once reconstituted as a potent threat to Republican supremacy. It was not yet a united force, and the issues upon which it had been swept into office were hardly new, but it was evident that Bryan's day had passed.

Bryan would remain the titular head of the party until 1912, to be sure, but the great Democratic sweep was not a Bryan victory, except as it was a vindication of the principles for which he had long fought. Actually, Bryan had bolted the party ticket in Nebraska[6] and had played a minor role in the campaign. New leaders, among them Woodrow Wilson of New Jersey, Governor Judson Harmon of Ohio, and Champ Clark of Missouri, had risen. Practically every Democratic newspaper in the country believed a reorganization of the party was in the offing and would culminate in the nomination of a new presidential candidate in 1912. "For the first time since Jackson's administration the Democratic party is emancipated and master of its own destiny," the leading eastern Democratic newspaper asserted. "All the shackles have been struck off. There is no load of sectional issues or dead issues or economic fallacies for [the party] to struggle under. As secession followed slavery to the grave . . ., so the Bryan socialism has followed silver, and the Democratic slate is wiped clean. The party is

---

[4] E.g., see Josephus Daniels, *The Wilson Era, Years of Peace—1910–1917* (Chapel Hill, N.C., 1944), p. 16, and Mary B. Bryan (ed.), *The Memoirs of William Jennings Bryan* (Philadelphia, 1925), p. 158.

[5] The Sixty-Second Congress, elected in November, 1910, was composed of the following: 227 Democrats, 162 Republicans, and 1 Socialist in the House of Representatives; 42 Democrats and 49 Republicans in the Senate.

[6] *The New York Times,* Sept. 21, 1910.

back to first principles again, under leadership that is fit to lead." [7] Moreover, when Bryan announced he was not in the running for a fourth nomination, all observers agreed that events during the next eighteen months would determine not only the question of leadership but also the fate of the Democracy.

Thus the Democratic preconvention campaign of 1911 and 1912 was no ordinary pre-election contest. As it became an all-out struggle for control of the Democratic party, it would be well to know the leading contenders, the issues, and the progress of that contest.

Woodrow Wilson, who had made an extraordinarily brilliant campaign for the governorship of New Jersey, quickly emerged as the most distinguished Democratic claimant. No man in the history of American politics had such a spectacular and rapid rise to political prominence. Born in Staunton, Virginia, on December 28, 1856, he grew up in the South during the Civil War and Reconstruction. After a brief attendance at Davidson College in North Carolina, he went to Princeton University in 1875 and was graduated in 1879. Next he studied law at the University of Virginia and during 1882–83 attempted a brief and impoverishing practice in Atlanta. Unhappy over his failure as a lawyer, Wilson went to the new Johns Hopkins University in Baltimore to study history and political science under the renowned Herbert Baxter Adams. His Ph.D. thesis, *Congressional Government,* published in 1885, was a brilliant analysis of the federal legislative system, strongly influenced by Walter Bagehot. From 1885 to 1888 he taught at Bryn Mawr College and from 1888 to 1890 at Wesleyan University. In the latter year he returned to Princeton as professor of jurisprudence and political economy and for the next twelve years won fame as a teacher and writer on political and historical subjects.

Elected president of Princeton in 1902, Wilson inaugurated a series of bold innovations that revitalized the University and marked him as one of the outstanding educational statesmen of his time. He revised the curriculum; he established the preceptorial system of guided study; and he brought to Princeton a large group of promising young teachers and scholars. At the same time, he became increasingly prominent throughout the country as a spokesman of Democratic conservatism— as a foe of Bryanism, of governmental regulation, and of the restric-

[7] New York *World,* Nov. 19, 1910; also *The New York Times,* Mar. 9, 1911.

tive practices of labor unions.[8] George Harvey, editor of the conservative *Harper's Weekly*, had begun a movement in 1906 and 1907 to make Wilson the Democratic presidential nominee in 1908 or 1912, but few persons took Harvey seriously until two events of profound importance in Wilson's own career occurred.

The first was the defeat of Wilson's program at Princeton after the first years of brilliant success. In 1906 and 1907 he attempted almost singlehanded to abolish the undergraduate eating clubs and to substitute in their stead quadrangles, or colleges, where undergraduates would live and eat together. He attacked the clubs on sound academic and intellectual grounds, not because they were allegedly centers of campus snobbery and exclusiveness; but the alumni and part of the faculty protested so violently that the trustees had to abandon Wilson in the fight. This was a humiliating defeat, and he contemplated resigning. But the really crushing blow came during the bitter fight in 1909 and 1910 over the establishment and control of a graduate college. Wilson's chief antagonist, Andrew F. West, Dean of the Graduate School, insisted that the graduate college be set apart under his control. Wilson, on the other hand, demanded that the graduate college be made the center of the University's intellectual life and subject to his control. As the bitterness of the controversy mounted, Wilson injected the personal issue and claimed he was fighting for democracy at Princeton. West, however, obtained the money to build the kind of college he wanted and won in the end.[9]

These tragic and bitter controversies left a deep scar on the University that did not heal for many years. They also highlighted grave defects in Wilson's character and quality of leadership—for example, his unfailing habit of converting differences over issues into bitter personal quarrels, his proud and unyielding stubbornness, and his inability to work with the opposition. But more important for the future of American politics, Wilson's defeat at Princeton made him willing to launch forth on the uncertain sea of politics.

The second decisive event that shaped Wilson's action at this important juncture in his career was his nomination for governor of New Jersey on the Democratic ticket in September, 1910. This maneuver

[8] Arthur S. Link, *Wilson: The Road to the White House* (Princeton, 1947), pp. 106–122, 126–127.

[9] For an account of the quadrangle and graduate college controversies, see *ibid.*, pp. 45–91.

was executed chiefly by Wilson's old booster, George Harvey, who convinced the leading Democratic boss, James Smith, Jr., that Wilson could be used to head off a growing progressive revolt within the party in the state. At the time of his nomination, Wilson was a political conservative, almost totally ignorant of the issues agitating the people. His political convictions, however, were never as fixed as his ambition; and as for the issues, he was a rapid learner. Cutting himself loose from the machine that nominated him, Wilson went over completely to the reform program that progressives of both parties had been pressing for a decade. His brilliant campaign swept him into the governorship by a fifty thousand majority and the Democrats into control of the lower house of the legislature.

It is no exaggeration to say that Wilson's meteoric rise electrified the nation,[10] while events of the next six months convinced many thoughtful observers that he was the bright hope of the Democracy. A few weeks after the election, Wilson broke openly with the bosses when he refused to support Smith's ambition to return to the United States Senate. By assiduous work among the politicians and by another appeal to the people, Wilson not only prevented Smith's election but also firmly established his personal control over the Democratic party in the state. Then, during the winter and spring of 1911, he subdued the bosses once again and pushed through a reluctant legislature practically the entire reform program—a direct primary system, corrupt practices legislation, workmen's compensation, and strict state control of railroads and public utilities. It was no wonder that Democratic progressives throughout the country were beginning to look upon Wilson, as one Texas editor later declared, as the "most hopeful figure in American politics." [11]

There is little doubt, also, that Wilson wanted the leadership of the Democratic party in the nation. A small group of hopeful president-makers gathered around him and began an organized campaign for his nomination in the spring of 1911.[12] For his part, Wilson campaigned strenuously in every section of the country before the end of

[10] New York *World,* Nov. 8, 1910; *Outlook,* XCVI (Nov. 5, 1910), 521; Baltimore *Sun,* Nov. 4, 1910; Philadelphia *North American,* Oct. 27, 1910.

[11] Galveston *Daily News,* Jan. 11, 1912.

[12] It is interesting that most of them were, like Wilson, Southerners living in the North. The leaders of the group were William F. McCombs, a young lawyer from Arkansas, who established Wilson headquarters at 42 Broadway, New York City, and who was general manager of the campaign; William G. McAdoo, former Georgian, who had built the Hudson Tubes; and Walter H. Page, *émigré* North Carolinian, who in 1911 was editor of *World's Work.*

the prenomination campaign. Up and down the country he went, pleading for support and setting forth his philosophy and program. By and large he talked in generalities, about returning the government to the people, the need for trust control and tariff and banking reforms, and the iniquity of special privilege legislation. Although few old-line politicians had committed themselves by the end of 1911, it seemed certain that Wilson would win the nomination without difficulty. No other serious contender seemed yet to be in sight.

The superficial success of Wilson's early campaign, therefore, made the rise of Champ Clark, Speaker of the House of Representatives, as the leading contestant for the Democratic nomination all the more startling. Clark was an old-time war horse from Pike County, Missouri, who had served in the House since the 1890's. A politician of the Bryan type, he had accumulated a consistent progressive record over the years. He had never originated any legislation or taken leadership in any important movement, however; and he was narrow and provincial in outlook, undistinguished by intellectual prowess, and so much addicted to alcohol as to be unfitted for the presidency of a great nation.[13] There is, therefore, little reason to doubt that the New York *World* was justified when it warned that Clark's nomination would spell disaster for the Democratic party and, if he were elected, for the United States.[14]

As Speaker of the House after March, 1911, Clark made hardly any popular campaign for the nomination, except occasionally to recite his stock lecture, "The Signs of the Times." In contrast, Wilson traveled tens of thousands of miles and made hundreds of speeches. Yet when the Democratic presidential primaries were held and the state conventions met in the spring of 1912, one after another of the states went for the Speaker. Clark had inherited most of Bryan's following in the Middle and Far West. He had the fervid support of William Randolph Hearst,[15] and the influence of the Hearst newspapers in his behalf in states like Illinois, California, and Massachusetts was decisive. Finally,

[13] For an excellent contemporary summary see Frank Parker Stockbridge, "Champ Clark, of Pike County," *World's Work*, XXIV (May, 1912), 27–36.
[14] New York *World*, Apr. 25, 1912; Herbert A. Hilary to Richard Olney, Apr. 17, 1912, the Papers of Richard Olney, in the Library of Congress; Olney to Hilary, Apr. 18, 1912, *ibid.; World's Work*, XXIV (June, 1912), 130; *Collier's Weekly*, XLVIII (Mar. 9, 1912), 9; *ibid.*, XLIX (June 22, 1912), 10.
[15] See Hearst's statements in Chicago *Examiner*, Sept. 26, 1911, and New York *American*, Mar. 14, 1912.

Clark had the support of most of the time-serving Democratic politicians and the state organizations, and their support was the critical factor in the success of his campaign.

While Clark gathered some 436 delegates pledged to support his nomination at the national convention in Baltimore in June, Wilson could count at the most only 248. The best the Wilson managers could hope for was that the support of the uninstructed Wilson delegates would give him control of at least one-third of the total convention vote of 1088. Wilson had made an especially hard fight to win his native South, but had to divide the Southern delegations with Clark and Oscar W. Underwood of Alabama, chairman of the House Ways and Means Committee.[16] For Wilson and his friends the days preceding the Baltimore convention were disheartening indeed. Wilson himself was ready to quit. Colonel Edward M. House, a quiet Texas politician who had joined the Wilson movement late in 1911, became discouraged and advised his friends to find another candidate to support if it seemed Wilson could not be nominated.[17]

It was easily the most critical time in the history of the Democratic party since 1896 when the national convention opened at Baltimore on June 25, 1912, for nothing less than control of the party and also of the federal government was at stake. From the very first day the convention was riotous and bitter. A member of the Nebraska delegation, Bryan led a revolt against the selection of the conservative Judge Alton B. Parker of New York as keynote speaker. The Wilson delegates supported Bryan in the fight, but the Clark men voted for Parker and he made his address. Next Bryan introduced a resolution pledging the party not to nominate any candidate subservient to "J. P. Morgan, Thomas Fortune Ryan, August Belmont, or any other member of the privilege-hunting and favor-seeking class" and demanding the withdrawal of delegates representing Wall Street interests. As Ryan and Belmont were both delegates, the resolution had considerable sting and evoked great controversy. It was adopted without the latter provision and Ryan and Belmont stayed on.

Bryan's courageous fight to expose and neutralize the reactionary

[16] Arthur S. Link, "The Underwood Presidential Movement of 1912," *Journal of Southern History*, XI (May, 1945), 230–245.

[17] E. M. House to C. A. Culberson, Apr. 23, 1912, the Papers of Edward M. House, in the Library of Yale University; House to Mary B. Bryan, June 22, 1912, *ibid*. Further references in this chapter to the writings of Colonel House have been drawn from this collection of papers.

element aroused the convention and the country, but it had little effect on the voting for a presidential candidate. In the early balloting Clark forged far in the lead. On the tenth ballot the boss of Tammany Hall, Charles F. Murphy, electrified the convention by delivering New York's ninety votes to Clark. It was the signal for a landslide, for the Speaker now had 556 votes, well over a majority. Under then existing rules he needed two-thirds for the nomination, to be sure, but not since 1844 had a Democrat obtained a majority in a national convention and then failed to win the necessary two-thirds.

The expected landslide did not materialize, however, because the Wilson delegates stood absolutely firm and because the Wilson and Underwood managers agreed to stand solidly together. Then began a long and grueling battle in which Wilson's managers undermined Clark's strength. On the fourteenth ballot Bryan came out against Clark and voted for Wilson, but his action was no great help to the Wilson leaders. They concentrated their efforts, not on the Bryan men, most of whom were fanatically loyal to Clark, but upon the boss-controlled delegations and upon the Underwood bloc. This strategy finally succeeded when Roger Sullivan, Illinois Democratic boss, delivered his delegates to Wilson on the forty-second ballot, and the Underwood men came to Wilson on the forty-sixth, thus nominating him. What had seemed impossible only a few days before was now a reality: one of the miracles of modern American politics.[18]

Thus control of the Democratic party was given over to its progressive element, and without any open rupture or more than the usual dissension. The Republican party, however, did not resolve its dilemma so happily. It will be recalled that the elections of 1910 had amounted to a mass repudiation of Taft's leadership and that the insurgents had made it plain soon afterward that they would not tolerate Taft's renomination. The Republican progressives now constituted a majority of the party in the Middle and Far Western states. They had a fairly coherent program of tariff and trust reform. All they lacked, therefore, was a dynamic leader of national standing to unite their ranks and lead their campaign. In 1910 and early 1911 many signs seemed to point to Senator Robert M. La Follette of Wisconsin as this leader. No Republican, not even Roosevelt, had carried the banner of progressivism so courageously and so faithfully as La Follette. He was, more-

[18] For the Baltimore convention, see Link, *Wilson,* pp. 431–465.

over, far and away the ablest of the Midwestern insurgents. He had led the fight against the Aldrich tariff betrayal and Ballingerism in 1909 and 1910; meanwhile, he had come forward with a comprehensive and rational program for financial and business control.[19]

It was Roosevelt and not La Follette, however, who dominated the progressive Republican situation, and until nearly the end of 1911 Roosevelt was undecided. He made friendly gestures in La Follette's direction, but his friends told him, and he agreed, that the Wisconsin senator could never defeat Taft. Many leading progressives turned to Roosevelt himself and pleaded with him to come out boldly and give them the only leadership that could win. He did not stop them when they began a high-pressure campaign for his nomination. Finally, in response to a prearranged appeal from seven Republican governors, dated February 10, 1912, Roosevelt on February 24 announced his candidacy and began a tremendous campaign to win delegates to the Chicago convention.[20]

The Republican preconvention campaign that followed, from March through May, was probably the bitterest in the history of the party. The Taft spokesmen searched Roosevelt's record and laid down a heavy barrage of personal abuse. Roosevelt replied in kind, giving more than he took. So enormous was the intraparty bitterness that some of the Republican state conventions were riotous brawls, with fistfights common. During April, May, and early June Roosevelt made a personal campaign that for strenuosity equaled Bryan's of 1896, and there seemed to be no doubt that his appeal was succeeding. He swept most of the states that held presidential primaries and even won Taft's native Ohio after a campaign into which both sides had poured all their resources. In thirteen states where the Republican voters had an opportunity to express a preference, La Follette won 36 delegates, Taft 48, and Roosevelt 278.[21]

But it was not enough. Taft had used the patronage steam roller to obtain control of the Southern delegations. He had the support of most of the delegates from boss-controlled states, like New York. Above all, he controlled the National Committee, which would organize the na-

[19] Alpheus T. Mason, *Brandeis, A Free Man's Life* (New York, 1946), pp. 366–374.

[20] *The Works of Theodore Roosevelt* (20 vols., New York, 1926), XVII, 149–150.

[21] Mowry, *Roosevelt,* pp. 220–236, is the best account of the Republican preconvention campaign.

tional convention and pass on the credentials of the delegates. Thus while the results of the preconvention campaign seemed confused, because one-fourth of the seats in the national convention were contested, actually the outcome was foregone before the convention met in Chicago on June 18. By the ruthless use of the same steam-roller

K. K. Knecht in the Evansville *Courier*

Roosevelt and Taft—1908 and 1912

tactics that Roosevelt had perfected in 1908, the Taft forces organized the convention and gave themselves 235 of the 254 contested seats. Roosevelt, who was then in Chicago directing his followers, gave the word and most of them walked out, whereupon the administration men proceeded to renominate Taft.

Convinced he had been cheated out of the nomination by corrupt and reactionary politicians, Roosevelt was now angry as only he could be and more than ever determined to run for President, even if that meant destroying the Republican party. His motives were obviously complicated, but prominent among them was his refusal to accept humiliation at the hands of the man he had put in the White House. Thus, in spite of the unwillingness of most of the insurgent leaders to follow him, Roosevelt went ahead relentlessly with his plans to organize a third party.

The outgrowth of his anger, the Progressive party, came into existence in Chicago on August 6 in one of the most remarkable political conventions the country had ever witnessed. Distinguished social and economic reformers like Jane Addams of Hull House in Chicago and George L. Record, resourceful progressive of New Jersey, disappointed politicians like the notorious William Flinn of Pittsburgh—all these and more made up the crowd that sang "Onward, Christian Soldiers," adopted the most significant platform since the Populist platform of 1892,[22] and nominated Roosevelt and Governor Hiram W. Johnson of California to head their ticket. Feeling, he said, like a bull moose, Roosevelt came to accept the nomination and delivered his "Confession of Faith," a statement of social and economic principles that was a classic synthesis of the most advanced thought of the time.[23]

The country witnessed during the summer and fall of 1912 the first serious three-cornered presidential contest since 1860. The Socialists, under the leadership of Eugene V. Debs, adopted an advanced platform and were making their strongest bid for power; but they were still

[22] The Progressive platform provided the basis for the future development of the progressive movement in the United States after 1912, just as the Populist platform of 1892 had earlier provided a foundation for the first phase of American progressivism.

The Progressive platform was most significant for the fact that the social justice group and other advanced progressives found approval for their objectives by a major, if ephemeral, party. Thus measures like the minimum wage for women, prohibition of child labor, workmen's compensation, and social insurance were embodied in the platform. On the political level the Progressives demanded the adoption of the initiative, referendum, and recall, the recall of judicial decisions, the institution of a nation-wide presidential primary, full publicity of campaign contributions and expenditures, and the like. In the economic field the major demands were for a federal trade commission to exercise sweeping regulatory authority over business and industrial activity and a tariff commission that would set tariff rates on a scientific basis and guarantee that benefits of protection accrued to workers as well as to employers.

[23] *Works,* XVII, 254–299.

a small minority of the voters. By the middle of August it was obvious that Taft simply was not in the running. He was in the race only to defeat Roosevelt anyway, and he could do this without strenuous effort. "I think I might as well give up so far as being a candidate is

WHERE WILL HE LAND ?

Denver *Post*

T. R. vaults the anti-third-term hurdle in 1912

concerned," he wrote as early as July 22. "There are so many people in the country who don't like me." [24] Except for his speech of acceptance, which he could not avoid making, the President refused to join in the speechmaking at all.

[24] Taft to Helen Taft, July 22, 1912, cited in Pringle, *Taft,* II, 817.

Wilson and Roosevelt carried the burden of the campaign, there-fore, and deserve most of our attention. Ideologically speaking, the progressive movement culminated and diverged in the philosophies and programs they set forth. Certain commentators, notably William Allen White, have referred to Roosevelt and Wilson as Tweedledum and Tweedledee, each in his own way setting forth an identical philosophy and program in 1912.[25] To say this is to miss a large part of the significance of the campaign, for Roosevelt's New Nationalism and what Wilson called the New Freedom mirrored a divergence in the progressive movement itself, a divergence far-reaching in its im-plications for the future development of governmental policies in the United States. As the campaign of 1912 became a full-dress debate over two conflicting progressive theories of government, it would be well to know what these theories were.

The New Nationalism was no mere campaign platform hastily con-trived for the purpose of catching votes. It was, rather, the consum-mation of a steady progression in the political thought of Roosevelt and a significant minority of progressive thinkers. During the last few years of his presidency Roosevelt had set forth his developing concept of the federal government as a dynamic force in the social and eco-nomic affairs of men. His Annual Message of 1908, for example, was a clarion call to progressives to re-examine the assumptions upon which their program rested. This, of course, was in the best Republican, nationalistic tradition. Although Roosevelt by 1909 had adopted a program demanding broad federal economic and social regulation, he had not yet formulated a coherent political philosophy to justify such a program. This task fell to a then obscure New York journalist, Herbert Croly, who published in 1909 his *Promise of American Life*. It was easily the best political treatise to come out of the progressive fer-ment.[26]

Croly's thesis not only summarized the most advanced progressive

---

[25] W. A. White, *Woodrow Wilson* (Boston, 1924), p. 264.

[26] Born in New York City in 1869, Croly was educated at Harvard and was editor of the *Architectural Record* from 1900 to 1906. He gained a pre-eminent position among intellectual progressives with the publication of *The Promise of American Life*. With the backing of Willard Straight of the Morgan firm, Croly in 1914 founded the *New Republic* and gathered around him some of the leading young thinkers in the country, including Walter Lippmann, Charles A. Beard, John Dewey, Walter Weyl, and Thomas N. Carver. His *Progressive Democracy*, published in 1914, was a second significant commentary on the American progressive movement.

thought of the time but also became the rationale of the New Nationalism and even of Wilsonian progressivism after 1915. It might, therefore, be characterized as the philosophical underpinning of the modern progressive movement. In American thought, Croly said, there had been two divergent views of the role the federal government should play. The first was the Hamiltonian belief that government should intervene directly to alter existing economic relationships or to establish new ones. The second was the Jeffersonian view that government should pursue a policy of strict *laissez faire* with regard to economic activity. The important historical fact about these two conflicting philosophies, Croly continued, was that the Hamiltonian concept of government had become identified in the popular mind with aristocracy and special privilege, while the Jeffersonian dogma of weak government had all along been identified with democracy and with a program of equal rights and opportunities. Croly admitted that the Hamiltonian philosophy had been used historically by the financial and industrial groups to justify special interest legislation, but he called boldly for an entirely new orientation in progressive thinking. What he demanded was nothing less than that the progressives abandon their Jeffersonian prejudices against strong government and adopt Hamiltonian means to achieve Jeffersonian, or democratic, ends.

It is impossible to measure the influence of *The Promise of American Life* on Roosevelt's developing progressivism. Roosevelt read the book with enthusiastic approval and it at least helped him systematize his own ideas. In any event, he at once began to translate Croly's abstruse and heavy language into living political principles that the rank and file could comprehend.[27] In a famous speech at Osawatomie, Kansas, on August 31, 1910, Roosevelt sounded the keynote of his two years' campaign. The old nationalism, he said, had been used "by the sinister . . . special interests." What he proposed was a new nationalism, a dynamic democracy, that would recognize the inevitability of concentration in industry and bring the great corporations under complete federal control, that would protect and encourage the laboring man, that, in brief, would do many of the things usually associated with the modern concept of the welfare state. "We are face to face with new conceptions of the relations of property to human welfare," he declared. ". . . Property [is] subject to the general right of the com-

[27] Henry F. Pringle, *Theodore Roosevelt, A Biography* (New York, 1931), pp. 540–541.

munity to regulate its use to whatever degree the public welfare may require it." [28]

This, in general, was also the program and theme Roosevelt set forth during the campaign of 1912. Needless to say, it attracted a large following, particularly among the social justice group and the social workers. As the campaign progressed, however, Roosevelt became increasingly radical and explicit. He began to place more emphasis upon the social justice objectives of his program—a minimum wage for women workers, a federal child labor law, a federal workmen's compensation act, federal intervention in labor disputes, an expanded federal health and conservation program, use of tariff protection to insure fair wages to workers in industry, and the like. In turn, he scoffed at Wilson as representing "rural Toryism," the mossback, worn-out Jeffersonian philosophy of *laissez faire*.

In contrast to his chief opponent, Wilson had no such well-defined program or philosophy when the campaign began. He was at another important crossroads in his career, but it was foregone in which direction he would travel. For, along with his general commitment to the ideal of social justice, he was still a progressive of the Jeffersonian persuasion, undisturbed by Croly's challenge. Fundamentally a state rights Democrat, he believed the federal power should be used only to sweep away special privileges and artificial barriers to the development of individual energies, and to preserve and restore competition in business. The idea of the federal government's moving directly into the economic field, by giving special protection to workers or farmers, was as abhorrent to Wilson in 1912 as the idea of class legislation in the interest of manufacturers or shipowners.

At first it seemed Wilson would make his campaign mainly on the tariff, but it did not take him long to discover that this was a worn-out issue and would evoke no popular response. He seemed to be searching for an issue more appealing when he met Louis D. Brandeis for the first time on August 28 at Sea Girt, New Jersey. One of the leading progressive lawyers in the country, Brandeis was also probably the chief spokesman of the philosophy of regulated competition, unhampered enterprise, and economic freedom for the small businessman. And it was Brandeis who clarified Wilson's thought and led him to believe the most vital question confronting the American people was preservation of economic freedom in the United States.[29]

[28] *Works*, XVII, 5–22.
[29] *The New York Times,* Aug. 29, 1912. Brandeis outlined his program for

Brandeis taught, and Wilson agreed and reiterated in his speeches, that the main task ahead was to provide the means by which business could be set free from the shackles of monopoly and special privilege. Roosevelt claimed that the great corporations were often the most efficient units of industrial organization, and that all that was necessary was to bring them under strict public control, by close regulation of their activities by a powerful trade commission. Wilson replied: "As to the monopolies, which Mr. Roosevelt proposes to legalize and to welcome, I know that they are so many cars of juggernaut, and I do not look forward with pleasure to the time when the juggernauts are licensed and driven by commissioners of the United States." Monopoly, he added, developed amid conditions of unregulated competition. "We can prevent these processes through remedial legislation, and so restrict the wrong use of competition that the right use of competition will destroy monopoly."

The divergence in Wilson's and Roosevelt's views on the role government should play in human affairs was more vividly revealed, however, by Wilson's savage attacks on Roosevelt's proposals for social welfare legislation. He objected to Roosevelt's labor program because it was paternalistic, because it would inevitably mean that workingmen would become wards of the federal government. Perhaps Roosevelt's "new and all-conquering combination between money and government" would be benevolent to the people, he said; perhaps it would carry out "the noble programme of social betterment" which so many credulously expected; but he did not believe paternalism was the answer for free men.[30]

And as the campaign progressed Wilson became more and more convinced that the struggle between the New Freedom and the New Nationalism was a struggle between two concepts of government so radically different that he prophesied slavery and enchainment for the people if Roosevelt were elected. "This is a second struggle for emancipation," he declared in a supreme outburst at Denver on October 7. ". . . If America is not to have free enterprise, then she can have freedom of no sort whatever."[31] It was Wilson's discovery that he was

trust control in a memorandum entitled "Suggestions for letter of Governor Wilson on Trusts," which he sent to Wilson on September 30, 1912. The memorandum is in the Woodrow Wilson Papers, in the Library of Congress.

[30] Speech at Buffalo, N.Y., Sept. 2, 1912, *The New York Times*, Sept. 3, 1912.

[31] Denver *Rocky Mountain News*, Oct. 8, 1912.

battling for the old American way of life and his conviction that economic democracy was absolutely essential to political democracy that gave ultimate meaning to his slogan "The New Freedom."

One of the most interesting developments of the campaign was the manner in which progressives reacted to Roosevelt's and Wilson's appeals. In the early weeks, before Wilson found himself and his great vital issue, progressives wondered whether he was a progressive after all. In contrast to Roosevelt's warm appeals for social justice, Wilson's early speeches seemed cold indeed. But as he gathered momentum, as he began to talk in glowing, if general, phrases of social righteousness and economic justice, many progressives claimed him as their new leader and hastened to his support: The significant development of the campaign was Roosevelt's failure to unite progressive Republicans and progressive Democrats. The Roosevelt that progressives knew had many sides, and a considerable portion of the progressives refused to believe he was now sincere. "I wish I could believe he intended to do a single honest thing," wrote Anna Howard Shaw, for example, "or that he would carry out a single plank in the platform if he were elected. . . . I cannot." [32]

By the middle of October there was not much doubt about the outcome of the contest. To be sure, Roosevelt had made a magnificent campaign and had won the support of most of the Republican progressives, especially in the Middle West. But he had failed to draw progressive Democrats away from Wilson, and that fact alone signified his inevitable defeat. More important for the future of American politics was the fact that he had signally failed to establish the Progressive party on a firm and lasting basis. As the election statistics revealed, there was little more to the new party than Roosevelt himself.

The results of the election, however, clearly demonstrated that the country was now overwhelmingly progressive in temper. Individuals might disagree over a definition for progressivism, but a large majority of them were discontented with Old Guard policies and in a rebellious mood. Wilson polled 6,293,019 popular votes, Roosevelt 4,119,507, and the Socialist candidate, Eugene V. Debs, 901,873. Even Taft, who received only 3,484,956 votes, would have denied he was a conservative. Because of the multiple division of the votes, Wilson's victory in the electoral college was of landslide proportions. Taft carried only

[32] A. H. Shaw to Jane Addams, Aug. 16, 1912, Jane Addams Papers, in the Swarthmore College Library.

"THEY WILL MISS ME WHEN I'M GONE"

Nelson Harding, Brooklyn *Daily Eagle*

The tariff issue in the 1912 campaign

Vermont and Utah and received eight electoral votes; Roosevelt won eleven of California's votes and all of Michigan, Minnesota, Pennsylvania, South Dakota, and Washington, for a total of eighty-eight votes. Wilson received all the rest, 435 electoral votes. The disruption of the G.O.P., however, gave control not only of the presidency but of Congress as well to the Democrats. At least for two years Wilson would be assured of a preponderant majority of seventy-three in the House of Representatives and a small but workable majority of six in the Senate.

Sweeping though the victory was, the Democrats could derive small comfort from a cold analysis of the returns. Wilson had not polled as many popular votes as Bryan had received in 1908. With a little more than 42 per cent of the popular vote, moreover, Wilson had clearly failed to establish his party as the majority party of the country, for the national Democratic ticket received clear majorities only in the eleven former Confederate states.

On the other hand, it is perhaps significant that neither Roosevelt nor Taft was responsible for the decrease in the Democratic vote in 1912. The combined popular vote given Wilson's two chief opponents in 1912 was also slightly less than Taft's total vote in 1908. In short, all major parties suffered a relative and absolute decline in 1912, because about half a million disgruntled progressives voted for Debs.

What was the meaning of Wilson's election, what did it signify for the future of the country? Certainly it was as much a political revolution as Jefferson's election had been. As in 1800, the election of 1912 effected an important shift in the geographical control of the federal government. For one thing, Southern influence had been decisive in nominating Wilson and directing his campaign, and Southerners would soon be given the same share in formulating national policies that their grandfathers once enjoyed. But the most significant result of all the preceding three or four years of political ferment was the emergence of Woodrow Wilson as a national leader. It was an open question whether the New Freedom program would satisfy progressive demands, but there could be no doubt that the Democratic party and the country now had a leader of resolution, ability, and boldness. Best of all, Wilson had made no binding commitments to any important economic interests. He would be embarrassed by no important political bargains. Few presidents have entered office so completely free to serve the general interest.

CHAPTER 2

The New Freedom

THE FEW months between the election and the inaugural afforded scant time to accomplish the gigantic task that lay ahead of Wilson and his advisers. They had to map the plans for a legislative program and to organize a government almost from the ground up. The prospect of a general housecleaning might warm the hearts of office-hungry worthies in Texas and Illinois, but it was intolerably annoying to the President-elect. Even before the election returns were complete, William F. McCombs, the erratic and morose Democratic national chairman, handed Wilson one list of names for the Cabinet and another of the faithful who expected appropriate rewards.[1] Within a few days some fifteen thousand supplicating letters poured in on Wilson at his home in Princeton, and it seemed that almost as many politicians descended upon him.

In the face of mounting demands for office, Wilson announced he would make no appointments until after his inauguration. Then, on November 16, he escaped with his family to his old refuge in Bermuda, in order, as he wrote, to get his head cleared for what was to follow. In this "lotus land" for a month, he was "free to do . . . quiet thinking and reflecting," to work out the program he had set his heart upon.[2] Meanwhile, he had commissioned his friend, Colonel Edward M. House, to find material for the Cabinet.

[1] New York *World,* Nov. 7, 1912.
[2] Wilson to W. J. Bryan, c. Nov. 15, 1912, Swem Notebooks, Ray Stannard Baker Collection, in the Library of Congress; Wilson to J. P. Tumulty, Nov. 27, 1912, *ibid.*

The friendship between Wilson and House was already an intimate one, although the two men had known each other hardly a year and even though House had played a minor role in the campaign. "Almost from the first our association was intimate; almost from the first, our minds vibrated in unison," House later recalled. "When we had exchanged thoughts with one another he translated our conclusions into action without delay. Nine times out of ten we reached the same conclusions." [3]

It was one of the most important friendships in history, but not "one of the strangest." [4] Like all great public men, Wilson needed a friend to whom he could unburden his secret thoughts and turn for advice and spiritual support. A man of intellect and moral strength, House was perfectly equipped to meet Wilson's peculiar needs. Wilson demanded the total loyalty of his friend, and House knew when to speak or be silent, when to agree or to demur. Yet in thus subordinating his will to Wilson's, House did not compromise his own integrity, judgment, or critical capacities. Because he understood the Wilsonian temperament and handled the President in a shrewdly calculated manner, House was able to retain Wilson's confidence and affection until new circumstances arose and a break came abruptly in 1919. From 1912 until 1917, however, House's influence grew steadily; and that influence by and large was salutary, for in times of crisis House proved a wise counselor and a stabilizing force.

The Cabinet that Wilson finally appointed was mainly of House's choosing and, with one or two exceptions, was perhaps as good as could be constructed from the material available. Because of his commanding influence in the party, Bryan received the appointment as Secretary of State. The Nebraskan was no great authority on foreign affairs. So much a believer in party government that he seemed almost a spoilsman, he made a number of appointments that did great damage to the foreign service. [5] In spite of his tenderness for "deserving Demo-

[3] E. M. House, "Memoirs of Colonel House," copy in the Papers of George Sylvester Viereck, in the Library of Yale University.

[4] As George Sylvester Viereck called it in *The Strangest Friendship in History* (New York, 1932).

[5] For example, W. W. Russell, an old career officer, was removed as Minister to Santo Domingo and replaced by James M. Sullivan, one of the worst officers in the history of the American diplomatic service. Or, again, Lewis Einstein, a brilliant young career diplomat, was removed as Minister to Costa Rica and replaced by Edward J. Hale, editor of Fayetteville, North Carolina, who had supported Wilson in the prenomination contest. For further elaboration see

crats," however, Bryan did surprisingly well; and if the world had remained at peace he would probably have served out his term, happy at his post. The conservative press ridiculed him for refusing to serve wine at state dinners and accused him of neglecting his duties to lecture for profit.[6] The truth was that Bryan was an indefatigable worker who gave assiduous attention to the detailed work of the Department and had a large part in the development of foreign policy. Moreover, he completely sublimated his personal ambitions to work loyally and well for the success of the President, at home and abroad, until differences over a matter of principle drove them apart in June, 1915.

Bryan was succeeded in the chief Cabinet post by Robert Lansing, who had served under him as Counselor for a little more than a year. In contrast to Bryan, Lansing was a professional at the practice of international law. A person of enormous reserve, he gave the superficial impression of a dignified law clerk; but the fire of strong conviction burned hot within him, even though his official statements rarely betrayed his secret thoughts. He often disagreed with the President's foreign policies but loyally strove to implement them, or to change them, if he could, by indirection.

The new Secretary of the Treasury, William G. McAdoo, was a Georgian transplanted to New York, who had played a prominent part in the preconvention campaign. In many respects McAdoo was the ablest and in some the most interesting member of the Cabinet. His restless, probing mind was unencumbered by economic or political theories, and during his tenure the Treasury Department launched new and interesting experiments for the benefit of businessmen and farmers. McAdoo was also the most ambitious, aggressive, and domi-

---

The New York Times, July 9, 1913, and George Harvey, "The Diplomats of Democracy," *North American Review,* CXCIX (Feb., 1914), 161–174.

If Bryan had been given a free rein, he would have also turned all Republicans out of the consular service, which President Theodore Roosevelt and Secretary of State Elihu Root had organized on a competitive and career basis. See the Diary of Edward M. House, in the Papers of Edward M. House, in the Library of Yale University, Apr. 18, 1913.

[6] Bryan frankly admitted that he found it necessary to lecture for profit in order to supplement his salary, which, he said, was inadequate to meet his obligations to church, charity, and education. See W. J. Bryan, "Making a Living," *The Commoner,* Aug., 1913. See also "The Bryan Scandal," *The Nation,* XCVII (Sept. 18, 1913), 256–257, and George Harvey, "Mr. Bryan Rides Again," *North American Review,* CXCIX (Mar., 1914), 321–334.

neering member of the Wilson circle. House thought, and probably correctly, that McAdoo was consumed by ambition to be President.[7]

For Attorney General, Wilson first thought of Louis D. Brandeis, the chief architect of the New Freedom. For a number of reasons House was opposed, and he finally persuaded Wilson that Brandeis was "not fit for that place." [8] Instead, Wilson allowed the Colonel to choose James C. McReynolds, a Kentuckian practicing law in New York, who had participated in the government's prosecution of the Tobacco Trust case and who was then thought to be a radical foe of monopoly.[9] Although he was not yet as cynical, irascible, and reactionary as he later became on the Supreme Court, McReynolds did not get on well with his colleagues. There was general relief—in the Cabinet—in 1914 when Wilson elevated him to the Supreme Court and appointed to his post Thomas W. Gregory, a Texan of high principles and even temper.

For Secretary of War, Wilson turned at the last moment to Lindley M. Garrison, a judge of the chancery court of New Jersey. Garrison vied with McAdoo for the reputation of the ablest Cabinet member. Utterly forthright, a superb administrator who quickly won the esteem of the military leaders, and loyal to the President, he was, however, inept in dealing with politicians, and Congressional leaders resented what they thought his overbearing manner. During the great battle over preparedness he resigned rather than compromise and was supplanted, early in 1916, by Newton D. Baker, Mayor of Cleveland.

Wilson rewarded his chief North Carolina supporter, Josephus Daniels, with the Secretaryship of the Navy. As editor of the Raleigh *News and Observer,* Daniels had been in the forefront of the progressive movement in his state, although he never allowed devotion to reform causes to stand in the way of his own advancement. The chief target of Republican ridicule, Daniels had nevertheless far more ability than his enemies admitted or his own benign countenance suggested. As Secretary of the Navy, he improved the conditions and opportunities of the enlisted men, fought the armor-plate monopoly to a standstill, and helped get through Congress in 1916 the greatest naval building program in the nation's history to that time. His studied but

[7] House Diary, July 7, Oct. 20, 27, Nov. 4, 1914, Aug. 27, 1916.
[8] *Ibid.,* Dec. 18, 1912, Jan. 10, 17, 23, 24, 1913.
[9] See, e.g., "J. C. M'Reynolds, the New Preceptor for the Trusts," *The New York Times Magazine,* Mar. 9, 1913.

sincere adulation of Wilson won for him the President's affection and enabled him to ride out many a hard storm of popular criticism.

Wilson and House went deliberately to Congress for a Postmaster General—Albert S. Burleson, another Texas veteran of many Congressional battles. Though he called himself a progressive, he never allowed principle alone to determine his course of action. He was a superb professional politician, utterly loyal to Wilson, who used the patronage ruthlessly to compel adoption of administration measures. Wilson's friends expected him to employ the appointing power to build up progressive factions in the states. It was Burleson, however, who persuaded the President that friendly support in Congress, even from old-line reactionaries, was more to be desired than control of the party by men who called themselves progressives. Thus the administration's great power was used to strengthen the factions already in control of the state organizations. In states like Virginia, North Carolina, Alabama, or Kentucky, where conservative Democrats were dominant, Burleson's policy operated to discourage and weaken the progressive faction.[10]

Franklin K. Lane, a California Democrat, was elevated from the Interstate Commerce Commission to the post of Secretary of the Interior. A brilliant conversationalist, letter writer, and wit, Lane was also the chief gossip of the Cabinet. Because Lane could not resist the temptation to divulge secrets to the newspapermen, Wilson had to stop saying anything important in the Cabinet meetings.[11] As Secre-

---

[10] Materials substantiating this generalization abound in the Wilson Papers. In Kentucky, for example, control of the patronage was turned over to Senator Ollie M. James and the congressmen, all identified with the liquor interests and all bitterly at odds with the antiliquor, Wilson-progressive faction. At the end of Wilson's first year as President, only one Wilson man had been named to federal office in the entire state. See Lexington *Herald*, Mar. 7, 1914, and Desha Breckenridge to W. F. McCombs, Mar. 7, 1914, the Woodrow Wilson Papers, in the Library of Congress.

The same situation existed in Virginia. In that state a large and active group of young progressive Democrats had revolted against the conservative organization and tried to carry their state for Wilson before the Baltimore convention. Yet this group of ardent Wilson supporters were denied any federal patronage once Wilson entered the White House; in fact, the federal patronage after 1913 was used to build the strength of the old machine. See J. G. Pollard *et al.* to Wilson, Jan. 5, 1914. *ibid.*

For details of a similar situation in Alabama, see Horace Hood to W. J. Bryan, Oct. 11, 1913, the Papers of Willian Jennings Bryan, in the National Archives.

[11] R. S. Baker, interviews with N. D. Baker, Apr. 6, 1928; with T. W.

tary of the Interior, Lane followed a middle course, although in the California oil lands controversy he supported the claims of private interests and became suspect among stanch conservationists.[12]

Lane's colleague in the Agriculture Department was David F. Houston, originally a North Carolinian but now a distinguished economist and president of Washington University in St. Louis. A close friend of House, Houston had met Wilson in December, 1911, and written a memorandum on the protective tariff for him. A classical economist and therefore a conservative, Houston presided over the Department during a time when the demands of farm groups for a larger measure of federal aid were growing irresistibly powerful. When the cotton market collapsed immediately after the beginning of the First World War, he successfully resisted the demands of the planters for far-reaching relief. He left his stamp upon the Federal Warehouse Act of 1914 and the Good Roads Act of 1916 in the large degree of federal control that these measures provided. Moreover, he opposed the rural credits bill, because it provided for governmental subvention to farmers, and blocked passage of the measure until 1916. A conservative in the field of federal economic policies, he none the less was an extraordinarily able administrator and brought his Department to a new peak of efficiency.

Wilson had given in to the pressure against making Brandeis Attorney General, but during February and early March, 1913, he seemed determined to bring the distinguished "people's lawyer" into his official family, as Secretary of Commerce. Indeed, the question of Brandeis' appointment came to be regarded by many progressives as a test of Wilson's sincerity.[13] On the other hand, when news of Brandeis'

Gregory, Mar. 14–15, 1927; with W. B. Wilson, Jan. 12–13, 1928, and with D. F. Houston, Dec. 1, 1928, Baker Collection.

[12] This was the longest and bitterest controversy that rent the administration before 1917. Presidents Roosevelt and Taft had withdrawn certain California oil lands from the public domain and constituted them a naval oil reserve. Meanwhile, a number of private parties had entered claims and protested the withdrawals. The Supreme Court in 1909 and 1915 denied the claims and upheld the withdrawals. In 1914 Lane drafted a General Leasing bill that would have provided relief by permitting private leasing of government oil lands, but not of such lands set aside for military or naval purposes. On the other hand, Daniels, Gregory, and conservation leaders like Gifford Pinchot and William Kent accused Lane of surrendering to private interests and bitterly opposed his leasing bill. In fact, this opposition was so vociferous that no leasing legislation was passed during the first administration.

[13] See, e.g., Norman Hapgood to House, Nov. 23, 1912, House Papers; also

probable appointment was published, Colonel House, the Irish politicians of Boston, and spokesmen of the great financial interests all combined to warn Wilson against making such a disastrous mistake.[14] Wilson wavered and then surrendered again. "The interests everywhere . . . and the country will think W[ilson] showed the white feather," lamented Norman Hapgood when the Cabinet list was published.[15]

Instead of Brandeis, Wilson finally chose William C. Redfield, a second-rate congressman from Brooklyn. Never much aware of issues or political principles, Redfield worked only to make his department the servant and protector of the American businessman. He will be remembered chiefly because he was the last important public man to wear side whiskers.

As for Secretary of Labor, there never seemed to be much doubt that the post should go to William B. Wilson, Democratic congressman from Pennsylvania and chairman of the House Labor Committee. A man of heroic stature, Wilson had begun his career as a miner at the age of nine. His qualities of leadership soon won him recognition among his fellows, and he helped organize the United Mine Workers of America, of which he was secretary-treasurer from 1900 to 1908. Hounded by employers because of his union activities, Wilson was once imprisoned for defying an injunction. As the first Secretary of Labor his was the task of organizing a new department. His first assistant, Louis F. Post, was a distinguished single taxer and friend of organized labor.

No account of the Wilson circle would be complete without some notice of Joseph P. Tumulty, Wilson's secretary from 1911 through 1921. Tumulty had joined the rising Democratic leader early in 1911 and had been his chief aide and adviser during the gubernatorial battles. Fiery, eloquent in an Irish way, and impulsive, Tumulty was passionate in his devotion to his chief. Wilson gave him a large share

W. J. Bryan to Wilson, Dec. 25, 1912; N. Hapgood to Wilson, Jan. 30, 1913; Felix Frankfurter to N. Hapgood, Feb. 12, 1913; Hamilton Holt to Wilson, Feb. 28, 1913, all in Wilson Papers. There are also many interesting items relating to this matter in the Papers of Louis D. Brandeis, in the Law School Library of the University of Louisville.

[14] On the grounds that Brandeis was not a Democrat, was too controversial a figure—as House thought—or else was so antagonistic to the business and financial interests that he could not be fair to them. House Diary, Jan. 23, 26, Feb. 13, 1913.

[15] Hapgood to L. D. Brandeis, Mar. 4, 1913, Brandeis Papers.

in determining patronage policies in the Northeast and Tumulty gave in return frequent advice, some of it foolish, on public opinion, legislative matters, and foreign policies. Tumulty was never popular among the official circle. After the election of 1916, House and Mrs. Wilson persuaded the President to ease Tumulty out of his job. Tumulty appealed pathetically to Wilson's better nature, and Wilson let him remain; but their relations were on a different basis after that.

Dominating the administration group was of course Wilson himself. In so far as he gave full rein to his subordinates and stood loyally by them, he was an excellent administrator. This was usually the case, especially in matters involving the prestige of the administration, or matters in which Wilson himself was not particularly interested. Moreover, he frequently took advice, and not a few of the administration's important policies were originated by Bryan, Lansing, McAdoo, and the others to a lesser degree.

There was, however, a less happy side to the Wilsonian character. Except for Colonel House, the group did not always enjoy satisfactory personal relations with their chief. Several of them bitterly resented Wilson's aloofness, his social *sang-froid*.[16] Worse still, practically all of them knew that when really vital questions were involved, Wilson did not want their advice unless it complemented his own thought or prejudices. Bryan, for example, realized this and resented Wilson's refusal to confide in him. Finally, Wilson's temperament put a heavy strain on his administrative talents. Because he valued loyalty and flattery over hardheaded frankness and cold and sometimes unpleasant logic, he was an extraordinarily poor judge of men.[17] Because he resented criticism, his advisers either told him what they thought he wanted to hear or else remained silent.[18]

[16] The Diary of Walter H. Page, in Houghton Library, Harvard University, n.d., but fall of 1916.

[17] John Sharp Williams, senator from Mississippi and a friend of Wilson, declared: "He was the best judge of measures and the poorest of men I ever knew." R. S. Baker, interview with John Sharp Williams, Mar. 11, 1927, Baker Collection. See also House Diary, Nov. 22, 1915, Sept. 6, Nov. 4, 1913, Nov. 14, 1914, Apr. 2, May 17, June 10, Aug. 27, 1916.

[18] The following description of Wilson's mental processes is the most illuminating this writer has read:

"When one comes to consider Mr. Wilson's mental processes, there is the feeling that intuition rather than reason played the chief part in the way in which he reached conclusions and judgments. In fact arguments, however soundly reasoned, did not appeal to him if they were opposed to his feeling of what was the right thing to do. Even established facts were ignored if they did

Personally, Wilson had changed little over the past ten years, except that advancing age had sharpened his traits of personality. He was still as much as ever intrigued by ideas and bored by details. A scholar rather than an intellectual, fascinated by ideas that had practical uses but not given to speculative thinking, intensive but restricted in his reading, Wilson's absorption with public affairs after 1910 demanded all his time and meager physical resources. His one great function, however, was to assimilate and synthesize ideas and proposals and then to use his incomparable power of leadership to translate them into statutory realities. Given favorable circumstances and a majority behind him, whether at Princeton, Trenton, or Washington, he usually succeeded.

Meanwhile, long before his inauguration, while he was in Bermuda and during the two and a half months after his return, Wilson worked intensively to lay the groundwork of his reform program. In Princeton and Trenton he conferred with Democratic leaders in Congress over the details of tariff and financial reform. He also made bold speeches in New York, Staunton, Virginia, Trenton, and Chicago, forecasting the realization of the New Freedom and warning the masters of capital not to use their great power to obstruct the fulfillment of that program. He did not believe, he said, that the businessman would use his power to start a panic in order to prevent the enactment of reform legislation. "If he does," Wilson warned, "I promise him, not for myself but for my countrymen, a gibbet as high as Haman." [19] There can be no doubt that he was imbued with high motives and a deep passion to set things aright.

Inaugural day dawned bright and clear—a good augury, some men thought, for the future of the first Democratic administration since 1897. In lofty and poetic phrases Wilson voiced his hopes of a new era

---

not fit in with this intuitive sense, this semi-divine power to select the right. Such an attitude of mind is essentially feminine. In the case of Mr. Wilson, it explains many things in his public career, which are otherwise very perplexing.

"In the first place it gave a superior place to his own judgment. With him it was a matter of conviction formed without weighing evidence and without going through the process of rational deduction. His judgments were always right in his own mind, because he knew that they were right. How did he know that they were right? Why he *knew* it and that was the best reason in the world. No other was necessary." "The Mentality of Woodrow Wilson," the Diary of Robert Lansing, in the Library of Congress, Nov. 20, 1921.

[19] This warning was given in his speech in New York Dec. 17, 1912, New York *World,* Dec. 18, 1912.

of social righteousness and iterated the partial program that had taken shape in his mind. The tariff would be lowered; the banking system would be overhauled and made the servant, rather than the master, of business. Strangely, he said nothing about strengthening the antitrust laws. Then, in a passage movingly beautiful, he ended: "This is not a day of triumph; it is a day of dedication. Here muster, not the forces of party, but the forces of humanity. Men's hearts wait upon us; men's lives hang in the balance; men's hopes call upon us to say what we will do. Who shall live up to the great trust? Who dares fail to try? I summon all honest men, all patriotic, all forward-looking men, to my side. God helping me, I will not fail them, if they will but counsel and sustain me!" [20]

No one who had read Wilson's writings could have doubted that he would inaugurate a new system of presidential leadership. From his youth he had been impressed by the almost fatal lack of responsibility in the presidential-Congressional system.[21] Until the early years of the twentieth century he believed the only way to obtain responsible government in the United States was adoption of the British Cabinet system. Roosevelt's success in arousing public opinion and bludgeoning Congress into action, however, apparently convinced Wilson that the President had all power sufficient for effective leadership, if only he called forth and used the power inherent in his office. The President, Wilson observed in 1907, "is . . . the political leader of the nation, or has it in his choice to be. The nation as a whole has chosen him, and is conscious that it has no other political spokesman. His is the only national voice in affairs. Let him once win the admiration and confidence of the country, and no other single force can withstand him, no combination of forces will easily overpower him." [22]

Wilson's strengthening and extension of the presidential powers constituted perhaps his most lasting contribution to American political practice. A strong believer in party government, he decided to work through and with his party in Congress, rather than to govern by a

[20] Ray S. Baker and William E. Dodd (eds.), *The Public Papers of Woodrow Wilson* (6 vols., New York, 1925–27), *The New Democracy,* I, 1–6.

[21] See, for example, his "Cabinet Government in the United States," *International Review,* VII (Aug., 1879), 146–163, or *Congressional Government* (Boston, 1885), the most famous of his earlier works.

[22] *Constitutional Government in the United States* (New York, 1908), p. 68. Wilson's views of the presidential office are best expressed in his letter to A. Mitchell Palmer, dated Feb. 5, 1913, printed in *The Public Papers, New Democracy,* I, 21–26.

coalition of progressives, as he might have done. Moreover, he conceived of himself as the responsible leader of his party, as the only leader who could speak for it and the country. Therefore, he felt himself personally charged with the introduction and sponsorship of important legislation; and for the first time in many years the Executive formulated a complete legislative program and worked closely with committee chairmen in giving body to it.

Wilson's methods and practice of leadership were spectacularly successful, to be sure; but they succeeded in large measure because of the peculiar circumstances that prevailed during his first administration. To begin with, because of the Republican rupture, the Democrats had a majority of seventy-three in the House during the critical first two years of the administration. Moreover, many of the Democratic members were new and inexperienced—114 of the 290 had been elected for the first time in 1912—and Wilson easily dominated them. In addition, the old-line Democratic leaders like Oscar W. Underwood, William C. Adamson, or Henry D. Clayton realized that the fate of their party depended upon their performance, and they willingly co-operated with the President to prove that they were not, as Republicans often charged, "the organized incapacity of the country." Finally, most of the Democrats in the Senate were able, responsible, and progressive, as eager as Wilson himself to give the administration success. The young, progressive group constituted a virtual galaxy: Joseph T. Robinson of Arkansas, Henry F. Ashurst of Arizona, Thomas J. Walsh of Montana, William Hughes of New Jersey, Henry F. Hollis of New Hampshire, Robert L. Owen of Oklahoma, and Atlee Pomerene of Ohio. Even the older, more conservative leaders in the Senate, like Furnifold M. Simmons of North Carolina, Thomas S. Martin of Virginia, John H. Bankhead of Alabama, or William J. Stone of Missouri, signified their readiness to follow the President. In these circumstances, Wilson's task was one mainly of uniting his forces and encouraging the strong Democratic determination to make good.

The first item on Wilson's legislative agenda was the smashing of the system of privileged tariff protection that the Republican party had carefully erected since 1861. On the day of his inauguration, Wilson called a special session of Congress, and on April 8 he went dramatically in person and delivered a short message before the two houses. Not since John Adams had a President appeared personally before the legislative branch. He wanted the congressmen and senators to see for themselves, he said, that he was a real person, "not a mere department of the Government hailing Congress from some isolated island of jealous power." He wanted them to think of him as a colleague in the great work of tariff reform they were now about to undertake. The following day he went to the Capitol and held the first of many conferences with Democratic leaders.[23] Thus Wilson not only asserted his personal leadership but also focused the attention of the country on Congress.

So largely has the tariff been eliminated from the politics of the present day that it would be easy to minimize the difficulties that Wilson and his supporters faced, or the critical character of this first struggle. Ever since the Civil War the high protective tariff had been to progressives one of the symbols of privilege. Cleveland had tried hard to lower the rates and had almost wrecked his party in the effort. Taft had promised tariff revision, and his failure had hastened the disruption of his party.

The bill that Chairman Oscar W. Underwood [24] of the Ways and Means Committee presented to the House on April 22 had been written for the most part two years before, when Congress had passed three Democratic tariff bills and Taft had vetoed them. Before Congress convened in special session in 1913 there had been months of new hearings and investigations. Wilson conferred frequently with Underwood while the measure was being written, and in the writing of the critical wool and sugar schedules he intervened in a decisive manner. Two years earlier Underwood had insisted upon moderate protection for wool and sugar; Wilson had supported him then, in the face of Bryan's demand for free wool. As in 1911, so again in 1913 the controversy over these two important products of Democratic states threatened to destroy party harmony. In the Ways and Means Committee the moderate protectionists had their way and voted a 15 per cent duty on raw wool. Then, for reasons that are not apparent, the

[23] *The New York Times,* Apr. 10, 1913.

[24] Chairman of the Ways and Means Committee and Majority Leader from 1911 to 1915, Underwood was probably the foremost authority in the country on tariff matters and one of the leading advocates of tariff reduction. Elected to the Senate in 1915, he served in that body until 1927. See Burton J. Hendrick, "Oscar W. Underwood, a New Leader from the New South," *McClure's Magazine,* XXXVIII (1912), 405–420, and Arthur S. Link, "The Underwood Presidential Movement of 1912," *Journal of Southern History,* XI (May, 1945), 230–245.

PLAYING TO THE GALLERIES

Nelson Harding in the Brooklyn Daily Eagle *satirizes protectionist arguments during the 1912 campaign.*

President called Underwood to the White House and sent him back to his Committee with instructions to obtain the adoption of free wool. As for sugar, the most Wilson would agree to was retention of a duty of one cent a pound for three years, after which it, too, must go on the free list. After a minor skirmish in the Commitee Wilson easily won his demand.

When Chairman Underwood presented his bill to the House of Representatives, competent observers agreed it was the most honest tariff measure that had been proposed since 1861.[25] By no means a free trade tariff, it aimed only at striking down the special advantages that the protectionist policy had conferred upon American manufacturers. The average ad valorem rate of the Payne-Aldrich tariff of 1909 was a little over 40 per cent; the Underwood bill brought rates down to about an average of 29 per cent and placed a whole host of important products on the free list. In brief, the aim of the Underwood bill was moderate protection by placing domestic industries in a genuinely competitive position with regard to European manufacturers. The duties were all ad valorem, with no devices to cover up exorbitant rates. In all cases where it could be shown that American products occupied a dominant position in the world market, rates were either abolished or drastically reduced. Agricultural machinery and most consumers' goods, such as food, clothing, and shoes, were put on the free list or given only incidental protection. All products manufactured by the so-called trusts, such as iron and steel and steel products, were also given free entry, thus satisfying the demands of the Midwestern insurgents.

Anticipating a decrease in customs receipts of about $100,000,000 because of the lower rates, the Ways and Means Committee added a provision for a graduated income tax that was drafted by Representative Cordell Hull of Tennessee, a leader in the struggle for tax reform. It was the first income tax under the Sixteenth Amendment, which had just been ratified on February 25, but exemptions were high and the graduated surtax was low.[26] Although the framers of the provision

[25] New York *World*, Apr. 8, 1913; *Harper's Weekly*, LVII (Apr. 19, 1913), 4; *Nation* (London), XIII (Apr. 12, 1913), 43–44; *Economist* (London), LXXVI (Apr. 12, 1913), 867–868; *World's Work*, XXVI (June, 1913), 137–138.

[26] A flat 1 per cent tax was applied on all incomes, individual and corporate, over $4,000. In addition, a surtax of 1 per cent on incomes from $20,000 to $50,000, 2 per cent on incomes from $50,000 to $100,000, and 3 per cent on incomes over $100,000 was added.

welcomed the opportunity to shift some of the tax burden from the poor to the wealthy, they had no intention of using the income tax to redistribute wealth or income.

This cautious beginning of a democratic tax policy apparently satisfied progressives in the House and was in time also approved by the Democratic members of the Senate Finance Committee. When the income tax provision of the Underwood bill came up for debate on the Senate floor on August 28, however, the Republican insurgents and radical Democrats, led by La Follette, George W. Norris of Nebraska, James K. Vardaman of Mississippi, and James A. Reed of Missouri, launched a stirring attack against it. La Follette demanded a maximum rate of 10 per cent, while Norris, in addition, proposed an inheritance tax ranging from 1 to 75 per cent. The Democratic radicals claimed a majority of the Senate caucus and threatened to rewrite the income tax provision if the Finance Committee did not surrender to their demands. So serious was the threat that Chairman Furnifold M. Simmons at once proposed a compromise, increasing the surtax to a maximum of 6 per cent on incomes over $500,000.[27] When the radicals still objected, Simmons hurriedly appealed to Wilson and Bryan for aid. In order to prevent party dissension, Bryan concurred in the compromise proposal, while the President agreed that it was wiser "to begin upon somewhat moderate lines." [28] In the face of this pressure, the Senate Democratic caucus approved the compromise on September 5 and it was adopted as one of the provisions of the final Underwood Act. Thus was the cautious first effort of the Ways and Means Committee transformed into the first serious attempt in the twentieth century to democratize the American tax structure.[29] The author of the original provision, Representative Hull, viewed the changes forced by the Senate progressives with delight. "I myself felt," he later recalled, "that if I should live two lifetimes I probably would not be able to

[27] Under the compromise proposal the surtax was 1 per cent on incomes from $20,000 to $50,000, 2 per cent from $50,000 to $75,000, 3 per cent from $75,000 to $100,000, 4 per cent from $100,000 to $250,000, 5 per cent from $250,000 to $500,000, and 6 per cent on incomes over $500,000.

[28] J. P. Tumulty to Wilson, Sept. 2, 1913; Wilson to Simmons, Sept. 4, 1913, both in Wilson Papers.

[29] For a more detailed account see Sidney Ratner, *American Taxation* (New York, 1942), pp. 324–333.

render public service equal to my part in the long fight for enactment of our income-tax system." [30]

The Underwood bill passed the House on May 8 by the resounding majority of 281 to 139. This, however, was as everyone thought it would be. Public attention now focused on the Senate. Would it betray party pledges as it had done during the passage of the Wilson-Gorman and Payne-Aldrich bills, by surrendering to the lobbyists and rewriting the measure in the interests of the manufacturers? It was a dangerous crisis, indeed, for Wilson's insistence on free wool and free sugar had embittered the very men whose votes were absolutely essential to the bill's success in the upper house.[31] In a canvass of the Senate on April 6, five Democrats from Louisiana, Arizona, Nevada, and Montana announced they would not support free sugar or free wool—and a change of three votes could turn a Democratic majority into a minority. Indeed, there was a grave danger that the Underwood bill would go the way of the Wilson and Payne bills, that Wilson's leadership would be repudiated in this first important test.

Confronted, therefore, with a perilous situation, Wilson at once took bold steps. First, he applied in full measure his great power of persuasion, by conciliatory but firm letters to and private conferences with the doubtful senators. "No party can ever for any length of time control the Government or serve the people which can not command the allegiance of its own minority," he wrote, for example, reminding a Louisiana senator of his duty to the party.[32] By the first of May it was evident that Wilson was winning his fight. On that day he conferred with six senators from the Western and Rocky Mountain states, and all of them agreed to support the Underwood bill when it came up in the Senate. One of them, Thomas J. Walsh of Montana, had declared only a week before that it was his duty to oppose free sugar and free wool; two weeks after his conference with Wilson he agreed that free sugar and wool would not bring disaster to his state. So confident was the President by the middle of May that he announced flatly that he would consider no compromise whatever on sugar and wool. When the

[30] Cordell Hull, *The Memoirs of Cordell Hull* (2 vols., New York, 1948), I, 71.

[31] The Democrats could not be sure of receiving a single progressive Republican vote, because by making the bill a strict party measure the President had alienated the Midwestern senators who had co-operated with the Democrats in passing the tariff bills of 1911.

[32] Wilson to J. R. Thornton, July 15, 1913, Wilson Papers.

Senate, in an important test vote on May 16, refused to instruct the Finance Committee to hold hearings on the Underwood bill, the administration forces had passed the first hurdle.

In spite of his victories in these preliminary skirmishes, Wilson knew the situation was still dangerous and uncertain. This was made all the more obvious when Senator Walsh, who had voted with the Democrats in refusing to force the Finance Committee to hold hearings, reversed his earlier position and announced publicly on May 19 that he would oppose free sugar and free wool. Besides, swarms of lobbyists had descended upon Washington and were hard at work on the senators from the West. The wool and sugar lobbyists, now joined by spokesmen of the cotton manufacturers, citrus fruit growers, and others, were in a state of high indignation and were bombarding senators with resolutions, petitions, and appeals.[33] Washington was so full of the representatives of special interests, Wilson said, that "a brick couldn't be thrown without hitting one of them." In a dramatic maneuver that gave fire and daring to his leadership, the President struck back. On May 26 he issued a public statement denouncing the "industrious and insidious" lobby. "It is of serious interest to the country," he declared, "that the people at large should have no lobby and be voiceless in these matters, while great bodies of astute men seek to create an artificial opinion and to overcome the interests of the public for their private profit." [34]

Reaction to Wilson's sensational statement was at first unfavorable, especially in the Senate, where Democratic leaders feared the President had overplayed his hand. In a move calculated to embarrass the administration, Senator Albert B. Cummins of Iowa proposed the appointment of a special committee to investigate the charge. The Democrats, of course, could not object; and when Senator La Follette suggested that all senators disclose their own property holdings that might in any way be affected by tariff reductions, no senator dared publicly to protest. What had begun as a political maneuver, therefore, soon turned into a sweeping investigation into the activities of private interests in behalf of legislation.[35]

[33] For accounts of the activities of the lobbyists, see New York *World*, Apr. 10, 22, 23, May 5, 18, 1913.

[34] *The New York Times*, May 27, 1913; printed in *The Public Papers, New Democracy*, I, 36.

[35] Senate Judiciary Committee, *Maintenance of Lobby to Influence Legislation, Hearings* . . ., 63d Cong., 1st sess. (4 vols., Washington, 1913).

The results were more favorable than Wilson or the progressives could have expected. The investigation proved that there was indeed an industrious lobby in behalf of sugar, whether insidious or not, and that an enormous amount of other lobbying was being carried on. But more important was the fact that each senator came before the committee and dutifully told how many shares of coal or steel stock, or how many acres of sugar or grazing land he owned.[36] For the first time in American history the economic interests of the members of the Senate were laid bare for the whole country to see. Under this glaring spotlight, the opposition of the Democratic senators, except for the two immovable Lousianians, wilted.

The first sign that the hardest phase of the struggle was over came when the Democratic caucus voted on June 25 to endorse free sugar and free wool. Although the Western senators dissented and grumbled, they made it plain they had no intention of carrying their fight to the Senate floor. On July 19 Chairman Simmons of the Finance Committee opened debate in the upper house; and if the Republicans had not sought to delay banking legislation by debating the tariff bill schedule by schedule, it might have been passed almost at once. As it was, the Republicans talked tariff all during the summer months. They made a final and unsuccessful effort on September 8 to break the now solid Democratic ranks—by offering an amendment for a gradual reduction of the wool duty. The following day the opposition collapsed and the Senate, forty-four to thirty-seven, passed the revised tariff bill. Among the Democrats, only the two Louisiana senators, Joseph E. Ransdell and John R. Thornton, voted against it.

When the Senate had finished its work, many observers could hardly believe what they saw. Instead of wrecking tariff reform, the Senate had actually effected a general reduction of 4 per cent in the Underwood rates, mainly by putting food and other farm products on the free list, thus bringing the general level of rates down to 24–26 per cent. Moreover, the Senate had increased the maximum surtax on

---

[36] For example, Senator Albert B. Fall of New Mexico revealed that he was a large owner of cattle, horses, sheep, and coal lands. Senator Asle J. Gronna of North Dakota said he owned a farm of nine thousand acres and had opposed the Canadian reciprocity treaty of 1911. Senator Henry F. Lippitt of Rhode Island admitted that he had extensive holdings in textile mills and that he had always favored a tariff on textile products. Senator Lee S. Overman of North Carolina said he and his wife owned shares in cotton mills, but that he stood with the President for tariff reductions.

incomes from 3 to 6 per cent. It was almost unbelievable. "I did not much think we should live to see these things," was Houston's surprised comment.[37] The House conferees accepted most of the Senate amendments and the revised bill was approved by the House on September 30 and by the Senate on October 2. A day later the President signed it in a pleasant ceremony at the White House. "It is hard to speak of these things without seeming to go off into campaign eloquence," he told an assembled throng of Democratic leaders, "but that is not my feeling. It is one very profound, a feeling of profound gratitude." [38]

What Wilson's victory in the tariff fight signified no one could doubt. Whether the operation of the Underwood law would in fact reduce the cost of living, as Democrats prophesied, was unimportant as compared with the fact that the party had proved itself free from shackling alliances with special privilege and capable of pulling together. As one editor put it: "This is no tariff by log-rolling, by manipulation, by intrigue, by bribery. It was bought by no campaign contributions. It was dictated by no conspiracy between corrupt business and corrupt politics." [39]

Significant, also, was the fact that by virtue of this victory Wilson's dominance in the Democratic party was firmly established. A weaker man would have failed where he succeeded and, as a London editor observed, the tariff victory raised Wilson "at a single stage from the man of promise to the man of achievement." [40] It was fortunate for the President that events turned out as they did, for another and more important struggle was already well in progress: the administration's campaign to free the nation's banks and businessmen from monopolistic control. It was a battle in which Wilson needed all the support he could find.

No objective stood higher on the Democratic reform schedule than banking and currency reform. In fact, there was by the beginning of 1913 complete agreement among informed circles that the most pressing economic need of the time was a fundamental reorganization of the nation's banking and money system.[41] Bankers and businessmen,

[37] David F. Houston to W. H. Page, c. Sept. 9, 1913, the Papers of Walter H. Page, in Houghton Library, Harvard University.
[38] *The New York Times*, Oct. 4, 1913.
[39] New York *World*, Oct. 4, 1913.
[40] London *Nation*, XIV (Oct. 11, 1913), 90.
[41] There are literally thousands of letters, written during December, 1912,

economists and leaders of both parties agreed that the national banking system, which had been established during the Civil War, was about as badly adapted to the financial needs of a great nation as any system could be. The national banking structure was disjointed and without any effective central control. The provisions for mobilizing the banking reserves of the country were entirely inadequate in periods of crisis; the money supply bore no necessary relation to the needs of business and industry.

The sharp bankers' panic of 1907 had reminded the country of the grave danger of attempting to get along with immobile reserves and an inelastic money supply. It had also evoked widespread discussion as to a remedy and the appointment of the National Monetary Commission, headed by Senator Nelson W. Aldrich. After studying intensively the banking systems of the world, the Commission offered its report and recommendations to Congress in 1911 and 1912.[42] Opinion was unanimous that financial reform was urgent, but the publication of the Aldrich report revealed a profound divergence over the kind of banking system the country should adopt.

The Aldrich plan was drawn up by Paul M. Warburg, of Kuhn, Loeb & Company,[43] and was cordially endorsed by the American Bankers' Association; in brief, it represented the ideal of almost the entire banking community. It provided for one great central bank, the National Reserve Association, with a capital of at least $100 million and with fifteen branches in various sections. The branches were to be controlled by the member banks on a basis of their capitalization. The National Reserve Association would issue currency, based on gold and commercial paper, that would be the liability of the bank and not of the government. It would also carry a portion of member banks' reserves, determine discount reserves, buy and sell on the open market,

---

and January and February, 1913, in the Papers of Carter Glass, in the Library of the University of Virginia, from businessmen, manufacturers, merchants, editors, or bankers, all strongly condemning the national banking and currency system and begging Glass and his House committee to lead the way in reforming the system. There would seem to be no doubt of the widespread nature of business discontent and of the conviction that banking and monetary reform was the most important need of the country.

[42] *National Monetary Commission,* Sen. Doc. 243, 62d Cong., 2d sess. (Washington, 1912). The Commission also published twenty-four monographs on all phases of banking problems and practices. These were published as Senate Documents from 1910 to 1912.

[43] At least, so Warburg told Colonel House. House Diary, Mar. 31, 1913.

and hold the deposits of the federal government. The branches and businessmen of each of the fifteen districts would elect thirty out of the thirty-nine members of the board of directors of the National Reserve Association.[44]

To progressive Democrats, the adoption of the Aldrich plan could mean only the perpetuation of existing Wall Street control—nothing less, in fact, than a resurrection of the second Bank of the United States, which Jackson had destroyed. After talking so much about the necessity for banking reform, Wilson and his party were now obliged to propose an alternative to the Aldrich plan, one that would avoid the danger of monopolistic control and at the same time satisfy banking and other conservative opinion that it was not a populistic, cheap-money scheme. Devising such an alternative and getting it adopted in the face of the united opposition of the banking community proved to be a task of infinite difficulty.

Soon after the election of 1912 a subcommittee of the House Banking Committee, headed by Carter Glass of Virginia, began to make plans for an exchange of views and hearings on currency legislation. There was, however, no agreement or even understanding among the Democratic leaders as to what kind of banking and currency system should be established. An ardent foe of the central bank plan, Glass was determined to establish such a loose and disconnected system of reserve banks that no one bank could ever become dominant. On the vital issue of control, however, he was thoroughly conservative. On the other hand, Bryan insisted that the government control the system and issue the currency—a proposition that caused conservative editors, and Democrats like Colonel House, to shudder. It was fortunate for the country that Wilson knew practically nothing about the details of the matter, had made no commitments on the basic issues, and stood free to serve as mediator among the rival Democratic factions.

Ten days after his return from Bermuda, Wilson called Glass and the subcommittee's expert, H. Parker Willis,[45] to Princeton for the first conference on the banking bill. Glass outlined his plan for a decentralized, privately controlled reserve system with possibly twenty

---

[44] For a brief analysis of the Aldrich plan see H. Parker Willis, *The Federal Reserve System* (New York, 1923), pp. 79–83.

[45] Formerly a professor of political economy at Washington and Lee and George Washington universities, in 1912 Willis was associate editor of the New York *Journal of Commerce*. He subsequently became secretary of the Federal Reserve Board and one of the leading authorities on the Federal Reserve System.

independent reserve banks. Wilson tentatively approved, but he asked
Glass and Willis to draw plans for a general supervisory board, what
he called the "capstone" of the system.[46] To Glass, Wilson's proposal
smacked of "dangerous centralization"; he was not at all convinced
any such "capstone" was necessary; but he and Willis proceeded
faithfully to follow the President-elect's instructions. By January 15,
1913, they had completed a tentative draft of the bill. Then, from
January 7 to February 17, the House subcommittee listened patiently
while bankers and businessmen voiced their eagerness for a strong and
highly centralized reserve system, privately controlled. When the
hearings were ended, Willis went carefully through the draft bill, re-
vising and strengthening its technical provisions in light of the bankers'
suggestions.

Thus, even before Wilson's inaugural, the administration had seemingly come to an agreement on the form and detail of the new banking
and currency bill. Working in close harmony with the bankers, Glass
and Willis had constructed a measure that, in Glass' words, would
"commend itself for soundness to the bankers of the country and . . .
secure the support of the business community." [47] In this objective they
had apparently succeeded, for leading bankers in New York, Chicago,
and St. Louis had promised cordial support. There had been no real
test of opinion among the Democrats, however, for the details of the
Glass plan had been kept a carefully guarded secret among Wilson,
Glass, Willis, and McAdoo. It did not seem to occur to Glass that his
plan might evoke hostility from the progressive element of the party.

The secret leaked when House sent a memorandum on the Glass
bill, which he had obtained from Wilson, to his friend, Paul M.
Warburg, one of the really competent authorities on banking practice
in the country.[48] From Warburg news of the plan spread through the
financial community and was blazoned in the press. Within a short

[46] Carter Glass, *An Adventure in Constructive Finance* (Garden City, N.Y.,
1927), pp. 81–84.

[47] Glass to Festus J. Wade, Jan. 24, 1913, Glass Papers.

[48] Formerly a partner in the banking house of M. M. Warburg & Company
of Hamburg, Germany, Warburg was at this time a partner in the New York
firm of Kuhn, Loeb & Company. He strongly favored a powerful central bank
with three or four branches, modeled after the German Reichsbank. Moreover,
he stood firmly against public control of the new system or governmental issue
of the currency. See his *The Owen-Glass Bill, Some Criticisms and Suggestions,*
written at Silas-Maria, Switzerland, July 15, 1913 (New York [?], 1913), and
Warburg to House, July 22, 1913, House Papers.

time a controversy of serious proportions was developing in the inner circle of the administration and in Congress—so serious that for a time it threatened to disrupt the party and destroy all hopes for financial reform.

The issue at stake was nothing less than the fundamental character of the proposed banking system. Glass and Wilson had agreed upon what was substantially a decentralized version of the Aldrich plan; there was not the slightest chance the progressive wing of the party would accept it. They demanded, instead, outright governmental control over the reserve system, and governmental issue of the currency. McAdoo, for example, came forward with an entirely new proposal to establish the system as an adjunct of the Treasury Department. Robert L. Owen, chairman of the Senate Banking Committee, and Samuel Untermyer, counsel for the Pujo "Money Trust" Committee, supported the McAdoo plan. Realizing that adoption of the Glass bill would signify repudiation of the Democratic platforms of 1896, 1900, 1908, and 1912, as well as his own convictions on the banking and money question, Bryan regretfully warned the President that he would have to oppose the measure.[49]

The administration was shaken during May and early June by these dissensions, but not, as Glass thought at the time and afterward, because a group of Greenbackers sought to wreck his constructive efforts. The trouble arose simply because the progressive element refused to stand by and see control of the banking system given over to private hands, especially if this were done by a "reform" administration. As the controversy developed, Glass appealed to his banker friends for support against McAdoo's "utter perversion of the true function of government." Bryan in effect replied that insistence upon the Glass bill would make any banking legislation impossible and wreck the Democratic party.[50]

Wilson was strangely surprised and of course profoundly disturbed by the dimensions of the struggle. By the middle of June it was plain the controversy would continue for months unless he could find a workable compromise and reconcile the opposing factions. If he had any genuine convictions on the basic issues, we do not know them.

[49] House Diary, May 11, 15, 19, 1913; House to Wilson, May 15, 1913, House Papers; Mary B. Bryan (ed.), *The Memoirs of William Jennings Bryan* (Philadelphia, 1925), p. 370.

[50] *Ibid.*, p. 371.

Probably he was undecided, even unconcerned, over what he thought was a question of detail. In any event, he had to either intervene quickly and decisively or else abandon his role as leader.

He could not decide, however, without consulting the man whose opinions on economic questions he respected above all others—Louis D. Brandeis. Brandeis came to the White House on June 11 and told the President frankly that Bryan and the progressives were right. The government alone should issue the currency, Brandeis insisted; and the government alone must control the banking system. "The conflict between the policies of the Administration and the desires of the financiers and of big business, is an irreconcilable one," he warned.[51] Brandeis' admonition must have persuaded Wilson that concessions to the progressive element had to be made. In several show-down conferences with Glass, Owen, and McAdoo June 17–19, the President announced that he would insist upon exclusive governmental control of the Federal Reserve Board and upon making Federal Reserve notes obligations of the United States. It was the absolute minimum that would satisfy the Bryan element, who wanted governmental operation of the entire system, and the most that Glass would concede, but it sufficed.

On June 23, therefore, Wilson went again to Congress and explained the administration's program for banking reform. "The control of the system of banking and of issue," he declared, "which our new laws are to set up must be public, not private, must be vested in the Government itself, so that the banks may be the instruments, not the masters, of business and of individual enterprise and initiative." [52] He must have reckoned on the opposition of the banking interests, but he was confident at least of the united support of his party in Congress. Actually, another revolt in the party was gathering, one that again threatened to split the party ranks in Congress and destroy all hopes of legislative action.

The revolt was brewing among the Southern agrarian spokesmen, the inheritors of the Jacksonian-Populist tradition, who demanded really thoroughgoing and radical reform.[53] Because the Glass bill did

---

[51] Brandeis to Wilson, June 14, 1913, Wilson Papers, embodying the substance of the views Brandeis had expressed at the conference of June 11, 1913.

[52] *The Public Papers, The New Democracy,* I, 39–40.

[53] For a further discussion of this group see Arthur S. Link, "The South and the New Freedom: An Interpretation," *The American Scholar,* XX (Summer, 1951), 314–324.

not provide for the destruction of interlocking arrangements among and the prohibition of restrictive practices by the great banks, they charged the administration with betrayal of the Democratic platform; because the bill authorized private control of the regional banks and the issuance of currency based in part upon commercial paper, they accused the Democratic leaders of surrendering control of the banking system and the money supply to private interests. Finally, because the Glass bill made no provision for short-term agricultural credit, these agrarian representatives accused the administration of selling out the farmers to the moneylenders. The leader of the rebels, Robert L. Henry of Texas, chairman of the powerful Rules Committee of the House, opened the battle on June 14 with a blast in the press.[54]

The administration went serenely on, however, unaware of the meaning or seriousness of the new revolt. Glass and Owen introduced identical bills on June 26; but when Glass asked for approval by his committee, the radical majority took charge. Over Glass' angry protest, they adopted an amendment prohibiting interlocking directorates. Rumors that they had even prepared an entirely new banking bill seemed to be borne out when the committee, on July 25, refused to report the Glass measure to the House Democratic caucus.

At this juncture Wilson entered the fight, pleading, cajoling, and promising that the interlocking directorate amendment would be incorporated in the antitrust bill. The rebels accepted the President's promise and then moved to their most important demand: provision for the discounting by reserve banks of short-term agricultural paper. It was when Representative J. Willard Ragsdale of South Carolina introduced a series of amendments on July 24 to encompass this objective that the really critical struggle began. The Eastern press scoffed at this proposal for "cotton currency" and "corn tassel currency" and predicted the administration would never surrender.[55] And when Wilson persuaded the Banking Committee to report the Glass bill to the Democratic caucus, observers were confident the President had stood firm.

---

[54] *The New York Times,* June 15, 1913. Other leaders of the agrarian faction were Representative Otis T. Wingo of Arkansas, James Willard Ragsdale of South Carolina, Joe Henry Eagle of Texas, Robert J. Bulkley of Ohio, and George A. Neeley of Kansas.

[55] *The New York Times,* July 26, 1913; Springfield *Republican,* Aug. 19, 1913; *Financial Age,* XXVIII (Aug. 23, 1913), 297; *Bankers' Magazine,* LXXXVII (Sept., 1913), 234–235.

The radicals, however, had meantime won Bryan to their side. After the first great compromise was effected, Bryan had heartily supported the Glass bill; but the radical leaders now convinced him their demand for short-term agricultural credit was reasonable, and he pleaded with Wilson at least not to oppose the demand when it was made in the caucus.[56]

For the President there now seemed no course open but to yield. When the Democratic caucus met from the eleventh through the twenty-eighth of August, the Southern and Western representatives combined to force an amendment for the discounting of short-term agricultural paper.[57] Even this concession, however, did not appease the more radical agrarians, who continued to attack the bill because it authorized so-called asset currency and private control of the reserve banks. At this critical stage in the caucus deliberation, Bryan issued a fervent appeal to the radicals to support the measure, assuring them that Wilson would fulfill his promise to destroy interlocking directorates.[58] Bryan's masterful plea ended the struggle. On August 28 the caucus, by 116 to 9, voted to approve the Glass bill with the agricultural credit and less important amendments. Not all the radicals were pacified; a few of them, like Representative Joe H. Eagle of Texas, continued to oppose the bill. But the great majority of them, including their leader, Representative Robert L. Henry, were satisfied and voted for the bill when it passed the House on September 18 by a vote of 285 to 85.[59]

During that epochal summer of 1913 Wilson and his advisers moved from crisis to crisis. No sooner had the administration done the things necessary to consolidate Democratic support behind the Glass bill than there arose a virtual storm of protest and abuse from bankers, business leaders, and their spokesmen in Congress, all of them up in arms denouncing the bill as socialistic, theoretical, vicious, as the "preposterous offspring of ignorance and unreason." Meeting in Boston in early October, the American Bankers' Association severely criticized the bill,

[56] Bryan to Wilson, Aug. 6, 1913, Wilson Papers.

[57] *The New York Times,* Aug. 15, 26, 1913; "Journal of the Democratic Caucus on Banking and Currency, August 11–28, 1913," in Glass Papers.

[58] Bryan to Carter Glass, Aug. 22, 1913, printed in *The Commoner,* Sept., 1913.

[59] Twenty-three Republicans and ten Progressives, most of them from the Middle West, supported the measure. Only three Democrats voted against it. *The New York Times,* Sept. 19, 1913.

and appointed a committee to wait upon the President. Even the so-called liberal bankers, George M. Reynolds, Sol Wexler, A. Barton Hepburn, and Festus J. Wade, who had helped frame the original measure, turned against it because of the provision for public control.

In the face of this torrent of abuse and criticism, Wilson stood immovable. For one thing, it was evident that the bankers were rapidly maneuvering themselves into an indefensible position as advocates of the private against the public interest. For another, the amended Glass bill had the warm support of all the independent and progressive newspapers and journals of the country, which kept hammering at the opposition all during the summer and fall.[60] Even more valuable and more surprising, however, was the support that some leaders of the business world gave the measure.[61]

These were all encouraging signs that the great mass of non-banking opinion in the country was behind the administration, and prospects for prompt action by the Senate seemed bright until three Democratic members of the Banking Committee—James A. O'Gorman of New York, James A. Reed of Missouri, and Gilbert M. Hitchcock of Nebraska—bolted their party and upset the legislative timetable. The Republican-Democratic coalition now dominating the Committee insisted, first, on holding a long series of new hearings, which proceeded at a leisurely pace from the first of September until October 25. Meanwhile, Wilson was at work almost constantly with Democratic leaders in the Senate, urging and pleading, even threatening to go to the people if the obstructionists persisted in blocking legislation. The party leaders were as indignant as the President, but they were helpless.

The situation changed suddenly around the middle of November, however, when O'Gorman and Reed, one intimidated and the other satisfied, surrendered and permitted the Democratic members of the Committee to make a report.[62] On November 22 the Committee re-

[60] E.g., Springfield *Republican,* June 20, 21, 23, 24, July 3, Aug. 7, Sept. 19, Oct. 7, 1913; *Harper's Weekly,* LVII (June 28, 1913), 3; *ibid.,* LVIII (Aug. 16, 1913), 4; *Outlook,* CIV (July 5, 1913), 490–491; *Saturday Evening Post,* CLXXXVI (Sept. 27, 1913), 26; St. Louis *Republic,* Sept. 29, 30, 1913; St. Louis *Star,* Sept. 3, 1913.

[61] The Merchants' Association of New York, for example, endorsed the Federal Reserve bill on October 9, while the constituent membership of the United States Chamber of Commerce approved it by a vote of 306 to 17. *The New York Times,* Oct. 10, 1913; New York *Journal of Commerce,* Oct. 15, 1913.

[62] Hitchcock's opposition stemmed in part from the fact that he was himself

ported three separate drafts of the Glass bill to the Senate, and debate was begun at once. The Senate leaders were determined to pass the bill before Christmas, and progress from this time on was uninterrupted. The Senate passed the Federal Reserve bill, fifty-four to thirty-four, on December 19;[63] three days later the conference committee agreed, and on December 23 the two houses ratified and the President signed the measure.

Thus it was that the greatest single piece of constructive legislation of the Wilson era was enacted, and almost exactly one year after that bleak afternoon when Wilson had held his first meeting with Glass and Willis in Princeton. Clearly the administration's whole concept and plan of banking and currency legislation had undergone profound alteration since that day. What had begun as a bill designed to serve only the business community and to reinforce private control over banking and the currency had metamorphosed, under progressive pressure, into a measure that offered substantial benefits to farmers as well as businessmen and allowed at least a modicum of public regulation.

The tide of progressive banking concepts had receded, however, once the bill left the House of Representatives. During the long struggle in the Senate, the Democratic leaders had felt themselves compelled to make concessions that gravely impaired the power of the Federal Reserve Board and enlarged the private influence. The Board, for example, was deprived of authority directly to set the discount rates of the several reserve banks and was empowered only to veto changes in existing rates; the gold reserve behind the Federal Reserve notes was

---

a banker and a spokesman of banking interests and in part from resentment at the administration's patronage policies in Nebraska.

Reed had apparently bolted because the President would not appoint his candidate as postmaster of Kansas City. Wilson finally named Reed's man.

O'Gorman, on the other hand, was determined to teach the President that he should not attempt to coerce the Senate. The New York senator, moreover, was working hand in glove with Tammany, and the administration's warfare on that organization had embittered him. When the administration-supported mayoralty candidate, John P. Mitchel, soundly thrashed the Tammany nominee in the New York election in November, however, O'Gorman began to view the President in a more favorable light. For an extended discussion see Charles W. Thompson's comments in *The New York Times Magazine,* Nov. 16, 1913.

[63] All Democrats present, including Hitchcock, voted for the amended bill. They were joined by six Republicans—John W. Weeks of Massachusetts, Thomas Sterling of South Dakota, John D. Works and George C. Perkins of California, Wesley L. Jones of Washington, and George W. Norris of Nebraska—and by the lone Progressive senator, Miles Poindexter of Washington.

increased from thirty-three to forty per cent, as a result of a single speech by Senator Elihu Root of New York; finally, the bankers won the addition of an Advisory Commission, composed of bankers, to the Board. Yet the Glass plan survived in its fundamental structure and purposes, in spite of the abuse hurled against it and in spite of the severity of the conservative attack in the Senate. The basic structure— twelve Federal Reserve banks, privately controlled, regulated and supervised in the public interest by the capstone of the Federal Reserve Board—still remained.

The creation of the Federal Reserve System was the crowning achievement of the first Wilson administration. The system was not created to prevent industrial depressions or banish poverty. The framers of the act hoped merely that it would provide the country with an absolutely sound yet elastic currency, establish machinery for mobilizing the entire banking reserves of the country in times of financial stringency, prevent the concentration of reserves and credit in New York City, and, finally, preserve private enterprise in banking on the local level while at the same time imposing a degree of public regulation. On the whole, they succeeded remarkably well.

CHAPTER 3

The New Freedom and the
Progressive Movement, 1913-16

THE UNSUCCESSFUL struggle of the progressives to achieve a reserve banking and currency system owned and operated exclusively by the government underscored the dilemma in which the American progressive movement found itself during the years immediately preceding the First World War. The great impulses of the several movements for social and economic justice were now pulsating more strongly than before; diverse groups were in the field, campaigning for stringent regulation of industry, woman suffrage, federal child labor legislation, and advanced governmental aid to labor, farmers, tenant farmers, and the unemployed. It was inevitable that these progressives [1] should sooner or later coalesce to put their program across. The important question was whether the New Freedom philosophy was sufficiently dynamic to accommodate the advanced pro-

[1] Diverse though they were, the several parts of advanced progressivism were clearly distinguishable by 1913. The more radical progressives included, first, the several important organized groups dedicated to the cause of social justice —the American Association for Labor Legislation, the Consumers' League, the organized social workers, the National Child Labor Committee, and the National Association for the Advancement of Colored People. The leaders of organized labor should also be included, even though they generally refused to associate themselves with the professional students of labor problems. Finally, there were the farm organizations, like the National Farmers' Union, and shortly afterward the Non-Partisan League, that were now demanding a dynamic program of governmental intervention in their behalf, especially the establishment of a governmental system of long-term rural credits.

gressive concepts; whether Wilson himself could abandon his liberal, *laissez-faire* rationale and become a progressive statesman; whether, in brief, there was room in the Democratic party for progressivism of this type.

Evaluating the New Freedom at the end of the first ten months of Wilson's incumbency, advanced progressives would have disagreed in their answer to that vital question. Most of them conceded that the Underwood tariff was a step in the right direction, even though it was in part based on *laissez-faire* assumptions. They viewed the Federal Reserve Act, however, with mixed reactions. Uncompromising progressives, like La Follette, and the irreconcilable agrarians denounced it because of the large measure of private control that it allowed,[2] while middle-of-the-road progressives approved it as beginning a new experiment in public regulation. Even so, they must have suspected that Wilson's concessions to the progressive concept had been made under duress and were not the result of any genuine convictions on his part.

That this suspicion was well founded was demonstrated time and again from 1913 to 1916, by the manner in which the President either obstructed or refused to encourage the fulfillment of a large part of the progressive platform. There was, for example, the way in which he maneuvered on the important question of the application of the anti-trust law to labor unions. Since 1906 the American Federation of Labor had waged a relentless campaign to obtain immunity from the application of the Sherman Law to its methods of industrial warfare, particularly the secondary boycott.[3] The Democratic platforms of 1908 and 1912 had endorsed labor's demands, and Democratic leaders in Congress from 1911 to March, 1913, had tried conscientiously, if unsuccessfully, to redeem their party's pledges.

Failing to get their contempt and injunction bills past the Republican opposition, the Democratic leaders had attached a rider to the Sundry Civil bill of 1913, prohibiting the Justice Department from using any funds therein appropriated in the prosecution of labor unions or farm organizations. President Taft promptly vetoed the bill, de-

---

[2] E.g., R. M. La Follette, "Legalizing the 'Money Power,' " *La Follette's Weekly*, V (Dec. 27, 1913), 1; Daniel T. Cushing, *The Betrayal of the People in the Aldrich-Wilson Federal Reserve Act and the Rural Credits Act* (Washington, 1916).

[3] For a brief account of this campaign see "The Twenty-Year Struggle for Adequate Eight-Hour Legislation," *American Federationist*, XX (Aug., 1913), 590–616.

nouncing the rider as "class legislation of the most vicious sort." When the same measure came up again in the special session in April, Wilson intimated to Congressional leaders that he would not oppose the exemption. News of Wilson's apparent approval and passage of the bill with the rider attached evoked a flood of petitions and appeals to the President from practically every spokesman of organized capital in the country, and from many of his personal friends as well. "The most vicious bill ever enacted by a Congress of the United States now awaits your approval or your dissent," exclaimed George Harvey, perhaps the most authoritative conservative spokesman in the country.[4]

Under such pressure Wilson weakened and then reversed his position. He signed the bill on June 23 but at the same time issued a statement explaining that the rider was merely an expression of Congressional opinion and that he would find money in the general funds of the Justice Department for the prosecution of any groups that broke the antitrust law. The explanation was not convincing, either to conservatives or to labor leaders. "He attempts to retain the support of those who insist upon this special privilege . . . by signing the bill," Taft commented, "and at the same time to mitigate the indignation of those who have regarded this as a test of his political character by condemning the rider in a memorandum and excusing his signature." [5] On the other hand, Samuel Gompers, president of the A.F. of L., had tried to make it plain that labor demanded nothing less than class legislation in its behalf; he later added that his union would not be satisfied until the principles embodied in the rider had been written into substantive law.

In this first critical test, however, Wilson had signified that he would adhere to the New Freedom doctrine of "special privileges to none," that he would no more approve special legislation on labor's behalf than such legislation in the interest of any other class. Using the New Freedom doctrine to thwart the demands of the farm groups was somewhat more difficult, however, as the agrarian spokesmen constituted perhaps a majority of the Democratic membership in Congress. Under heavy pressure, Wilson had consented to the addition of the short-term

[4] "An Appeal to the President," *Harper's Weekly*, LVII (May 17, 1913), 3–4; also "Six Months of Wilson," *North American Review*, CXCVIII (Nov., 1913), 576–587.

[5] W. H. Taft to Gus J. Karger, June 25, 1913, the Papers of William Howard Taft, in the Library of Congress.

agricultural credit amendment to the Glass bill; but this had not involved federal subvention to farmers, nor did it satisfy farm groups throughout the country. Their chief objective was the establishment, underwriting, and operation by the federal government of a system of long-term credits. The question had been under discussion for many years; all three major parties promised some form of federal aid in their platforms of 1912. By 1913 the movement was so powerful that no one expected the new administration to resist it.

Indeed, at the beginning of the serious discussions of the rural credits question it appeared that no occasion for controversy would arise. In the spring of 1913 Congress authorized the appointment by the President of a Rural Credits Commission to study the problem and bring in a recommendation. The Commission studied rural credits systems in Europe during the summer; then its chairman, Senator Duncan U. Fletcher of Florida, framed a bill that would establish a system of privately controlled land banks, operating under federal charter.[6] Secretary of Agriculture Houston endorsed the bill and Wilson added his warm approval. In fact, he conferred with the joint subcommittee of the House and Senate banking committees that had charge of the legislation and urged prompt passage of the Fletcher bill.

Encouraged by the President's friendly attitude, the joint subcommittee at once set to work and came up, around May 1, 1914, with a bill that adopted more or less the framework of the system proposed in the Fletcher plan but added a provision requiring the government to furnish the capital of the land banks, to purchase their bonds if private investors did not, and to operate the system. It was practically the same rural credit bill that was finally passed in 1916. The reporting of this, the so-called Hollis-Bulkley bill, set off a significant controversy in the administration, significant because it pointed up Wilson's limited view of the proper function of government. The root of the difficulty was that the farm spokesmen were convinced a rural credits system without governmental support and sponsorship would never succeed in making farmers independent of private moneylenders, while Wilson and Houston were just as strongly convinced this was no kind of business for the federal government to engage in.

Houston cogently expressed this sentiment in a speech before the National Grange at Manchester, New Hampshire, in November, 1913. "I am not impressed," he said, "with the wisdom and the justice of

[6] Introduced on August 9, 1913.

proposals that would take the money of all the people, through bonds
or other devices, and lend it to the farmers or to any other class at a
rate of interest lower than the economic conditions would normally
require and lower than that at which other classes are securing their
capital. This would be special legislation of a particularly odious type,
and no new excursions in this direction would be palatable when we
are engaged in the gigantic task of restoring the simple rule of equity." [7]

The controversy came to a head when Representative Robert J.
Bulkley insisted on introducing the joint subcommittee's bill, in spite
of the indignant protests of Carter Glass and other administration
leaders. To head off the revolt, Majority Leader Underwood called a
caucus of the House Democrats. To the assembled throng Glass read a
fervent appeal from the President declaring he would gladly approve
the Hollis-Bulkley bill without the governmental aid feature. But,
Wilson added, "I have a very deep conviction that it is unwise and
unjustifiable to extend the credit of the Government to a single class
of the community." This, he continued, was a clear and permanent
conviction, one that had come to him, as it were, "out of fire." [8]
Obviously threatening a veto of the Hollis-Bulkley bill, Wilson's letter
angered the agrarian spokesman, who avowed there would be no rural
credits legislation at all until the President changed his mind. Nor was
there any such legislation, until new political circumstances prevailed in
1916 and Wilson abruptly reversed his position.

Wilson's momentary defeat of the rural credits measure pleased the
private investors, but it generated a good deal of bitterness among the
rural leaders of the country. Efforts of Democrats like Glass and Bryan
to justify the President's stand in terms of "sound Democratic doctrine" [9] made little sense to editors of farm papers and presidents of
granges and farmers' unions. When Congress reconvened in December,
1914, Senator Henry F. Hollis warned the President that he and
Bulkley planned to renew their campaign, even though Wilson's
Annual Message had relegated rural credits legislation to the scrap
heap.[10] Pressure from the rural sections mounted during the following

[7] Quoted in *Commercial West*, XXIV (Nov. 22, 1913), 7–8.
[8] Wilson to Glass, May 12, 1914, the Woodrow Wilson Papers, in the
Library of Congress.
[9] Glass to D. C. Pryer, July 9, 1914, the Papers of Carter Glass, in the
Library of the University of Virginia; Glass to Herbert Myrick, May 18, 1914,
ibid.; "Rural Credits Legislation," *The Commoner*, June, 1914.
[10] Hollis to Wilson, Dec. 11, 1914, Wilson Papers. In his Annual Message of

months. Without warning to administration leaders, the Senate on February 25, 1915, adopted an amendment to the agricultural appropriation bill providing for the establishment of a rural credits system in the Treasury Department. A few days later, on March 2, the House approved the Hollis-Bulkley bill, but the session expired before the conference committee could agree, and the President was spared the embarrassment of vetoing a bill that had overwhelming support in Congress and among the farmers of the country.

Thus Wilson successfully stood off the movements designed to swing the influence and financial support of the federal government to labor unions and farmers in their struggle for advancement. His strong conviction that there were definite limits beyond which the federal authority should not be extended was demonstrated, again, in the manner in which he thwarted the campaign of the social justice groups to commit the administration to a positive program of social legislation.

One of the chief objectives of the reformers, for example, was a federal child labor law. A model bill, drafted by the National Child Labor Committee, was introduced in the House by Representative A. Mitchell Palmer on January 26, 1914. It would be incorrect to say Wilson opposed it; he simply refused to support it because he thought it was unconstitutional.[11] And so long as he withheld his aggressive support the bill would never get past the Senate.

Another social justice objective was woman suffrage. Here, again, Wilson did not openly fight the cause but rather refused to aid it. And Southern opposition in Congress was so strong that without Wilson's most determined effort applied in its behalf a suffrage amendment could never obtain the necessary two-thirds vote. Wilson probably did

---

December 8, 1914, Wilson had declared: "The great subject of rural credits still remains to be dealt with, and it is a matter of deep regret that the difficulties of the subject have seemed to render it impossible to complete a bill for passage at this session. But it can not be perfected yet, and therefore there are no other constructive measures the necessity for which I will at this time call your attention to." Ray S. Baker and William E. Dodd (eds.), *The Public Papers of Woodrow Wilson* (6 vols., New York, 1925–27), *The New Democracy*, I, 220.

[11] In early January, 1914, a delegation of leaders in the child labor reform movement requested an interview with the President. "Glad to see these gentlemen," Wilson replied, in a note to Tumulty, "but they ought to know, in all frankness, that no child labor law yet proposed has seemed to me constitutional." Wilson to Tumulty, inscribed at the bottom of Tumulty to Wilson, Jan. 24, 1914, Wilson Papers.

not believe it was proper for a lady to vote, but the excuse he always gave the delegations of suffragettes who visited him was that he was bound hand and foot in the matter because the Democratic platform had not approved a suffrage amendment.[12] Some of the interviews were not pleasant affairs, as the ladies could be brutally frank. For example, Mrs. Glendower Evans of Boston, who had escorted a large delegation of working women to the White House on February 2, 1915, reminded the President that in 1912 he had led her to believe he would support woman suffrage. Wilson replied that he had then spoken as an individual, but that he was now speaking as a representative of his party. "Of course," Mrs. Evans shot back, "you were gunning for votes then." Wilson's face turned red, but he managed a weak smile. On the occasion of the sixth visitation by petitioning females, however, he finally confessed that he was "tied to a conviction" that the states alone should control the suffrage.

A third item of the program supported by many leaders of the social justice movement was the imposition of some restriction on the enormous numbers of immigrants then coming to American shores. Restriction or, if possible, putting an end altogether to immigration had long been a prime objective of the A.F. of L. and other labor groups, whose spokesmen claimed unrestricted immigration operated to depress wages in the United States. Appalled by the dire effects of unrestrained immigration on American institutions, a number of leading sociologists and social workers supported the movement.[13] Moreover, the restrictionists were also strongly supported by anti-Catholic and anti-Jewish elements.

The device favored by the restrictionists and exclusionists of that day, the literacy test, was embodied in the Burnett general immigration bill, which the House approved on February 4, 1914, and the Senate on January 2, 1915. From the beginning of the debates in the House, Wilson had intimated he would veto the immigration bill if it included the literacy test. After the House passed the bill, he frankly warned Senate leaders that he would veto the measure if they did not strike

[12] *The New York Times,* Dec. 9, 1914; Elizabeth Glendower Evans, "An Audience at the White House," *La Follette's Weekly,* VI (Feb. 14, 1914), 5, 15.

[13] Among them were Henry P. Fairchild of Yale, Edward A. Ross of Wisconsin, Jeremiah W. Jenks of New York University, Thomas N. Carver of Harvard, Dean Leon C. Marshall of the University of Chicago, and Robert A. Woods of South End House, Boston. See H. P. Fairchild to Wilson, Mar. 17, 1914, Wilson Papers.

out the disputed provision.[14] Whether he thus acted out of conviction or for reasons of expediency, it is impossible to say,[15] but when the Senate approved the Burnett bill *in toto* he replied with a ringing veto. "Those who come seeking opportunity are not to be admitted unless they have already had one of the chief of the opportunities they seek, the opportunity of education," he asserted. "The object of such provisions is restriction, not selection."[16] Two years later, in January, 1917, Congress re-enacted the Burnett bill. Wilson replied again with a stirring veto, but this time the forces of restriction were not to be denied victory, and the House on February 1 and the Senate on February 5 overrode the veto.

One great measure of social justice, the Seamen's bill, had the President's approval in the beginning, as its purpose was only to free American sailors from the bondage of their contracts and to strengthen maritime safety requirements. Any recital of how this measure was passed should begin by taking account of the devotion and twenty years' unrequited labor of the president of the Seamen's Union, Andrew Furuseth—"one of the heroes of the world, who . . . forfeited money, position, comfort and everything else to fight the battle of the common sailor."[17] Furuseth finally found sponsors for his bill

[14] Wilson to Senator E. D. Smith, Mar. 5, 1914, *ibid.*

[15] Senator John Sharp Williams urged Wilson not to veto the Burnett bill. Wilson's reply indicated that political considerations were uppermost in his mind. He wrote: "I find myself in a very embarrassing situation about that bill. Nothing is more distasteful to me than to set my judgment against so many of my friends and associates in public life, but frankly stated the situation is this: I myself personally made the most explicit statements at the time of the presidential election about this subject to groups of our fellow-citizens of foreign extraction whom I wished to treat with perfect frankness and for whom I had entire respect. In view of what I said to them, I do not see how it will be possible for me to give my assent to the bill. I know that you will appreciate the scruple upon which I act." Wilson to Williams, Jan. 7, 1915, *ibid.*

[16] *The Public Papers, New Democracy,* I, 254.

It should be pointed out here that during this long controversy a number of the social justice leaders strongly opposed any form of restriction. See, e.g., Jane Addams to Wilson, Jan. 29, 1915, Wilson Papers; Stephen S. Wise to Wilson, Jan. 29, 1915, *ibid.; The Public,* XVIII (Feb. 5, 1915), 121.

The large employers of labor and their spokesmen, the spokesmen of the Italian-, Polish-, Hungarian-, and Russian-American societies, and the representatives of the Jewish community in the United States, however, were the real leaders in the fight against any form of restriction. The author could find no evidence that the Catholic Church entered the controversy on the political level.

[17] William Kent to Norman Hapgood, June 16, 1914, the Papers of William Kent, in the Library of Yale University.

in the Sixty-Second Congress, Representative William B. Wilson and Senator La Follette. It passed the House in 1912 and the Senate in 1913, only to receive a pocket veto from President Taft in the closing days of his administration.

Had the Seamen's bill been merely a matter of domestic concern it would probably have been promptly re-enacted by the Sixty-Third Congress and signed by the President. Before the international ramifications of the measure were brought home to him, for example, Wilson was cordially disposed and promised to support the bill. Trouble arose, however, because the measure in effect abrogated the contractual obligations of alien seamen on foreign ships in American ports, thus violating treaties with all the maritime powers.[18] Moreover, the United States had consented to send delegates to an international conference on safety at sea in London in November, 1913; it seemed hardly courteous for the nation that had taken the initiative in calling the conference to act unilaterally before it could meet.

The envoys of several of the great powers expressed these objections emphatically to the Secretary of State, but Wilson was not disturbed until John Bassett Moore, Counselor of the State Department, called his attention to them on October 16, 1913. By this time it was too late to stop action by the Senate, which on October 23 adopted the Furuseth bill sponsored by La Follette. The administration blocked action by the House, however, and the American delegates, Furuseth among them, went to the London conference unembarrassed by any prior action by their government. Furuseth resigned and came home when the conference adopted safety requirements that did not meet the standards of his own bill. The rest of the American delegates stayed on, however, and helped draft a Convention that imposed uniform and generally rigid safety standards on the vessels of all maritime powers.

The administration was now in another dilemma. Should the United States ratify the Convention on Safety at Sea unconditionally, which would mean abandoning the Furuseth bill, or should it ratify with a reservation that would leave room for the passage of that measure? Wilson let the State and Commerce departments, which in-

---

[18] The United States had entered into treaties with the maritime powers providing for the arrest of foreign seamen who deserted while their ships were in American ports. The Seamen's bill would have unilaterally abrogated these treaties.

sisted on unconditional ratification, make the decision; and he reversed his own support of the Furuseth bill and applied administration pressure toward speedy ratification of the Convention. Thus a bitter controversy ensued between the administration and some of the progressive leaders in Congress. In the end the progressives won. The House passed a modified version of the Furuseth bill on August 27, 1914; the Senate in December ratified the Convention with a sweeping reservation; and three months later both houses ratified the conference report.

Events now moved swiftly to a conclusion. Bryan urged the President to give the bill a pocket veto,[19] and the newspapers on March 1, 1915, predicted that this would be the measure's fate. Furuseth appealed in a moving letter, begging Wilson to approve the legislation for which he had fought so long, and Wilson replied in words indicating he had no alternative but to follow the advice of the State Department. The same day, March 2, La Follette, Furuseth, and Senator Owen called on Bryan. Bryan had never heard of Furuseth, but he was so shaken by the old sailor's plea that he at once reversed his position.[20] La Follette added his personal promise that Congress would give the State Department ample time in which to abrogate old treaties and negotiate new ones. Wilson signed the Furuseth bill on March 4, but apparently not without considerable soul searching. "I debated the matter of signing the bill very earnestly indeed . . .," he explained, "and finally determined to sign it because it seemed the only chance to get something like justice done to a class of workmen who have been too much neglected by our laws." [21]

The dearth in administration circles of any impelling passion for social justice was nowhere better illustrated than in the government's policy toward Negroes during Wilson's magistracy. During the campaign of 1912 Wilson had appealed for Negro support, and spokesmen for the cause of racial democracy, among them being Oswald Garrison Villard, William E. B. Du Bois, and William Monroe Trotter, had

[19] On the grounds that passage of the bill would require the United States to denounce unilaterally some twenty-two treaties with maritime nations. Bryan to Wilson, Feb. 27, 1915, the Papers of William Jennings Bryan, in the National Archives. See also Bryan to Wilson, Mar. 1, 1915, Wilson Papers, and Robert Lansing to Bryan, Mar. 1, 1915, ibid.

[20] Bryan also urged the President to suggest that the Seamen's bill be amended so as to give the State Department time in which to abrogate the treaties. Bryan to Wilson, Mar. 2, 1915, ibid.

[21] Wilson to Newton D. Baker, Mar. 5, 1915, ibid.

accepted his promises and worked for his election. Soon after Wilson's inauguration, Oswald Garrison Villard, one of the founders of the National Association for the Advancement of Colored People and publisher of the New York *Evening Post* and the *Nation,* called at the White House and presented a plan for the appointment of a National Race Commission to study the whole problem of race relations in the United States. Wilson seemed "wholly sympathetic" to the suggestion, and Villard left for a visit to Europe, confident Wilson would soon be ready to appoint the Commission.[22] He returned in July and tried several times to see the President, but Wilson refused to grant him an interview. Finally, when Villard appealed in personal terms, Wilson had to tell him that the political situation was too delicate for any such action, that the appointment of the Commission would incite the resentment of Southerners in Congress, whose votes he needed for the success of his legislative program.[23]

Villard's disappointment over Wilson's abandonment of the Race Commission was nothing, however, as compared with his consternation at the way in which Southern race concepts had gained ascendancy in Congress and in the administration. Southerners were riding high in Washington for the first time since the Civil War, demanding segregation in the government departments and public services and the dismissal or down-grading of Negro civil servants.

Throughout his incumbency, Wilson stood firm against the cruder demands of the white supremacists, but he and probably all of his Cabinet believed in segregation, social and official. The issue first arose on April 11, 1913, when Burleson suggested segregating all Negroes in the federal services. If there were any defenders of the Negro or any foes of segregation in the Cabinet they did not then or afterward raise their voice.[24] Shortly afterward the Bureau of the Census, the Post Office Department, and the Bureau of Printing and Engraving quietly began to segregate workers in offices, shops, rest rooms, and res-

[22] O. G. Villard to R. H. Leavell, May 15, 1913, the Papers of Oswald Garrison Villard, in Houghton Library, Harvard University. Villard's plan was explained in *A Proposal for a National Race Commission to be appointed by the President of the United States, Suggested by the National Association for the Advancement of Colored People* (n.p., n.d.).

[23] Villard to Wilson, Aug. 18, 1913, Villard Papers; Wilson to Villard, Aug. 21, 1913, *ibid.* Wilson made this point even clearer in a conversation with John Palmer Gavit on October 1, 1913, for an account of which see Gavit to Villard, Oct. 1, 1913, *ibid.*

[24] The Diary of Josephus Daniels, in the Library of Congress, Apr. 11, 1913.

taurants. Employees who objected were discharged.[25] Moreover, federal Post Office and Treasury officials in the South were given free rein to discharge and down-grade Negro employees. The postmaster of Atlanta, for example, discharged thirty-five Negroes. "There are no Government positions for Negroes in the South," the Collector of Internal Revenue in Georgia announced. "A Negro's place is in the cornfield." [26]

There had been segregation in the government departments before, to be sure, but it had been informal and unofficial. Now it seemed that for the first time since the Civil War the federal government had placed its approval on the Southern caste system. Needless to say, Negroes throughout the country were shocked and confused by this action of an administration that promised a new freedom for all the people. "I have recently spent several days in Washington, and I have never seen the colored people so discouraged and bitter as they are at the present time," the great leader of the Negroes wrote.[27] "We had looked forward in the hope that under your guidance all this would be changed," another Negro leader wrote the President, "but the cold facts presented to us show that these cherished hopes are to be dashed to the ground and that for a while longer we must continue to drink from this bitter cup." [28]

The anger of the Negro leaders at the new segregation policies was the natural reaction of a group who had hopefully supported the man they were sure would deal with them compassionately. More surprising, however, was the manner in which a large part of the progressive leadership of the North and Middle West rose in fervent protest. Villard and his *Nation* and New York *Evening Post* and the National Association for the Advancement of Colored People first sounded the alarm, and the storm of protests from editors, clergymen, and civic leaders that followed gave ample proof that the old spirit of equalitarianism was not dead.

Wilson was visibly surprised and greatly disturbed by the furor his

[25] May Childs Nerney to Oswald G. Villard, Sept. 30, 1913, Wilson Papers, is the report by an investigator for the National Association for the Advancement of Colored People. For other analyses see J. P. Gavit in New York *Evening Post,* Oct. 21, 1913, and William Monroe Trotter, "Federal Segregation Under Pres. Wilson," Boston *Guardian,* Oct. 25, 1913.

[26] Atlanta *Georgian and News,* Oct. 7, 1913.

[27] Booker T. Washington to O. G. Villard, Aug. 10, 1913, Wilson Papers.

[28] W. F. Powell to Wilson, Aug. 25, 1913, *ibid.*

subordinates had provoked. From the beginning of the controversy, however, he contended that segregation was being instituted in the interest of the Negroes, and throughout he stoutly maintained this position. "I would say that I do approve of the segregation that is being attempted in several of the departments," he wrote, for example, to the editor of the influential *Congregationalist*.[29] Moreover, when the militant Boston Negro spokesman, William Monroe Trotter, headed a delegation to carry a protest to the White House and spoke rashly, the President virtually ordered him out.

In every respect the whole affair was tragic and unfortunate—one of the worst blots on the administration's record. It was more than even Wilson's staunchest editorial supporter, Frank Cobb, could stomach. "It is a small, mean, petty discrimination," he cried in protest, "and Mr. Wilson ought to have set his heel upon this presumptuous Jim-Crow government the moment it was established. He ought to set his heel upon it now. It is a reproach to his Administration and to the great political principles which he represents." [30]

Although the President never set his heel upon Jim Crow, the forthright protests of the liberal North had some effect. The Treasury Department reversed its policy and began quietly to eliminate segregation. But more important was the fact that the segregation movement in other departments was entirely checked. Jim Crowism was not rooted out of the federal government, to be sure, but at least the white supremacists were less bold and far less successful after 1913.

The segregation affair caused many progressives to wonder what kind of progressive Wilson was. Their confusion was compounded, moreover, by the perplexing reversals that Wilson executed when he proceeded to complete his legislative program by fulfilling his pledges to strengthen the antitrust laws.

Wilson had fabricated the New Freedom program in 1912 largely out of promises to destroy monopoly and restore free competition. He had, moreover, evolved a fairly definite remedy, which was to rewrite the rules of business practice so clearly that there could be no doubt as to their meaning, and to enforce these rules by the normal processes of prosecution and adjudication. Not until the middle of November, 1913, however, when the Underwood bill was passed and the Federal Reserve bill was safely on its way to passage in the Senate, did Wilson

[29] Wilson to Rev. H. A. Bridgman, Sept. 8, 1913, *ibid*.
[30] New York *World*, Nov. 13, 1914.

give any thought to details. On November 20 he began a long series of conferences with Democratic leaders in Congress, seeking their views and requesting them to submit their recommendations. The news that the President was determined to carry through with antitrust legislation also provoked the introduction of a bewildering variety of bills when Congress convened in December.

By the middle of December most of the recommendations were in, and it was evident that progressive opinion was divided over the remedy. The main body of Democrats desired merely an interpretative amendment of the Sherman Act, to define precisely the prohibitions against restraint of trade, to outlaw interlocking directorates of all kinds, and to narrow and clarify the "rule of reason," promulgated by the Supreme Court in 1911.[31] A minority of Democrats and practically all progressive Republicans, on the other hand, agreed with Theodore Roosevelt that this was a naïve solution, that it would be impossible to define by statute every conceivable restraint of trade. They wanted instead a powerful, independent trade commission armed with broad authority and capable of suppressing unfair competition whenever it arose and under whatever guise.[32]

Wilson had to choose, therefore, between what he called the "two ways open to us"—in brief, to choose between the solution he had offered in 1912 and the program that Roosevelt and his friends championed. He pondered this question during his vacation at Pass Christian, Mississippi, over the Christmas holidays, and if there was any doubt in his mind it was quickly resolved. He would press ahead for legislation along New Freedom lines, in spite of the great pressure that was being brought to bear upon him by personal friends and spokesmen of the great business interests to abandon his efforts, in spite of the seeming surrender of the House of Morgan, when it announced on

---

[31] The rule of reason, first promulgated by the Supreme Court in the Standard Oil case in May, 1911 (221 U.S. 1) and shortly afterward reaffirmed in the American Tobacco case (221 U.S. 106), represented a triumph for Chief Justice Edward D. White, who, since 1897, had contended that the framers of the Sherman Act had intended to outlaw only unreasonable, or direct, restraints of trade, not reasonable restraints that were normally ancillary to most contracts.

Some Democrats, notably John Sharp Williams and Bryan, wanted to abolish the rule of reason altogether and outlaw every restraint of trade, whether direct or ancillary. See J. S. Williams to Wilson, Jan. 13, 1914, Wilson Papers.

[32] For an analysis of such proposals see J. E. Davies to Wilson, Dec. 27, 1913, and "Memorandum of Recommendations as to Trust Legislation by Joseph E. Davies, Commissioner of Corporations," both in *ibid.*

January 2, 1914, its withdrawal from thirty directorships in banks, railroads, and industrial firms.[33]

Soon after his return to Washington, Wilson had full-dress conferences with Congressional leaders, who agreed to support the program the administration had formulated. Then, appearing for the fifth time before a joint session, the President explained in unusual detail the kind of legislation he had in mind. He brandished no flaming sword against business, however, but offered an olive branch of peace and the hope of permanent accommodation. "The antagonism between business and Government is over," he said several times, as if to emphasize that he was speaking for the best business thought of the country.[34]

Wilson's program was embodied in three bills, originally drawn by Chairman Henry D. Clayton of the House Judiciary Committee, which were soon combined into one measure, known as the Clayton bill. It enumerated and prohibited a series of unfair trade practices, outlawed in unqualified terms interlocking directorates and stockholdings, and gave private parties benefit of decisions in suits that the government had originated. A fourth bill, prepared by Representatives Clayton, James H. Covington, and William C. Adamson and Senator Francis G. Newlands, created an interstate trade commission to supplant the Bureau of Corporations. The new commission would be no independent arbiter of business practices, however, but would serve merely as the right arm of the Justice Department in antitrust matters. Actually, it was the Bureau of Corporations, under a new name and with a little more power—as Wilson said, no "dangerous experiment," but a "safe and sensible" agency that all Democrats could approve. A final feature of the program was the bill prepared by Representative Sam Rayburn of Texas and Louis D. Brandeis, to give the Interstate Commerce Commission control over the issuance of new securities by the railroads.[35]

This, therefore, was the substance of the original Wilson program for

[33] *The New York Times,* Jan. 3, 1914.

[34] *The Public Papers, New Democracy,* I, 81–88.

[35] This measure passed the House on June 5, 1914, but later died in the Senate, in part a casualty of the panic that the war evoked. During the early months of the war the American security markets were in a chaotic condition; the New York Stock Exchange was closed; and the railroads were in a state approaching insolvency. Administration leaders decided, therefore, to drop the Rayburn bill entirely.

trust reform. No sooner was it proposed, however, than there arose a storm of confusing dissent and criticism. The "Money Trust" expert, Samuel Untermyer, rushed to Washington and pointed to many weaknesses in the Clayton bill. Brandeis, who was now spending most of his time in Washington, was evolving an entirely new solution, the cornerstone of which was the strengthening of small business by fair-trade price laws. Progressives and the representatives of small business were up in arms in protest against the plan for a weak interstate trade commission. And to compound the difficulty, Democratic leaders in Congress began to quarrel among themselves over jurisdiction and details. It seemed no one knew what to do or how to do it.

The most serious controversy of all, however, was that which occurred when the labor leaders and spokesmen in Congress read the Clayton bill and found nothing in it to give labor unions exemption from the application of the antitrust laws. Gompers and his colleagues in the A.F. of L. had supported Wilson in 1912 and had confidently expected the administration to stand by the Democratic platform pledges to exempt labor and farm organizations from the penalties of the Sherman law. They were now up in arms, threatening the Democrats with loss of labor's vote if these demands were not conceded. "Without further delay," Gompers declared, "the citizens of the United States must decide whether they wish to outlaw organized labor." [36]

In this bitter controversy Wilson and his Congressional leaders stood absolutely firm. The most they would concede was a compromise amendment providing for jury trials in cases of criminal contempt, circumscribing the issuance of injunctions in labor disputes, and declaring that neither farm nor labor unions should be considered as illegal combinations in restraint of trade when they lawfully sought to obtain legitimate objectives.[37] This did not go far enough to suit the

---

[36] New York *World*, Mar. 1, 1914.

[37] Wilson was emphatic in declaring that the provision did not authorize labor unions to use methods of industrial warfare that had previously been condemned by the courts. *The New York Times*, June 2, 1914; New York *World*, June 2, 1914.

Representative E. Y. Webb of North Carolina, who framed the compromise provision, further explained:

"The framers of the Sherman law never intended to place labor organizations and farmers' organizations under the ban of that law. The existence of a labor of farmers' union never has been unlawful, and is not unlawful today, but it was decided to place in the statutory law of the country a recognition of the rights of those organizations to exist and carry out their lawful purposes.

labor leaders, whose spokesmen in Congress [38] went to the White House on April 30 and threatened to join the Republicans in defeating the administration's antitrust program if labor's demand for complete immunity were not granted. Wilson would not budge, however, and the labor congressmen and union officials had to accept the compromise, which was better than nothing.

With the compromise labor provision included, the House passed the Clayton bill, along with the interstate trade commission and railroad securities bills, by overwhelming majorities on June 5, 1914. The House's action brought to an end the New Freedom phase of antitrust legislation, that is, of legislation based upon the assumption that all that was required was merely to make more specific the prohibitions against restraint of trade. From this point forward, progress away from this concept was uninterrupted, until in the end Wilson accepted almost entirely the New Nationalism's solution for the regulation of business by a powerful trade commission. The metamorphosis in administration policy was gradual, and the story of how it evolved is complicated; but the major reasons for the change are clear.

To begin with, there is much evidence that Wilson was growing uncertain as to the manner in which the broad objectives of his program should be accomplished. His attitude toward the industrial problem was conditioned by his belief that the vast majority of businessmen were honest and desired only the public good. Thus his objective was chiefly to strengthen the altruistic tendencies in the business community; and he began to wonder whether this could be done by rigid, inflexible laws that might only further alienate and confuse the honest businessman.

On the other hand, a large minority of the Democrats—the Southern agrarians and the Bryan followers—proposed legislation to destroy the oligarchical economic structure: stringent federal regulation of stock exchanges; [39] a graduated corporation tax that would bear so heavily

---

"After the original Section 7 of the Anti-trust bill was drawn, certain representatives of labor contended that the section did not give labor all it was entitled to and demanded that we should make the section provide that the anti-trust laws should not apply to labor organizations. The acceptance of this amendment would have placed labor organizations beyond the pale of the anti-trust law entirely, which neither the president nor the members of the [Judiciary] committee would agree to." *The New York Times,* June 14, 1914.

[38] Representatives David J. Lewis of Maryland, Edward Keating of Colorado, Isaac R. Sherwood of Ohio, and John J. Casey of Pennsylvania.

[39] This was one of the recommendations of the Pujo Committee and was strongly supported by Samuel Untermyer and Senator Robert L. Owen of

on the great combinations as to put them out of business; limiting a corporation or holding company usually to about one-third the total product of any given industry; [40] abolition of the "rule of reason"; and the complete destruction of the complicated network of interlocking relationships among banks, railroads, corporations, and insurance companies.[41] This program went far beyond anything Wilson envisaged at any time. For example, he did not object to bigness per se; he only wanted to prevent the great interests from using their power to stifle new growth and competition. And he was beginning to doubt that the Clayton bill and the weak interstate trade commission bill offered an effective remedy.

In the second place, the spokesmen of the business community, particularly the United States Chamber of Commerce, had embraced the ideal of the "self-regulation" of business. What they desired most was legislation prohibiting unfair trade practices, with a trade commission to pass upon the legality of practices and to serve as a friendly adviser to businessmen. The suggestion found strong support in the Senate and among progressives generally, as it seemed to offer a simple solution to a perplexing difficulty.

Just at the moment when Wilson seemed most confused and uncertain, Louis D. Brandeis took up the strong trade commission idea and persuaded the President to adopt it also. Since October, 1913, Brandeis had been hard at work, in Boston and Washington, on the antitrust question. His close friend and associate, George L. Rublee of New York, had joined the "people's lawyer," and together the two men drafted a Federal Trade Commission bill that was introduced by Representative Raymond B. Stevens, Democrat of New Hampshire. The Stevens bill in general terms outlawed unfair trade practices and established a trade commission endowed with plenary authority to oversee business activity and by the issuance of cease and desist orders to prevent the illegal suppression of competition.

Oklahoma. Early in the Congressional discussions of antitrust legislation the President let it be known he did not favor the stock exchange bill. *The New York Times,* Jan. 23, 1914.

[40] The report of the House committee, headed by A. O. Stanley of Kentucky, which investigated United States Steel in 1911–12, proposed that there should be a presumption of restraint of trade when a single corporation or holding company controlled at least 30 per cent of the output of a single industry. *House Report,* No. 1127, 62d Cong., 2d sess. (Washington, 1912), p. 214.

[41] This was the desire and determination, often voiced, of practically all the so-called radical Democrats in the House of Representatives.

Wilson and Congressional leaders first learned the details of the Brandeis-Rublee plan in the latter part of April, 1914. The chairman of the House Commerce Committee, William C. Adamson of Georgia, was aghast at the proposal, declaring it proposed giving an administrative agency power to make law. Wilson said nothing at first, but after the antitrust bills were safely through the House he called Brandeis, Rublee, and Stevens to the White House on June 10 and told them he had decided to make the Stevens bill the cornerstone of his antitrust program. How the President was won over to the idea of a strong trade commission is nowhere evident. In any event, three days after the White House conference the Senate Interstate Commerce Committee reported the Federal Trade Commission bill with the Stevens bill as an amendment. There then followed several weeks of debate in the Senate, during which time Wilson, Brandeis, and Rublee worked feverishly to overcome old-line Democratic and conservative opposition to Section 5, empowering the Commission to issue cease and desist orders. After adopting amendments guaranteeing broad court review of the Commission's orders, the Senate passed the bill on August 5 by a bipartisan vote of fifty-three to sixteen. The House agreed a month later, and the measure became law on September 10. "If the bill is wrong I shall be much to blame," Rublee wrote. "I drafted the conference report which was agreed to. Section 5 is exactly as I wanted it to be." [42]

Meanwhile, after he espoused the Brandeis-Rublee plan, Wilson seemed to lose all interest in the Clayton bill. It was cut adrift in the Senate, with the result that one after another of its strong provisions was so weakened as to make it in many particulars almost innocuous. For example, instead of forbidding exclusive selling contracts, interlocking directorates, or interlocking stockholdings outright, the words "where the effect may be to substantially lessen competition or tend to create a monopoly in any line of commerce," or words of similar purport, were inserted after all the prohibitions.[43]

"When the Clayton bill was first written," Senator James A. Reed of Missouri exclaimed, "it was a raging lion with a mouth full of teeth. It has degenerated to a tabby cat with soft gums, a plaintive mew, and

[42] Rublee to Brandeis, Oct. 6, 1914, the Papers of Louis D. Brandeis, in the Law School Library of the University of Louisville.

[43] For a good analysis of the weakening of the Clayton bill see Henry R. Seager and Charles A. Gulick, Jr., *Trust and Corporation Problems* (New York, 1929), pp. 420–422.

an anaemic appearance. It is a sort of legislative apology to the trusts, delivered hat in hand, and accompanied by assurances that no discourtesy is intended." [44] Wilson, too, complained that Senator Culberson, chairman of the Judiciary Committee, had made the bill "so weak that you cannot tell it from water." [45] Of course this was largely true, but it was true because the administration had put all faith in the trade commission plan and had given up its effort to prohibit restraints of trade by statutory action.

Farm and labor leaders, meanwhile, had been striving mightily with the Senate to win the concessions the President and House of Representatives had denied them. On July 30, Gompers, Frank Morrison, secretary-treasurer of the A.F. of L., the legislative representatives of the railroad brotherhoods, the general counsel of the Farmers' Union, and the secretary of the Farmers' National Congress addressed an important appeal to the Senate Judiciary Committee. The letter reviewed the labor provisions of the Clayton bill, as it had passed the House, and pointed out specifically the changes that were necessary to satisfy labor and farm demands. The effect of the suggested changes would have been to give to labor and farm organizations the immunity from the penalties of the Sherman law they were seeking.

A comparison of the labor-farm demands with the labor provisions of the Clayton bill as it passed the Senate and conference committee reveals that the Senate, like the President and the House of Representatives, stood absolutely firm in resisting these demands. The Senate made one change that became famous but was not important. At the suggestion of Senator Albert B. Cummins, it amended the provision to read, "The labor of human beings is not a commodity or article of commerce," which phrase was nothing more than a pious expression of senatorial opinion and did not change labor's standing before the law.[46]

In any event, the labor provisions of the act apparently pleased everyone. Gompers hailed them as labor's "Magna Carta" [47] and after-

[44] *The New York Times,* Sept. 29, 1914.
[45] The Diary of Edward M. House, in the Papers of Edward M. House, in the Library of Yale University, Oct. 2, 1914.
[46] That the labor provisions of the Clayton Act did not confer immunity from prosecution on farm and labor unions was the opinion of practically every responsible contemporary observer. See, e.g., the cogent essay, " 'Labor Is Not a Commodity,' " *New Republic,* IX (Dec. 2, 1916), 112–114, or W. H. Taft to G. W. Wickersham, Oct. 31, Nov. 8, 1914, Taft Papers.
[47] "Labor's Magna Carta—Demand It," *American Federationist,* XXI (July, 1914), 553–557; *ibid.* (Oct., 1914), 866–867.

ward tried desperately to convince himself and the country that labor was freed from the restraints of the antitrust laws. On the other extreme, the general counsel of the American Anti-Boycott Association was also entirely satisfied with the legislation. "The bill makes few changes in existing laws relating to labor unions, injunctions and contempts of court," he observed, "and those are of slight practical importance." [48]

With the appointment of the Federal Trade Commission on February 22, 1915, the administration launched its experiment in the regulation of business enterprise. It is well, however, to understand the spirit in which the experiment was conceived and the purposes that Wilson and his colleagues hoped to accomplish. They were chiefly purposes friendly to business. As Redfield later put it, Wilson hoped to "create in the Federal Trade Commission a counsellor and friend to the business world. . . . It was no large part of his purpose that the Federal Trade Commission should be primarily a policeman to wield a club over the head of the business community. Rather the reverse was true and the restraining powers of the Commission were thought a necessary adjunct which he hoped and expected to be of minor rather than of major use." [49]

Progressives like Brandeis and Rublee, who hoped the Commission would become a dynamic factor in American economic life, were bitterly disappointed when it failed to do anything constructive during the first years of its life. Brandeis later correctly observed that Wilson had ruined the Commission by his choice of commissioners. "It was a stupid administration," he recalled.[50] The chairman, Joseph E. Davies of Wisconsin, lacked force and judgment. In fact, the only really competent appointee, Rublee, was prevented from serving because the Senate refused to confirm his nomination.[51] Davies proved so incompetent that in June, 1916, the majority of the Commission deposed him and made Edward N. Hurley, a Chicago industrialist, chairman. Hurley

[48] Daniel Davenport, in Springfield *Republican*, Oct. 11, 1914.

[49] W. C. Redfield, "Woodrow Wilson: An Appreciation," in the Ray Stannard Baker Collection, in the Library of Congress; see also A. W. Shaw, MS of interview on Jan. 4, 1915, with Wilson, in Wilson Papers.

[50] R. S. Baker, interview with L. D. Brandeis, Mar. 23, 1929, Baker Collection.

[51] Jacob H. Gallinger of New Hampshire, minority leader in the Senate, objected to the appointment on personal grounds and the Senate refused to confirm Rublee, in spite of the President's strenuous efforts to obtain confirmation.

was certainly abler than Davies; but he devoted his talents to making the Commission useful to businessmen and to preaching the doctrine of co-operation between government and business. And under his leadership, the Commission practically abandoned its role as watchdog of business practices. It was little wonder, therefore, that, on reviewing the situation on the eve of America's entry into the war, Rublee concluded that the Commission was on the rocks.[52]

The weakening of the administration's antitrust program was only the first sign of a general reaction that began to set in around the beginning of 1914 and increasingly affected the administration and the President. The chief cause of the ebbing of the reform impulse was the insidious depression that began during the fall of 1913 and mounted in severity during the late winter and spring of 1914. It was a world-wide phenomenon, the result of the tightening of credit in Europe because of the Balkan Wars and the fear of a general war.[53] But in the United States the Republicans blamed the Underwood tariff and Wilson's antitrust measures. Business failures increased, production sagged, and unemployment was widespread and especially acute in the large cities.[54] Wilson and administration leaders like McAdoo tried to persuade themselves and the public that no real depression existed. Actually, however, they were seriously alarmed, and their concern inevitably evidenced itself in administration policies.

To begin with, in the spring of 1914 the President embarked upon a campaign calculated to win the friendship of businessmen and bankers and to ease the tension that had existed between the administration and the business community. The accommodation of the antitrust program to the desires of the business world was the first step, along with Wilson's repeated expressions of confidence in and friendship for businessmen. Next the President began to welcome bankers

[52] George Rublee to E. M. House, Jan. 26, 1917, Wilson Papers.

[53] See the excellent analysis by S. S. Fontaine, in New York *World*, Jan. 3, 1915.

[54] Incomplete surveys revealed that in New York 23.7 per cent of 115,960 families investigated in January-February, 1915, had members unemployed. The Bureau of Statistics of Massachusetts reported that returns received from labor organizations in the state, representing 66 per cent of the total trade-union members, showed 18.3 per cent unemployed on December 31, 1914. See Mayor's Committee on Unemployement, New York City, *Report of the Mayor's Committee on Unemployment* (New York, 1916), and Bureau of Statistics, Labor Division, Commonwealth of Massachusetts, *Thirtieth Quarterly Report on Unemployment in Massachusetts, Quarter Ending June 30, 1915* (Boston, 1915).

and business leaders to the White House. In the palmy days of 1913 he had not wanted their advice; now he welcomed J. P. Morgan, delegations of businessmen and bankers from Illinois, and Henry Ford. Thirdly, Wilson let it be known in the financial circles of New York and Boston that he had never really been an enemy of big business, but only of business that grew "big by methods which unrighteously crushed those who were smaller." [55]

It was about this time, also, that Attorney General McReynolds, with Wilson's approval, began to use a new method in dealing with alleged combinations in restraint of trade. He announced that any large corporation that felt doubtful of the legality of its corporate structure might seek the friendly advice and help of the Justice Department in rearranging its affairs. Several great combinations, notably the American Telephone & Telegraph Company and the New Haven Railroad, came to terms with the administration and received its blessing.[56] Whether such policy was wise or foolish depended upon one's point of view; in any event, there was no trust-busting ardor in the Wilson administration.

Wilson climaxed his little campaign to win the friendship of the business classes by turning over control of the Federal Reserve Board, in effect, to their representatives, as if he were trying to prove the sincerity of his recent professions. For several months McAdoo and House had engaged in a tug of war over the selection of the Board, McAdoo arguing that the appointees should be men in sympathy with the ad-

[55] Wilson to A. S. Burleson, July 27, 1914, Wilson Papers. See also Wilson to H. L. Higginson, Oct. 23, 1914, *ibid.;* E. M. House to J. C. McReynolds, Jan. 7, 1914, House Papers.

[56] For details and consequences of the A. T. & T. settlement, see *The New York Times,* Dec. 20, 21, 1913.

The New Haven settlement was reached only after long and bitter negotiations. There was first a thorough investigation into the affairs of the railroad by Joseph W. Folk, special prosecutor for the Interstate Commerce Commission. This was followed by an agreement for the dissolution of the vast New Haven empire, the terms of which were agreed to by railroad and Justice Department officials on January 10, 1914. *Ibid.,* Jan. 11, 1914. The New Haven officers objected, however, to the government's demand that they dispose of the Boston & Maine Railroad at once. *Ibid.,* July 21, 22, 23, 1914. The government replied by instituting a suit to compel dissolution, whereupon the railroad officials surrendered and accepted the Justice Department's terms. *Ibid.,* Aug. 12, 1914.

It should be added that when officials of the United States Steel Corporation, notably Henry C. Frick, endeavored to reach agreement with McReynolds, the Attorney General refused to approve the proposed settlement on the ground that it would not restore genuine competition in the industry. House Diary, Mar. 22, 24, 26, Sept. 30, 1913.

ministration's broad policies, House advising that the President choose leading bankers and businessmen. Actually, there never was much doubt in Wilson's mind as to the wise course to follow; and when the membership of the Board was announced it evoked almost unanimous approval from bankers and business leaders. Progressives, on the other hand, were shocked and astonished. "Why, it looks as if Mr. Vanderlip [president of the National City Bank of New York] has selected them," one progressive Republican senator exclaimed.[57]

The degree to which Wilson had outraged progressive sentiment, however, did not become apparent until the President sent the nominations to the Senate on June 15. Insurgent anger in the upper house centered on two of the nominees—Thomas D. Jones of Chicago and Paul M. Warburg. A former trustee of Princeton University and a close friend of Wilson, Jones was one of the owners of the so-called Zinc Trust and a director of the International Harvester Company, then under state and federal indictment for being an illegal combination. Warburg was a partner in Kuhn, Loeb & Company, one of the great Wall Street banking houses.

In reply to attacks on his friend Jones, Wilson addressed a public letter to the Senate Banking Committee, defending him and explaining that he had become a director of the Harvester Trust to help bring that corporation into conformity with the law. Jones came before the Committee, however, and affirmed that he had not gone on the board of the corporation to reform it and approved everything the Trust had done since he became a director. The upshot was that the Banking Committee refused to approve Jones' nomination and Wilson had to ask him to withdraw from the contest. The Warburg affair, on the other hand, developed differently, and with certain comic aspects. Much insulted by the senatorial opposition, Warburg at first refused to appear before the Committee. Finally the President persuaded him to swallow his pride and the Senate confirmed his appointment.

The startling aspect of the Jones-Warburg affair, however, was Wilson's own reaction to it and the manner in which he came forward as the champion and defender of big business. "It would be particularly unfair to the Democratic Party and the Senate itself to regard it as the enemy of business, big or little," he declared, while the fight was in progress.[58] When it became obvious that the Senate would re-

[57] Boston *Advertiser*, May 6, 1914.
[58] *The New York Times,* July 9, 1914.

fuse to confirm Jones, Wilson's anger became intense. In a commiserating letter to Jones, he lashed out at the Senate insurgents, and at progressives in general. "I believe that the judgment and desire of the whole country cry out for a new temper in affairs," he wrote. ". . . We have breathed already too long the air of suspicion and distrust." In short, there was no room in this year of New Freedom grace for "class antagonism," for the very dynamic quality that had given impetus and force to the American progressive movement.[59]

Wilson's temper soon cooled, and a week later the attention of the country was diverted to other matters by the outbreak of the war in Europe. Then followed a period of political confusion, during which partisan passions subsided. As it turned out, these developments at home and abroad were a godsend to the Democrats during the ensuing Congressional campaign. The Republicans did not wage a vigorous fight, and there seemed to be a general disposition to stand by the President during a time of peril. The most important Democratic asset, however, was the continued disruption of the Republican party, with Roosevelt and the Progressives making one last and futile effort to establish themselves as a major party.[60]

In spite of all these advantages, the Democrats made such a poor showing in the state and Congressional elections on November 3 that their defeat in 1916 seemed almost certain. The Democratic majority in the House was reduced from seventy-three to twenty-five; there was no change of voting strength in the Senate; but the Republicans swept back into or stayed in power in states like New York, Illinois, Pennsylvania, Ohio, Kansas, New Jersey, Connecticut, Wisconsin, and South Dakota. It seemed as if the progressive tide was beginning to recede, and everywhere progressive leaders were disheartened. "The cataclysm was just about what I expected," Roosevelt lamented.[61] "We are saddened by many defeats," Brandeis added.[62] Wilson, too, was heartsick and wondered whether all the effort of the preceding two years had been worth while. "People are not so stupid not to know," he declared, "that to vote against a Democratic ticket is to vote indirectly against

[59] Wilson to T. D. Jones, July 23, 1914, printed in *ibid.*, July 24, 1914.

[60] George E. Mowry, *Theodore Roosevelt and the Progressive Movement* (Madison, Wis., 1946), pp. 300–303.

[61] Roosevelt to Archie B. Roosevelt, Nov. 7, 1914, the Papers of Theodore Roosevelt, in the Library of Congress.

[62] L. D. Brandeis to Gifford Pinchot, Nov. 4, 1914, Brandeis Papers.

me." [63] He changed his mind soon, however, and boasted that the Democrats had won a great victory.

In the autumn of 1914 Wilson, moreover, thought his program to effect a fundamental reorganization of American economic life was complete and that the progressive movement had fulfilled its mission. "We have only to look back ten years or so to realize the deep perplexities and dangerous ill-humors out of which we have at last issued, as if from a bewildering fog, a noxious miasma," he wrote in a public letter to McAdoo in November, 1914, announcing the consummation of the New Freedom program. "Ten or twelve years ago the country was torn and excited by an agitation which shook the very foundations of her political life, brought her business ideals into question, condemned her social standards, denied the honesty of her men of affairs, the integrity of her economic processes, the morality and good faith of many of the things which her law sustained." And so things stood until the Democrats came to power and the New Freedom legislation righted fundamental wrongs. The nightmare of the past years was over now, and the future would be a time of co-operation, of new understanding, of common purpose, "a time of healing because a time of just dealing." [64]

Advanced progressives were puzzled by Wilson's remarkable letter. Did the President mean what he had said? Was the progressive movement over? If so, then where could the social justice element go? Herbert Croly, chief editor of the *New Republic*, which had just begun its distinguished career, voiced the apprehensions that many progressives felt when he wrote:

How can a man of . . . [Wilson's] shrewd and masculine intelligence possibly delude himself into believing the extravagant claims which he makes on behalf of the Democratic legislative achievement? . . . How many sincere progressives follow him in believing that this legislation has made the future clear and bright with the promise of best things? . . .

President Wilson could not have written his letter unless he had utterly misconceived the meaning and the task of American progressivism. After every allowance has been made for his justifiable pride . . . , there remains an ominous residue of sheer misunderstanding. Any man of President Wilson's intellectual equipment who seriously asserts that the fundamental wrongs of

[63] House Diary, Nov. 4, 1914.
[64] Wilson to W. G. McAdoo, Nov. 17, 1914, printed in *The New York Times*, Nov. 18, 1914. See also Wilson to Powell Evans, Oct. 20, 1914, Wilson Papers.

a modern society can be easily and quickly righted as a consequence of a few laws . . . casts suspicion either upon his own sincerity or upon his grasp of the realities of modern social and industrial life. Mr. Wilson's sincerity is above suspicion, but he is a dangerous and unsound thinker upon contemporary political and social problems. He has not only . . . "a single-track mind," but a mind which is fully convinced of the everlasting righteousness of its own performances and which surrounds this conviction with a halo of shimmering rhetoric. He deceives himself with these phrases, but he should not be allowed to deceive progressive popular opinion.[65]

Croly's analysis of the superficial character of Wilson's progressivism was essentially correct. There is little evidence that Wilson had any deep comprehension of the far-reaching social and economic tensions of the time. As Croly said, Wilson was intelligent and sincere. But that did not make him a prophet or a pioneer, or even a progressive of the advanced persuasion. He had not taken office to carry out a program of federal social reform. He had promised to lower the tariff, reorganize the currency and banking system, and strengthen the antitrust laws, in order to free the nation's energies and unleash the competitive urges of the people. He had done these things, and with a minimum of concession to advanced progressive concepts. He had, moreover, turned over control of the public agencies established by the new legislation—the Federal Reserve Board and the Federal Trade Commission—to cautious men. To try to portray such a man as an ardent social reformer is to defy the plain record.

This, however, is only one chapter in the history of the journey of the Democratic party on the road leading to the New Deal and the Fair Deal. Events and circumstances sometimes cause men to change their minds or to adopt policies they have previously opposed. The process of reform was but temporarily halted in 1914, only to be reactivated by 1916. But before we tell this story we must first give some account of other events more portentous for the immediate future of the American people.

[65] "Presidential Complacency," *New Republic,* I (Nov. 21, 1914), 7.

CHAPTER 4

Missionary Diplomacy

"IT WOULD be the irony of fate if my administration had to deal chiefly with foreign affairs," Wilson remarked to a Princeton friend just before he went to Washington.[1] As it turned out, fate was not only ironical, but in a sense also cruel, for the new administration had to cope with foreign problems of such magnitude as had not confronted the nation since the early years of the nineteenth century. With the outbreak of the war in Europe, the difficulty became almost more than the administration could handle; but even from the first months of his presidency, Wilson was perplexed by one crisis after another in foreign relations.

Wilson and Bryan shared with most of their predecessors ignorance of and indifference to foreign affairs. To a remarkable degree, however, they also shared certain assumptions and ideals, which provided the dynamic for their foreign policy. They were both moralists, who thought of foreign policy in terms of the eternal verities, rather than in terms of the expedient. They were both dedicated to the democratic ideal, at least theoretically, and obsessed with the concept of America's mission in the world. Finally, they were both fundamentally missionaries, evangelists, confident that they comprehended the peace and well-being of other countries better than the leaders of those countries themselves. This urge to do good, to render disinterested service, was so compelling that it motivated interference in the internal affairs of

[1] To E. G. Conklin, cited in Ray Stannard Baker, *Woodrow Wilson: Life and Letters* (8 vols., Garden City, N.Y., 1927–39), IV, 55.

other nations on such a scale as the United States had not heretofore attempted.

The missionary impulse helps explain much that is baffling about Wilson's foreign policy, but it is not a full and sufficient explanation. To a varying degree, many other factors were involved—naïveté, the desire to protect American economic interests, imperialistic ambitions—but these operated subconsciously in Wilson's and Bryan's minds. Paramount in their motivation was the ambition to do justly, to advance the cause of international peace, and to give to other peoples the blessings of democracy and Christianity.

The most typical manifestation of missionary diplomacy[2] was Bryan's great campaign during 1913 and 1914 to negotiate treaties of conciliation with the nations of the world.[3] It had long been an obsession with the Nebraskan to promote the cause of peace,[4] and one of the conditions upon which he accepted the Secretaryship of State was that Wilson should give him a free hand in negotiating the peace treaties. The first was signed with Salvador on August 7, 1913, and during the following year twenty-nine others were negotiated, including treaties with Great Britain, France, and Italy. Significantly, the German government refused to sign a treaty. Hardheaded realists like Theodore Roosevelt might condemn the plan as futile and dangerous, but Bryan was sure he had struck a blow for peace, and to the end of his life he was prouder of this achievement than of anything else he did during his long career.

Another early evidence of the power of the missionary urge was the abrupt manner in which the administration withdrew support from the Six-Power Consortium, which had been formed in 1911 to make a

---

[2] The author wishes to explain that he does not use this term in its technical meaning—that is, diplomacy aimed at protecting missionaries and church missions abroad. He means, simply, diplomacy motivated by a desire to help other nations.

[3] These "cooling off" treaties, as they were called, provided for the submission of all disputes, even those involving questions of national honor, to permanent commissions for investigation. Neither party would declare war during the "cooling off" period, which was usually one year. After the investigation was completed, the parties could accept or reject the commission's findings. Bryan explained the details of his plan in a speech in New York City on May 9, 1913, for which see *The New York Times,* May 10, 1913.

[4] Bryan first suggested his peace plan in February, 1905, and from that time forward he pressed it vigorously. He tells the history of the idea in his letter to Harry Walker, Jan. 20, 1915, the Papers of William Jennings Bryan, in the Library of Congress.

loan of $125 million to the Chinese government for the construction of the Hukuang Railway.[5] The visit to the State Department on March 10, 1913, by representatives of the American banking interests involved precipitated the first discussion of the project in administration circles. There is strong evidence that the American bankers were anxious to be rid of their commitment and that the European bankers, too, were lukewarm because Russian and Japanese banking interests had been admitted to the Consortium.[6] Secretary of State Philander C. Knox had insisted upon American admission to the Consortium and participation by the American banking group in order that the State Department might be in a position to protect American interests and the Open Door in China. There seems, however, to have been no serious consideration by the new administration of these larger economic and strategic interests, only the moral judgment that, as the President told the Cabinet, "we ought to help China in some better way." [7] In any event, on March 18 Wilson issued a public statement explaining the American withdrawal. The United States could not approve the loan agreement, he declared, because the conditions attached to it touched "very nearly the administrative independence of China itself" and would lead to intolerable interference in Chinese affairs by foreign agents. The United States, he added, earnestly desired to help the struggling Chinese people in every way consistent with their own principles, but not by thwarting the Chinese efforts at independence and self-government.

Experienced and cynical diplomatists thought they saw some Machiavellian purpose in Wilson's action. The German Under-Secretary for Foreign Affairs, for example, suspected that the American bankers wanted to withdraw from the Consortium, and that Wilson used their withdrawal as a means of winning good will in China. The suspicion credited Wilson with a sophistication in foreign affairs that he did not yet possess. The way in which the withdrawal evoked the

[5] The Consortium was first composed of British, French, and German bankers. Upon the demand of President Taft and the State Department in 1909, an American banking group was admitted in 1911, and Russian and Japanese interests were included soon afterward.

[6] Chief of the Banking House, M. M. Warburg & Company, in Hamburg, Max Warburg, to the Undersecretary in the Foreign Office, Zimmermann, Mar. 20, 1913, in *Die Grosse Politik der Europäischen Kabinette, 1871–1914* (40 vols. in 54, Berlin, 1926), XXXII, 380–382.

[7] The Diary of Josephus Daniels, in the Library of Congress, Mar. 12, 1913, relating Cabinet discussions of the same date.

overwhelming approval of missionaries and the American religious press was good evidence that Wilson and Bryan had simply voiced the revulsion all moralists felt against what seemed to be a conspiracy to control the government of China. As the President expressed it at a Cabinet meeting, "If we had entered into the loan with other powers we would have got nothing but mere influence in China and lost the proud position which America secured when Secretary Hay stood for the open door." [8]

The administration's ambition to deal justly with China could be satisfied, therefore, only if the United States played a lone hand in the Far East, free from allegedly sinister European influences. A few weeks later, moreover, the President insisted upon recognizing the new Republic of China unilaterally and without prior agreement among the powers.

Friendly feeling and good intentions did not always suffice to settle delicate diplomatic questions, as was evidenced when a serious controversy with Japan arose at the time the administration was considering other aspects of the Far Eastern question. The dispute had its origin in the efforts of Progressive and Democratic politicians in California to curry favor with the farm and labor vote in that state by enacting legislation prohibiting Japanese ownership of land.[9] The controversy soon deepened into a major international crisis, because the California leaders proceeded ruthlessly and deliberately to humiliate the Japanese people.

In this development, unfortunately, Wilson and Bryan were not blameless. To begin with, they did not at first take the affair seriously or realize its international ramifications. In the second place, they acted throughout the episode as if California were a sovereign nation, at liberty to defy the treaty obligations of the United States.[10] Even more important, however, was the fact that they actually encouraged the Californians in their designs. When Democratic leaders in the state

[8] Daniels Diary, Mar. 28, 1913.
[9] The Democrats made an even more strenuous anti-Japanese campaign in 1912 than the other two major parties. See J. O. Davis, chairman of the Democratic state central committee, to J. P. Tumulty, Jan. 4, 1913, Papers of the Department of State, in the National Archives.
[10] "I do not feel by any means as confident as you do," Wilson wrote a young professor of jurisprudence at Princeton, "as to the power of the Federal Government in the matter of overriding the constitutional powers of the states through the instrumentality of treaties." Wilson to Edward S. Corwin, Apr. 19, 1913, the Woodrow Wilson Papers, in The Library of Congress.

expounded upon the Japanese peril, the President replied that he understood. "I have only hoped," he added, "that the doing of the thing might be so modulated and managed as to offend the susceptibilities of a friendly nation *as little as possible.*" [11] He then proceeded to volunteer a means by which the Japanese in California might be excluded from landownership without violating the Japanese-American Treaty of 1911.[12]

The affair seemed to be progressing smoothly when the California Assembly on April 16 passed an alien land bill that prohibited Japanese landownership in the indirect manner that Wilson had suggested.[13] Underneath the surface, however, an international crisis of the first order was in the making. The Japanese representatives in Washington and the American Chargé in Tokyo had repeatedly warned the State Department of the inevitable Japanese reaction; but it was not until public opinion in Japan erupted in full fury around the middle of April that the Washington government awoke to a realization that the two countries might be moving toward a break in relations.

The crisis was made all the more acute, moreover, when the leaders in the California Senate announced on April 21 that they intended to ignore the cautiously worded Assembly bill and to substitute a measure aimed specifically at the Japanese, by prohibiting landownership by all persons "ineligible to citizenship." This, and a rising war fever in

[11] Wilson to James D. Phelan, Apr. 9, 1913, *ibid.;* italics mine.

[12] William Kent, who acted as intermediary between the President and Governor Hiram Johnson, tells the story: "I was in Washington and had an interview with President Wilson. He suggested the extremely irritated state of affairs with Japan, admitted and endorsed the state's right to handle its own land questions, but deferentially submitted the fact that it might be framed in less offensive form. The result of our conference was, that it should be suggested that a bill might be drawn excluding from land ownership those who had not made application for American citizenship, thereby leaving the way open for bona fide prospective citizens to participate in the privilege of owning California land, but excluding those who had no such intent, necessarily including the Japanese whose first papers would not be accepted." William Kent, "Some Reminiscences of Hiram Johnson," in the Papers of William Kent, in the Library of Yale University. See also Kent to Johnson, Apr. 7, 1913, and Wilson to Kent, Apr. 10, 1913, both in Wilson Papers.

[13] This was the so-called Thompson-Birdsall bill, which was modeled after the Alien Ownership Act of the District of Columbia of March 3, 1887, and which prohibited aliens from owning land for more than one year unless they declared their intentions of becoming United States citizens. *The New York Times,* Apr. 17, 1913; Boston *Transcript,* Apr. 16, 1913.

Japan, impelled the President at last to take a hand. Firstly, on April 22 he addressed a public appeal to the Californians, urging them to exclude Japanese from landownership only by polite and indirect means, and not to embarrass the federal government by making the bill openly discriminatory.[14] Secondly, Wilson decided to send Bryan to California to plead the cause of national honor personally before the California lawmakers.[15]

Bryan left for Sacramento on April 24 with only the power of an ambassador, to plead but not to coerce. In the capital he addressed the legislature and conferred with the Governor and legislators, begging that they defer legislation until the State Department had had an opportunity to negotiate the question and, if that were impossible, that they adopt a law that would not openly discriminate against the Japanese. The Californians, however, knew what they wanted and were determined to get it. They conceded the right of Japanese subjects to lease agricultural property for short periods; but they insisted on denying the privilege of landownership to persons "ineligible to citizenship"—words that could only excite and insult the people of Japan. In one last, desperate stroke, Bryan appealed to Johnson to veto the bill, but the Governor, in a telling reply, refused.

Meanwhile, relations with the Japanese government were rapidly approaching the point of tension. On May 9, the day the California legislature passed the alien land bill, the Japanese Ambassador, Viscount Chinda, lodged his government's protest with the State Department. It was politely worded, but it left no doubt that the Imperial Government felt sorely aggrieved.[16] The American naval chiefs, fearful of a surprise attack on the Philippines, on May 13 urged the immediate distpatch of three American warships in the Yangtze River to those islands. The following day, the Joint Board of the Army and Navy reiterated the recommendation and Admiral Bradley A. Fiske warned that war with Japan was "not only possible, but even probable." [17] These recommendations precipitated a spirited discussion in

[14] Wilson to Hiram Johnson et al., Apr. 22. 1913, printed in The New York Times, Apr. 23, 1913.

[15] The decision was made at a Cabinet meeting on April 22. See the Daniels Diary, Apr. 22, 1913, for an account of these Cabinet discussions.

[16] Chinda to Bryan, May 9, 1913, Papers Relating to the Foreign Relations of the United States, 1913 (Washington, 1920), pp. 629–631.

[17] Daniels Diary, May 15, 1913; B. A. Fiske to Josephus Daniels, May 14. 1913, the Papers of Josephus Daniels, in the Library of Congress.

the Cabinet on May 16. Garrison favored strong action and approved the Joint Board's recommendation, while Daniels argued that moving the warships would only irritate the Japanese without making it possible to defend the Philippines if war occurred. Wilson, of course, made the final decision. He not only decreed that no ships should be sent to the Philippines but also directed the Joint Board to hold no further meetings until he so ordered.

From this time on, the state of high tension gradually diminished, and by the end of May the jingoists in both countries seem to have given up hope. But it would be a grave error to assume that friendly relations were restored by the administration's attempts to conciliate the Japanese. Many notes passed between the two foreign offices during the remainder of 1913 and the first half of 1914. In August, 1913, the Japanese proposed a treaty guaranteeing the mutual right of land-ownership by the citizens of both countries, and the Imperial Foreign Office repeatedly urged the extreme necessity of satisfying Japanese public opinion on this point. In turn, Wilson and Bryan promised to negotiate such a treaty as soon as it were politically possible to do so. But the time never seemed to come. The Yamamoto ministry fell on April 16, 1914, when the Diet rejected its naval budget, and Foreign Minister Makino was succeeded by Baron Kato in the new Okuma ministry. Shortly afterward, Kato abruptly brought the negotiations with the United States to an end. Japanese resentment had in no wise abated; the Imperial government had simply concluded that further parleys were useless and humiliating.

The spreading of the First World War to the Far East, a development that Bryan tried unsuccessfully to prevent, brought a new tension in the troubled relations between Japan and America. The Japanese expelled the Germans from the Shantung Province and gave evidence of their intention to remain there permanently. What the American leaders suspected—that Japan would seize this opportunity to extend her control over China proper—was borne out when, in the early weeks of 1915, the Japanese government presented a series of demands, twenty-one in number, to the Republic of China.[18] This move so

---

[18] Reinsch to Secretary of State, Jan. 23, 24, 26, 27, Feb. 1, 1915, *Papers Relating to the Foreign Relations of the United States, 1915* (Washington, 1924), pp. 79–82.

The first fourteen demands, embodied in Article I–IV of a treaty proposed by the Japanese government, transferred German interests in the Shantung Province to Japan, extended Japan's control in South Manchuria, and pro-

alarmed some State Department officials that discussions in the administration were begun at once. In the beginning of the crisis, however, the President signified he would move cautiously and not in a manner antagonistic to Japan. The charge that Japan had made demands that would have seriously compromised Chinese independence had only been alleged, not proved; and the allegation seemed false when Baron Kato informed the American Ambassador in Tokyo that the Imperial government had made no secret demands on China, had no desire to impair Chinese independence or to abrogate the rights of other nations in China, and desired only to strengthen its paramount interests in Manchuria and the Shantung Province. Wilson and the State Department officials knew they would have to make a frank avowal of their attitude, but they apparently had no intention of entering the negotiations as special defenders of China. In fact, they were ready to admit Japan's paramount interests in Manchuria and the Shantung Province and discussed using such recognition as a bargaining weapon in reaching a settlement of the California question.[19]

As a preliminary move, Bryan addressed a long note to the Japanese Ambassador on March 13, 1915, unequivocally reminding the Imperial government that the United States had large commercial and religious interests in China, which it had no intention of abandoning.[20] Not yet alarmed, Wilson and Bryan were confident a friendly agreement with Japan was possible.

But at the very moment when it appeared that American influence in the Japanese Foreign Office was having a moderating effect, the

---

hibited China from leasing any ports or harbors to foreign countries. The remaining seven demands, embodied in Article V, would have made China virtually a protectorate of Japan if the Chinese government had accepted them. In these provisions Japan demanded, among other things, that China employ Japanese administrative, military, and financial advisers; that China and Japan jointly police the important areas of China; that China purchase half her arms and munitions from Japanese firms, and that Japan be given important economic privileges. The proposed treaty is printed in *ibid.,* pp. 93–95.

[19] Wilson to Bryan, Feb. 25, 1915, *Papers Relating to the Foreign Relations of the United States, The Lansing Papers, 1914–1920* (2 vols., Washington, 1939–40), II, 407. See also E. T. Williams to Bryan, Feb. 26, 1915, the Papers of William Jennings Bryan, in the National Archives, and Lansing to Bryan, Mar. 1, 1915, *ibid.*

[20] Bryan to Chinda, Mar. 13, 1915, State Dept. Papers. The Japanese reply was "Unofficial Memorandum left by Ambassador Chinda Mch 22—1915 at my [Bryan's] request after he had delivered its contents as an oral communication," in Bryan Papers, National Archives. For Wilson's comment thereon, see Wilson to Bryan, Mar. 24, 1915, *ibid.*

situation suddenly worsened. On March 31 the Chinese and Japanese negotiators in Peking reached a deadlock and observers predicted that Japan would soon present an ultimatum. Then, on April 5, the American Chargé at Peking made a full report to Wilson on the negotiations then in progress in the Chinese capital. Contrary to Baron Kato's assurances, he wrote, the Japanese had presented secret and sweeping demands to the Chinese government; the Chinese had resisted this attack on their independence and had expected diplomatic support from the United States. Nine days later came a report from Reinsch, the American Minister in Peking, that destroyed any chance that the United States would come to a friendly understanding with Japan. The Japanese Minister, Reinsch reported, had told the Chinese negotiators that it was futile for them to expect support from the United States. Moreover, the authoritative Tientsin *Times* had quoted a prominent Japanese to the effect that "the Secretary of State is so much under the influence of Baron Chinda that he is not saying a word against the wishes of Japan." [21]

Wilson's comment on Reinsch's dispatch indicated that he had lost confidence in the good faith of the Japanese government and was now determined to take a strong stand in behalf of the Chinese cause. On April 27, therefore, Bryan informed Ambassador Chinda that the State Department could no longer refuse to take a public position, since its silence had been interpreted as acquiescence in the Japanese demands.[22] Moreover, the State Department issued a statement for the American press, declaring that the United States had never contemplated surrendering its treaty rights in China.[23] When the Japanese Cabinet, on May 4, voted to send an ultimatum to China and the Chinese began to make preparations to defend their capital, Bryan addressed a long memorandum to the Japanese government, setting forth the American objections to the demands, especially the secret demands included in Article V of the treaty Japan was attempting to force on China. The following day, he addressed a personal message to Count Okuma, the Prime Minister, urging patience and a peaceful policy.[24]

[21] Reinsch to Secretary of State, Apr. 14, 1915, State Dept. Papers.
[22] Bryan to Chinda, Apr. 27, 1915, Bryan Papers, National Archives. For Wilson's comment, see Wilson to Bryan, Apr. 27, 1915, *Lansing Papers,* II, 417–418.
[23] *Foreign Relations, 1915,* p. 143.
[24] Bryan to Chinda, May 5, 1915, Bryan Papers, National Archives; Bryan to Chargé Wheeler, May 6, 1915, *Lansing Papers,* II, 422–423.

The upshot of the State Department's strong stand was that the Japanese gave in under the American pressure and abandoned for the time being the demands included in Article V, while the Chinese consented to the remainder. It was a signal triumph for missionary diplomacy. Bryan, moreover, had the last word in the controversy. He addressed an identic note to China and Japan, solemnly declaring that the United States could not "recognize any agreement or undertaking which has been entered into or which may be entered into between the Governments of Japan and China, impairing the treaty rights of the United States and its citizens in China, the political or territorial integrity of the Republic of China, or the international policy relative to China commonly known as the open door policy." [25] Whether unwittingly or not, the Secretary of State was expounding a policy to which his government would adhere in future years and which eventually would prove to be one of the causes of war with the Japanese Empire.

The significant point of Wilson's and Bryan's position during this crisis was that they were considerably more sympathetic to the Japanese at the outset of the affair than has heretofore been thought; that they were in no wise endeavoring to thwart Japanese attempts to strengthen their position in South Manchuria or even to legitimize their seizure of the Shantung Province; and that they finally took a firm public stand in defense of Chinese so-called sovereignty only after they were convinced the Japanese were using American friendship for Japan to intimidate the Chinese and compel them to surrender the vestiges of their independence. Had the Japanese Foreign Office been less devious in its diplomacy or more moderate in its aspirations, the story might well have had a different ending.[26]

Another international difficulty, for example, was promptly and effectively settled because there was good faith and mutual trust on both sides—the Anglo-American dispute over the free use of the Panama Canal by American ships engaged in the coastwise trade. Congress had exempted coastwise ships from the payment of tolls in August, 1912, and the Democratic and Progressive platforms had both strongly approved the exemption. On October 14, 1912, the British Foreign Office lodged a strong protest against the exemption, asserting that its effect would be to violate the Hay-Pauncefote Treaty of 1901,

[25] Bryan to Guthrie, May 11, 1915, *Foreign Relations, 1915,* p. 146.
[26] For extended discussions of this episode, see Essay on Sources, "The United States and the Far East, 1910–17."

which promised equal rates for all nations,[27] and proposing that the matter be arbitrated.

The issue did not involve the vital interests of either country, to be sure, but to many Americans and practically all Britons it involved the good faith and honor of the United States. As the American Ambassador, Walter Page, wrote from London, "Everywhere—in circles the most friendly to us and the best-informed,—I received commiseration because of the dishonourable attitude of our Government about the Canal Tolls." [28] Although he had approved the exemption during the campaign of 1912, Wilson was soon persuaded that national honor required repeal of the disputed provision.[29] In the first weeks of the administration, the British Ambassador, James Bryce, pressed Bryan hard for prompt action; but Bryan had to tell him the President could not then risk disrupting his party. In the following November, Sir William Tyrrell, secretary to the British Foreign Minister, came to America to discuss the Mexican situation and to reiterate the British point of view in the tolls controversy. He left with personal assurances from the President that the United States would, in good time, live up to its treaty obligations.[30]

It was not until the Federal Reserve Act had been passed and the antitrust discussions had been launched, however, that Wilson was ready to carry out his plan. On January 26, 1914, he met the Senate Foreign Relations Committee in a three-hour conference and frankly reviewed the critical state of foreign affairs. He pointed to the tensions with Japan and the support the Japanese government was extending to the Huerta regime in Mexico; to the tolls dispute with Britain; and to the generally perilous world situation. One way to clean at least part of the American slate, he said, was to repeal the exemption clause and

[27] "The canal shall be free and open to the vessels of commerce and of war," the treaty read, "of all nations observing these rules, on terms of entire equality, so that there shall be no discrimination against any such nation, or its citizens or subjects, in respect of the conditions or charges of traffic, or otherwise."

[28] Page to Wilson, Sept. 10, 1913, the Papers of Walter H. Page, in Houghton Library, Harvard University.

[29] He had come to this decision at least by January, 1913. See the Diary of Edward M. House, in the Papers of Edward M. House, in the Library of Yale University, Jan. 24, 1913, and Henry White, *The Roster of the Round Table Dining Club* (New York, 1926), pp. 21–25.

[30] For details of this conference see House to W. H. Page, Nov. 14, 1913, House Papers.

to come to a friendly understanding with the British government on other matters. A week and a half later he came out publicly for repeal of the exemption provision, which, he said, was "in clear violation of the terms of the Hay-Pauncefote Treaty."

For a time it seemed the President might encounter grave difficulty in obtaining repeal by the House, for Speaker Clark and Majority Leader Underwood both refused to follow his lead, asserting that they would not be parties to the violation of the solemn pledge given in the platform of 1912. Warned that repeal would fail unless he took personal leadership of the fight, Wilson on March 5 laid his case clearly and ably before a joint session, ending with a cryptic reference to the Mexican difficulty: "I ask this of you in support of the foreign policy of the administration. I shall not know how to deal with other matters of even greater delicacy and nearer consequence if you do not grant it to me in ungrudging measure." [31]

The subsequent battle in the House came dangerously close to disrupting the Democratic ranks, and the bolt of Clark and Underwood caused observers to wonder if the President had lost his once firm control over the lower house. The bad feeling was aggravated, moreover, when Republican Anglophobes charged that Wilson had promised repeal of tolls exemption in return for the withdrawal of British support from Huerta.[32] Republican hopes of a Democratic rupture, however, soon vanished. On March 31 the House passed the Sims bill to repeal the exemption provision, 247 to 162, with only Clark, Underwood, the Tammany representatives, and Irish-American spokesmen from Boston and Chicago, among the Democrats, dissenting.[33] In the Senate the fight was more prolonged and bitter than in the House. Led by Senator James A. O'Gorman of New York, the Irish-Americans

[31] Ray S. Baker and William E. Dodd (eds.), *The Public Papers of Woodrow Wilson* (6 vols., New York, 1925–27), *The New Democracy*, I, 92–93. For significant British comment see *Pall Mall Gazette* (London), Mar. 6, 1914; *Daily Post* (Birmingham), Mar. 6, 1914; *Westminster Gazette* (London), Mar. 6, 1914; *The Times* (London), Mar. 6, 1914; *Morning Post* (London), Mar. 7, 1914; *Observer* (London), Mar. 8, 1914.

[32] Wilson and Sir Edward Grey both indignantly denied the accusation. New York *World,* Mar. 20, 1914; *The New York Times,* Mar. 31, June 30, 1914.

[33] New York *World,* Apr. 1, 1914; *The New York Times,* Apr. 1, 1914. It was perhaps a victory for principle, but one should not assume that devotion to principle alone motivated the Democrats. The dispenser of the patronage, Postmaster General Burleson, also had something to do with the victory in the House. See R. S. Baker, interview with A. S. Burleson, Mar. 17–19, 1927, Ray Stannard Baker Collection, in the Library of Congress.

and other enemies of England enjoyed a field day and gave free rein to their opinions. After two months of bitter skirmishing and debate, the administration forces and Republican advocates of repeal won easily enough when they were able to obtain a vote.[34]

The significance of the President's personal victory in the tolls fight was not lost upon the country or the rest of the world: it was a clear vindication of the principle of honor and decent dealing among nations, and it came about in spite of all that purveyors of prejudice and local patriots could do. Administration policies in the Caribbean area, on the other hand, pose a more difficult problem of interpretation. Here was another important testing ground of Wilsonian idealism; here the difficulties of squaring generous professions with the necessities of power politics first became apparent.

Latin America—indeed, the entire civilized world—confidently expected that the coming to power of the Democrats in 1913 would signify the beginning by the United States of a policy of nonintervention in Latin American affairs.[35] Since 1898 the Democratic party, and particularly its chief spokesman before 1912, Bryan, had consistently opposed the extension of American control over the Caribbean region, whether by outright military force or by so-called dollar diplomacy. After 1912, moreover, Wilson, Bryan, and, later, Lansing gave eloquent voice to the doctrines of nonintervention and the absolute equality of the states of the Western Hemisphere. The President went even further in his promise of a new Latin American policy when, at Mobile on October 27, 1913, he prophesied the freeing of the southern republics from the strangle hold of foreign concessionaires.[36]

So much for the promise, which was bright. What does the record say about the performance? To state a complex matter briefly, the administration, with the best intentions, found itself so entangled by previous commitments and especially by its own inconsistencies that it violated all its generous professions in its relations with Mexico, Central America, and the island countries. The years from 1913 to 1921 witnessed intervention by the State Department and the navy on a scale that had never before been contemplated, even by such alleged imperialists as Theodore Roosevelt and William Howard Taft.

[34] On June 11, 1914, by a vote of fifty to thirty-five.

[35] For an example of such expectations see *La Follette's Weekly*, V (Mar. 29, 1913), 9.

[36] *The Public Papers, New Democracy*, I, 64–69. For a further discussion of the circumstances and significance of this address, see below, pp. 116–118.

The most important reason for this wide disparity between profession and practice was the fact that the administration inherited a Caribbean policy, the object of which was the protection of the future Panamanian life line, which could not be reversed without a radical change in foreign policy. The Roosevelt and Taft administrations had used private bankers to consolidate American control in the Caribbean. Bryan earnestly sought to persuade the President to inaugurate a new policy—to use the financial resources of the United States to free Latin America from private banker control. If Wilson had meant to undertake a new policy and hasten the day when the New World would be free of European financial exploitation, he would have considered Bryan's proposal. However, it was too bold, too unprecedented, too "radical," and Wilson rejected it. Thus Bryan thought he had no alternative but to continue to use the old instrumentalities. Certainly it was not at that time possible for him to think in terms of complete nonintervention. American naval power was not sufficient to allow such a luxury.

In the second place, Wilson and Bryan were confident that the well-being of the Caribbean archipelago was absolutely dependent upon American supremacy in the area. Moreover, as evangels of democracy, they thought they could teach the Mexican, Central American, and Caribbean peoples how to elect good leaders and establish stable institutions. Intervention, therefore, was always rationalized in terms of the good neighbor rescuing his helpless friends from foreign dangers and internal disorders. Because he thought in these terms, it did not occur to Bryan that he might be pursuing a conventionally imperialistic course, even when, for example, he began a diplomatic campaign to establish a string of new American naval bases in the Caribbean.

Thirdly, Bryan was often extraordinarily naïve in his estimate of character and motivation. If a man came from a respectable middle-class family or were a good friend and loyal Democrat, then Bryan thought he was as guileless as Bryan himself. Sometimes this was not true, and Bryan often took advice that was hardly disinterested.

The formulation of Bryan's Nicaraguan program provides an illustration of how these several factors combined to determine policy. In 1909 Secretary Knox had established a Conservative government, headed first by Juan J. Estrada and then by Adolfo Díaz, in Managua and had persuaded American bankers to underwrite the regime.[37] In

[37] During a revolution against the Nicaraguan dictator, José Santos Zelaya,

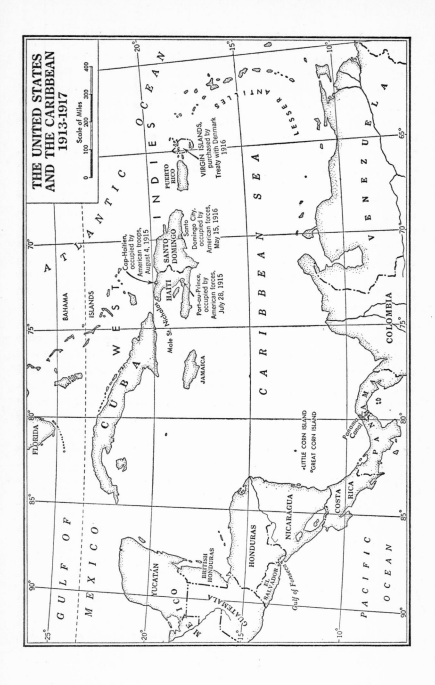

THE UNITED STATES
AND THE CARIBBEAN
1913-1917

Scale of Miles
0   100   200   300   400

ATLANTIC OCEAN

WEST INDIES

LESSER ANTILLES

BAHAMA ISLANDS

FLORIDA

GULF OF MEXICO

CUBA

JAMAICA

Cap-Haïtien,
occupied by
American troops,
August 4, 1915

Mole St. Nicholas

HAITI

SANTO
DOMINGO

Santo
Domingo City,
occupied by
American forces,
May 15, 1916

Port-au-Prince,
occupied by
American forces,
July 28, 1915

PUERTO
RICO

VIRGIN ISLANDS,
purchased by
Treaty with Denmark
1916

CARIBBEAN SEA

VENEZUELA

COLOMBIA

LITTLE CORN ISLAND
GREAT CORN ISLAND

Panama Canal

PANAMA

COSTA RICA

NICARAGUA

HONDURAS

BRITISH
HONDURAS

YUCATÁN

MEXICO

GUATEMALA

EL SALVADOR

Gulf of Fonseca

PACIFIC OCEAN

addition, Knox had negotiated a treaty with Nicaragua by which that country agreed to sell an option on its canal route to the United States for three million dollars, which sum was to be used to put Nicaragua's finances in order. The Democrats defeated ratification of the treaty in the Senate, but no sooner had Wilson come into office than the Díaz government opened a campaign for the renegotiation of the treaty. The turning point in the negotiations came on June 9 and 11, 1913, when Charles A. Douglas, close friend of Bryan and counsel for the Nicaraguan government, presented a draft treaty to the State Department. It provided for American purchase of the canal option for three million dollars and American supervision of the disbursement of the purchase money; but, more important, it empowered the United States to intervene in Nicaragua to maintain orderly government, to protect property, and to preserve Nicaraguan independence. It is clear from this and other correspondence that the idea of making Nicaragua a protectorate of the United States was conceived by the American bankers, Douglas, and the Díaz regime, chiefly as a means of keeping an unpopular government in power.

How was Bryan persuaded to approve a treaty embodying a policy that he had strenuously opposed most of his adult life? He approved the treaty because it seemed the only possible way to preserve American influence and to prevent civil war and possible anarchy in Nicaragua.[38] He approved it, also, because he trusted his friend Douglas. It was no accident that the Díaz government chose Douglas to plead their cause before the Secretary of State.

The details of the subsequent negotiations are too involved to be told here. Suffice it to say that the inclusion in the treaty of the provision for American control of the internal and external affairs of

---

in 1909, the State Department gave the revolutionists material aid. Zelaya was driven from the country and a Conservative and minority government, with intimate business connections in the United States, was established. This was followed by the inauguration of an American receivership of the customs and the refinancing of Nicaragua's foreign debt by the American bankers, Brown Brothers and J & W Seligman. In 1912 a revolt against the Conservative government was suppressed with the help of some 2,700 American marines, who stayed on in the capital until 1925. For monographic treatments of this subject see Essay on Sources, "The United States, the Caribbean, and Latin America, 1910–17."

[38] Bryan explained and defended the treaty in Bryan to Wilson, June 16, 1913, Jan. 15, June 12, July 8, Sept. 30, 1914, Wilson Papers; Bryan to Wilson, Jan. 23, 1914, Jan. 22, 1915, Bryan papers, National Archives; Bryan to W. J. Stone, July 2, 1914, State Dept. Papers.

Nicaragua aroused the hostility of the rest of Central America and also of the Democratic members of the Foreign Relations Committee. They, in fact, refused to ratify the treaty until that provision was eliminated.[39] Actually, the removal of the objectionable clause made no difference at all in the State Department's policy, which continued to be one of active intervention in Nicaraguan affairs.

The effect of Bryan's Nicaraguan policy [40] was, in brief, to fasten upon the people of Nicaragua a regime they did not like and the life of which depended upon the military and financial support of the United States. Even so, as it developed, the policy was also aimed at freeing Nicaragua from banker control and at establishing conditions in which orderly government might be maintained.

Bryan's policy toward the Dominican Republic had much the same objectives, but it was wrecked by the machinations of the gentleman he sent as Minister to that country, in one of the most disgraceful chapters in the history of the American foreign service. Because of his tenderness for "deserving Democrats," especially for veterans of the campaign of 1896, Bryan made many unfortunate appointments on the ministerial level. Most of them, however, were mere incompetents, not scoundrels. The worst mistake of all was the appointment of James M. Sullivan of New York City and Connecticut to Santo Domingo. A former prize-fight promoter and a lawyer of poor reputation, Sullivan by any criteria hardly measured up to the standards of the foreign service. Bryan did not know it then, but the fact came out later through the revelations of the New York *World* and a presidential commission of inquiry,[41] that the man who engineered Sullivan's appointment was William C. Beer, New York agent of Samuel M. Jarvis and his Banco Nacional of Santo Domingo. Jarvis coveted the

[39] The Senate ratified the treaty on February 18, 1916. For accounts of the struggle for ratification see Bryan to Wilson, July 31, 1913, Wilson Papers; *The New York Times,* Aug. 3, 1913; New York *World,* Aug. 3, 1913; B. W. Long, memorandum of conversation with W. J. Stone, dated Dec. 16, 1915, State Dept. Papers.

[40] The writer uses this term deliberately, as the Nicaraguan policy was the work of Bryan and the State Department and Wilson had nothing to do with formulating it. In fact, the President gave Bryan and the Department a free hand in the formulation of all policies relating to the Caribbean republics. He had some reservations about the Nicaraguan treaty, and he seemed to sense that there was some inconsistency about the Department's policies and his own high-sounding phrases about nonintervention and equality of states. He did not, however, allow these doubts to disturb him unduly.

[41] New York *World,* Dec. 7, 8, 9, 10, 13, 1914.

deposits of the American Receiver-General of the Dominican customs.
He supported Sullivan's candidacy in return for Sullivan's help in getting the deposits transferred from the agent of the National City Bank
of New York in Santo Domingo to his own Banco Nacional.

The funds of the Receiver-General were, accordingly, transferred
soon after Sullivan reached Santo Domingo. If this had been the
Minister's only manipulation, however, his record would not have been
exceptionally bad. The funds, in any event, were soon transferred
back to the bank from which they had been taken.[42] But Sullivan also
entered into some kind of alliance with the then President, José Bordas
Valdés. The extent to which the Minister personally profited from the
arrangement is not known; however, his cousin, Timothy Sullivan,
who accompanied him to Santo Domingo, received a large share of
the government's construction contracts, and it is possible the Minister
received a favor or two.

The Sullivan affair might have had a comic aspect, in view of the
Minister's foibles and his long-winded reports to the Department, if a
revolution had not broken out against Bordas in September, 1913.
As it was, Sullivan kept his friend in power for almost a year, in the
face of overwhelming popular hostility. He threatened the rebels with
punishment by the United States; he constantly misrepresented the
Dominican situation in his reports to the Department. In spite of the
open support that the United States extended to the Bordas government, the rebels triumphed everywhere outside the capital, until in
desperation Bordas had to call for American military aid. By mid-
summer, 1914, the situation in the republic was rapidly approaching
a state of anarchy and State Department officials concluded that only
complete military occupation by American forces would suffice to
restore order.

Wilson finally intervened to end the civil war. Firstly, Sullivan was
dismissed and replaced by the career officer, William W. Russell, who
had preceded him. Secondly, the President sent a commission to Santo
Domingo under instructions to confer with all the Dominican leaders,
to request these chieftains to agree upon a provisional president, and
to warn the Dominicans that if they did not settle their quarrels peace-

---

[42] It soon became evident the Banco Nacional was utterly unreliable and
unsafe, and the funds were transferred back to the National City Bank's agent,
S. Michelena. See W. W. Vick to Frank McIntyre, Feb. 19, 1914, State Dept.
Papers; Sullivan to Secretary of State, May 25, 1914, *ibid.;* L. M. Garrison to
Bryan, June 4, 1914, *ibid.;* Frank McIntyre to Bryan, June 10, 1914, *ibid.*

fully he would occupy their country with American military forces.[43] The commission found a provisional president apparently acceptable to all factions, and elections were held the following November under American supervision, at which one of the revolutionary leaders, Juan Y. Jiménez, was elected President. Unfortunately, however, Jiménez was too old and feeble to cope with the still explosive and complicated situation. On May 2, 1916, the opposition elements in the Dominican Congress voted to impeach the President, and when sharp fighting broke out three days later he resigned. After repeated warnings by Minister Russell, American marines were landed at the capital on May 15 and took possession of the city. As it turned out, this was merely the beginning of what became by the end of 1916 the full-fledged occupation of the country and the establishment of a military government under the command of the senior naval officer, Captain Harry S. Knapp.

American relations with Santo Domingo's neighbor, Haiti, during the Wilson period began differently but ended in the same way, except that the Haitians, with their long and proud tradition of independence, fiercely resisted the American occupation. Soon after Wilson's inauguration, a new President, Michel Oreste, was elected by the usual methods and inaugurated in Port-au-Prince. For a few months affairs went smoothly, and then the inevitable [44] revolution broke out in Le Plaine du Cul de Sac and spread to Cap Haitien. Oreste abdicated on January 27, 1914, and American sailors were landed temporarily at Port-au-Prince. Oreste was succeeded by two revolutionary chiefs, the brothers Zamor, Charles and Oreste, the latter being elected President on February 8, 1914.

The downfall of the Oreste regime—the fourth to be overthrown in two and a half years—provoked discussions in the State Department of

[43] Bryan to John Franklin Fort, Aug. 10, 1914, Wilson Papers. The "Plan of President Wilson" is printed in *Papers Relating to the Foreign Relations of the United States, 1914* (Washington, 1922), pp. 247–248.

[44] Inevitable because revolution was the instrument usually employed to accomplish political change in Haiti. Control of the customs houses was the chief objective of all Haitian politicians. A military chieftain would seize control of the government and appropriate the customs revenues. Then another chieftain would organize a "revolution" to oust the "tyrant," and when this "revolution" had succeeded the new dictator would proceed to loot the Treasury. Under such an arrangement the democratic procedures established in the Haitian constitution were obviously inoperative. See Boaz W. Long to Secretary of State, Jan. 23, 1914, and B. W. Long, "Revolution in Haiti," memorandum dated Feb. 9, 1914, both in Wilson Papers.

the need for American control of Haitian affairs. Prominent in these discussions was the agent of the National City Bank of New York in Haiti, Roger L. Farnham, and Boaz W. Long, Chief of the Latin American Affairs Division, who also had intimate connections with Wall Street. Farnham and Long suggested this would be the proper time to seize control of the Haitian customs houses, to press for a naval base at Môle St. Nicholas,[45] and in general to bring Haiti under as complete American control as was feasible. These plans were momentarily abandoned, however, when the Department learned that the Germans in Haiti were intriguing against the new Zamor government. Instead of attempting immediately to establish a protectorate, the Department recognized the Zamor regime on March 1, 1914, and gave it open support.

Once the Zamor government was apparently securely in power, however, Bryan and the Latin American Affairs Division began to mature the so-called Farnham plan for American control of the Haitian custom houses and financial affairs.[46] A convention along the lines of the Dominican-American Convention of 1907 was drafted, and Farnham went to Haiti to promote its acceptance by the native leaders.[47] In a conference with Farnham and the American Consul at Cap Haitien, Charles Zamor, brother of the President, accepted the plan on behalf of the government. Moreover, he agreed that on the occasion of the next revolutionary disturbance, the United States should land occupation forces. An outbreak did occur in Port-au-Prince on July 19 and State Department officials urged that the time for full-scale intervention had come. The Zamor brothers, however, had found elsewhere the money they needed to stay in power, and they

[45] Acquisition of this naval base was one of Bryan's first projects. He not only recognized the strategic value of the base but was also anxious to prevent any European nation, particularly Germany, from obtaining a foothold in Haiti. In June, 1913, Bryan sent former Governor John E. Osborne of Wyoming to Haiti to negotiate the cession of a strip of land twenty miles wide running ten miles beyond the eastern line of the harbor. Bryan to Wilson, June 14, 1913, Wilson Papers; Bryan to Wilson, June 20, 1913, Bryan Papers, National Archives.

[46] The French and German governments, incidentally, asked for a share in the control of the Haitian customs and were told decisively that the United States would not consent to such an arrangement. Bryan to Wilson, Mar. 24, 1914, and Wilson to Bryan, Mar. 26, 1914, both in Wilson Papers.

[47] Bryan to Livingston, American Consul, Cap Haitien, July 10, 1914, State Dept. Papers. A copy of the proposed treaty was sent to Minister Blanchard on July 2, 1914, and is printed in *Foreign Relations, 1914*, pp. 349–350.

now repudiated their acceptance of the proposed convention. The State Department, therefore, held off and did not intervene.

The situation in Haiti grew utterly hopeless, however, in September and October, 1914. When it was apparent their government was doomed, the Zamor brothers appealed to the American Minister for help. They were now ready to accept the proposed treaty if the United States would maintain them in power. It was too late. President Zamor fled the capital on a Dutch boat on October 29, while his brother, Charles, and his so-called Cabinet sought refuge in the French legation. A few days later the successful revolutionary chief, Davilmar Théodore, entered Port-au-Prince and took possession of the government.

Immediately the State Department applied pressure upon the new Théodore government for the negotiation of the treaty. When Acting Foreign Minister Bobo refused and offered instead to grant large commercial and mining concessions to the United States in return for American financial assistance, Bryan was so offended by the proffered bribe that he replied that the United States had no desire to force its influence on Haiti. The Théodore government soon proved incompetent and corrupt, and when another revolution broke out in Cap Haitien in early January, 1915, Bryan and the President agreed that American intervention could not long be postponed. They sent former Governor John Franklin Fort of New Jersey and Charles C. Smith to Haiti to negotiate the convention; but before the commission arrived in Port-au-Prince, Théodore had fled and General Vilbrun G. Sam had been elected President. Sam and his Foreign Minister, Duvivier, talked informally with the commissioners but refused officially to negotiate, on the ground that the Americans were not properly accredited to a sovereign government.

During the following months, Wilson and Bryan pondered a course of action. Although he still supported the proposed treaty, the Secretary was reluctant to force it on the Haitians and tried to find an alternative to military action; the President, on the other hand, was completely out of patience and anxious to bring the matter to a head. The excuse for such action arose when the Haitian situation exploded again in June and July, 1915, after Bryan had resigned. When a revolution under Dr. Rosalvo Bobo threatened the capital, President Sam executed 160 political prisoners, including former President Zamor, who had returned to Haiti. The people of Port-au-Prince rose in righteous anger, dragged Sam and his executioners from their refuge in the French legation, and hacked their bodies to pieces.

This final display of anarchy spelled the doom of Haitian independence. Marines and bluejackets landed at Port-au-Prince on July 28 and encountered slight resistance in occupying the city. A week later American sailors were landed at Cap Haitien, the nest of revolutionary disorders. From this point on, the task was mainly one of subduing the *cacos,* the professional soldiers, who resisted the American forces and took refuge in the mountainous parts of the country. The process of pacification, which had begun so easily, soon became almost a war of extermination, as the Haitians fought back fanatically, and the job was not completed until some two thousand of them had been shot.

Meanwhile, on August 9, 1915, Admiral W. B. Caperton took control of the Haitian government. Three days later the Admiral allowed the National Assembly to elect a pro-American, Sudre Dartiguenave, President of Haiti. The State Department now moved firmly to press a treaty upon the government, an arrangement providing not only for American financial supervision but also for the disarming of the so-called army and the establishment of a native constabulary under American control. When Dartiguenave balked at signing the treaty, Secretary of State Robert Lansing threatened to establish complete military government or else to put another puppet in power.[48] After much parleying, in which the Haitians got nowhere, Dartiguenave signed the treaty making his country a protectorate of the United States on September 16, 1915.[49]

To such extremes of intervention, invasion, and military occupation did missionary diplomacy carry the United States. By 1917 the close bonds between Nicaragua and Santo Domingo and the United States had been immeasurably strengthened, while a new protectorate [50] in Haiti had been added to the State Department's realm. Nor would the process have stopped here, if Bryan had had his way; for he originally

[48] Lansing to Davis, Aug. 24, 1915, *Foreign Relations, 1915,* pp. 437–438.

[49] Printed in *ibid.,* pp. 449–451. The treaty was ratified by the Haitian Senate on November 12, 1915, and by the United States Senate on February 28, 1916.

[50] The writer uses the word "protectorate" in its popular sense. Technically and legally, Nicaragua, Santo Domingo, and Haiti were not protectorates of the United States. In reality, however, they were.

dreamed of making quasi protectorates of all the Central American republics.

Whether in the long run the achievements of missionary diplomacy justified the unfortunate consequences is a matter of opinion. Certainly in the more important case of Mexico, which will be examined in the next chapter, the constructive accomplishments were few and the unfortunate results were many.

The one saving feature of the policy, the feature that in the end prevented it from becoming pure imperialism, was its peculiar motivation. Important in this motivation was the administration's desire to preserve the stability of the Caribbean area in order to preclude the excuse for European intervention, it is true. But just as important was Bryan's and Wilson's conviction that the great American democracy could not in Christian conscience refuse to offer a friendly hand to peoples ravaged by endemic civil war, disease, and starvation. Actually, this was the most important immediate motive for intervention in Santo Domingo and Haiti, for in 1915–16 there was no danger of any early European intervention. Moreover, had the people of these two republics demonstrated even a slight capacity to govern themselves and to discharge their international responsibilities, intervention in their affairs by the United States would not have occurred.

It can be said, also, that missionary diplomacy was not motivated by any ambition to promote the exclusive material interests of the United States. On the contrary, Bryan was often more regardful of the rights and interests of the Caribbean peoples than were their so-called governments. For example, on one occasion Bryan advised the Cuban government not to agree to the terms of a loan it was negotiating with Wall Street firms, because the conditions of the loan restricted Cuba's ability to borrow in the future. "It is the policy of this Government," he added, "to treat all Americans alike and to give all an equal opportunity . . .; but in advising the Latin American states it is our desire to look at the question from their standpoint and to give them every assistance." [51] On several occasions, moreover, Bryan intervened to prevent the Díaz government of Nicaragua from granting exclusive concessions and undue privileges to American bankers. When the Nicaraguan government negotiated a loan in September, 1913, Bryan wrote: "We have put in everything [in the loan agreement] that we

[51] Bryan to Minister W. E. Gonzales, Nov. 21, 1913, Bryan Papers, Library of Congress.

can think of that will protect Nicaragua. . . . The Nicaraguan representatives in Washington would have willingly made a contract less favorable to Nicaragua. In fact, they complained a little at the restrictions that I imposed, but I told them that I would not recommend anything to you that could, in my judgment, be criticized." [52] Soon afterward Bryan prevented Nicaragua from granting a ninety-nine-year contract to Brown Brothers, banking firm of Baltimore, for the construction and operation of a railroad. He objected because the concession was exclusive and too long lived.[53] Finally, when the Haitian government of Davilmar Théodore tried to bribe the State Department by an offer of exclusive concessions for Americans, Bryan replied in a ringing affirmation of the principle that undergirded his diplomacy: "Our obligation to the American people requires that we shall give all legitimate assistance to American investors in Haiti, but we are under obligations just as binding to protect Haiti, as far as our influence goes, from injustice or exploitation at the hands of Americans." [54] A poor principle, indeed, upon which to build an American imperialism!

In fact, it was Wilson's and Bryan's great hope that their policies would lead to peace and unity throughout the Western Hemisphere. In their relations with the stable governments of South America they gave full evidence that they regarded them as equals, deserving of the respect and treatment of sovereign neighbors. This conviction was given dramatic expression in 1914, when the President accepted Argentina's, Brazil's, and Chile's offer of mediation soon after the occupation of Vera Cruz, when it appeared war between the United States and Mexico was inevitable. A year later Wilson went even further and sought the advice and support of the leading Latin American governments in his handling of the Mexican problem.

But the act which, more than any other, helped restore the moral prestige of the United States in the eyes of South America was the negotiation of a treaty with Colombia in 1913–14 to repair the damage done by Theodore Roosevelt's aggression in practically seizing the Canal Zone in 1903.[55] It was an act of honest and humble statesman-

[52] Bryan to Wilson, Sept. 3, 1913, Wilson Papers.

[53] I am not disposed to favor anything down there, Bryan added, "that I would not favor here and an exclusive franchise is abhorrent, especially when running ninety-nine years." Bryan to Wilson, Oct. 4, 1913, *ibid.*

[54] Bryan to Blanchard, Dec. 19, 1914, *Foreign Relations, 1914,* p. 371.

[55] In Article I of the treaty the United States expressed "sincere regret that anything should have occurred to interrupt or to mar the relations of cordial

ship, sincerely meant. The idea of the great and powerful government of the United States in effect apologizing to the helpless government of Colombia for a past wrong stirred a wave of warm and friendly feeling in South America. The publication of the treaty of course nearly gave Roosevelt apoplexy,[56] and his friends in the Senate prevented its ratification.[57] The good intentions of the administration had been made clear, none the less.

Wilson climaxed his hemispheric diplomacy by taking leadership in a movement to unite the American republics in a great Pan-American alliance, binding them to a "mutual guarantee of territorial integrity and of political independence under republican forms of government," to settle all disputes by peaceful means, and mutually to refrain from aiding the enemies of any signatory government.[58] Such a pact had been suggested by Representative James L. Slayden of Texas in 1910–11 and formally proposed a year later by the Colombian government. The Taft administration had scoffed at the Colombian proposal; but as soon as Wilson came into office, Slayden and the Colombian Minister renewed their campaigns for a nonaggression pact. Wilson took up the idea enthusiastically; the State Department drafted a treaty and circulated it among the Latin American governments. Practically all the small republics hastened to approve the pact; the Brazilian government strongly supported it. Argentina, however, was lukewarm, while Chile, because of her long-standing boundary dispute with Peru, was

---

friendship that had so long subsisted between the two nations"—an obvious apology for the Panama affair. Moreover, the United States offered the Colombian government free use of the Canal and an indemnity of $25 million. The treaty is printed in *ibid.*, pp. 163–164.

[56] Roosevelt demanded a speedy hearing by the Foreign Relations Committee. "I ask for this hearing," he wrote, "because I regard the proposed Treaty as a crime against the United States, an attack upon the honor of the United States, which, if true, would convict the United States of infamy, and a serious menace to the future well-being of our people." Theodore Roosevelt to the Chairman of the Senate Committee on Foreign Relations, July 11, 1914, the Papers of Theodore Roosevelt, in the Library of Congress.

[57] Led by Senator Henry Cabot Lodge, the Republicans defeated ratification of the treaty in 1914 and again in 1917, although on the latter occasion Lansing warned the Foreign Relations Committee that ratification was vital to the security of the United States. A treaty awarding Colombia $25 million, but without the so-called apology, was negotiated and approved by the United States Senate in April, 1921.

[58] These were the provisions of the proposed treaty. A copy is printed in Charles Seymour (ed.), *The Intimate Papers of Colonel House* (4 vols., Boston, 1926–28), I, 233–234.

positively opposed. The State Department was never able to crack the hard shell of Chilean resistance, and so the pact failed.

Although the Pan-American Pact clearly forecast the League of Nations Covenant and the Good Neighbor Policy of a later President, the historian must be allowed a few doubts as to the administration's sincerity in proposing it. There is no evidence that Wilson, Bryan, or Lansing was prepared to do more than pay lip service to the Pan-American ideal, especially where the Caribbean and Central American countries were concerned. Nor were they ready to renounce the so-called right of intervention, in spite of the solemn pledges contained in the Pan-American Treaty. The truth was they were trying to reap the benefits of the Good Neighbor Policy without being willing to abide by that policy's fundamental principles. One of the chief tasks of subsequent administrations was to liquidate the remaining vestiges of missionary interventionism, in order that genuine Pan-American unity might become a living reality.

CHAPTER 5

Mexico: Interference and Defeat, 1913-17

MISSIONARY diplomacy found its apogee in Wilson's efforts to shape the Mexican Revolution into a constitutional and moralistic pattern of his own making. In spite of the President's frequent denials that he ever had intervened or ever would intervene, this effort involved interference by the United States in Mexican affairs on an unprecedented scale. Wilson's broad objective—the establishment of a constitutional government in Mexico, responsive to the economic and social needs of the people and amenable to his direction—was always paramount in his thought and policy. And Wilson had a sincere passion to help the struggling Mexican masses win land and liberty. The root of his difficulty and the chief cause of his failure was that in working toward a commendable objective he used the wrong tactics, with the result that by the end of his administration the United States had hardly a friend left in Mexico.

Wilson, of course, inherited and did not create the Mexican problem. The old regime under Porfirio Díaz had been overthrown in 1911 by a reformer, Francisco I. Madero. Mystic, idealist, and dreamer though he was, Madero none the less tried to destroy the backbone of the old system—the landed aristocracy, the professional politicians allied with the business interests, the Church, and the army. And because he was attempting to reconstruct the bases of Mexican society the inevitable counterrevolutions occurred, and, in the end, Madero was betrayed, deposed, and murdered by his chief general, Victoriano Huerta.

Events of the "Tragic Ten Days" in Mexico City, February 9–18,

1913, during which Huerta executed his coup, shook the Western world and set off a chain of events that culminated in one of the significant revolutions of the twentieth century. That fact was not, however, apparent at the time. The only reason President Taft did not heed the advice of his Ambassador, Henry Lane Wilson, to extend immediate recognition to the Huerta government was that the State Department planned to use recognition as a bargaining weapon in obtaining favorable settlement of certain outstanding disputes with Mexico.[1] Following traditional practice, England, France, Germany, Japan, and the other powers extended recognition, as Huerta seemed the only person capable of preserving order and protecting foreign interests.

This, therefore, was the state of affairs when Wilson and Bryan took control of the foreign policy of the United States in March, 1913. Ambassador Wilson began to bombard them with urgent pleas for recognition. Learned specialists in the State Department argued correctly that Huerta had observed constitutional requirements in assuming power, that the United States had always extended *de facto* recognition to revolutionary governments, and that the Huerta regime was in fact the only government in Mexico. Moreover, practically the entire American colony in Mexico City and powerful financial interests in the United States brought strong pressure to bear upon the administration to force recognition.[2] Wilson, however, would not be hurried or persuaded by these advices and pleas. To him, as to Bryan,[3] the issue

[1] The Diary of Chandler P. Anderson, in the Library of Congress, Mar. 15, 1915. Former Secretary of State Knox told Anderson that if he and Taft had realized that Wilson would not recognize Huerta, they would have done so themselves. See also W. H. Taft to W. V. Backus, July 10, 1916, the Papers of William Howard Taft, in the Library of Congress.

[2] Especially active in this regard were E. N. Brown, president of the National Railways of Mexico, and James Speyer, of Speyer & Company, New York bankers with large interests in Mexican bonds. See the Diary of Edward M. House, in the Papers of Edward M. House, in the Library of Yale University, Mar. 27, Apr. 1, 1913; W. A. Tucker to E. M. House, Apr. 17, 1913, House Papers; James Speyer to J. B. Moore, May 1, 31, 1913, Papers of the Department of State, in the National Archives; Speyer to W. G. McAdoo, May 5, 1913, *ibid.*

[3] From the beginning of their administration, Wilson and Bryan were in complete accord in dealing with the Mexican problem. The State Department records reveal that although Wilson took the initiative in determining policy and made all important decisions, Bryan heartily concurred and faithfully executed his chief's policies. The present writer does not know of a single important disagreement between the two men over Mexican policies.

was clear: a constitutional, popular government had been overthrown by a military usurper, and the rightful rulers of Mexico had been murdered. To recognize such a *coup d'état* in a country as important as Mexico would be to sanction and encourage government by assassination throughout the Western Hemisphere. "I will not recognize a government of butchers," Wilson said privately.[4] Through the press he let it be known he would not appoint a successor to Ambassador Henry Lane Wilson, as such an act would imply tacit recognition of the Huerta government.[5]

It is plain Wilson's decision was dictated chiefly by the moral revulsion he felt against the bloody means Huerta had used to rise to power. There was, however, another reason why the administration hesitated to accord a hasty recognition to the provisional government in Mexico. On the day after Huerta's coup, the standards of a new revolution were unfurled in the northern states of Coahuila and Chihuahua. The leader was the Maderista Governor of Coahuila, Venustiano Carranza, a bespectacled, scholarly-looking man with a great white beard, whose childlike face failed to reveal his inflexible character. Calling themselves Constitutionalists and the rightful heirs of Madero, the anti-Huertistas met at Guadalupe and pledged themselves to carry on the struggle, under the leadership of the First Chief, Carranza, until Huerta was overthrown and constitutional government was re-established. Although it was impossible to measure the proportions or predict the future of the Constitutionalist movement during March-May, 1913, it was evident Huerta's claim that he had pacified Mexico was false.

[4] Charles Willis Thompson to "Rube" Bull, May 22, 1913, the Papers of Charles Willis Thompson, in the Library of Princeton University.

[5] New York *World,* Mar. 13, 1913; *The New York Times,* May 17, 1913. On March 11 Wilson issued a public statement declaring that the United States could not approve Latin American governments established by fraud and violence and in defiance of the wishes of the majority. "We can have no sympathy with those who seek to seize the power of government to advance their own personal interests or ambition," he warned. *Ibid.,* Mar. 12, 1913. This statement, however, was not meant to apply to the situation in Mexico. It was issued because the administration had received advice from American diplomatic officials in Nicaragua that revolutionary leaders in that country were contemplating an uprising against the Díaz government. Miguel Alvarez S. to Dr. Salvador Castrillo, Nicaraguan Minister to the United States, Feb. 1, 1913, State Dept. Papers; Minister George F. Weitzel, from Managua, to Secretary of State, Feb. 18, Apr. 4, 1913, *ibid.* The Diary of Josephus Daniels, in the Library of Congress, Mar. 11, 1913, gives details of the Cabinet discussions of the same date.

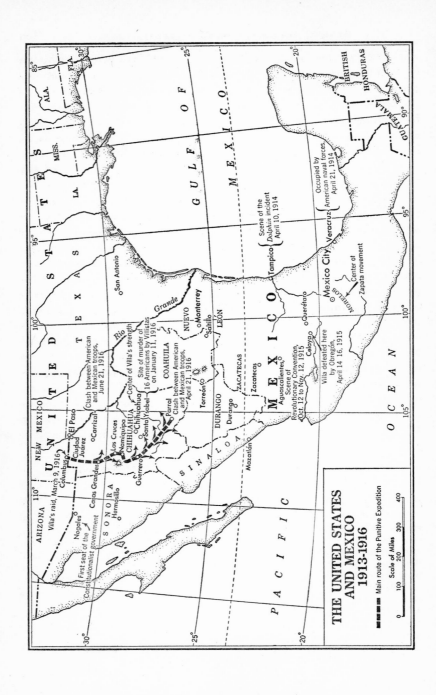

THE UNITED STATES
AND MEXICO
1913-1916

Main route of the Punitive Expedition

Scale of Miles
0   100   200   300   400

In the face of this uncertain situation, Wilson and Bryan wisely decided to wait and see whether Huerta could extend his control over all of Mexico and whether he would hold constitutional elections, as he had said he would do. Meanwhile, the United States would not formally recognize the provisional government, although it would deal with it, through Ambassador Wilson, "on the basis of the fact of its existence." [6]

At this point in the administration's deliberations, that is, in early May, the spokesmen of several corporations with large material interests in Mexico—the Southern Pacific Railroad, Phelps, Dodge & Company, the Greene Cananea Copper Company, and Edward L. Doheny's Mexican Petroleum Company—came forward with a plan that seemed to offer a practical solution. They proposed that the State Department agree to recognize Huerta, provided Huerta hold an election before October 26, 1913, the date the leaders of the provisional government had already agreed upon. The Constitutionalists, moreover, should suspend hostilities, join in the election, and agree to support the President thus chosen. Wilson was so impressed by the proposal that he at once drafted a plan for a settlement that provided for recognition of Huerta by the United States, on the condition that Huerta hold an early and fair election; the plan also envisaged suspension of hostilities, participation in the election, and submission to the new government on the part of the Constitutionalists.[7] Wilson also drafted a note to Ambassador Wilson, setting forth the terms of his settlement, but for reasons that are not evident he did not send the note or formally offer his plan to the provisional government.[8]

Meanwhile, before he settled upon any policy, Wilson endeavored to obtain a true estimate of the Mexican situation. As early as March 7 there had been disturbing reports reflecting on the integrity of Ambassador Wilson, reports to the effect that he had actually aided and abetted the Huerta *coup d'état*.[9] These and subsequent revelations

[6] This policy was announced in the press on May 17, 1913, although Ambassador Wilson was apparently not informed of it until July 10. *The New York Times,* May 17, 1913; Bryan to H. L. Wilson, July 10, 1913, *Papers Relating to the Foreign Relations of the United States, 1913* (Washington, 1920), p. 809.

[7] "Mexico. Settlement," MS drafted by Wilson, c. May 8–10, 1913, the Woodrow Wilson Papers, in the Library of Congress. Wilson planned to negotiate with the Constitutionalists through a special envoy.

[8] The text of this draft is printed in R. S. Baker, *Woodrow Wilson: Life and Letters* (8 vols., Garden City, N.Y., 1927–39), IV, 248–249.

[9] New York *World,* Mar. 7, 8, 12, 1913. The extent to which Ambassador

convinced the President that Henry Lane Wilson was thoroughly untrustworthy, and it is doubtful that thereafter he even read the Ambassador's dispatches. Instead, the President by-passed the Ambassador by sending a trusted friend, William Bayard Hale,[10] on a secret mission to Mexico City to investigate and report. Hale's vivid and dramatic dispatches from the Mexican capital during the summer of 1913 reiterated a single theme, that the Huerta government could not possibly survive and that only the election of a constitutional government could avert full-scale American intervention.[11]

Shortly before Hale's dispatches began to come to the President, the Southern Pacific-Phelps, Dodge & Company group brought forward on May 26 a revised plan for a settlement of the civil war in Mexico. These spokesmen did not now advise recognition of Huerta; they merely proposed that the State Department use its good offices to mediate between the provisional government and the Constitutionalists, who were daily gaining strength, to effect a fair and nation-wide election. Soon afterward Hale's reports began to come in, and on June 14 the administration made its first formal and outright declaration of policy. Huerta was told that if he gave satisfactory assurances that an early and free election would be held and observed his promise not to

---

Wilson encouraged the Huerta-Díaz cabal has never been determined. It is evident from Wilson's own dispatches, however, that he was strongly opposed to Madero, knew well in advance about the plot to overthrow the legal government and did not inform the constitutional authorities, and actually brought Huerta and Felix Díaz together in the American Embassy and persuaded them to sign the "Pacto de la Ciudadela" on February 18, 1913, by which an agreement on the composition of the provisional government was reached. See especially H. L. Wilson to Secretary of State, Mar. 12, 1913, *Foreign Relations, 1913*, pp. 768–776.

[10] A former Episcopal clergyman, William Bayard Hale was in 1910–13 one of the leading journalists in the United States. As a reporter for Walter Page's *World's Work*, Hale had come to know Wilson intimately in 1911. In 1912 Hale edited Wilson's major campaign addresses in a volume entitled *The New Freedom*, which was published in 1913. Hale's brilliant style and quick intelligence made a deep impression on Wilson. In so far as the present writer can ascertain, Hale's reports from Mexico City were generally credible.

[11] Hale to Ben G. Davis (for the Secretary of State), June 3, 22, 25, July 2, 8, 9, 12, 15, 16, 17, 24, 29, Aug. 5, 1913, State Dept. Papers.

It should be added that Bryan also sent a secret envoy to Mexico—Reginaldo F. Del Valle of California. Del Valle first conferred with Constitutionalist leaders, including Carranza, in northern Mexico; he then went to Mexico City, where he acted so indiscreetly that Bryan was forced to recall him. See Del Valle to Ben G. Davis, June 8, 9, 12, 17, 23, 1913, *ibid.;* Davis to Del Valle, July 8, 15, 1913, *ibid.; El Diario* (Mexico City), July 7, 1913.

be a candidate,[12] the United States would attempt to bring the warring factions in Mexico together in a common program and government.

This first message to the Huerta government was merely suggestive of a larger program of interference in the affairs of Mexico, along the lines of the second Southern Pacific-Phelps, Dodge & Company proposal, that the President was preparing to undertake. That the program involved interference that neither side in Mexico had asked for or wanted did not seem to disturb the President, who apparently thought a strong policy would bring prompt submission. Firstly, he called Henry Lane Wilson home and then dismissed him. Secondly, he sent John Lind, former Governor of Minnesota and a close friend of Bryan, to the Mexican capital to press his proposal for the election of a constitutional government the United States could recognize.[13] Thirdly, the President addressed a circular note to the powers, requesting them to urge upon Huerta the necessity of accepting American mediation.[14] When news of Lind's mission reached Mexico City, Huerta blustered and informed the American Chargé, Nelson O'Shaughnessy, that Lind would not be welcomed unless he came properly accredited. "I will resist with arms any attempt by the United States to interfere in the affairs of Mexico," he threatened.[15]

Huerta's outburst was, of course, not seriously meant. But his anger and the astonishment that most Mexicans, including the Constitutionalists, felt were not without good cause. Wilson's missionary diplomacy succeeded, to be sure, when all the President had to do was to order the occupation of some small republic and establish a puppet government. Mexico, however, was not Nicaragua or Santo Domingo. Mexico was a nation, whose citizens cherished their independence and

[12] The statement, "that Huerta will observe his original promise and not be a candidate at that election," reveals a puzzling misconception on Wilson's part regarding Huerta's position. Huerta had never promised that he would not be a candidate, yet during the future negotiations Wilson acted as if he had.

[13] Wilson's instructions to Lind, embodying the plan, are printed in *Foreign Relations, 1913*, pp. 821–822. Specifically, Wilson proposed (1) that there should be an immediate armistice in Mexico, (2) that there should be an early and free election, in which all parties would participate, (3) that Huerta should bind himself not to be a candidate for the presidency, and (4) that all factions should agree to abide by the results of the election and co-operate in supporting the new administration.

[14] Circular note to governments with representatives in Mexico, Aug. 8, 1913, Wilson Papers.

[15] *The New York Times,* Aug. 9, 1913.

sovereignty more than their lives. To these proud people Wilson's assumption of the right to tell them who should or should not be their President was, in any event, intolerable. The method Wilson used, moreover—that of sending an unofficial agent to a government the United States would not recognize—only increased Mexican resentment and added to the general irony of the situation.

Arriving in Mexico City on August 11, the following day Lind discreetly presented the President's proposal to the Foreign Minister of the *de facto* government, Federico Gamboa. Gamboa pleaded movingly for recognition, or at least abstention from interference in Mexican affairs by the United States. He declared, moreover, that Mexico regarded the President's proposal as an unwarranted meddling in the domestic affairs of a sovereign neighbor. Lind replied firmly. The United States, he said, would never recognize the provisional government. Moreover, he continued, in a thinly veiled threat, if Huerta rejected the President's mediation, Wilson might be compelled to lay the whole matter before Congress and might also allow the Constitutionalists to buy arms in the United States. Day after day the parleys proceeded stubbornly, amid alarming rumors in both countries of an impending break or outright American military intervention. On August 22 Lind went his limit and held out the promise that, if Huerta accepted Wilson's proposal, the State Department would help the Mexican government obtain a loan in the United States. Gamboa replied that he dared not transmit this offer, or bribe, to his chief.[16]

Then, after Lind had broken off the negotiations and left for Vera Cruz, the Foreign Minister delivered his final reply. Indignantly repudiating the right of an American President to determine Mexican affairs, Gamboa added: "If even once we were to permit the counsels and advice (let us call them thus) of the United States of America not only would we as I say above, forego our sovereignty but we would as well compromise for an indefinite future our destinies as a sovereign entity and all the future elections for president would be submitted to the veto of any President of the United States of America. And such an enormity, Mr. Confidential Agent, no government will ever attempt to perpetrate and this I am sure of unless some monstrous and almost impossible cataclysm should occur in the conscience of the Mexican

[16] Lind to Secretary of State, Aug. 12, 1913, State Dept. Papers; Lind to Secretary of State, n.d., but received Aug. 15, 1913, *ibid.;* Lind to Secretary of State, Aug. 18, 22, 1913, Wilson Papers. Of course Gamboa did transmit the offer to Huerta.

people." However, Gamboa continued, the fact was that under the Mexican Constitution Huerta could not be a candidate to succeed himself. Huerta had done nothing to raise the suspicion that he would be a candidate. "On what then is the gratuitous suspicion of the President of the United States of America based and his demand which is absolutely inadmissible?" Finally, Gamboa rejected Lind's offer of an American loan with the following barb: "When the dignity of the nation is at stake I believe that there are not loans enough to induce those charged by the law to maintain it to permit it to be lessened." [17]

Expressed though it was in proud words, Gamboa's note in effect conceded Wilson's most important demand, that Huerta eliminate himself from the Mexican presidency at an early date. Before the note arrived in Washington, however, Wilson went before a joint session, in the afternoon of August 27, for the first time to explain his Mexican policy to Congress and the country. He outlined the proposal that Lind had presented to Huerta and declared that Huerta had flatly rejected it. The United States, therefore, would now pursue a policy of "watchful waiting," would urge American citizens to withdraw from Mexico, and would "follow the best practice of nations in the matter of neutrality by forbidding the exportation of arms or munitions of war of any kind" to either side in the civil war that was mounting in intensity.[18]

The arrival during the evening of August 27 of Gamboa's note, together with assurances from Lind that the United States had won a substantial victory, greatly eased the tension in Washington and set Wilson and Bryan to making further plans to bring peace and stability to Mexico. The next four or five weeks were a virtual honeymoon period in Mexican-American relations. When Huerta expressed a desire to send a confidential agent to Washington, Bryan replied encourag-

[17] Gamboa to Lind, Aug. 26, 1913, transmitted in O'Shaughnessy to Secretary of State, Aug. 27, 1913, original in *ibid.*

[18] The address is printed in Ray S. Baker and William E. Dodd (eds.), *The Public Papers of Woodrow Wilson* (6 vols., New York, 1925–27), *The New Democracy,* I, 45–51.

Up to this time the provisional government had been able to purchase arms in the United States, while the Constitutionalists, whose belligerent status the United States had not recognized, could not. Wilson's careless assertion that "the best practice of nations in the matter of neutrality" was the application of an arms embargo was grossly false. Two years later friends of Germany, who were urging an arms embargo, quoted it over and over, and with telling effect.

ingly.[19] Then, on September 16 Huerta announced to the Mexican Congress his ardent desire to turn the government over to a constitutional successor, and Lind and Bryan were greatly relieved. But the most encouraging development of all was the nomination of Gamboa for the presidency by the Catholic party on September 24. "I feel that we have nearly reached the end of our trouble," wrote Bryan in strong approval of the Foreign Minister,[20] while the State Department announced it would approve Gamboa's election, even if the northern states in revolt against Huerta did not participate.[21]

Just at the moment, however, when it appeared that Huerta would yield power to Gamboa and that the United States would throw its moral and financial support behind the new government, a catastrophic chain of events was set in motion upon the arrival in Mexico City of a new British Minister, Sir Lionel Carden. Carden was the mouthpiece of S. Weetman Pearson, Lord Cowdray, who had enormous oil interests in Mexico, and there is some ground for believing that the British Foreign Office for a time allowed Cowdray to dictate its Mexican policy.[22] Nor was there much doubt that Cowdray, through his agents in Mexico, exercised great influence over the Huerta government. In any event, Carden's arrival coincided with Huerta's most appalling act since the murder of Madero.[23] On October 10 the

[19] O'Shaughnessy to Secretary of State, Sept. 1, 1913; Bryan to Lind, Sept. 8, 1913, both in State Dept. Papers.

[20] Bryan to Wilson, Sept. 25, 1913, Wilson Papers; also Bryan to Lind, Sept. 26, 1913, State Dept. Papers.

[21] New York *World,* Sept. 26, 1913. It should be added, however, that the State Department was doing its best at this time to bring about an armistice in the fighting and to obtain the participation of the Constitutionalists in the coming presidential election, scheduled to be held October 26, 1913.

[22] This was Wilson's and Bryan's firm conviction. See, e.g., Daniels Diary, Apr. 18, 1913, for Cabinet discussions of this point; also House Diary, Oct. 30, 1913. Sir Edward Grey emphatically denied the charge in *Twenty-Five Years, 1892–1916* (2 vols., New York, 1925), II, 98–100.

In any event, the major factor in British policy was Mexican oil, as the British navy had recently converted from coal burners to oil burners. With its production of twenty-five million barrels in 1912, Mexico was practically the sole source of oil for the British navy. British policy, therefore, was naturally directed at preserving a steady flow of petroleum. The provisional government in Mexico City could and did give guarantees that this vital British interest would be protected.

[23] Lind was convinced that Carden knew beforehand of Huerta's coup of October 10 and that the British Minister timed the presentation of his credentials with reference to it. Lind to Secretary of State, Oct. 23, 27, 1913, State Dept. Papers.

usurper fell upon the Chamber of Deputies, composed mainly of Maderistas, arrested and imprisoned 110 members, and inaugurated a full-fledged military dictatorship. The following day, October 11, Carden went ostentatiously to the Presidential Palace and presented his credentials to Huerta.

Huerta's act of violence and Carden's open approval shocked and angered Wilson and impelled him to adopt a new course of action. Firstly, the President accused Huerta of personal bad faith and told him the United States would not approve any election he might hold. Secondly, the President addressed a circular note to the governments with representatives in Mexico, asking them to withhold recognition from the new regime. Thirdly, two weeks later, on November 7, he warned these governments that it was "his immediate duty to require Huerta's retirement from the Mexican government" and that the United States would "now proceed to employ such means as may be necessary to secure this result." [24]

A significant exchange among Wilson, Bryan, and Counselor John Bassett Moore preceded the sending of the circular note of November 7. Following Carden's recognition of Huerta's *coup d'état* of October 10, Wilson wrote on his own typewriter an outline of a circular note he wished the State Department to prepare. In his outline, the President accused the European powers of keeping Huerta in power, "without regard to the wishes or purposes of the United States." Would they co-operate with the United States, Wilson continued, "or is their policy and intention to antagonize and thwart us and make our task one of domination and force?" To England, Wilson wanted it said that "The bottom was about to drop out when Sir Lionel Carden appeared upon the scene and took charge of its rehabilitation." Finally, Wilson wrote, he wanted the note to be *"as strong and direct as the courtesies and proprieties of pacific diplomacy permit."* [25]

Bryan thereupon proceeded to write a draft of the note Wilson had requested, and the President went over Bryan's draft, making certain textual changes in his own handwriting. In this note the United States

[24] Bryan to American Embassy, Oct. 13, 1913, *ibid.;* Bryan to certain diplomatic officers, Oct. 24, Nov. 7, 1913, *Foreign Relations, 1913,* pp. 849, 856.

[25] Undated memorandum in State Dept. Papers. Wilson's anger stemmed chiefly from his belief that the British government was supporting Huerta in order to protect Cowdray's oil concessions. He told Colonel House he was determined to expose this alliance between the provisional government and Cowdray. "He said it was his purpose to build a fire back of the British Ministry through the English public." House Diary, Oct. 30, 1913.

accused the powers of allowing their citizens to assist and encourage Huerta, in return for commercial concessions. The United States, therefore, "in the name of the people of the western hemisphere, whose lands have been dedicated to free and constitutional government, ask them [the powers] to withdraw that recognition which has exerted so baneful an influence." [26]

The note, if sent as drafted, might well have provoked a severe crisis with the British government and certainly would have earned for its authors a reputation for blustering diplomacy. Fortunately, however, Bryan handed the note to Moore for its polishing, with the suggestion that the Counselor add a paragraph invoking the Monroe Doctrine. Moore now proceeded to do a courageous, but dangerous, thing: he forthwith gave Wilson probably the severest tongue-lashing the President ever received. The states of this hemisphere are independent, Moore pointed out, and "it has therefore never been considered necessary for foreign Powers to ask our consent to their recognition of an American government." Before accusing the powers of improper motives in recognizing Huerta, Moore added, the President should remember that actually the United States had been conducting diplomatic relations with the provisional government for many months. Seventeen governments had recognized Huerta. They thought they were doing the proper thing. As for Great Britain, he concluded, it would be unwise to impugn British motives in view of the grievances the British government had against the United States. Sending the proposed note, therefore, would only stir up resentment abroad and would in the end defeat the President's purpose.[27]

The significant point of this episode is that the gist of Wilson's emotional memorandum and projected note was incorporated in the famous speech he delivered at Mobile on October 27, in which he heralded the day when Latin America would be emancipated from the control of foreign concessionaires. If one reads "Mexico" for "Latin America" and "Great Britain" for "foreign interests," the subtle meaning of Wilson's words becomes evident. Moreover, Wilson was indirectly assuring the Mexicans that in the campaign he was about to undertake against Huerta he would avoid intervention that carried with it acquisition of territory and would seek only to make possible the development of constitutional government in Mexico.

[26] Draft of note, in State Dept. Papers.
[27] John Bassett Moore to Wilson, Oct. 28, 1913, *ibid.*

During the six months from November, 1913, until nearly the end of April, 1914, Wilson bent all his energies and employed all the diplomatic resources of the United States to force Huerta from power, by all means short of war. His campaign was two-pronged: to isolate Huerta diplomatically, and then to encourage the Constitutionalists in their war against Huerta.[28]

As the German government quickly signified its willingness to follow the President's lead, Wilson brought his greatest pressure to bear upon the British Foreign Office. In cold truth, the British were forced to choose between the friendship of the United States and that of Huerta. The Foreign Secretary, Sir Edward Grey, was frankly fearful of what would happen to British property in Mexico if the Constitutionalists succeeded. If Huerta were eliminated and the Constitutionalists obtained control, would the United States assume responsibility for the protection of British property in Mexico? These questions were discussed and answered when Grey sent his secretary, Sir William Tyrrell, to Washington for talks with the President and Colonel House. Tyrrell promised that the Foreign Office would withdraw its recognition and support from Huerta. For his part, Wilson assured Tyrrell that he would "teach the South American republics to elect good men" and that the United States would work to establish a government in Mexico "under which all contracts and business and concessions will be safer than they have been," as well as to protect all foreign property in Mexico during the civil war.[29]

However doubtful Grey might have been about the President's ability to carry out these promises,[30] in the then perilous state of European

---

[28] It should be pointed out, however, that before undertaking this campaign, Wilson made another strenuous effort to persuade Huerta to retire in favor of a provisional government of elder statesmen, which should hold new elections. "This Government cannot too earnestly urge him [Huerta] to make the inevitable choice wisely and in full view of the terrible consequences of hesitation or refusal," Wilson warned. Bryan to American Embassy, Nov. 1, 1913, *ibid*.

When Huerta signified his readiness to agree (O'Shaughnessy to Secretary of State, Nov. 13, 1913, *ibid*.), Wilson proceeded to draw up a contract providing for Huerta's retirement, for the formation of a provisional government acceptable to the United States, and for American recognition of the new provisional government. Bryan to O'Shaughnessy, Nov. 14, 1913, *ibid*. At this point, however, Huerta balked and announced to the world his determination to fight on.

[29] Burton J. Hendrick, *The Life and Letters of Walter H. Page* (3 vols., Garden City, N.Y., 1924–26), I, 204; Wilson to Tyrrell, Nov. 22, 1913, Wilson Papers.

[30] Wilson's promise was, of course, a vitally important one. But the President made it on the assumption that he could create and control a Mexican govern-

affairs he had no alternative but to co-operate. In the event of a general European war, which seemed, in the offing, American friendship would be worth more than Mexican oil. Accordingly, Carden was soon bridled by the Foreign Office, the British withdrew recognition of Huerta, and British policy in Mexico, generally, was thereafter subordinated to the personal wishes of the President of the United States.

Meanwhile, the steady progress of the Constitutionalist armies toward Mexico City encouraged Wilson to believe they might be the instrument he could use to encompass Huerta's downfall, without the military intervention of the United States. The Constitutionalist chieftain, Venustiano Carranza, established a provisional government at Hermosillo, in Sonora, on October 17, and already claimed control of most of the large northern states. There was no doubt in the minds of many observers that the Constitutionalists were carrying the torch of the Madero Revolution and were fighting to achieve the aspirations of the Mexican masses. The chief question in Wilson's mind, however, was whether they had the capacity to govern Mexico and whether he could control them. To find the answer, in mid-November Wilson sent his trusted confidential agent, William Bayard Hale, to Nogales, Mexico, with a message of supreme importance for Carranza. It proposed nothing less than the joint co-operation of the United States and the Constitutionalists in the war against Huerta.[31]

---

ment, and the assumption was unwarranted by the circumstances. As will be shown, Wilson tried hard enough to bring the Constitutionalists under his control but failed.

[31] The author was not able to find a copy of Wilson's message to Carranza. Fortunately, however, the President outlined his plan to Colonel House, as follows:

"The President has in mind to declare war against Mexico even though actual armed entrance into Mexico is not made. His purpose in this is to keep the powers from interfering and entirely out of the situation. He will first blockade the ports, thereby cutting off all revenue from the Mexican Government which will have a tendency to break down Huerta's resistance.

"He has in mind also throwing a line across the southern part of Mexico, and perhaps another line just south of the Northern States. He plans to send troops to the Northern States, if they [the Constitutionalists] consent, in order to protect the lives and property of foreign citizens. These troops would be stationed at strategic points, but would not be intended to contend against either the Constitutionalists or Federals [the Huerta forces] unless some overt act was made by one or the other.

"It is his purpose to send six battleships at once. . . . The President seems alert and unafraid. He realizes that his course may possibly bring about a coalition of the European Powers against this Government, but he seems ready to throw our gauntlet into the arena and declare all hands must be kept off excepting our own." House Diary, Oct. 30, 1913.

The Nogales conference was significant, not only because of Wilson's offer of support to the Constitutionalists, but also because in the course of the negotiations he clearly revealed the pattern of his future relations with the Constitutionalist movement. In brief, in return for American support, he insisted on guiding the Revolution into orderly and democratic channels by obtaining Carranza's promise that the rebels would participate in new elections, provided a provisional government of elder statesmen were established. Carranza, on the other hand, made it abundantly plain that the Constitutionalists did not want the advice and support of the United States and would oppose the entry of American troops into Mexico by force, if that were necessary. They wanted from the American government only one thing—recognition of their belligerent status, with the accompanying privilege of buying arms and ammunition. Moreover, they were determined to effect a thoroughgoing revolution; they would not compromise with the old regime by co-operating with a facsimile of it in holding national elections; and they would use constitutional processes only after they had occupied all of Mexico. Once Wilson's plan was made clear to Carranza, he broke up the conference by demanding diplomatic recognition and by refusing further to see Hale. Hale, in turn, accused the First Chief of a lack of candor and left in a huff for Washington. "You know the world is full of all kinds of people," he told reporters at Nogales, Arizona. "Some of them are not only impossible, but highly improbable. Please understand that I am not speaking of the gentlemen across the border who are with such admirable skill preventing their friends from helping them." [32]

For two months after the Nogales conference Wilson withheld any form of support from the Constitutionalists. By the beginning of 1914, however, it was evident the President would have to either allow them to obtain arms and supplies or else carry out his threats to depose Huerta by the military force of the United States. As Wilson was not yet ready to intervene in an active way, he had no alternative but to lift the arms embargo. In late January, therefore, the State Department undertook official negotiations with Luis Cabrera, Carranza's agent in Washington, and obtained from him the promise that the provisional Constitutionalist government would respect property rights and "just and equitable" concessions. Following this exchange, the

[32] *The New York Times,* Nov. 20, 1913. Hale's reports are Hale to Secretary of State, Nov. 12, 14, 15, 16, 17, 18, 19, 1913, State Dept. Papers.

President on February 3 took the fateful step of revoking the embargo; thus, in the eyes of the world, he identified the United States with the cause of the Mexican Revolution.

Wilson, his advisers, and the Constitutionalists all confidently predicted the speedy triumph of the revolutionary forces as the result of the President's action. Events did not turn out that way, however, for by lifting the arms embargo Wilson spurred Huerta and his government to new endeavors and caused the landed aristocracy, the business and banking elements, and the Church for the first time to throw their full support to Huerta. By the end of March, therefore, Huerta's end seemed no nearer than it had been two months before. From Wilson's point of view, this was a catastrophic development, for, as Lind wrote almost daily from Vera Cruz, it was now up to the President to fulfill his pledges to Mexico and the world.

But how could this be done? How could Huerta be deposed, if not by the direct military intervention of the United States, which was what the Constitutionalists had threatened to oppose by force of arms? There seemed no other way, yet Wilson shrank from the extreme alternative, as if his former threats had been mere bluff. Then an opportunity to intervene, and with some show of excuse, presented itself when an otherwise minor incident occurred on April 10 at Tampico, held by the Huertistas but then under siege by a Constitutionalist army. The paymaster and crew of the U.S.S. *Dolphin* were arrested by a Mexican colonel when they landed their whaleboat without permission behind the federal lines. As soon as the Huertista commander, General Morelos Zaragoza, learned of the incident, he immediately released the Americans and sent a personal apology to Admiral Henry T. Mayo, commander of the American squadron off Vera Cruz.[33]

The affair would have ended with Zaragoza's apology had not the Washington administration been looking for an excuse to provoke a fight. On his own volition, Admiral Mayo demanded a twenty-one-gun salute to the American flag, and Wilson backed up the demand. There followed a serious of ridiculous exchanges between Mexico City and Washington, in which the latter converted the arrest of the paymaster and his crew from the petty incident it was into a deliberate affront

---

[33] Morelos Zaragoza, "Truth of the 'Dolphin' Incident at Tampico," *El Excelsior* (Mexico City), Dec. 6, 1931, gives the Mexican side; Clarence A. Miller, Consul at Tampico, to Secretary of State, May 21, 1914, State Dept. Papers, is a splendid report of the incident and its aftermath. Miller's account generally agrees with Zaragoza's.

to the honor of the United States and on April 18 issued an ultimatum to Huerta to salute the American flag at once or take the consequences.

The logic behind Wilson's demand was difficult for the Mexicans to perceive. The United States had refused to recognize the Huerta government yet was dealing with it as if it were enough of a government to discharge an official international obligation. The humor of the situation was not lost upon Huerta, who replied that he would salute the American flag, but only if an American warship returned the salute, volley for volley. As this would have been tantamount to recognizing the provisional government, Wilson refused. Then in Hot Springs, Virginia, he announced on April 19 he would go before Congress the following day. In Washington naval and military leaders laid plans for a general blockade and possible war operations, the first step of which would be the occupation of Vera Cruz. Arriving in Washington early in the morning of April 20, the President at once held hurried conferences with the Cabinet, Congressional leaders, and his military and naval advisers. At three that afternoon he went before a joint session, related the details of the Tampico affair and the subsequent negotiations, accused the Huerta government of deliberately insulting the United States, and asked for Congressional authority to use the armed forces to obtain redress.[34]

While both houses were debating resolutions conferring the authority Wilson had requested, news reached the State Department in the early morning of April 21 of the impending arrival at Vera Cruz of a German steamer, the *Ypiranga,* with an enormous load of ammunition for the Huerta government. In order to be able legally to prevent the entry of these supplies, which might soon be used against American forces, and without waiting for Congressional sanction, Wilson at daybreak ordered the navy to occupy Vera Cruz.[35] A landing was easily effected and by the following day, April 22, all of the city was in American hands, although Mexican naval cadets and civilians offered spirited resistance and suffered 126 killed and 195 wounded.[36] American casualties were nineteen dead and seventy-one wounded.

It is clear Wilson contemplated only this limited punitive action

[34] *The Public Papers, New Democracy,* I, 99–103.
[35] *The New York Times,* Apr. 22, 1914. The *Ypiranga,* incidentally, slipped out of Vera Cruz harbor, moved down the coast to Puerto México, and discharged her cargo there.
[36] This was the official American count. Fletcher to Secretary of the Navy, Apr. 24, 1914, Wilson Papers.

against the *de facto* government,[37] in order to hasten its downfall. Because he had not been frank with Congress and the people, because he insisted he was punishing an individual, Huerta, for a personal insult,[38] no one outside high administration circles understood the reason for the Vera Cruz action. Indeed, in the eyes of the civilized world the President appeared ridiculous, as a person willing to make war over an obscure point of honor. As one London editor put it, "If war is to be made on points of punctilio raised by admirals and generals, and if the Government of the United States is to set the example for this return to mediaeval conditions it will be a bad day for civilization." [39] No wonder the public at home was also dazed, when Wilson told them over and again that he had a passion for peace and justice and an abhorrence of war.[40] Nor was the confusion abated when Car-

[37] As was evidenced by his instructions to General Frederick Funston, when the army relieved the navy of the duty of occupying Vera Cruz. See Chief of Staff, Memorandum for the Adjutant General, Apr. 26, 1914, *ibid.*

[38] On April 20, just before he addressed the joint session, Wilson told reporters: "What, then, is the purpose of our naval operation in Mexico? It is not, as you gentlemen seem to think—not this act, that is—the elimination of Huerta. Its purpose is to compel the recognition of the dignity of the United States." "President Wilson on His Foreign Policy," *World's Work*, XXVIII (Oct., 1914), 489–490.

In his message to the joint session, Wilson added: "I therefore come to ask your approval that I should use the armed forces of the United States in such ways and to such an extent as may be necessary to obtain from General Huerta and his adherents the fullest recognition of the rights and dignity of the United States." *The Public Papers, New Democracy,* I, 102.

The present writer finds it difficult to believe that Wilson was speaking frankly, that he was actually willing to go to war to compel an unqualified salute.

[39] *Economist* (London), LXXVIII (Apr. 18, 1914), 906–907.

The action at Vera Cruz provoked a series of anti-American demonstrations throughout Latin America—in Montevideo, Santiago, Chile, Costa Rica, Guatemala, and elsewhere, while the authorities in Buenos Aires prevented a public demonstration. Except for the Brazilian newspapers, the Latin American press generally condemned the occupation of Vera Cruz as another manifestation of American imperialism. As for European opinion, the British Foreign Office welcomed the occupation of Vera Cruz as heralding full-scale occupation of Mexico by American forces, while Conservative journals and newspapers, including *The Times* (London), also approved. The German government and press were generally favorable to the United States, but Russian editorial comment was mordant. See, e.g., *Novoe Vremya* (St. Petersburg), 9/22, 15/28 Apr. 1914; *Retch* (St. Petersburg), 9/22 Apr. 1914; *Russkoe Slovo* (Moscow), 11/24 Apr. 1914.

[40] *The New York Times,* Apr. 21, 1914. Perhaps a word about American reaction to the Vera Cruz action is in order. A small Republican interventionist group in the Senate, led by Henry Cabot Lodge of Massachusetts and

ranza and his lieutenants, with one notable exception, condemned the seizure of Vera Cruz as wanton aggression against the Mexican people. Indeed, only by the most strenuous effort were hostilities with the Constitutionalists avoided.[41]

Albert B. Fall of New Mexico, tried unsuccessfully to obtain adoption of a resolution empowering the President to send the armed forces anywhere into Mexico to compel respect for American lives and property. It is doubtful, however, if Lodge and Fall spoke for a majority even of their own party. Certainly they did not bespeak the sentiments of the American people. As it was manifested in newspapers, mass meetings, and resolutions and letters, the preponderant American sentiment was decidedly pacific. It is even doubtful that most articulate leaders and spokesmen approved the Vera Cruz action; they certainly regarded the prospect of a general war with utter repugnance. From the crisis over the flag salute through the occupation of Vera Cruz, peace groups, labor unions, Socialist organizations, and diverse groups of plain citizens held mass meetings and flooded congressmen and the President with appeals for peace. For a few samples of such appeals see Resolutions adopted by the Commission on Peace and Arbitration of the Federal Council of Churches of Christ in America, Apr. 21, 1914, in the Papers of Elihu Root, in the Library of Congress; Massachusetts Federation of Churches to Wilson, Apr. 22, 1914, Wilson Papers; Executive Committee of the Socialist Party to Wilson, Apr. 22, 24, 1914, *ibid.;* Andrew Carnegie to Wilson, Apr. 21, 1914, *ibid.;* O. G. Villard to Wilson, Apr. 23, 1914, *ibid.;* John W. Foster to Elihu Root, Apr. 24, 1914, Root Papers; Moorfield Storey, president of the Anti-Imperialist League, to Wilson, Apr. 25, 1914, Wilson Papers; Charles W. Eliot to Wilson, Apr. 29, 1914, *ibid.* There is, moreover, no evidence that men with large material interests in Mexico, or their spokesmen, except for William R. Hearst, were in any way agitating for a war. The *Financial World,* XXII (Apr. 18, 1914), 2, and *Financial Age,* XXIX (Apr. 25, 1914), 673, condemned Wilson's policy and declared the financial community did not want war. Former President Taft declared that Wilson was attempting to provoke war for political purposes. Taft to Mabel T. Boardman, Apr. 19, 1914, Taft Papers. Senator Elihu Root wrote that he was heartsick at the thought of war with Mexico. Root to A. T. Mahan, Apr. 27, 1914, Root Papers. There seems no reason to continue to pile evidence on evidence to prove this point.

[41] On April 23 Carranza addressed a letter to the President and the Secretary of State, in which he declared: "The invasion of our territory and the permanency of your forces in the Port of Vera Cruz are a violation of the rights that constitute our existence as a free and independent sovereignty, and will drag us into an unequal war which until today we desired to avoid." Carranza, moreover, demanded that the United States evacuate Vera Cruz at once. Carranza to Carothers, for Wilson and Bryan, Apr. 22, 1914, printed in *The New York Times,* Apr. 23, 1914. In reply, Wilson and Bryan assured the First Chief that their intentions were friendly and called upon him to affirm that the Constitutionalists would not resist the efforts of the United States to obtain redress from Huerta. Bryan to Letcher, Consul at Chihuahua, Apr. 24, 1914, State Dept. Papers. In addition, supporters of the Constitutionalist movement in the United States brought immediate pressure to bear upon Carranza to show a more friendly attitude and assured him that the American government had no intention of subverting Mexican sovereignty. C. A. Douglas to Pesqueira, Apr. 23,

It came as a great relief to the American people, therefore, when the Brazilian, Argentine, and Chilean envoys in Washington on April 25 offered to mediate the dispute and Bryan and Huerta accepted. The offer did not come any too soon, for Wilson's decision on April 23 to send an occupation army into Vera Cruz brought the military leaders prominently into the administration's deliberations and was further provocation to the Huerta government. At a Cabinet meeting on April 24, for example, Secretary of War Garrison urged the President to order the army to move toward Mexico City as rapidly as possible. At a White House conference that evening the President, Bryan, Garrison, and Daniels discussed plans for a general war, while Garrison and Daniels at once set their staffs at work on campaign plans. It should be noted, however, that throughout these discussions Bryan argued consistently against further preparations or provocations.

On the face of it, it was somewhat absurd for the United States to negotiate on the high level of international mediation with a government it had refused to recognize. But Wilson was not disturbed by a seeming inconsistency, for he never had any intention of submitting to a genuine mediation. On the contrary, he expected to use the mediation as a means of eliminating Huerta and establishing a provisional government that would turn Mexico over to the Constitutionalists.[42]

1914, copy in *ibid.;* S. G. Hopkins to Carranza, Apr. 24, 1913, copy in the Papers of Hugh L. Scott, in the Library of Congress.

Meanwhile, Carranza's chief general in the north, Francisco Villa, who was already laying plans to seize control of the Constitutionalist movement, publicly declared he would not join Carranza in war against the United States. New York *World,* Apr. 24, 1914. Privately, Villa assured Wilson that Carranza had spoken only for himself and that he, Villa, entirely approved the seizure of Vera Cruz. Carothers to Bryan, Apr. 25, 1914, transmitting Villa to Wilson, Apr. 25, 1914, State Dept. Papers.

Villa's defection from the otherwise solid Constitutionalist ranks precluded any action by Carranza. On April 28 the two men met at Chihuahua City and agreed that the Constitutionalists should not oppose American forces unless they invaded Constitutionalist territory. *The New York Times,* Apr. 29, 1914; New York *World,* Apr. 29, 1914.

[42] In a confidential memorandum for the ABC mediators, written probably on April 25, 1914, Wilson warned that no settlement of the Mexican problem would be acceptable to American public opinion or the American government that did not provide for "the entire elimination of General Huerta" and the establishment of a provisional government in Mexico City representative of all factions. Undated memorandum in the Wilson Papers. Moreover, the American commissioners at the peace conference that met soon afterward at Niagara Falls, Canada, constantly pressed Wilson's plan for the creation of a provisional government controlled by the Constitutionalists. Obviously, the American ob-

The American and Mexican delegates met at Niagara Falls, Canada, under the ABC sponsorship, from May 20 until July 2, 1914. As the talks droned on, the Constitutionalists drove nearer and nearer Mexico City. Huerta notified the commissioners that he was about at the end of his rope and would soon have to abdicate. The only significant aspect of the conference, therefore, was Wilson's attempt to compel the Constitutionalists to cease fighting and submit to American guidance in establishing a provisional government. After much parleying, Carranza reluctantly sent a delegation to Niagara Falls, which met secretly with the American commissioners on June 16. Carranza's envoys frankly declared that the First Chief did not want American help, would oppose any form of mediation of the civil war itself, and would not accept Mexico City if it were offered to him by outsiders.

Carranza's absolute refusal to allow Wilson to use the ABC mediation to settle the civil war and to impose a program for the economic and social reconstruction of Mexico [43] was final and complete proof that the Revolution was out of American control. And it was out of control at the very moment when the cumulative effect of American policies was making possible the triumph of the revolutionary forces. In short, Wilson had made possible the success of a movement for which he had assumed responsibility before the British government,

---

jective was either to persuade Huerta to abdicate peacefully and to turn over the government to his enemies or else, as General Hugh L. Scott, American Chief of Staff, put it, "to kill time until Villa takes the City of Mexico." Scott to Mary L. Scott, May 19, 1914, Scott Papers.

[43] At least since the early winter of 1913–14, Wilson and his chief advisers had given much study to the economic and social aspects of the Mexican problem. This shift from a moralistic to a sociological approach brought with it an increasing awareness on the administration's part that the basic causes of disorder in Mexico were the illiteracy, abject poverty, landlessness, and exploitation of 80 per cent of the Mexican people. In a long conversation with Samuel G. Blythe on April 27, for example, Wilson revealed an acute comprehension of the underlying causes of the Revolution and of the aspirations of the Mexican masses. S. G. Blythe, "Mexico: The Record of a Conversation with President Wilson," *Saturday Evening Post,* CLXXXVI (May 23, 1914), 2–4. In a memorandum that he prepared on May 4, 1914, for the guidance of the President and the Secretary of State, Counselor Robert Lansing also revealed a thorough understanding of the important causes of Mexico's difficulties. Robert Lansing, "The Mexican Situation," May 4, 1914, State Dept. Papers. Consequently, the American commissioners at the ABC conference pressed hard for a comprehensive program for the reconstruction of Mexico, a program that emphasized land reform. The insuperable obstacle was, of course, Carranza's refusal to admit that the Washington government knew more about the Mexican problem than the Constitutionalists did.

yet over which he could exercise no real direction. There was nothing he could do, therefore, except to acquiesce and to make it plain that the United States would not tolerate wholesale executions or confiscations when the Constitutionalists captured their capital. On July 15 Huerta abdicated; a provisional government was speedily formed to arrange the surrender, and on August 20 the First Chief, his lieutenants, and his armies triumphantly entered the City of Mexico.

"With the retirement of Huerta . . . prospects are bright for the triumph of President Wilson's moral-suasion peace policy," wrote one optimistic editor,[44] and many commentators throughout the world agreed. Yet the new era of peace and reconstruction, the end of Mexico's suffering and of Wilson's perplexities, was not yet; for almost immediately after Huerta's downfall there occurred a tragic split in the ranks of the Constitutionalists that was to plunge Mexico into civil war for another three years. The disruption of the revolutionary movement was, of course, long in the making and the product of many forces. The root of the trouble, however, was the personal rivalry between the First Chief and his most spectacular general, Francisco, or "Pancho," Villa.[45] Born a peon, Villa, who had spent most of his early life an outlaw and a bandit, joined the Madero forces in 1911 and two years later threw in his lot with Carranza. Where Carranza was stolid, Villa was volatile and violent, the personal embodiment, as it were, of the hatred the peons bore toward the great landowners and professional politicians. Ignorant and illiterate though he was, Villa soon demonstrated astonishing military skill and a dashing leadership; and, as general of the Division of the North, he became the dynamic force behind the Constitutionalist movement in the northern states.

Unfortunately for his distracted country, Villa was also consumed with an ambition to become ruler of Mexico, and during the early months of 1914 he schemed to wrest control of the revolutionary armies from Carranza. There was almost a complete rupture between the two leaders in April, 1914, but American diplomatic officers in the field, especially George C. Carothers, who was attached to Villa's headquarters, temporarily patched up the break. Then, during the first two months after the Constitutionalists assumed power, Villa carefully garnered supplies and built up his forces.

From its consular agents in Chihuahua and Juarez, the Washington

[44] Dallas *Baptist Standard*, XXVI (July 23, 1914), 4.
[45] Villa's real name was Doroteo Arango.

government knew about the impending rupture long before it occurred. From Wilson's and Bryan's point of view, Villa's revolt was
not altogether unfortunate, because it afforded an opportunity to dis-
place Carranza as leader of the Revolution with Villa, who had
studiously manifested his willingness to follow Wilson's advice. The
deposing of Carranza and the enthroning of Villa now became the
chief objective of the American government.[46] In August, 1914, the
administration embarked upon its new policy, one ill conceived and
unfortunate in its consequences.

As the first step, John Lind was dismissed as adviser to the State Department, because he was too friendly to Carranza and too hostile to
the Roman Catholic Church. He was replaced by Paul Fuller, a member of the New York law firm of Coudert Brothers, a leading Roman
Catholic layman, and an authority on Latin American affairs. As the
second and more important step, Fuller was sent with secret instructions from Wilson on confidential missions to Villa's headquarters and
to Mexico City to propose the calling of a convention representing the
revolutionary armies and the subsequent creation of a new provisional
government. At Santa Rosalia on August 16, Fuller conferred with
Villa and obtained from him oral and written promises of his willingness to co-operate and his purpose to help establish speedily a constitutional government and then to retire from political life. The American
agent added also a flattering description of Villa's personal qualities—
his quiet demeanor, gentleness, and self-effacement.[47] That Villa's

[46] How did it happen that Wilson and Bryan turned against Carranza and
threw their support to Villa, whose violent character and consuming ambition
for personal power had already been made plain to them in numerous ways?
Their dislike of Carranza is not hard to understand, as the First Chief time and
again had demonstrated his stubborn refusal to take their advice or even to
reciprocate their early friendship. Wilson's and Bryan's support of Villa
stemmed chiefly from the fact that Villa had been careful to give them the
impression that he would establish a government they could control. The two
Americans did not forget, moreover, that Villa's firm stand had prevented
Carranza from making trouble at the time of the Vera Cruz affair. Further-
more, there was a strong pro-Villa clique in the administration, headed by
George C. Carothers, Consul accredited to Villa's headquarters, and General
Hugh L. Scott, Chief of Staff, who pleaded Villa's cause and played upon the
President's prejudices against Carranza. Finally, Villa had enjoyed a friendly
press in the United States and had been depicted as a natural leader of the
downtrodden Mexican masses. It was assumed Villa would effect land reform
more quickly than Carranza.

[47] Paul Fuller, "Memorandum for the President," dated Aug. 20, 1914, State
Dept. Papers. Villa's written affirmation was "Statement by General Villa of

promise to retire from public life was given or received sincerely might be doubted, as Fuller later declared that the object of his mission was "conciliation and mediation between the hostile elements, directed chiefly to bringing about a convention which would place Villa in control." [48]

Fuller went next to Mexico City, by way of Vera Cruz. Arriving in the capital on September 4, he proceeded to lecture the Foreign Secretary in the provisional government on correct democratic procedures. In conference with Carranza on September 5, Fuller found the First Chief accommodating, friendly, and willing to co-operate in President Wilson's plan and to retire from the leadership of the Constitutionalist movement after the new government was established. Obviously Carranza was in a perilous situation and dared not risk the consequences of open defiance, as his chief lieutenant, Álvaro Obregón, had come out in support of the President's plan. On September 8 Fuller had his last conference with Carranza, and agreement was made for the calling of the convention and the speedy establishment soon afterward of a civil government, representing all factions. Thus it seemed the way was finally open for the retirement of Carranza and the seating of a new coalition, headed by Villa.

That Villa was all along jockeying for supremacy was evidenced when he issued a declaration of war against Carranza on September 23, three weeks before the convention was to assemble. The convention, none the less, met at Aguascalientes from October 12 through November 12. Middle-of-the-road leaders like Obregón and Pablo Gonzáles, who sincerely desired the retirement of Carranza and Villa and a genuine reconciliation of all factions, tried vainly to heal the breach. At the insistence of the Villistas, delegates from the Zapatista revolutionary movement [49] were admitted, whereupon the Villistas joined

the purposes and intentions of his Division of the North with reference to the new government in Mexico, August 18, 1914," enclosed in Villa to Wilson, Aug. 18, 1914, *ibid.* One is tempted to believe that Fuller helped Villa write this statement.

[48] Anderson Diary, Feb. 20, 1915.

[49] In 1910 Emiliano Zapata began a revolutionary movement in the state of Morelos, southeast of Mexico City, against the Díaz regime, which he continued against the Madero government. The Zapatistas' first objective was destruction of the great estates and the distribution of land among the peons, which objective was set forth in the Plan of Ayala, adopted November 28, 1911. See E. Zapata to Wilson, Aug. 23, 1914, Wilson Papers, and "Plan for the liberation of the natives of the State of Morelos belonging to the Insurgent Army . . .," dated Nov. 28, 1911, and "Act of Ratification of the Plan of Ayala," dated July 19, 1914, copies in *ibid.*

with them to dominate the convention, depose Carranza, establish a new government, and elect General Eulalio Guiterrez, a Villa follower, President.

Along with other lesser chieftains, Carranza's two stalwarts, Obregón and Gonzáles, co-operated with the Villista-Zapatista majority and even tried to persuade Carranza to withdraw. But it was evident to the First Chief that the new convention government was merely a front for Villa, and he defied the convention and declared war on the usurpers of Aguascalientes. At this point, when it was clear they would have to choose personally between Villa and their chief, a majority of the able generals, including Obregón and Gonzáles, unhesitatingly repudiated the convention and rushed to Carranza's side. Carranza then moved his capital from Mexico City to Vera Cruz, recently evacuated by the American forces; Villa and Zapata met in the City of Mexico and established the convention government there, and the civil war was begun all over again.

If the State Department had remained absolutely neutral in the ensuing conflict, its duration would have been considerably shortened. Instead of remaining aloof, the Washington government threw its moral and diplomatic support behind the convention, or Villa, government. As it turned out, Wilson and Bryan could have made no more unrealistic decision or worse diplomatic blunder. They bet on the wrong man, in spite of the fact that their agents at Aguascalientes told them Carranza still commanded the loyalty of a large majority of the revolutionary forces and that Villa was surrounding himself with the worst elements in Mexico.

Events soon demonstrated the error of the administration's policy. While Villa sat in Mexico City and waited for the Carranzistas to disintegrate, the First Chief set to the task of rebuilding his armies and broadening his program. The "Additions to the Plan of Guadalupe" of December, 1914, the decree of January 6, 1915, restoring land to the villages, and various labor decrees mobilized broad public support behind the Constitutionalists and set in motion a social revolution that is still in progress. Then, in January, 1915, under Obregón's masterful generalship, Carranza began a campaign that inflicted a series of crushing blows on the Villistas, culminating in a great defeat of Villa's army at Celaya, April 14–16, 1915. From this time on, Villa fought a desperate retreat northward, until he found refuge in his native stronghold of Chihuahua.

The period of the rapid destruction of Villa's power, from January to September, 1915, was a time of divided counsels and confusion in the Washington government. The administration quickly shifted from support of the Villa convention government to a policy of strict neutrality, and Wilson forthrightly and courageously insisted that the Mexicans be allowed to settle their own problems in their own way.[50] The war in Europe made this policy of abstention easier, as there was now no possibility of immediate European interference. On the other hand, demands at home for intervention mounted so rapidly during the first nine months of 1915 that the administration was subjected to pressures almost irresistible. Some business elements may have desired the military occupation of Mexico, but if they did their spokesmen were remarkably silent. Since 1913 the Hearst newspapers had been trying frantically to generate a war fever; they now redoubled this effort. But more important were the powerful new voices in the interventionist camp. On December 6, 1914, Theodore Roosevelt opened his campaign for intervention with a strong blast in *The New York Times Magazine*.[51] His assertion that Wilson was responsible for most of the trouble in Mexico, because he had made the civil war possible by his support of the Constitutionalist movement, was soon echoed by influential spokesmen, some of whom had previously been friendly to the administration.[52] Even more important a factor in the new campaign for intervention, however, were the hierarchy and laymen of the Roman Catholic Church.[53]

Confronted with a rapidly changing situation in Mexico that he did not understand, Wilson in February, 1915, sent another agent, Duval West of San Antonio, to Mexico; but West returned to report that no

[50] Especially in his Jackson Day address at Indianapolis, January 8, 1915, *The Public Papers, New Democracy,* I, 236–251.

[51] Theodore Roosevelt, "Our Responsibility in Mexico," *The New York Times Magazine,* Dec. 6, 1914.

[52] E.g., Chicago *Daily Tribune,* Dec. 7, 1914; W. H. Taft to M. T. Herrick, Dec. 14, 1914, Taft Papers; *Outlook,* CIX (Jan. 20, 1915), 127, CX (May 5, 1915), 10–12; *Independent,* LXXXI (Jan. 25, Mar. 22, 1915), 112–113, 407; Louisville *Courier-Journal,* Apr. 17, 1915; *New Republic,* III (June 12, 1915), 133.

[53] E.g., sermon by Joseph Schrembs, Bishop of Toledo, in the Baltimore Cathedral, Sept. 27, 1914, New York *World,* Sept. 28, 1914; American Federation of Catholic Societies to Wilson, Sept. 29, 1914, Wilson Papers; Cardinal O'Connell of Boston, in New York *World,* Nov. 16, 1914; John Ireland, Archbishop of St. Paul, to Theodore Roosevelt, Dec. 7, 1914, the Papers of Theodore Roosevelt, in the Library of Congress.

faction was strong enough to dominate the country and establish order. West also brought back a tragic report of a Mexico ruined and devastated, her industries and railroads destroyed, her people near starvation. The worst aspect of the tragedy was that there seemed to be no hope. The administration pondered the alternatives and concluded that the only effective solution was the establishment and maintenance by the United States of a government capable of restoring order and suppressing the civil war. This, clearly, was what the President had in mind when, on June 2, he issued a warning to the Mexican leaders to stop fighting or else to face American intervention. Villa replied by offering to make peace with Carranza, while the First Chief emphatically repudiated the President's right to interfere.[54]

At this point, when it seemed the administration would at last succumb to interventionist pressures and temptations, the situation took a new turn. In the first place, it became increasingly evident during the summer and early fall that Duval West's estimate had been incorrect. The unpleasant truth was that Carranza was growing stronger daily and that intervention by the United States would entail a war with Mexico that no one in administration circles wanted. Secondly, at the same time the United States became embroiled in a diplomatic crisis of the greatest magnitude with Germany over the use of the submarine against merchant shipping. As war with Germany became a possibility, administration leaders recognized the necessity of avoiding a second possible war with Mexico. Thirdly, and most important, the German government undertook to provoke a war between the United States and Mexico, in order to weaken American pressure against free use of the submarine.[55]

In early June, 1915, moreover, a new Secretary of State, Robert Lansing, took the helm at the Department of State. In decisions affecting Mexico, Bryan had always followed Wilson's lead, without attempting to take the initiative. Lansing, however, pursued a more vigorous policy. Earlier, in March, he had suggested that the ABC powers be brought into the administration's consultations, and in August he began a series of conferences with the ABC Ambassadors, the Ministers from Bolivia, Uruguay, and Guatemala, and Paul Fuller

[54] "I think I have never known of a man more impossible to deal with on human principles than this man Carranza," Wilson wrote soon afterward. Wilson to Lansing, July 2, 1915, the Ray Stannard Baker Collection, in the Library of Congress.
[55] These intrigues are discussed more fully below, pp. 200–201.

that lasted into October. At the outset of these deliberations, Lansing and his colleagues agreed Carranza should be eliminated and a new provisional government, representing all factions, should be established.[56] On August 11 the conferees addressed an appeal to the various Mexican leaders, urging them to compose their differences under the auspices of the Pan-American council.[57] Villa agreed at once to a mediation that would save a remnant of his shattered power, but the Carranzistas replied with one voice that their only leader was the First Chief, who would transmit their refusal to submit to any form of mediation.[58] Finally, Carranza sent his refusal to Washington on September 10, at the very time his armies were capturing Torreón, the Villista stronghold in the North.

Impressed by the unity in the Constitutionalist ranks and by Carranza's capture of Torreón, Lansing decided the First Chief should be recognized. Moreover, the German intrigues in Mexico had convinced him there was no alternative.[59] First, however, he had to persuade the Latin American envoys, who represented reactionary governments and were extremely hostile to the Mexican Revolution, to concur. "It was a situation which required delicate handling because a false move would defeat the object for which the Conference was called," Lansing wrote soon afterward. "The plan of carrying on the negotiation which I determined to follow . . . to bring the desired result, the recognition of

[56] Lansing to Wilson, Aug. 6, 1915, *Papers Relating to the Foreign Relations of the United States, The Lansing Papers, 1914–1920* (2 vols., Washington, 1939–40), II, 544. On the other hand, Wilson did not agree that the Pan-American conferees should insist upon Carranza's elimination. He was so impressed by the First Chief's growing power that he was willing to consider the possibility of recognizing him. Wilson to Lansing, Aug. 11, 1915, *ibid.,* p. 549.

[57] Printed in *Papers Relating to the Foreign Relations of the United States, 1915* (Washington, 1924), pp. 735–736.

[58] *The New York Times,* Aug. 22, 1915.

[59] Lansing wrote (the Diary of Robert Lansing, in the Library of Congress) on October 10, 1915:

"Looking at the general situation I have come to the following conclusions:

"Germany desires to keep up the turmoil in Mexico until the United States is forced to intervene; *therefore, we must not intervene.*

"Germany does not wish to have any one faction dominant in Mexico; *therefore, we must recognize one faction as dominant in Mexico.*

"When we recognize a faction as the government, Germany will undoubtedly seek to cause a quarrel between that government and ours; *therefore, we must avoid a quarrel regardless of criticism and complaint in Congress and the press.*

"It comes down to this: Our possible relations with Germany must be our first consideration; and all our intercourse with Mexico must be regulated accordingly."

Carranza, was to lay a foundation in philosophy, which would appeal strongly to the Latin mind." Lansing's strategy was to convince his colleagues that Mexican sovereignty now resided in the revolutionary armies, and that the Carranza faction was *de facto* sovereign because it controlled most of the country.[60]

Lansing's strategy succeeded on October 9, and ten days later the United States and its six Latin American associates formally recognized the government of Venustiano Carranza as the *de facto* government of Mexico. The Villa clique in Washington, headed by the Chief of Staff, General Hugh L. Scott, were of course angered, but the Roman Catholic hierarchy and journalistic spokesmen were even more outraged and replied with a savage attack on the administration that continued through the election of 1916.[61] The Catholic leaders felt insulted, not only because the Carranzistas were avowedly anticlerical and had committed outrages against priests, nuns, and church property, but also because these same Catholic leaders had earlier attempted to persuade Wilson and Bryan to bring pressure to bear upon the Constitutionalists to repeal the Reform Laws of the Juarez era, and Wilson and Bryan had refused.[62] Whether the Catholic hierarchy would have preferred Villa to Carranza, it is impossible to say.[63] In any event, the powerful hostility of the Catholic Church to the administration's policy, already manifested, was intensified. Wilson, in turn, resented the Catholic criticism and contemplated striking the hierarchy a public blow, but apparently thought better of it.[64]

[60] *Ibid.*

[61] E.g., *America*, XIII (Oct. 2, 1915), 614; *ibid.*, XIV (Oct. 16, 1915), 14; *ibid.* (Oct. 23, 1915), p. 38; Brooklyn *Tablet*, Oct. 16, 1915; New Orleans *Morning Star*, Oct. 16, 1915.

[62] The Rev. Francis C. Kelley, of the Catholic Church Extension Society of Chicago, was the hierarchy's intermediary with the administration. See D. F. Malone to Wilson, Apr. 22, 1915, Wilson Papers. Kelley wrote a long letter, setting forth the official Catholic position and objectives on February 23, 1915. The author was unable to find this letter, but Bryan described it in a letter to Wilson, Apr. 19, 1915, the Papers of William Jennings Bryan, in the National Archives. "Father Kelley's letter is on the whole quite moderate I think," Bryan commented, "but there is one proposition in it which would seem to be untenable, namely, that the revolutionists should be asked to *repeal the laws which they have there on the separation of church and state.*"

[63] Villa's chief agent in the United States, Felix A. Sommerfeld, obtained from Villa a promise not to molest the Church and negotiated with the Rev. Francis C. Kelley, the chief Catholic spokesman in the United States on Mexican matters. F. A. Sommerfeld to H. L. Scott, Feb. 18, 1915, Scott Papers.

[64] "The President was very firm in his determination to strike the Catholics a

Relations between the United States and the Carranza government were friendly, if not cordial, during the first three months after recognition. Then, in early January, 1916, occurred the first in a series of events that was to culminate in the two nations' drawing to the verge of war. The entire cause of the trouble was Villa, who, after Carranza's recognition, turned violently on his erstwhile friends and began a campaign to exterminate Americans in the Northern states. On January 11, 1916, Villistas stopped a Mexico Northwestern train at Santa Ysabel, fifty miles west of Chihuahua City, removed seventeen Americans, and shot sixteen of them on the spot. Coinciding as it did with the opening of the campaign of 1916, the massacre evoked a strong demand in Congress for intervention, and even Wilson's stalwart spokesman in the Senate, William J. Stone, wavered. It required the full force of administration influence to block passage of a resolution authorizing the President to use the military forces in Mexico.[65]

Villa, however, was now deliberately attempting to provoke such intervention as a means of discrediting Carranza and regaining his lost power. When the Santa Ysabel massacre failed to bring results, the bandit chieftain made a desperate raid on American territory, at Columbus, New Mexico, on March 9, burning the town and killing nineteen Americans. Some observers thought he had been seized with what Mexicans called *Delirio de Grandeza* and had gone mad with an obsession to kill Americans. Whatever his motivation, Villa this time achieved his objective, for the demand in the United States for military action against the Villistas was now so strong that the administration could hardly resist it. Instructions were sent immediately to military commanders in Texas to assemble an expedition for the pursuit of Villa. The President, however, would not allow this so-called Punitive Expedition to cross the border until he had been assured the Mexican authorities approved such action.[66] At the same time, in re-

public blow, provided they carried their arrogance too far." House Diary, Dec. 16, 1914 [1915].

[65] *The New York Times,* Jan. 14, 15, 1916. The interventionists did, however, obtain passage of a resolution by the Senate calling on the Secretary of State to submit a report on the number of Americans killed in Mexico since the beginning of the Revolution. The resolution and the State Department's reply are printed in *Papers Relating to the Foreign Relations of the United States, 1916* (Washington, 1925), pp. 463–464, 469–478.

[66] This approval was given orally by the Mexican Secretaries for Foreign Relations, War, and Marine on March 15. Silliman to Secretary of State, Mar. 15, 1916, *ibid.,* p. 491.

sponse to a suggestion from Carranza, Lansing negotiated on March 13 a protocol with Eliseo Arredondo, Mexican Ambassador-designate in Washington, empowering either nation in the future to pursue bandits across the international boundary. Finally, the Punitive Expedition, under the command of Brigadier General John J. Pershing, was sent across the border on March 15, 1916, but with the most explicit instructions to commit no acts of aggression against the Carranza forces.

At the same time that Lansing initialed the protocol, the administration announced that the agreement was "in full force" and that it authorized the entry of the Punitive Expedition into Mexican territory. The Washington government was acting in good faith, but its assertions were incorrect. In the first place, the protocol had not been ratified by the Mexican government when the Expedition crossed the border; in the second, it authorized only temporary crossings *in the future*. Actually, the protocol was not officially ratified by the *de facto* government until March 24, and by this time Pershing's force was far into Mexico.

When he proposed authorizing the mutual right of hot pursuit across the border, Carranza was thinking in terms of small forces, whose stay in the neighboring territory would be limited to a few days. The entry of Pershing's large force [67] greatly alarmed him, and he at once began a diplomatic campaign to compel the Expedition's retirement. During the first few weeks of the chase, however, the Carranzistas restrained their irritation and even made a show of co-operating with Pershing. There would have been no difficulty if Villa had been less elusive; several times Pershing came within an ace of capturing him and destroying his band, but Villa always somehow contrived to escape southward, drawing Pershing behind him. By April 8 the Punitive Expedition, now 6,675 strong, had penetrated more than three hundred miles

---

Before this word had come from the Mexican capital, then at Querétaro, Wilson told Tumulty that if the Mexicans showed an intention to resist the Punitive Expedition he would not allow Pershing to cross the border. Tumulty to Wilson, Mar. 15, 1916, Wilson Papers; House Diary, Mar. 17, 1916. This was a time of renewed crisis with Germany, and, as House expressed it, the President was determined to avoid war with Mexico because Germany ardently desired such a war. *Ibid.,* Mar. 29, 1916.

[67] In the beginning the Expedition contained a little over 5,000 officers and men. By April 5 there were 251 officers and 6,424 men in the force. On April 18 an additional 2,300 troops were sent to Pershing. By June 19, at the height of the Mexican-American tension, Pershing's force numbered 11,635—385 officers and 11,250 men.

deep into the heart of Mexico. To sensitive Mexicans this was alarming enough; worse still, the Expedition gave no signs of halting, was being constantly reinforced, and was rapidly assuming the appearance of an army of occupation in the northern states. Carranza had never agreed to the Expedition's entry; he now decided he could remain acquiescent no longer, and on April 13 Arredondo presented his chief's protest, a virtual demand for the withdrawal of the Expedition from Mexican soil.

By mid-April, therefore, it was evident the two governments had unintentionally blundered into an exceedingly dangerous situation. By now Mexican public opinion was so hostile to the Expedition that Carranza could not long remain in power if he did not take drastic steps to compel its withdrawal. On the other hand, the Washington government were now convinced Carranza either could not or else did not wish to control the bandit gangs in northern Mexico. The longer the Expedition stayed in Mexico, the less willing the Carranzistas were to pursue the Villistas, which fact only deepened American suspicion that the Carranza commanders were contemplating an attack on the Expedition. Moreover, the Republicans were now launching a bitter campaign against the administration's Mexican policy. Carranza's demand for the withdrawal of the Expedition evoked indignant protests from leaders of the President's own party, who realized withdrawal at this time might have disastrous political consequences.

Neither Carranza nor Wilson wanted war, yet a situation was rapidly developing in which conflict between the American and *de facto* forces was inevitable. This unhappy truth was demonstrated by an incident that occurred on April 12 and that prompted Carranza to demand the withdrawal of the expeditionary force. A detachment of American troops entered the town of Parral to purchase supplies. Mexican soldiers opened fire upon the Americans as they were leaving, and in the ensuing exchange forty Mexicans and two Americans were killed. The issue, therefore, was now clearly drawn. In the face of an inflamed Mexican public opinion, Carranza could not acquiesce in the shedding of Mexican blood on Mexican soil. On the other hand, Wilson could not give the appearance of allowing a Mexican mob to drive the United States Army out of Mexico. Carranza's demand, therefore, was refused.

Immediately after the Parral incident the two governments made one desperate effort at agreement, in order to avert the likelihood of hostilities, when Generals Hugh L. Scott and Frederick Funston conferred with General Álvaro Obregón, Mexican War Minister, in Juarez and El Paso. It was evident from the War Department's instructions to Scott that the administration sought only the protection of the border

HUMANITY
NEUTRAL RIGHTS
INTERNATIONAL LAW

Kirby in the New York *World*

The class in reading and writing

and the suppression of the Villa marauders. But the President insisted that these objectives could be obtained only through the effective co-operation of the Mexican and American forces, operating on Mexican soil. Obregón, on the other hand, demanded the complete and immediate withdrawal of the Expedition. Scott and Funston finally drew Obregón into a secret conference and persuaded him to sign an agreement providing for the gradual withdrawal of the Punitive Expedition and an effective campaign against the Villistas by the *de facto* government. Wilson immediately approved the protocol; Carranza, however, rejected it because it did not stipulate a definite date for the complete evacuation of the Expedition, and he countered with the suggestion that the two governments co-operate in policing the border. In the end, the most Scott and Funston could get from Obregón was a promise that the Mexicans would in good faith try to clean out the Villistas.

As it turned out, Villa had other plans. Almost at the very moment Obregón was giving his pledge, the bandit leader executed a daring raid fifteen miles across the Rio Grande, on the little settlement of Glen Springs, Texas, killing three soldiers and a boy and capturing one soldier. There were new demands in Congress for full-fledged intervention, and the Governor of Texas called for the occupation of all northern Mexico. And when the President sent a new detachment into Mexico to pursue the Glen Springs raiders, Carranza concluded the time for a showdown had come—by diplomacy if possible, by war if that were necessary. On May 22 he addressed a long and bitter note to the Secretary of State, accusing the American government of bad faith, requesting the United States frankly to avow its intentions, and declaring that Washington could prove it did not want war only by immediately withdrawing the Punitive Expedition.

Carranza's note was delivered at the State Department on May 31. From this time forward it seemed events were out of control, that the two nations were plunging headlong toward a war that neither of them wanted, and that the most tragic chapter in twentieth-century American history was about to open. Firstly, the American military leaders began to draw plans for a Mexican campaign. "I would like plans prepared by the War College for the invasion of Mexico on the lines of the various railways from the north," Scott ordered.[68] Secondly, Carranza instructed his commanders to prevent new American expeditions from entering Mexico and to resist the Punitive Expedition if it moved in any direction but northward, toward the border. Thirdly, the President on June 18 called out practically the entire National Guard, some 100,000 men, to protect the border,[69] and sent additional warships to

[68] H. L. Scott, "Memorandum for Chief, War College Division," June 16, 1916, Scott Papers.
[69] *The New York Times,* June 19, 1916. Scott later wrote (to Robert

1. WOODROW WILSON

Painting by Sir William Orpen, courtesy of Bernard Baruch, Jr., photographed by Fernand Bourges.

2. WILLIAM HOWARD TAFT, President of the United States, 1909-1913, and Sympathetic Critic of Wilson's Policies, 1913-1917.

3. THEODORE ROOSEVELT, Leader of Republican Progressives and Wilson's Chief Critic on Foreign Policy.

4. GIFFORD PINCHOT

5. SEN. JONATHAN P. DOLLIVER

LEADERS
OF THE
REPUBLICAN
INSURGENTS

6. SENATOR WILLIAM E. BORAH

7. Wilson Being Inaugurated by Chief Justice Edward D. White, March 4, 1913.

8. Wilson and His Cabinet, 1913. Reading from left to right: President Wilson, William G. McAdoo, James C. McReynolds, Josephus Daniels, David F. Houston, William B. Wilson, William C. Redfield, Franklin K. Lane, Albert S. Burleson, Lindley M. Garrison, William J. Bryan.

9. LOUIS D. BRANDEIS, one of the Chief Architects of the New Freedom.
Appointed to the Supreme Court in 1916.

10. OSCAR W. UNDERWOOD

11. CHAMP CLARK

MAKERS

OF

AMERICAN

DOMESTIC

POLICY

1913-1917

12. CARTER GLASS

13. WILLLIAM J. BRYAN
Secretary of State, 1913-1915

14. ROBERT LANSING, Counsellor of t
State Department, 1914-1915, and Secr
tary of State, 1915-1920.

MAKERS

OF

AMERICAN

FOREIGN

POLICY,

1913-1917

15. EDWARD M. HOUSE, Adviser to the
President, 1913-1919

16. FRANCISCO VILLA

17. VICTORIANO HUERTA

LEADING
CONTENDERS
IN MEXICO,
1913-1915

18. GENERAL VENUSTIANO
CARRANZA with His Staff

19. **Brigadier General John J. Pershing**, Commander of the Punitive Expedition.

20. "Horse Marines" in Vera Cruz, April 24, 1914.

21. Pershing and the Staff of the Punitive Expedition. Reading from left to right: Col. L. G. Berry, Col. De R. C. Cabell, Lt. M. C. Schellenberger, Gen. Pershing, Lt. George E. Patton, Maj. J. L. Hines, Maj. J. B. Clayton, Capt. W. B. Burt.

23. Theobald von Bethmann-Hollweg, Imperial German Chancellor.

22. Sir Edward Grey, British Foreign Secretary.

TWO LEADERS OF THE OPPOSING EUROPEAN ALLIANCES

24. The Great Preparedness Parade, 150,000 Strong, Passing in Front of the New York Public Library, May 13, 1916.

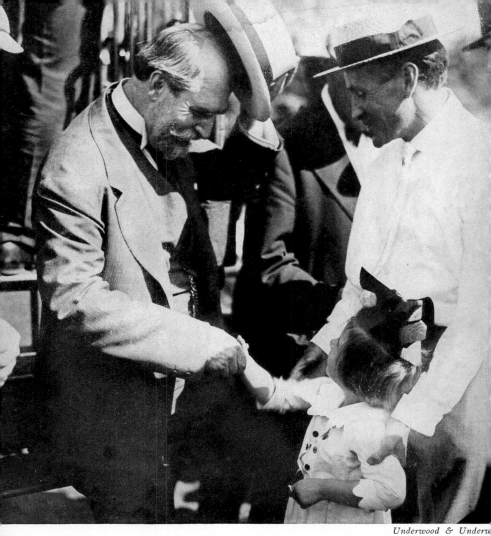

Underwood & Underw

25. CHARLES EVANS HUGHES Appeals for Votes in 1916

Brown Brothers

26. GOVERNOR HIRAM JOHNSON Is Not Amused

27. Wilson on Campaign Tour, 1916

28. Wilson Reads His War Message to Congress, April 2, 1917

both coasts of Mexico. Fourthly, on June 19 occurred a clash between Mexican soldiers and American sailors at the port of Mazatlán, on the west coast.[70] Finally, on June 20, the Secretary of State addressed the reply of the United States to Aguilar's note of May 22. Lansing recounted the destruction of American life and property in Mexico, by Mexican citizens; he accused Carranza of being unable or unwilling to punish the perpetrators of these outrages; he reviewed the diplomatic exchanges since the sending of the Punitive Expedition; he told the Mexican government that the Expedition would not be withdrawn, and he ended with the warning that any attacks by the *de facto* forces on American troops would "lead to the gravest consequences." [71]

The incident that seemed inevitably to lead to "the gravest consequences" occurred on June 21, only a few hours after Lansing's stinging rebuke was delivered in Mexico City. On June 15, Pershing, then encamped at Dublan, received a report that a large force of *de facto* troops were concentrating against him. The General sent two troops of cavalry under one Captain Boyd and Captain Lewis S. Morey to investigate, with Boyd in command. The American party came upon a detachment of 250 Mexicans near Carrizal. Wishing to push on beyond, to Ahumada, Boyd negotiated briefly with the Mexican commander, General Félix G. Gómez. Gómez informed Boyd he could not allow him to pass through the town but offered to request such permission from his superiors. Convinced the Mexicans would not resist, Boyd ordered his men to charge the Mexican troops, who meanwhile had taken a strong position. Instead of running, as Boyd expected, the Mexicans replied gallantly, surrounded the American force, killing twelve, including Boyd, and capturing twenty-three soldiers and an interpreter. General Gómez and twenty-nine Mexicans were killed.[72]

Leonard, Dec. 11, 1916, Scott Papers): "The Mexicans had an idea that we were afraid of them; some 20,000 of them were congregating around Pershing within striking distance; some 14,000 were below Douglas, Arizona, and our line was thin everywhere. . . . Obregon was boasting that he would be in San Antonio within two weeks."

[70] For details see *The New York Times*, June 20, 1916; Flagship *San Diego* to Secretary of the Navy, June 21, 1916, Wilson Papers; Josephus Daniels to Wilson, July 21, 1916, the Papers of Josephus Daniels, in the Library of Congress, and Daniels to Secretary of State, July 19, 1916, *ibid.*, endorsing report by Commander A. G. Kavanagh of the U.S.S. *Annapolis*.

[71] Lansing to Secretary of Foreign Relations, June 20, 1916, *Foreign Relations, 1916*, pp. 581–592.

[72] The foregoing is based upon the following accounts, all of which agree remarkably: (1) report by Captain Morey, written immediately after the

Was this the first incident in the war that all responsible officials in Washington now expected? So it seemed, for the first accounts of the clash told of a treacherous ambush of the American troops. Charging the Mexican government with "deliberately hostile" purposes, Wilson demanded the immediate release of the prisoners. A few hours later, he called Congressional leaders to the White House and told them American troops had been deliberately attacked at Carrizal and that he would soon appear before a joint session. Next, he prepared the message he would deliver, in which he reviewed the recent history of the troubles with Mexico, disavowed any intention of seeking to intervene in Mexican internal affairs, declared the United States had no alternative but to clear the northern states of the bandit gangs, and asked Congress to empower him to use the armed forces for such a purpose.[73]

Such action, even the publication of Wilson's message, would have meant a war that would end only in the occupation of practically every square mile of Mexico by American soldiers. And yet, because of the force of public opinion in the United States, because Wilson never lost control of the military services, and because neither Carranza nor Wilson wanted war, war was averted. Captain Morey's report, which proved that the Americans had been the aggressors at Carrizal, was published in the newspapers on June 26. It was taken up by the American Union Against Militarism, a pacifist organization, which printed it and a fervent plea against war in full-page advertisements in all the metropolitan newspapers. As a result, Wilson was immediately overwhelmed with a flood of telegrams, letters, and petitions; and from the replies he made to the appeals for peace it is evident that he was shaken and deeply moved. Not slowly, but almost at once, good sense returned to official circles in Washington. And when Carranza, on June 28, ordered the release of the American soldiers, tension eased perceptibly. Two days later, in a speech before the New York Press

battle, printed in *Foreign Relations, 1916,* p. 596; (2) report written by the interpreter, Lemuel Spillsbury, printed in *The New York Times,* June 25, 1916; (3) official Mexican report, Lt. Col. Genovevo Rivas to General Gonzáles at Juarez, c. June 21, 1916, printed in *El Pueblo* (Mexico City), July 1, 1916; (4) official United States Army report, E. A. Garlington, Inspector General, "Fourth Endorsement on the Report of investigation of the encounter between American and Mexican forces at Carrizal, Chihuahua, June 21, 1916," dated Oct. 2, 1916, Wilson Papers.

[73] The manuscript copy of Wilson's address, "To the Congress. June, 1916," is in *ibid.*

Club, Wilson reciprocated with a forthright, passionate plea for peace. "Do you think the glory of America would be enhanced by a war of conquest in Mexico?" he asked.[74] An answer was given in Mexico City on July 4, when Carranza suggested direct and friendly negotiations to end the causes of the Mexican-American tension.

The upshot was the signing soon afterward of an agreement for the appointment of a Joint High Commission to investigate and recommend. Wilson welcomed the negotiations, as they afforded some relief from the Republican attacks during the presidential campaign then in progress. Carranza welcomed the conference because it afforded him an opportunity to hold elections, the first step in the establishment of a constitutional government. From September 6, 1916, through January 15, 1917, the commissioners—Secretary of the Interior Franklin K. Lane, the Reverend Doctor John R. Mott, former Judge George Gray, Luis Cabrera, Ignacio Bonillas, and Alberto J. Pani—met in New London, Atlantic City, and Philadelphia. All phases of the Mexican problem were thoroughly discussed. The Mexicans pressed for an agreement promising the immediate withdrawal of the Punitive Expedition. The Americans, on the other hand, insisted on discussing internal conditions in Northern Mexico, taxes on American mining properties in Mexico, and the protection of British and American oil properties. The Mexican commissioners finally surrendered to the extraordinarily heavy pressure being put upon them and, on November 24, signed a protocol for the withdrawal of the Expedition within forty days, only provided conditions in the Northern states warranted such action.

A new crisis was created, however, when Carranza, on December 27, rejected the protocol and announced he would approve no agreement that did not first provide for the immediate evacuation of Mexican territory by the forces of the United States. As accord on that issue was impossible, the Joint High Commission broke up January 15, 1917. It had preserved the peace, and that fact alone justified its existence; and it had helped Wilson win the election by neutralizing the Mexican issue during the campaign. But with the breakup of the Commission the Washington government was back at the point from which negotiations had begun. In brief, the United States now had either to withdraw the expedition or else to break relations and attempt to occupy

[74] New York *World*, July 1, 1916.

the Northern Mexican states. With the possibility of soon becoming involved in the European war staring him in the face, there was never much doubt in Wilson's mind what the national interest compelled him to do. The decision was made by January 18, when Secretary of War Baker informed the military commanders that the President would soon order the return of Pershing's command to Texas. By January 27 the withdrawal had begun and a near-tragic chapter in Mexican-American relations was finished.

The *de facto* government, meanwhile, had proceeded serenely and quite independently to establish a constitutional government. On October 22, 1916, the Mexican people elected a constituent assembly that met in Querétaro in December and January and adopted a new and advanced Constitution. Next, on March 11, a new Congress and a constitutional President, Carranza, were elected; finally, the United States extended *de jure* recognition by sending Henry P. Fletcher as Ambassador to Carranza on March 13, 1917.

The recognition of Carranza's *de jure* government and the withdrawal of the Punitive Expedition were the outward and visible signs of the First Chief's victory, not only at home, but also over an equally stubborn man in the White House. Since the first days of the Constitutionalist movement, Carranza had never once wavered in his determination to preserve the integrity and independence of the Revolution. Neither Wilson's blandishments nor threats had moved him. The result was that Mexico was now free to undertake its great experiment and its long and difficult progress toward democratic institutions.

The tragedy was that Wilson had in large measure made this opportunity possible, yet had interfered in the wrong way so often that he embittered Mexican-American relations for many years to come. Even so, future generations may forget his mistakes and the Mexican people may some day remember that he, almost alone, stood off Europe during the days of the Huertista tyranny, withstood the powerful forces in the United States that sought the undoing of the Revolution, and refused to go to war at a time when it might have insured his re-election.

CHAPTER 6

American Neutrality, 1914-15

TO SAY that the outbreak of the First World War in August, 1914, came as a shock to the American people would be to make an understatement of heroic proportions. In the summer of that momentous year most Americans were still living in the confident international community of the nineteenth century and were totally unprepared for the impending catastrophe. Americans read with horrified interest about the assassination on June 28 of the Austrian Archduke and his wife, but they were unaware that this spark would set off a general conflagration. When war came and the international structure fell crashing in ruins, thoughtful men in the United States, indeed, in all the world, were stunned and perplexed. As one sensitive North Carolinian expressed it, "This dreadful conflict of the nations came to most of us as lightning out of a clear sky. The horror of it all kept me awake for weeks, nor has the awfulness of it all deserted me." [1]

Yet events compelled Americans to examine closely the basic causes and issues of the war. During the first months, indeed, during the long period from August, 1914, to April, 1917, the American people were deluged with a flood of appeals, both at home and abroad, in behalf of the opposing alliances. So much that is superficial has been written on the subject of propaganda and the formation of American attitudes that perhaps a few corrective generalizations are in order. Firstly, it is doubtful that Americans of this period were as naïve about the origins of the war as a later generation believed. On the contrary, many

[1] Robert N. Page to Walter H. Page, Nov. 12, 1914, the Papers of Walter H. Page, in Houghton Library, Harvard University.

molders of opinion had a sophisticated understanding of the intricate causes of the war.[2] To be sure, some influential newspapers and spokesmen in the United States immediately branded Germany as the aggressor;[3] but other distinguished leaders in church and secular affairs argued persuasively that Germany was least guilty.[4] Secondly, the Germans had a full and free opportunity to present their case before the American public and did present it in a variety of ways, especially through the regular channels of opinion.[5] Far from being inept and

[2] Colonel House's comment, which is too long to be printed here, is particularly significant, as it revealed an acute understanding of European politics and the background of the war. The Diary of Edward M. House, in the Papers of Edward M. House, in the Library of Yale University, Apr. 15, 1915. See also, for example, Benjamin Ide Wheeler to F. K. Lane, Sept. 5, 1914, copy in the Woodrow Wilson Papers, in the Library of Congress; C. W. Eliot to Wilson, Aug. 20, 1914, *ibid.; Saturday Evening Post,* CLXXXVII (Aug. 29, 1914), 20; *ibid.,* June 19, 1915, p. 22; George Harvey, "Europe at Armageddon," *North American Review,* CC (Sept., 1914), 321–332; *The Presbyterian,* LXXXIV (Sept. 30, 1914), 3; *ibid.,* Dec. 2, 1914, p. 3; Pastoral Letter of the Methodist Episcopal Bishops, May 12, 1915, in New York *Christian Advocate,* XC (May 20, 1915), 677.

[3] E.g., New York *World,* Aug. 4, 5, 1914; *Outlook,* CVII (Aug. 15, 1914), 891–893; *ibid.,* CVIII (Sept. 30, 1914), 245–249; W. H. Taft to Mrs. W. A. Edwards, Sept. 2, 1914, the Papers of William Howard Taft, in the Library of Congress; O. G. Villard to E. W. Hilgard, Sept. 18, 1914, the Papers of Oswald Garrison Villard, in Houghton Library, Harvard University; Henry A. Wallace to W. H. Page, Aug. 2, 1915, Page Papers; Henry Watterson, in Louisville *Courier-Journal,* July 4, 1915. Elihu Root's views are given fully in the memorandum of an interview of c. Aug. 4, 1914, that Hamilton Holt sent to Root on Aug. 7, 1914, the Papers of Elihu Root, in the Library of Congress.

[4] *Lutheran Church Work,* III (Sept. 3, 1914), 8–9; *ibid.,* Oct. 1, 1914, pp. 8–9. Rear Admiral French E. Chadwick carried on a long campaign to convince the public that Britain was chiefly responsible for the war. For samples of his propaganda see Chadwick to Wilson, Aug. 23, Sept. 12, Dec. 16, 1914, Feb. 19, 1915, Wilson Papers; Chadwick to O. G. Villard, Jan. 4, 1915, Villard Papers. Professor John W. Burgess of Columbia University was another ardent defender of Germany. See, among others, his articles in the Boston *Evening Transcript,* Aug. 19, 1914; Newport (R.I.) *Daily News,* Sept. 12, 1914; New York *Evening Mail,* Aug. 14, 1915; letter to editor of the Springfield *Republican,* reprinted in *The Open Court,* XXVIII (Oct., 1914), 587–595. Perhaps the most influential German apologist in the United States, however, was the Rev. Dr. Walter Rauschenbusch, leader of the social gospel movement. His "Be Fair to Germany," reprinted from the *Congregationalist* by the *Lutheran Church Work,* III (Nov. 19, 1914), 8–10, is typical of his appeals.

[5] The British cut the cable between Germany and the United States immediately after the declaration of war; but the lack of direct cable connection between Berlin and New York was no deterrent to the sending of news from Germany. A great amount of literature came through the mails during the first year of the war; American correspondents sent their dispatches through either

unsuited to the American mentality, much of the German propaganda was skillfully executed and made a deep impression on the American mind, especially when it appealed to the deep-rooted American hatred of Russian despotism and anti-Semitism and the American fear of future Russian aggression.[6]

The fact is, the Germans and their champions in the United States went to greater expense and effort to influence American opinion, at least before the German propaganda machine was exposed in August, 1915, than did their enemies. That they failed to persuade a majority of Americans that their cause was just does not necessarily signify that they blundered. They failed because a majority of thoughtful Americans had made up their minds on the causes and issues of the war before the German or British propaganda agencies set effectively to work. American attitudes were of course conditioned by the background of German-American rivalries, by the fear that Germany had naval ambitions in the Caribbean, and by a deep-rooted distrust of the Kaiser and the military clique that controlled Imperial Germany. But most important, Germany's actions immediately before and after the outbreak of the war confirmed the deepest American suspicions. Germany's and Austria's refusal to submit the Serbian question to arbitration, it was thought, had made a general war inevitable, while Germany's ruthless breach of treaty pledges in violating Belgian neutrality was regarded as a defiance of the moral conscience of the world. Thus the preponderant American opinion was determined during the first months of the war, not by atrocity stories,[7] British propaganda, and

---

Rotterdam, Copenhagen, or London, but in the latter case the British censors often did not interfere. Finally, American correspondents could always use the wireless for important dispatches, and a large quantity of news came by this route.

[6] For samples of German propaganda in the United States, see the Essay on Sources, "Propaganda and American Opinion on the War—German Propaganda."

[7] Before the publication of the Bryce *Report* on May 13, 1915, no person of consequence in the United States took the atrocity stories seriously, mainly because American correspondents with the German armies in Belgium and France denied them emphatically. See Roger Lewis *et al.*, in New York *World*, Sept. 7, 1914; John T. McCutcheon, in *ibid.*, Sept. 19, 1914; Joseph Medill Patterson, in *ibid.*, Sept. 25, 1914; Arno Dosch, "Louvain the Lost," *World's Work*, XXVIII (Oct., 1914), A–H; Arthur Sweetser, "A Diary from the Front," *ibid.*, XXIX (Jan., 1915), 350–356; Irvin S. Cobb, "Being a Guest of the German Kaiser," *Saturday Evening Post*, CLXXXVII (Oct. 24, 1914), 14; A. Sweetser, "With the Germany Army in Its Dash Toward Paris," *Outlook*, CIX (Jan. 27, 1915), 186–190.

hysterical fear, but upon a fairly keen analysis of the international situation and sure knowledge of German actions. And this opinion was confirmed and strengthened by subsequent events, especially the ruthless submarine campaign.[8]

The fact that probably a majority of Americans were mildly proAllied by the autumn of 1914 did not mean, however, that they wanted to intervene in any fashion. At this time, at any rate, opinion was almost unanimous that the United States had no vital stake in the war and that wisdom dictated a policy of complete neutrality. Therefore, when the President issued an official proclamation of neutrality and backed it up on August 18 with a personal appeal to his fellow countrymen for impartiality of thought as well as of action, even ardent believers in the British cause like Charles W. Eliot applauded.[9]

The publication by the Bryce Commission of its *Report*, however, created an entirely new situation. James Bryce, Sir Frederick Pollock, and the other members of the Commission were venerated in the United States, and their names gave authority to a superficially convincing document, the main thesis of which was that the German army had used cruelty as a deliberate policy in Belgium. Coming as it did after the second greatest atrocity of the war—the sinking of the *Lusitania*—the *Report* caused many Americans to wonder or to believe that there was a firm basis of truth in many of the atrocity charges. For American comment see New York *World*, May 13, 1915; *The Nation*, C (May 20, 1915), 554–555; *Independent*, LXXXII (May 24, 1915), 309–310; *Outlook*, CX (May 26, 1915), 150–151; *World's Work*, XXX (June, 1915), 134; *Collier's*, LV (June 5, 1915), 15.

It would be easy, however, to overestimate the importance of the Bryce *Report*. We know, for example, that Wilson steadfastly refused to listen to, much less believe, the atrocity charges. Southerners with long memories pointed out that General Sherman had used a deliberate policy of cruelty to civilians to shorten the Civil War. And most Americans had made up their minds by the time the Bryce *Report* was issued.

[8] Oswald Garrison Villard, certainly not an interventionist, best expressed the preponderant American opinion in reply to the German naval attaché, who had asserted that the American people were being misled by British lies. "I am frant to admit," Villard replied, "that it is no longer possible for the bulk of the papers to deal with judicial minds with the situation; for the bulk of them it has been impossible since Belgium, but I insist that the responsibility rests with Germany alone and that their acts in Belgium, in Louvain and the sinking of the Lusitania readily account for this partisanship of our press. Germany has affronted the moral, neutral sentiment of the world, and that cannot be explained away by dismissing our sources of information as English lies, etc." Villard to Karl Boy-Ed, Oct. 28, 1915, Villard Papers.

[9] Wilson also forbade army and navy officers publicly to discuss the issues of the war. Later he went so far as to make an appeal to motion-picture audiences to refrain from demonstrating in any way in favor of either side. Wilson to Bryan, Sept. 11, 1914, Wilson Papers. On another occasion, he refused to accept a cutting from a rosebush from the battlefield of Verdun because to do so might be "unneutral." Wilson to B. R. Newton, June 9, 1916, *ibid*.

Shattering though the war was to American dreams of the progressive betterment of mankind, it had also a profound impact on the domestic economy and created problems that demanded prompt attention. Rumors of war, for example, sent prices on the New York Stock Exchange on July 30 tumbling an average of nearly five points, and the pressure of European liquidation was so enormous that the Exchange closed the following day. A panic was averted by Secretary McAdoo's decisive action in making available an almost unlimited quantity of so-called "emergency currency," authorized by the Aldrich-Vreeland Act, until the Federal Reserve System could go into operation.[10] Moreover, closing prices on the Stock Exchange were used to determine the value of securities offered as collateral for loans from national banks, thus freezing, as it were, stock and bond prices at an almost normal level.

Effective co-operation between bankers and the Treasury saved the national financial structure until the day, in the spring of 1915, when Allied war orders began to pour in upon American manufacturers and stimulated a boom of great proportions. But when a similar crisis demoralized the cotton market and caused prices to drop from ten-eleven to four-five cents a pound, the government at first failed to do anything. Facing economic ruin, the cotton planters and their spokesmen were up in arms all over the South and in Washington, imploring the administration to use governmental resources to stabilize cotton prices, by "valorizing" the price of cotton.[11] There was even a short-lived filibuster in Congress in October, but the strongest pressure Southerners could muster brought no substantial relief. The most the administration would do was to allow the issuance of emergency currency against cotton in licensed warehouses, but on the basis of 75 per cent of the current price, to approve a federally licensed warehouse system, and to promote the establishment by private bankers of a national pool of $150 million to stabilize cotton at six cents a pound. So onerous were the terms under which planters could borrow from the national

[10] To September 10, 1914, some $256,170,000 of the emergency currency was issued.

[11] Representatives of the cotton growers met with Secretary McAdoo at a conference in the Pan-American Building in Washington on August 24–25, 1914. The cotton spokesmen proposed that the federal government peg the price of cotton at its normal level of ten cents a pound and allow state banks to issue emergency currency, in the form of loans to planters, based upon ten-cent cotton. *The New York Times,* Aug. 25, 26, 1914; New York *Journal of Commerce,* Aug. 25, 1914.

pool, however, that only seven loans, totaling $28,000, were made; and it is a safe assumption the South lost about half the value of the cotton crop of 1914 without benefit of any decisive action by the administration.

Southerners, therefore, complained bitterly that the administration was mindful of business and banking interests and callous to the desperate needs of the farmers. These complaints were not without substance. In numerous ways besides the issuing of emergency currency and the pegging of security prices the administration evidenced its readiness to soften the impact of the war on the business and commercial classes, if not actually to take advantage of the war situation to give a peculiar advantage to those interests.

Thus, on July 31 the President called Congressional leaders to the White House, warned them that the outbreak of war would demoralize the sea lanes until the British navy had cleared them of German raiders, and urged the passage of emergency legislation to increase the American merchant marine.[12] In response to this appeal, the Senate on August 3 passed a bill authorizing the use of naval vessels as cargo carriers. It was never approved by the House; but the administration obtained drastic alterations in the ship registry law, making it easy for foreign ships to hoist the American flag.[13] The administration, moreover, obtained Congressional approval for the establishment in the Treasury Department of a War Risk Insurance Bureau to provide

[12] He was obviously thinking of blockade and contraband in traditional terms, as he pointed out that American ships alone would be available to carry food, cotton, and other raw materials to the Central Powers. W. C. Adamson, undated memorandum in the Baker Collection; also New York *World*, Aug. 1, 1914.

[13] As the bill approved on August 18, 1914, did not even require American ownership of a majority of stock in corporations applying for American registry, it was a clear violation of international custom and law and later evoked strong protests from the British government. See Joint Neutrality Board, "Note to the French Ambassador Concerning Purchase of German Merchant Ships," dated Sept. 16, 1914, copy in the Papers of Chandler P. Anderson, in the Library of Congress.

Fortunately for the United States, the German owners of vessels in American harbors dared not risk losing their property and did not openly take advantage of the new provision. Thus most of the vessels that changed their registry were American-owned ships previously under British, Belgian, and German registry, and the United States was spared the necessity of defending the right of German shipowners to operate under the American flag. The right of American citizens to buy German vessels and operate them in the European trade was a different matter and will be discussed later.

marine insurance at standard rates for American shipowners and shippers.

The administration's early position on the question of loans by American bankers to belligerent governments should also be understood as part and parcel of a great effort to protect the much damaged domestic financial structure. In early August the French government asked J. P. Morgan & Company to float a $100 million loan in the United States. There were good economic reasons why the loan should not be made: the security markets were disorganized and there was widespread fear that foreign creditors would demand large quantities of gold in return for American securities and payment of outstanding obligations. In refusing to approve the French loan, the administration was protecting the American gold reserve. Unfortunately, however, the President allowed the Secretary of State to inject an irrational and unneutral meaning into the State Department's refusal to approve the transaction, and to trumpet it abroad as the official position of the American government. "There is no reason why loans should not be made to Governments of neutral nations," Bryan was allowed to say in an official statement, "but in the judgment of this Government loans by American bankers to any foreign nation which is at war is [sic] inconsistent with the true spirit of neutrality." [14] Moreover, in a signed article in his monthly, *The Commoner,* for September, 1914, Bryan went further and declared, "Money is the worst of contrabands—it commands all other things." [15]

While the State Department's ban did not violate international law, it was a deviation from traditional practice and, further, was unneutral, in that it operated to the disadvantage of Great Britain, a sea power, and to the great advantage of Germany, a land power. Moreover, it was an economically unrealistic policy, because if it had been faithfully adhered to it would have ended by destroying the only foreign trade in which the United States could then engage on a large scale—trade with its natural customers, Britain and France.

As these facts became evident after the panic in Wall Street had

[14] Bryan's statement of August 15, 1914, printed in *The New York Times,* Aug. 16, 1914.

[15] Bryan expressed these sentiments also in Bryan to Wilson, Aug. 10, 1914, Wilson Papers. One is tempted to believe that had this issue not arisen at the time of Mrs. Wilson's death, when he was almost beside himself with grief, the President would not have allowed Bryan to lead him into approving this mistaken policy.

passed, the economic impossibility and strategic unwisdom of maintaining Bryan's ban on loans also became apparent, and the State Department began a retreat that ended in complete revocation of the prohibition. In mid-October the Department shifted its position and made it plain it would not attempt to obstruct future loans to the belligerents. A short time later, on October 23, the President told Lansing, then Counselor, that he would not oppose an extension of commercial credits, information that was at once relayed to the National City Bank and the Morgan firm. The bankers, however, seemed still uncertain of the administration's attitude, especially regarding the floating of outright loans, and they moved with extreme care to avoid offending public opinion. Before the spring of 1915 only a few small short-term commercial credits had been advanced by the New York banks. As exports began greatly to exceed imports, however, larger credits had to be advanced, and the bankers demanded explicit assurances of approval from the State Department before they undertook to finance the growing war trade. The issue came to a head in March, 1915, when the Morgan firm sought official approval for a $50 million commercial credit to the French government. Every responsible person knew there was no difference between a credit of this kind and a "loan," but Bryan saved face by announcing on March 31 that the Department would not object to such credit arrangements, although it had in the past disapproved "loans."

The administration's most important effort to meet the economic needs created by the war situation was its vigorous, almost frantic campaign to obtain passage of a bill to provide $30 million for the purchase of a governmentally owned and operated shipping line. The author of the ship purchase bill introduced in August, 1914, was McAdoo, who brought the President to his side and led the fight for its adoption. As the bill provided for the purchase, not for the construction, of ships, the question of what ships would be purchased immediately arose. Obviously, the only vessels available in quantity were the German ships, totaling half a million tons, lying in American harbors. Wilson was reluctant to take the step, but McAdoo convinced him there was no other way to get the ships quickly. Moreover, as McAdoo pointed out, the government "would not . . . be confined to the purchase of German ships only." [16]

Wilson's insistence on pushing the measure provoked a bitter fight in

[16] McAdoo to Wilson, Nov. 21, 1914, *ibid.*

Congress. The Republicans, led by Henry Cabot Lodge and Elihu Root, opposed the bill because it would project the government into the business field. They opposed it, also, because they suspected the administration planned to buy the German ships and operate them in the Atlantic trade; [17] and this, they asserted, would inevitably involve the United States in a serious and entirely needless dispute with the British government.[18] Administration spokesmen were not frank with Congress and refused to affirm or deny the charge that they contemplated purchasing the German ships. Like most other leaders, Bryan saw the issue clearly and begged the President to come out frankly and tell the American people and the Allies that he had no intention of buying the disputed vessels. But Wilson would not surrender. On the contrary, he grew sullen and bitter and privately charged Lodge and Root with lack of conscience and with using "insincere and contemptible methods of fighting." After the defeat of the bill in early March, 1915, moreover, he wrote a long and bitter indictment of the Republican senators and the seven Democrats who had joined them in defeating the measure.[19] Someone must have persuaded him to withhold the statement, for it was never published.

The administration, meanwhile, had been maneuvering to take a definite diplomatic position in relation to the belligerents. As the German government early announced its intention to adhere to the Declaration of London [20] in its maritime warfare and adhered to this

[17] Lodge, moreover, believed McAdoo was involved in some understanding, probably corrupt, with Kuhn, Loeb & Company, which firm, he thought, would handle the sale of the ships. See Lodge to Theodore Roosevelt, Jan. 15, 20, 26, Feb. 5, 8, 19, Mar. 1, 1915, the Papers of Theodore Roosevelt, in the Library of Congress; Lodge to Henry L. Higginson, Jan. 8, 25, 1915, the Papers of Henry L. Higginson, in Houghton Library, Harvard University; Lodge to John T. Morse, Jr., Jan. 28, 1915, the Papers of John T. Morse, Jr., in the Massachusetts Historical Society.

[18] Lodge's and Root's fear was well grounded, as was evidenced by the bitter protest of the British Foreign Secretary, Sir Edward Grey, against the ship purchase bill (Grey to Spring Rice, Jan. 22, 1915, House Papers). It is certain the British would not have acknowledged the legality of the American government's purchase of the German vessels. Moreover, the British would probably have seized the ships if the government shipping corporation had tried to use them in the Atlantic trade. This action, in turn, would have compelled the United States either to abandon its shipping venture or else to resort to strong diplomacy or force to maintain its illegal position.

[19] "Statement about the shipping bill," c. Mar. 4, 1915, in Wilson Papers.

[20] Drawn up by the representatives of the maritime powers at the London Conference of 1909, the Declaration represented the culmination of liberal

promise until February, 1915, the administration's early troubles were all with Great Britain—over the contraband list, the status of American-owned ships formerly under German registry, and the searching and detention of American ships by British naval craft. Determined to use their naval supremacy to the fullest advantage, the British Cabinet, by Order in Council on August 20, 1914, began the process of tightening the noose around the Central Powers. Slowly, gradually, this economic warfare was intensified, until soon Germany was denied access, even through neutral ports, to neutral sources of copper, oil, food, cotton, and other vital raw materials. But the Cabinet always operated with a keen eye on American reactions. The British policy, in brief, was to exercise the maximum restraint of neutral trade compatible with retaining the friendship of the United States. By the beginning of 1915 the structure of the British system of maritime controls was fairly complete, although it was strengthened considerably as new opportunities arose.

The important question was whether the American government would acquiesce in the British system or attempt to enervate it by insisting, to the point of war, upon freedom of trade with Germany in so-called noncontraband commodities. At first Wilson endeavored to persuade the Foreign Office to accept in full the Declaration of London, with one modification, as the code governing British sea operations. Wilson's proposal would have given the British only slight control over the transit of goods into Germany through neutral ports and would have denied to the British their most effective weapon—their control over the contraband list.[21] Grey pointed out this elemental, but important, fact to Page when he rejected the President's suggestion. In their subsequent negotiations with the British Foreign Office, there-

---

nineteenth-century thought on the subject of maritime warfare. Its provisions regarding contraband were most explicit and generous to land powers, as it forbade placing food and raw materials on the list of absolute, or prohibited, contraband. The Declaration was never ratified by the British Parliament and was, therefore, never an integral part of international law.

[21] Specifically, Wilson proposed that the British government accept the Declaration of London, with the reservation that when the territory of a neutral country was used as a base for the transit of supplies to Germany, "such port or territory has acquired enemy character in so far as trade in *contraband* is concerned and that vessels trading shall be thereafter subject to the rules of the declaration governing trade to enemy's territory." (Italics mine.) Acting Secretary of State to Page, Oct. 16, 1914, *Papers Relating to the Foreign Relations of the United States, 1914, Supplement* (Washington, 1928), pp. 249–250.

fore, the Washington government had to appeal to traditional international law, much controverted though it was.

In actual fact, however, the President was unwilling at this time to make a serious issue with the British over the important aspects of their economic warfare. On December 26, 1914, for example, the State Department sent a firm note to the Foreign Office protesting ship seizures and detentions, but it was cordial in tone. For obvious reasons, however, Grey was anxious to come to an informal understanding with Wilson and to accomplish this end sent a message of great importance to the President by Chandler P. Anderson, then in the State Department. Firstly, Grey wanted Wilson to have a clear understanding of the Allied war aims, which he specified in detail.[22] Secondly, he wanted the President to know that the British government was doing its best to meet American objections to the manner in which the Order in Council of August 20, 1914, was being enforced. When Anderson relayed Grey's message to Wilson, the President replied that there were "no very important questions of principle" involved in the Anglo-American disputes, and that they could all be settled by arbitration or adjudication after the war was over.[23]

Just at the moment, therefore, when it seemed Wilson and Grey had found a basis of mutual adjustment, a new issue of serious proportions arose and revived smoldering grievances. It was the much debated question of the purchase of the German ships in American ports by American citizens or by German-controlled dummy corporations, which was raised when the Hamburg-American Line sold a freighter, the *Dacia*, to Edward N. Breitung, mine operator and banker. As Breitung was acting for the German government and planned to buy all the German vessels in the United States if the *Dacia* purchase went unchallenged, the British Cabinet became enormously agitated and

[22] At this time they included restitution of and reparation for Belgium, the return of Alsace-Lorraine and an indemnity for France, and the transfer of Constantinople and the Dardanelles to Russia.

[23] The Diary of Chandler P. Anderson, in the Library of Congress, Jan. 9, 1915. Anderson himself had argued to this effect earlier in his "Memorandum of reasons why the United States should acquiesce without protest but reserving all rights in regard to Great Britain's interference with shipments from the United States to neutral countries of supplies available for war purposes, the ultimate destination of which is Germany," dated Oct. 21, 1914, Anderson Papers. Anderson gave Wilson a copy of this memorandum, but if Wilson read it he was not impressed. He told Anderson on January 9, 1915, that he did not remember it.

warned they would seize the vessel and bring it before the Prize Court.[24] Even more excited were the British editors, some of whom hinted that the United States would force a break in relations if the State Department attempted to protect the *Dacia*.[25] Although the Department was moderate and conciliatory throughout the controversy, the *Dacia* affair stirred British resentment as no other incident before 1916 did; and the fact that their government sidestepped the issue by allowing the French to seize the ship did not appease the anger of the British people.[26]

The dispute over the transfer of German ships to American registry was soon obscured, however, by a new and startling development—the German submarine challenge to the British maritime system and to traditional concepts of international law, which compelled a re-examination of Wilson's whole plan of neutrality. Hereafter it would be impossible for the United States to acquiesce in the British system without seriously impairing the continuance of friendly relations with Germany. In other words, as the two giants fought desperately for survival impartiality was no longer possible for the United States. Any American action against one belligerent was bound to benefit the other; American acquiescence in the maritime measures of one belligerent would injure the other.

It is, of course, clear that Britain and Germany were determined to exert the maximum economic pressure compatible with achieving their supreme goals,[27] and that the policies of the one were not necessarily

[24] See e.g., Page to Secretary of State, Jan. 15, 18, 1915, *Papers Relating to the Foreign Relations of the United States, 1915, Supplement* (Washington, 1928), pp. 679–680, 682–683.

[25] See especially the vitriolic editorial in the *Spectator* (London), Jan. 23, 1915; also, *Morning Post* (London), Jan. 14, 1915; *Standard* (London), Jan. 16, 1915; *Westminster Gazette* (London), Jan. 16, 1915.

[26] The *Dacia* affair led Grey to send an extraordinary message to the British Ambassador, Sir Cecil Spring Rice, to be shown only to Wilson and House. In this dispatch, Grey made a sweeping indictment of the allegedly unneutral conduct of the Wilson administration, for blocking private loans to the Allies, refusing to allow the export of submarine parts, trying to obtain passage of the ship purchase bill, promoting the sale of German ships, and for not discouraging the movement to apply an embargo on the export of munitions. Grey to Spring Rice, Jan. 22, 1915, House Papers. Page also summarized the British grievances in a frank personal letter to the President, Jan. 26, 1915, Wilson Papers.

As for the *Dacia*, she was confiscated by the French government, was renamed the *Yser*, and was sunk by a submarine in the Mediterranean on November 9, 1915.

[27] Thus, for Great Britain, this meant using the maximum pressure against

dependent upon the policies of the other.[28] In diplomatic practice, however, the doctrine of *retaliation* and *reprisal* is often invoked to justify policies unpleasant to third parties. Thus after January, 1915, the Germans used the illegal British measures as an excuse for instituting illegal measures of their own, which action in turn furnished further excuse to the British for intensifying their maritime controls.

The question of how far each of the contenders should go in their maritime warfare was raised in such a way, however, as to confuse the American government and public. In January, 1915, the W. L. Greene Commission Company of St. Louis shipped a large cargo of food to Germany on the *Wilhelmina,* owned by the Southern Products Trading Company. Actually, German interests were behind the entire transaction. Four days after the *Wilhelmina* sailed, the Bundesrat, or Federal Council, impounded all foodstuffs within the German Empire, and this action gave the British Cabinet an excuse to prohibit all shipments of food from the United States to Germany. The Bundesrat thereupon rescinded its order, in so far as it applied to food imported from neutrals; but the British stood by their decree and seized the *Wilhelmina* off Falmouth on February 11.

In reply and allegedly in retaliation against the British food blockade, the German Admiralty on February 4, 1915, announced a submarine blockade of the British Isles. All enemy vessels within the war zone would be destroyed, the German proclamation warned, while neutral vessels in the zone would be in grave danger because of the British misuse of neutral flags.[29] During the ensuing weeks German spokesmen explained and appealed to the American people for understanding. The German government, they said, had adopted extreme measures only to force the British to abandon their blockade aimed at starving German

Germany compatible with retaining American friendship, which was absolutely essential to an Allied victory. For Germany, it meant adjusting its sea warfare to the demands of the United States until it was considered more advantageous to have the United States in the war than to forgo longer the unrestricted use of the submarine.

[28] In other words, the British would have instituted a total blockade of Germany and neutral European ports whether or not the Germans resorted to the submarine weapon, while the Germans would have used the submarine regardless of British measures.

[29] Gerard to Secretary of State, Feb. 4, 1915, *Foreign Relations, 1915, Supplement,* p. 94. In a concurrent memorandum, the Imperial Chancellor explained that the submarine blockade was being undertaken as reprisal against British violations of the laws of sea warfare. "Memorandum of the German Government . . . .," dated Feb. 4, 1915, *ibid.,* pp. 96–97.

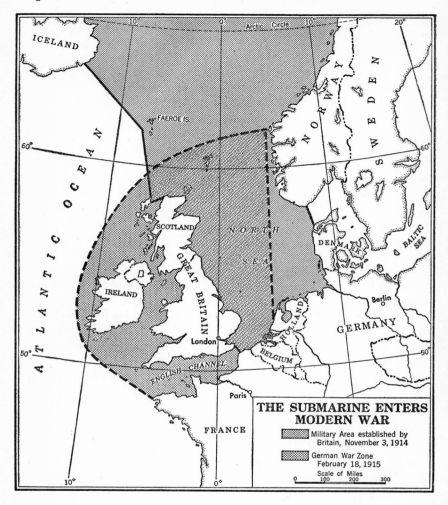

THE SUBMARINE ENTERS
MODERN WAR

Military Area established by
Britain, November 3, 1914

German War Zone
February 18, 1915

Scale of Miles

women and children. Germany would, therefore, it was officially announced, abandon the submarine blockade if Britain would abandon her food blockade.[30]

[30] Official statement of Admiral Behncke of the Marine Department, presented to the United States naval attaché on February 16, 1915, and printed in *The New York Times,* Feb. 17, 1915; Gerard to Secretary of State, Feb. 12, 1915, *Foreign Relations, 1915, Supplement,* p. 102; Bernstorff to Secretary of State, Feb. 15, 1915, *ibid.,* pp. 104–105.

As was later revealed, this German offer was not seriously intended. The Germans were simply using a bluff, a paper blockade, to try to compel the British to relax their controls, not only on food, about which they were not seriously worried, but also on other so-called noncontraband raw materials. If the Germans had been able to institute an effective blockade of the British Isles at this or any other time, they would have done so and would thereby have brought the war to a speedy conclusion.

This fact, however, was not apparent to most American leaders, some of whom, like Bryan, took seriously the German cry of "starvation." As correspondents and diplomatic officers pointed out time and again, there was an ample supply of food in the Empire before 1917, and the British food blockade was a failure. The head of the German War Food Office, Dr. Batocki, summarized the situation when he declared on January 27, 1917:

> There is absolutely no question of our ability to pull through. Despite the blockade and the practically complete stoppage of our imports, despite the partial failures of some of our own crops last year, we have enough food. We do not pretend that it is all we should like to have. There are numerous things which we enjoy, but they are not necessary. We eat them with pleasure when we have them. But we do not starve without them, nor do we lose health and vigor for the lack of them. . . . I tell you there is absolutely no question of starvation for the German people. In point of fact, there is less starvation in Germany today than there is in the United States with your congested cities and your great centres of poverty and distress.[31]

The German "war zone" decree and accompanying "offer" raised a challenge and presented an opportunity to the State Department that it did not fail to grasp. To answer the challenge to American interests implicit in the warning to neutral vessels, Lansing and Wilson at once prepared a reply, advising the German authorities that the United States would not tolerate unrestrained attacks on American vessels, would hold the Imperial government to "a strict accountability" for illegal destruction of American ships and lives, and would take measures necessary to defend American rights on the seas.[32] Although

[31] *The New York Times,* Jan. 28, 1917.
[32] Secretary of State to Gerard, Feb. 10, 1915, *Foreign Relations, 1915, Supplement,* pp. 98–100. Lansing's original draft of this note, dated February 6, 1915, with Wilson's penciled emendations, is in the Wilson Papers.

Lansing wondered whether any protest should be made [33] and the note was weak, in that it was confined entirely to German attacks against American vessels and said nothing about attacks upon belligerent merchant ships upon which Americans might be traveling or working, American commentators hailed the note as a forthright and courageous reply.[34] Actually, in the subsequent negotiations and after several American ships had been destroyed, the Imperial government backed down in its threat against American vessels, so that the later and great controversies centered around an entirely new issue—the alleged rights of Americans traveling and working on Allied merchantmen.

On the other hand, the Washington administration also seized the opportunity presented by the German offer to abandon the submarine blockade, provided the British gave up their "hunger blockade," to attempt to persuade the British Cabinet to relax their controls. From the point of view of American neutral interests, such a move became highly desirable when the British Cabinet on March 11 issued a new Order in Council interdicting *all* neutral commerce to Germany, through German or neutral ports. So hostile was the reaction in American circles that the administration could not well ignore this extension of Britain's sea dominion. Even before the new British Order was issued, the President had instructed Page and House, then in London, emphatically to urge the Cabinet to accept the German offer. Under increasing American pressure, Grey finally agreed in May to accept, with reservations, the proposed arrangement, and Wilson and House were delighted. It later turned out, however, that both Wilson and the German Foreign Office insisted that the British allow free entry into Germany, not only of foodstuffs, but also of all noncontraband products, and this the British adamantly refused to do.

Meanwhile, Wilson and his advisers had been moving in another direction to solve their dilemma—in the direction of ending the war by mediation. At the outset of hostilities the President had offered his good offices as mediator, and although this offer was rejected peace rumors and discussions persisted. Most of them came to nothing, but out of the talks begun by the New York banker, James Speyer, in September, 1914, grew the idea that England and Germany might come to an understanding under the aegis of Wilson and House.[35] As time passed,

[33] Lansing to Wilson, Feb. 7, 1915, *ibid.*

[34] E.g., New York *World,* Feb. 12, 1915; *The Nation,* C (Feb. 18, 1915), 186.

[35] Speyer dined with Ambassador von Bernstorff on September 5, 1914, on

the pressure on the President to take some positive steps to end the war mounted, while his own thoughts turned irresistibly in the same direction.[36] Thus, in mid-December, 1914, Wilson asked Colonel House to begin serious discussions with the British and German Ambassadors and then to go to Europe to carry the conversations to the point of definite agreement. Bernstorff was positive his government would agree to evacuate and indemnify Belgium, while Grey sent word to Spring Rice that the Allies could not refuse a reasonable German offer.[37] It was with high hopes, therefore, that House sailed from New York on January 30, 1915.

House was received cordially in London, but his early progress was interrupted by the controversy over the submarine blockade, the British retaliatory measures, and considerable opposition within the British Cabinet to the idea of any peace discussions.[38] From London House went to Paris and thence to Berlin for long talks with all the leading civilian officials. To the British he had suggested general disarmament and an international organization as a basis for the peace settlement; to the Germans he held out the bait of freedom of the seas and an end to British navalism. Friendly and hopeful though the German officials were, they frankly admitted they could not dare publicly to agree to evacuate and indemnify Belgium. House left Berlin, however, with the understanding that he would endeavor to persuade the British government to "consent to freedom of the seas as one of the peace conditions," while the German leaders should begin to prepare their people to

---

which occasion Bernstorff told him he believed the Kaiser would be willing to discuss measures of peace through mediation. Speyer went at once to Washington and relayed the conversation to Bryan, who began serious intergovernmental discussions.

[36] For example, he told House on September 28, 1914, that Grey should be warned of the grave danger of postponing peace discussions, because if Germany and Austria were crushed it might become impossible to restrain Russia. House Diary, Sept. 28, 1914.

[37] *Ibid.*, Dec. 17, 20, 1914. Grey revealed his great enthusiasm for the peace project in a conversation with Sir Horace Plunkett on February 6, 1915. See the Diary of Horace Plunkett, microfilm copy in possession of Herbert Brayer, Evanston, Ill., Feb. 6, 1915.

[38] House to Wilson, Feb. 8, 9, 15, 18, 23, Mar. 1, 5, 9, 1915, Wilson Papers; House Diary, Feb. 10, 11, 13, 14, 17, 18, 20, 24, 25, Mar. 4, 5, 7, 8, 9, 1915.

"E. M. House went to Paris this morning, having no peace message from this Kingdom whatever. This kind of talk here now was spoken of by the Prime Minister [Asquith] the other day as 'the twittering of a sparrow in a tumult that shakes the world.'" The Diary of Walter H. Page, in Houghton Library, Harvard University, Mar. 11, 1915.

accept the idea of giving up Belgium. After House left Berlin and had gone to Paris, the Foreign Secretary, Gottlieb von Jagow, revealed to him the terms Germany would be willing to accept. They included German retention of Namur, Liége, and the Valley of the Meuse, an indemnity from France, and acquisition of part of the Belgian Congo. House repeated the terms to Delcassé, the French Foreign Minister, who remarked that if the Germans wanted their indemnity they would have to come to Paris to get it.

Back in London in late April, the Colonel set to work at once to persuade the British Cabinet that freedom of the seas was as essential to British as to German security. Grey, personally, was not opposed, provided Germany consented to general disarmament and gave definite guarantees for the future. What progress House made, however, was shattered by the ruthless sinking of the British liner *Lusitania* by a German submarine on May 7, 1915. If that were the German idea of "freedom of the seas," then the British wanted none of it. Moreover, as the German-American negotiations over the *Lusitania* proceeded, House became momentarily convinced his country would soon be drawn into the war.[39] He left England on June 5, therefore, more an emissary of war than of peace, his mission a failure because neither coalition was yet willing to admit that it could not achieve by war what it had failed to achieve by diplomacy.

At the very time House was in Berlin, the German admirals were setting in motion the underseas campaign that would inevitably bring their government into collision with the United States. The first important issue arose when a submarine sank the British steamer *Falaba* on March 28, 1915, without giving the passengers and crew time to escape. One American, Leon C. Thrasher, was drowned.

The Thrasher case assumed an extraordinary significance when it became evident during the ensuing discussions that the administration was constructing a future policy regarding submarine warfare. The debate in the State Department revealed at once a profound divergence in the administration. The distinguished international lawyer, Chandler P. Anderson, then acting in an advisory capacity, argued that the case did not involve an affront to the United States, as Thrasher's death was incidental to the destruction of the *Falaba*.

[39] At times he thought the United States should enter the war. For revealing statements by House, see the Plunkett Diary, June 1, 4, 1915; also House to Wilson, June 16, 1915, Wilson Papers.

Under international law, Anderson asserted, the United States was warranted in asking only for pecuniary damages. Bryan reinforced Anderson's argument by a series of letters and memoranda, in which he raised many extraneous issues,[40] but the chief purport of which was that the United States should grant the same freedom to violate international law to Germany that it had given to Britain. In opposition, Lansing, Counselor of the Department, argued that the attack on the *Falaba* was such a flagrant violation of international law that the United States could not avoid asking the German government to disavow the act, punish the submarine commander, and pay damages. He frankly admitted that such demand might lead to war. Lansing, moreover, was supported by an unequivocal declaration by the Joint Neutrality Board that American interests were vitally involved in the case and that "the action of the commanding officer of the German submarine appears to the Board not only illegal but revoltingly inhuman." [41]

The final decision, of course, rested with the President. From the outset of the discussions he seemed to agree with Lansing; even so, he was reluctant to raise a serious issue with the German government, especially since he thought there was some chance that House's mission would succeed. The collapse of the peace negotiations and the growing truculence, not to say insolence, of the German government,[42] however, must have made a deep impression on him. On April 22 he finally gave his decision: he would avoid discussing the issue on merely tech-

[40] Chief among which was the question whether the British were arming their merchant ships and whether this did not provide justification for unrestricted submarine warfare.

[41] Memorandum of the Joint Neutrality Board, Apr. 8, 1915, Wilson Papers.

[42] Bernstorff, for example, on April 6 gave out a statement from his government disavowing any responsibility for the safety of neutrals on board belligerent ships. *The New York Times,* Apr. 7, 1915. On April 4, moreover, the Ambassador presented to the State Department a long memorandum accusing the United States of virtual unneutrality because it acquiesced in British violations of international law and allowed the export of munitions to Germany's enemies. *Foreign Relations, 1915, Supplement,* pp. 157–158. Without consulting the State Department, Bernstorff gave the memorandum to the newspapers on April 11. This move, which, incidentally, he made on the direct order of the Foreign Office, was clearly an appeal to the American people over the heads of their leaders and a direct encouragement to the movement then getting under way in the United States with the help of German money to force Congress to apply an embargo on munitions exports. The Department's reply, probably drafted by Wilson, was a masterful refutation of the German accusations. Secretary of State to Bernstorff, Apr. 21, 1915, *ibid.,* pp. 160–162.

nical grounds and would "put the whole note on very high grounds,—not on the loss of this single man's life, but on the interests of mankind which are involved and which Germany has always stood for; on the manifest impropriety of a single nation's essaying to alter the understandings of nations; and as all arising out of her mistake in employing an instrument against her enemy's commerce which it is impossible to employ in that use in accordance with any rules that the world is likely to be willing to accept." [43] After having come to this decision, however, Wilson six days later admitted he was not sure what the administration should do. "Perhaps it is not necessary to make formal representations in the matter at all," he wrote to Bryan.[44]

To follow Bryan's advice and say nothing about Thrasher's death would have been the easy way out, and Wilson might have followed such a course had not events taken a sudden, spectacular turn. That a profoundly serious crisis was impending was evidenced when, on May 1, the German Embassy published a formal warning to Americans against traveling on belligerent merchantmen. Before the administration could come to a decision on a *Falaba* note or comment on the remarkable German warning, there occurred the dramatic and catastrophic event—the sinking of the *Lusitania* on May 7—that forced the President to make some kind of reply to the German challenge.[45]

Americans were shocked and horrified at what they considered the deliberate murder of almost twelve hundred noncombatants, including 128 Americans, on the high seas, by direct order of the German government. But except for a small group of ardent nationalists headed by Theodore Roosevelt, few Americans wanted to go to war to avenge the

[43] Wilson to Bryan, Apr. 22, 1915, *Papers Relating to the Foreign Relations of the United States, The Lansing Papers, 1914–1920* (2 vols., Washington, 1939–40) I, 378.

[44] Wilson to Bryan, Apr. 28, 1915, *ibid.*, p. 380.

[45] I do not have space to go into the many facets of the controversy that has since grown up over the sinking of the *Lusitania*. Whether the great North Atlantic liners were legitimate prey of the submarines—since they were prime carriers of contraband—became obscured by the methods the Germans used to destroy them. There are, however, a few points that might be cleared up. Firstly, the *Lusitania* was not armed. Secondly, she was not actually an auxiliary cruiser. Thirdly, she carried some 4,200 cases of small arms, which was a small part of her cargo of contraband. Fourthly, the submarine commander, Schwieger, knew well that he was aiming at a great passenger ship. He apparently fired only one torpedo and was astonished when the ship sank rapidly. See "Admiralstab d. Marine. Kriegstagebuch. U. 20. Kptltn. Schwieger. vom 18.3.15. bis 31.8.15 Bd. 3," from the Kriegsarchiv der Marine, Berlin, photostat in the Wilson Papers.

OCEAN STEAMSHIPS.

CUNARD

EUROPE VIA LIVERPOOL
LUSITANIA

Fastest and Largest Steamer
now in Atlantic Service Sails
SATURDAY, MAY 1, 10 A. M.
Transylvania, Fri., May 7, 5 P.M.
Orduna, - - Tues.,May 18, 10 A.M.
Tuscania, - - Fri., May 21, 5 P.M.
LUSITANIA, Sat., May 29, 10 A.M.
Transylvania, Fri., June 4, 5 P.M.

Gibraltar—Genoa—Naples—Piraeus
S.S. Carpathia, Thur., May 13, Noon

NOTICE!

TRAVELLERS intending to
embark on the Atlantic voyage
are reminded that a state of
war exists between Germany
and her allies and Great Britain
and her allies; that the zone of
war includes the waters adja-
cent to the British Isles; that,
in accordance with formal notice given by the Imperial German Government, vessels flying
the flag of Great Britain, or of
any of her allies, are liable to
destruction in those waters and
that travellers sailing in the
war zone on ships of Great
Britain or her allies do so at
their own risk.

IMPERIAL GERMAN EMBASSY

WASHINGTON. D. C., APRIL 22. 1915.

Two notices concerning the same sailing

wrong. The great majority applauded when Wilson acted deliberately
during the crisis, even when he declared in a speech at Philadelphia on
May 10 that "There is such a thing as a man being too proud to
fight." [46] From governors, senators, congressmen, and other spokesmen

[46] *The New York Times,* May 11, 1915. Although the foregoing generalization is correct, it should also be pointed out that the sinking of the *Lusitania*
convinced a small but significant segment of thoughtful American opinion that
Imperial Germany was a menace to the peace of the world and that the
philosophy of ruthlessness had so captured the German mind that the United
States could not survive in a world dominated by the Prussian military class.
Lansing, for example, who had heretofore taken a realistic view of the German
violations of American rights (Diary of Robert Lansing, in the Library of Congress, May 3, 1915), was now firmly convinced that German success "would
mean the overthrow of democracy in the world, the suppression of individual
liberty, the setting up of evil ambitions, the subordination of the principles of
right and justice to physical might directed by arbitrary will, and the turning
back of the hands of human progress two centuries." *Ibid.,* July 11, 1915. Elihu
Root, also, found evidence in the *Lusitania* disaster that the war was a struggle
between democracy and military despotism. Anderson Diary, May 15, 1915.

came fervid appeals for peace. From Senator Thomas S. Martin and Representative Hal D. Flood, two powerful Democratic leaders, came an explicit warning that the country did not want war and that the President might find it impossible to obtain a war resolution from Congress.

It should not, however, be assumed that in the subsequent negotiations with the German government Wilson's strong arm was paralyzed by popular and Congressional opposition to a belligerent policy. The President was confident there would be no real diplomatic crisis and, in any event, contemplated no stronger step than severing relations with Germany.

During the discussions over the writing of the first *Lusitania* note, Lansing took a consistently strong stand, while Bryan sought to find some way to mitigate the severity of the language. In his note to the German government of May 13, 1915, the President now took the high ground he had earlier decided to take in composing a *Falaba* note and had then abandoned. He reviewed the submarine actions culminating in the sinking of the *Lusitania* and virtually demanded that the Imperial government abandon submarine warfare altogether against unarmed merchantmen.[47] Under pressure from Bryan, Wilson agreed to issue a statement suggesting arbitration of the dispute; but under stronger pressure from Lansing, Garrison, Burleson, and Tumulty, Wilson recalled the statement, which had already been cabled to Berlin.[48] The note, therefore, was delivered at the Foreign Office in all its naked severity. When Von Jagow replied evasively,[49] Bryan pleaded for compromise even more strongly than before. Wilson stood firm, however, and Bryan resigned rather than sign the second note, in which the President appealed to the Imperial government to renew its allegiance to "the rights of humanity, which every Government honors itself in respecting."[50] Von Jagow's reply, again, was evasive and unsatisfactory, and for a third time Wilson addressed the German govern-

[47] Bryan to Gerard, May 13, 1915, *Foreign Relations, 1915, Supplement,* pp. 393–396.

[48] This was the famous "postscript" episode, about which there was much controversy later. For details see L. M. Garrison to R. S. Baker, Nov. 12, 30, 1928, Ray Stannard Baker Collection, in the Library of Congress; House Diary, Nov. 3, 1916; Bryan to Wilson, May 13, 1915, the Papers of William Jennings Bryan, in the National Archives; Bryan to Gerard, May 13, 1915, *ibid.*

[49] Gerard to Bryan, May 29, 1915, *Foreign Relations, 1915, Supplement,* pp. 419–421.

[50] Lansing to Gerard, June 9, 1915, *ibid.,* pp. 436–438.

ment. He was both conciliatory and peremptory. He admitted that it might be possible for submarine warfare to be conducted within the rules of visit and search, and he invited the German government to join him in achieving freedom of the seas. But he ended with the warning that a repetition of ruthless sinkings would be regarded by the United States as "deliberately unfriendly," in other words, would lead to diplomatic rupture and possibly to war.[51]

The summer of crisis was a time of alarm, confusion, and divided counsels among the American people. After his resignation, Bryan set out upon a peace campaign, which added new impetus to the already widespread antiwar sentiment. There were increased demands that the administration adopt a stern attitude also toward the British. The movement for an arms embargo, liberally financed by the German Embassy, was gaining new converts, while German- and Irish-American spokesmen grew frantic in their rage against the President's policy. On the other hand, anti-German sentiment undoubtedly increased by leaps and bounds as a result of the failure of the *Lusitania* negotiations. Moreover, the secrets of the German propaganda machine, headed by Privy Councillor Heinrich Albert in New York City, were revealed when United States secret-service agents picked up a brief case that Albert left on an elevated train and the contents were published in the New York *World* and the Chicago *Tribune*. Nor was the excitement allayed when the Austrian Ambassador, Dr. Constantin Dumba, was sent home for trying to persuade Austro-Hungarian subjects to quit working in American munitions plants. Even more irritating to inflamed American sentiment were the rumors and reports of German intrigues and machinations against the neutrality and peace of the United States. Many thoughtful men looked with shame and disgust at a nation "too proud to fight," so weak that it could not protect its rights on the seas or preserve its neutrality at home, so divided from within that its government could not speak with authority abroad.

In Germany, too, the popular temper was inflamed [52] and demanded

[51] Lansing to Gerard, July 21, 1915, *ibid.*, pp. 480–482.

[52] On two counts, mainly: (1) the export of munitions to the Allies, which infuriated the German people, and (2) the widespread impression that the United States was trying to force Germany to give up her most effective naval weapon without at the same time compelling Great Britain to adhere to international law. For able analyses of German opinion and samples of German editorial opinion, see J. C. O'Laughlin to Wilson, Feb. 1, 1915, Wilson Papers; O'Laughlin to Tumulty, Apr. 16, 1915, *ibid.;* New York *World*, Apr. 17, 1915; *The New York Times*, June 30, 1915; Von Reventlow in New York *World*,

that the Imperial government resist inflexibly the American demands. Official spokesmen had so aroused the people against the alleged "hunger blockade" and predicted so confidently the success of the submarine campaign that the government feared disastrous consequences if it should yield. However, as it became apparent that concessions might be necessary to maintain peaceful relations with the United States, the moderate editorial spokesmen in Germany defied public opinion and boldly championed conciliation and compromise.

In the meantime, the Washington government waited to see what events would bring. On June 30, 1915, a British passenger liner, the *Armenian,* was sunk off the coast of Cornwall; but when it developed that the ship had attempted to escape after warning was given, no issue arose. On July 17 another British liner, the *Orduna,* was attacked, though the torpedo missed its mark and the German Admiralty denied official knowledge of the incident. Then on August 19 came the event that ended the President's time of waiting—the torpedoing without warning of the White Star liner *Arabic* off Fastnet, with the loss, among others, of two American lives.[53] Wilson evidently resolved to obtain full satisfaction or else to break relations, although he was not yet thinking in terms of war.[54] The tension was relieved on August

---

July 4, 1915; Karl Boy-Ed to O. G. Villard, Nov. 6, 1915, Villard Papers; *Kölnische Zeitung,* 1st morning ed., Feb. 3, 1915; *Frankfurter Zeitung,* 2d morning ed., Feb. 14, 1915; *Deutsche Tageszeitung* (Berlin), morning ed., Feb. 14, 1915; *Vossische Zeitung* (Berlin), Apr. 22, 1915; *Berliner Lokal-Anzeiger,* morning ed., Apr. 22, 1915; *Kölnische Zeitung,* noon ed., May 18, 1915; *Kreuzzeitung* (Berlin), June 4, 1915.

The incident that had probably the most unfortunate effect on German-American relations was the publication by the Cleveland Automatic Machine Company in the *American Machinist,* XLII (May 6, 1915), 26–27, of an advertisement depicting a machine that manufactured high-explosive shells. The advertisement went on to describe in a gory way the deadliness of the shrapnel thrown out as the shell exploded. A facsimile was printed in the German press (e.g., *Frankfurter Zeitung,* 3d morning ed., June 26, 1915) and evoked a wave of resentful criticism of the United States. See *Deutsche Zeitung* (Berlin), evening ed., June 25, 1915; *Berliner Tageblatt,* evening ed., June 25, 1915; *Tägliche Rundschau* (Berlin), morning ed., June 26, 1915; *Kölnische Zeitung,* evening ed., June 25, 1915. Copies of the advertisement were also laid on the desks of every member of the Reichstag.

[53] The *Arabic* was another important carrier of contraband. For a description of her cargoes on her last three voyages from New York to Liverpool, see the New York *World,* Aug. 20, 1915. She was westbound when she was sunk.

[54] There appeared in the Baltimore *Sun,* August 24, 1915, an article purporting to describe the plans for a war with Germany that the Army War College had drawn up. Wilson read the report, became much agitated, and

25, when the German Chancellor declared that the submarine commander must have exceeded his instructions, and that if investigation proved a German submarine had sunk the *Arabic* the Imperial government would not hesitate to give complete satisfaction to the United States. Rumors that Germany had begun a diplomatic retreat were confirmed when it became known that the Imperial government, on June 6, had ordered its submarines to spare large passenger liners. More important for the United States was the outcome of an Imperial conference at Pless Castle on August 26, at which the Emperor took Chancellor von Bethmann-Hollweg's side and ordered the abandonment of unrestricted warfare against all passenger ships. The decision was telegraphed at once to Bernstorff, who, under strong pressure from Lansing, on September 1 gave a written promise that "Liners will not be sunk by our submarines without warning and without safety of the lives of noncombatants, provided that the liners do not try to escape or offer resistance." [55]

The giving of the so-called *Arabic* pledge, the later explicit disavowal of the sinking of the ship, and the generous pledges given concerning American ships in the war zone [56] added up to a remarkable diplomatic achievement for the President and sufficed at least to preserve peace between the two governments. This, however, was no lasting and complete settlement of the submarine troubles, for the reluctant *Arabic* pledge applied only to passenger vessels and left uncertain the status of merchantmen and armed merchant and passenger ships. Moreover, the *Lusitania* issue still hung fire, and German refusal to give satisfaction prevented cordial relations. Most important, Wilson's confidence in the good faith and integrity of the German government had been severely shaken, if not destroyed.

Meanwhile, the administration had not relaxed its pressure on the British government, although the dire crisis with Germany precluded strong and effective measures to compel the British to abandon their illegal blockade. The gravest threat to Anglo-American relations was

---

ordered the Assistant Secretary of War to investigate. "No such plans have ever been prepared, nor even contemplated by the General Staff," the Chief of the War College replied. W. W. Macomb, Chief, War College Division, Memorandum for the Chief of Staff, Aug. 24, 1915, Wilson Papers.

[55] *The New York Times,* Sept. 2, 1915.

[56] Given in the so-called *Frye* note of September 19, 1915. Gerard to Secretary of State, Sept. 20, 1915, *Foreign Relations, 1915, Supplement,* pp. 551–552.

the possibility that the Southern contingent in Congress might join with the German- and Irish-American elements to force the application of an arms embargo in retaliation against British suppression of the cotton trade with Central Europe. The British Foreign Office made arrangements to provide for that part of the crop of 1914 that had been sold to German buyers; [57] but as the crop of 1915 blossomed in the fields and picking time drew near, a wave of hysteria swept over the South, out of fear that the British would suppress exports to Europe altogether and the South would have to endure another year of depression. That the situation was full of danger was evidenced by a widespread campaign throughout the South for retaliation against the British government.[58] The pro-British senator from Mississippi, John Sharp Williams, spoke truthfully when he declared that every politician in the South had to be anti-British.[59]

Rumors that the British would put cotton on the list of absolute contraband and refuse to support the price of the staple leaked to the Washington administration in July. Greatly excited, Wilson declared such action would have a "fatal effect" on American opinion and would probably lead to "action by Congress cutting off munitions." The warning was at once relayed to the British Cabinet. So great was the popular demand in Britain for making cotton absolute contraband—that is, for suppressing completely the cotton trade with Germany—that the government could no longer resist it. The Foreign

[57] After the promulgation of the Order in Council of March 11, 1915, declaring a virtual blockade of Germany, the British Cabinet's policy regarding the shipment of cotton to the Continent was designed to prevent such shipments without unnecessarily offending American cotton growers. All cotton sold to German buyers before March 2 was given free transit; but the British reserved the right to buy the cotton at the contract price. This arrangement would not, however, apply in the future. Official statement of the British Foreign Office, *The New York Times,* May 21, 1915.

[58] On June 28, for example, the Georgia legislature petitioned the President to use every means, "diplomatic if possible, retaliatory if necessary," to open American trade in cotton with neutral European ports. *Ibid.,* June 29, 1915. See also "Preamble and Resolution adopted by the Board of Directors of the New Orleans Cotton Exchange," dated June 30, 1915, in the Papers of Albert S. Burleson, in the Library of Congress; resolution adopted by the State Council of the North Carolina Farmers' Union, c. July 3, 1915, Wilson Papers; resolutions adopted by the Savannah Cotton Exchange, July 8, 1915, *ibid.;* officers of the National Farmers' Union to Wilson, Aug. 13, 1915, *ibid.;* resolution adopted by the Texas Farmers' Union, Aug. 6, 1915, *ibid.;* A. F. Lever, E. J. Watson, and Wade Stackhouse to Wilson, July 12, 1915, *ibid.* New York *World,* July 22, 1915, gives a long and able analysis of Southern sentiment.

[59] Williams to Wilson, June 29, 1915, Wilson Papers.

Office, therefore, sought and obtained an understanding with the American government that solved the dilemma. A secret agreement, officially unknown to Wilson and Lansing, was negotiated by Ambassador Cecil Spring Rice and Sir Richard Crawford of the British

McCutcheon in the Chicago *Tribune*

Embassy with W. P. G. Harding of the Federal Reserve Board and Theodore Price, a financial reporter of New York City. It provided in effect that the British government would buy enough cotton to stabilize the price at ten cents a pound.[60] The agreement was never published,

[60] For details of the cotton agreement see Anderson Diary, July 22, 30, 1915; Page to Secretary of State, Aug. 13, 1915, Wilson Papers; New York *Tribune*, Nov. 20, 1915.

and for a time after the British put cotton on the absolute contraband list the pressure from Southerners for retaliation was enormous. But in almost no time cotton prices began to rise as a result of British buying, and the cotton crisis was soon passed.

It was fortunate for the British that they were able thus easily to eradicate the most rankling cause of American resentment before the summer of 1915 had ended. For the fact was, as the Germans lamented time and again, that the United States had by now become virtually an arsenal of the Allies. This was a natural consequence of the British control of the seas and was in no respect the outcome of American sentiments. The important fact was, however, that Allied buying in the United States had become so heavy by August, 1915, that the British were near the end of the resources from which they could obtain dollars.[61] Allied purchases would have to be drastically curtailed if Britain and France did not obtain a large loan in the United States to finance the war trade. But the New York bankers who stood ready to float such a loan refused to commit themselves to the undertaking unless the State Department explicitly approved. The trouble was, as McAdoo pointed out in a long letter to Wilson, that Bryan had committed the administration and even the President personally to a policy of discouraging outright loans. Had a strictly neutral course been adopted in the beginning, the administration would not have discouraged loans to the belligerents and would not now find itself caught in a trap from which escape was difficult.

In the end, the State Department specifically reversed the Bryan doctrine—which Bryan himself had in effect reversed on March 31, when he approved large commercial credits—and declared that it had no objection to the loan. Certain New York bankers may have had strong pro-Allied sentiments, although that fact did not prevent them from demanding and obtaining a commission of 2 per cent, in addition to an interest rate of nearly 5½ per cent. It is clear, however, that the administration made its decision to approve the loan on two grounds only: firstly, that negotiation of the loan was essential to the maintenance of the war trade, and therefore to the prosperity of the United States, and secondly, that to prohibit the loan would be an unneutral

---

[61] By the end of May the British economic situation was becoming almost desperate. By this date Britain was purchasing $50 million to $75 million monthly in excess of her ability to pay in gold, goods, and services.

act, so discriminatory as to deprive Britain of her legitimate advantage as mistress of the seas.

On September 10, 1915, a distinguished Anglo-French commission arrived in New York City and subsequently negotiated with a group of bankers, headed by J. P. Morgan, for a loan of $500 million. Popular opposition, generated by the Hearst press and the German- and Irish-American groups, was so great that the campaign to sell the bonds to the public did not come off well.[62] During the next year and a half the British government borrowed a billion dollars, the French government three hundred millions, and the Canadians over four hundred millions more. All the later loans, however, were secured 100 per cent by high-grade American and South American securities, and none was sold by public campaign.

The summer of 1915 was a time not only of uncertainty and alarm but also of decision. Anglo-American relations were considerably improved by the cotton agreement and by the State Department's reversion to a neutral position on loans to the belligerents. The first great submarine crisis had been weathered by a mixture of firmness and pacific diplomacy, but German-American relations were still in a precarious state. The great crisis through which the American people had passed had stimulated new fears and suggested remedies so conflicting that it was evident the nation was on the verge of one of the bitterest and most portentous debates in its history. In fact, the great debate over foreign policy and preparedness had already begun, and the administration could not long ignore it.

[62] The syndicate managing the loan was unable to sell $187 million of the bonds, which had to be taken by the participating banks.

CHAPTER 7

The Preparedness Controversy, 1914-16

D URING the first months of the war, before the submarine issue was raised, American sentiment was overwhelmingly neutral and pacific. Even those persons who believed in a vague way that the United States had some interest in the European settlement were reassured by the knowledge that the Allies were bound to win. This conviction of the certainty of an Allied victory, held by civilian and military leaders alike, conditioned all American attitudes on questions of foreign policy and preparedness. No catastrophe such as the fall of France in 1940 occurred before April, 1917, to shock Americans out of their complacency; nothing compelled them to calculate seriously the consequences of German domination of Europe.[1]

A few observers like Ambassador Walter H. Page and Charles W. Eliot sensed that the issues involved in the conflict were freighted with momentous consequences for the United States. Page and a few other like-minded citizens frankly declared at the outset of the war that American and British interests were so closely intertwined that the destruction of British naval power and the triumph of a dynamic, militaristic Imperial Germany would constitute a grave threat to the future security of the United States.[2] Such voices, however, were ob-

---

[1] For a significant commentary on this point, see Edward H. Buehrig, "Wilson's Neutrality Re-Examined," *World Politics,* III (Oct., 1950), 1–19.

[2] See, e.g., H. L. Higginson to E. M. House, Sept. 1, 1914, the Papers of Edward M. House, in the Library of Yale University; Walter H. Page to House, Sept. 22, 1914, *ibid.;* Henry Van Dyke to Wilson, Sept. 10, 1914, the Woodrow Wilson Papers, in the Library of Congress; *Collier's,* LIII (Sept. 12, 1914), 16; Stuart H. Perry, "After the War," *North American Review,* CC (Nov., 1914), 732–741; *Outlook,* CVIII (Nov. 4, 1914), 521–524.

scured by the more vociferous and more representative spokesmen, who affirmed the total separation of American and European interests. This, after all, was the ideological base upon which American neutrality rested.

Even so, after the war's first shock wore off, impartiality in thought became impossible for many sensitive Americans, who refused to close their minds to the issues of the greatest catastrophe that had visited the world in a century. It was inevitable that as German methods and ambitions unfolded, these observers should begin to calculate the value of neutrality. The first important manifestation of this sentiment came during the debate provoked by Theodore Roosevelt's charge,[3] later reiterated by Senators Root and Lodge and other Republican leaders, that the administration had virtually acquiesced in Germany's invasion of Belgium by not protesting that violation of the Hague Convention.[4]

The great submarine crisis of 1915 and the concurrent revelations of German intrigues against American peace and neutrality, however, caused an even more significant turn in this segment of American opinion. The conviction that the United States could probably not avoid intervention, especially if the Allies weakened, now spread irresistibly among leaders like Root, Lansing, Roosevelt, George Harvey, editor of the *North American Review,* Lawrence Abbott, an editor of the *Outlook,* and Paul Fuller, prominent New York attorney. The rationale of these interventionists and near-interventionists of course varied. Some were sheer idealists, who believed the American democracy could not refuse to aid the European democracies in their death grapple with imperialistic autocracy; some, like Roosevelt, were realists, who thought a firm defense of American rights on the seas would lead inevitably to war.[5]

[3] "Fear God and Take Your Own Part," *The New York Times Magazine,* Nov. 8, 1914.

[4] The controversy rather fizzled, however, when Norman Hapgood pointed to Roosevelt's earlier articles in the *Outlook,* August 22 and September 23, 1914, in which Roosevelt had declared that the United States should adhere to a strict neutrality and bore no responsibility for Belgium's fate. Norman Hapgood, "The Real Hughes Idea," *Harper's Weekly,* LXII (Mar. 18, 1916), 271. As the *New Republic,* VI (Mar. 25, 1916), 204, pointed out, the truth was that everyone—Wilson, Roosevelt, and Root included—thought in August, 1914, that noninterference was the proper course to follow.

[5] For expressions of the interventionist attitude, see Lawrence Abbott to T. Roosevelt, Dec. 23, 1914, the Papers of Theodore Roosevelt, in the Library of Congress; Paul Fuller, for the American Rights Committee, "A Memorial to the President of the United States," dated Nov. 29, 1915, Wilson Papers, and the

In December, 1915, a little group of New York interventionists formed the American Rights Committee,[6] which, with the New York *Tribune,* then edited by Ogden Reid, and similar groups in Boston and Cambridge, waged a valiant but generally futile campaign to fire the American war spirit.[7] Calling upon the President to break relations with the German government, these idealists devoted their talents to the hopeless task of persuading the American people that a complete Allied victory was essential to the preservation of democracy and civilization. As the President turned a deaf ear to their pleas and succeeded, in spite of extraordinary provocations, in preserving neutrality, the interventionists turned on him in disgust and contempt.[8] Their sentiments were nowhere more accurately expressed than in the following tribute by the novelist, Owen Wister:

> To WOODROW WILSON. FEB. 22, 1916.
> History has lashes that have flayed the names
>   Of public cowards, hypocrites, poltroons,
> You go immune, cased in your self-esteem;
>   The next world cannot scathe you, nor can this;
> No fact can stab through your complacent dream;
>   Nor present laughter, nor the future's hiss.
> But if its fathers did this land control
>   Dead Washington would wake and blast your soul.[9]

titles cited in the Essay on Sources, "German-American Relations, 1914–17—American Comment on Germany—General" and "American Public Opinion on the War, 1914–17—Representative American Comment on the War."

[6] Prominent in this organization were George Haven Putnam, Henry L. Stimson, Everett V. Abbott, Lawrence F. Abbott, Frederick R. Coudert, Professor Franklin H. Giddings, Lawrence Godkin, Charles P. Howland, and, before his death, Paul Fuller.

[7] For representative editorials in the New York *Tribune,* see the issues of Dec. 29, 1915, Jan. 1, 4, 26, 1916.

[8] Theodore Roosevelt, for example, from the early days of the submarine crisis, accused the President of cowardice and of being a "Byzantine logothete" because he wrote notes instead of taking strong action to defend American rights. The following comment (Roosevelt to Archibald B. Roosevelt, May 19, 1915, Roosevelt Papers) is typical: "There is a chance of our going to war; but I don't think it is very much of a chance. . . . As a nation, we have thought very little about foreign affairs; we don't realize that the murder of the thousand men, women and children on the Lusitania is due, solely, to Wilson's abject cowardice and weakness. . . . He and Bryan are morally responsible for the loss of the lives of those American women and children. . . . They are both of them abject creatures and they won't go to war unless they are kicked into it."

[9] Printed in the Springfield *Republican,* Feb. 24, 1916.

For all the depth of their conviction and the ardor of their pleading, however, the interventionists remained only a fractional minority before March, 1917, devoid of influence on the masses of people. Their organization, the American Rights Committee, never gained a foothold outside the Northeast and was in no sense comparable in power and influence to the Committee to Defend America by Aiding the Allies of the period 1939–41. The crisis in German-American relations in 1915 was chiefly significant, therefore, not because it stimulated the interventionists to greater efforts, but because it provoked among many Americans an awareness of the military impotence of their country. In fact, an important public debate over the question of increased armaments had been maturing for months before the submarine controversy erupted. For example, Theodore Roosevelt and his editorial organ, the *Outlook,* assumed leadership of the preparedness movement in November and December, 1914,[10] while in the latter month Senator Lodge's son-in-law, Representative Augustus P. Gardner, tried vainly to force a Congressional investigation of the military and naval establishments. Moreover, on December 1, 150 public leaders gathered in New York City and organized the National Security League, frankly dedicated to the task of preparing the United States for a possible war with Germany. Meanwhile, the two stalwart champions of the services, the Navy League and the Army League, had redoubled their propaganda.

This early preparedness agitation, however, fell on deaf ears in the administration and country and aroused the bitter antagonism of the progressive and peace groups. In October, 1914, the President laughingly called the preparedness talk "good mental exercise," and in his Annual Message of December 8 he reaffirmed the traditional position. "We shall not alter our attitude . . .," he declared, "because some amongst us are nervous and excited." [11] Secretary Daniels announced happily that the navy was in "fine shape," even though the General Board had advised differently.[12] Every effort by the preparedness

[10] *Outlook,* CVIII (Nov. 25, Dec. 9, 16, 30, 1914), 663–666, 813–814, 865–866, 986–988.

[11] Ray S. Baker and William E. Dodd (eds.), *The Public Papers of Woodrow Wilson* (6 vols., New York, 1925–27), *The New Democracy,* I, 223–227.

[12] The navy had suffered a severe decline in efficiency as a result of the concentration of the Atlantic fleet in Mexican waters since February 10, 1913. Target practice had been so neglected that a large proportion of the men of the fleet had never heard a ship's guns fired. The crews of the *Texas* and the *New York,* the largest and most powerful of the battleships, had never fired a gun.

advocates met not only with strong administration opposition in Congress but also with intimations by Wilson that he suspected some lobby was stirring up an artificial alarm. Thus, when the President and his defense secretaries conferred with Democratic leaders in January, 1915, over the army and navy appropriations for 1915, opinion was unanimous that, in view of the decrease in federal revenues, the military budgets would have to be cut instead of increased.

In reply, the preparedness spokesmen increased the tempo and broadened the scope of their activities and propaganda during the early months of 1915. A stream of articles and books, depicting the nation's military weakness and forecasting the invasion of American territory by hostile forces, began to pour forth. Then, after the *Lusitania* disaster, this stream became a mighty flood. Motion-picture producers, too, entered the struggle, with *The Battle Cry of Peace* and *The Fall of a Nation,* both of which portrayed invasions of the United States by soldiers with a goose step and German-style mustaches. Not in many years had the American people been subjected to such pressure by an organized minority.[13]

As the conviction grew after the *Lusitania* incident that the United States had a vital interest in the conduct of the belligerents and the outcome of the war, preparedness became a virtual crusade. Defense societies were swamped with applications for membership. When the Navy League asked for $25,000 for a campaign to compel Congress to appropriate half a billion dollars for "an adequate navy," the sum was oversubscribed in twenty-five minutes.[14] In a stirring manifesto issued two days after the sinking of the *Lusitania,* the National Security League appealed to the American people to examine their defenses and compel Congress to strengthen them, while the Navy League on May 11 demanded that Congress be called into special session and vote $500 million for naval expansion. In mid-June the National Security League convoked a great preparedness assemblage

---

Moreover, because of their prolonged stay in the tropics and their long absence from home, the men were in bad spirits. A. F. Nicholson, senior member of the General Board, to Secretary of the Navy, Sept. 9, 1914, Wilson Papers.

[13] Needless to say, none of this literature was Allied propaganda. It was, instead, thoroughly indigenous. For the literature of preparedness, see the Essay on Sources, "The Preparedness and Peace Movements, 1914–17—The Literature of Preparedness."

[14] At a meeting of 100 of New York City's wealthiest men, on June 10, 1915. New York *World,* June 11, 1915.

in New York City, which was attended by public leaders from twenty-five states. By September, twenty-two governors had joined the organization.

It was evident, therefore, that a powerful movement had been set on foot that could not long be ignored by the political leaders. Although the various defense societies had made an honest effort to be non-partisan, practically all their chief spokesmen were Republicans associated with the great financial and industrial interests. As many observers pointed out, the danger seemed grave indeed that the Republicans would capture the preparedness movement and succeed in identifying the Democratic party with national weakness.

As he was ever mindful of the desirability of keeping the Democratic party in power, the significance of the preparedness agitation could not have been lost upon the President. It would, however, probably be more accurate to say that the submarine crisis and the exasperatingly futile *Lusitania* negotiations were the chief reasons why Wilson decided to reverse his position on the armaments question. In any event, he became a convert to preparedness reluctantly and only after much soul searching. On July 21, 1915, he asked Secretaries Garrison and Daniels to investigate and recommend programs adequate to satisfy the needs of security. Shortly afterward, he advised Congressional leaders that the administration would soon reverse its position.

As they had long been at work on comprehensive plans, the General Board of the Navy and the Army War College speedily answered the President's request of July 21. Garrison and Daniels evidently exercised little restraint, but rather gave their subordinates a free hand in constructing what they thought were ideal programs. The General Board submitted a long-range program, aimed at achieving naval equality with the British by 1925. Approved by the President on October 15, this plan envisaged the construction, during the first five years, of ten battleships, six battle cruisers, ten cruisers, fifty destroyers, one hundred submarines, and lesser craft, at a cost of $500 million. Even the Navy League had not asked for more. Although the army plan was a compromise between what the War College wanted and what Garrison thought it could get, in certain respects it was even more astonishing than the General Board's recommendations. The army plan proposed not only substantial increases in the Regular Army, which everyone expected, but also virtually to scrap the National Guard as the first line of defense and to substitute instead a national reserve force, the Continental Army, of 400,000 men.[15]

Although the administration's defense program had been described piecemeal by the newspapers during October, it was not until November 4, 1915, that the President presented it formally to the country. The occasion was an address before the Manhattan Club in New York City, in which he explained the program and urged its adoption.[16] The Navy League and other defense organizations rallied at once to the President's side; but it was as yet impossible to ascertain Congressional or popular opinion. From the violent protests and criticisms of the antipreparedness forces, however, it was evident that one of the hardest battles of the decade impended.

To understand the intensity and significance of the struggle that followed, it is necessary first to appreciate the character of the progressive-pacifistic movement of these years. The humanitarian spirit that had given momentum to the progressive movement stemmed from definite beliefs about America and her place in the family of nations. To begin with, progressivism concentrated largely on economic and social justice at home. This emphasis grew into such an obsession that progressivism became tantamount to provincialism. To be sure, a small Eastern minority, led by Roosevelt, were internationally minded; but to the large majority of progressives, particularly in the South and Middle West, America's unique mission was to purify and offer herself to decadent Europe, an example of democracy triumphant over social and economic injustice. This self-purification involved also an end to America's experiment in imperialism and a weakening of American naval power. The second major progressive assumption concerned the place of war in modern society. Wars were mainly economic in causation and necessarily evil because bankers with money to lend, munition-makers with sordid profits to earn, and industrialists with markets to win were the chief promoters and beneficiaries of war.

It followed from these two assumptions that the path of progressive righteousness led straight to disarmament, an international system based upon compulsory arbitration, and an unequivocal repudiation of war. To these progressives, therefore, the call of duty was unmistakably clear in the summer and fall of 1915. The forces against which they had been battling at home since 1898—the big navy imperialists,

[15] There is a comprehensive analysis of the administration's defense program in *The New York Times,* Nov. 6, 1915.
[16] *The Public Papers, New Democracy,* I, 384–392.

the armor-plate monopoly, the big industrialists, and the bankers—
were arrayed solidly in support of a great military effort. This fact
alone would have sufficed to arouse the hostility of progressives, but
more important was their repudiation of the principle of using power

Robert Carter in the New York *Evening Sun*

Preparedness: Wilson reverses himself in midstream

as an instrument of diplomacy. To them preparedness signified turning
America into an armed camp, the glorification of force, and, worst of
all, an end to the reform movement at home. Little wonder it was
that in the ensuing battle almost every leader of the American progressive movement was found in the antipreparedness ranks.

The antipreparedness forces had not been entirely inactive before the summer of 1915. At the same time the National Security League was organized, a group of Eastern peace leaders, including Oswald Garrison Villard, George Foster Peabody, Jane Addams, Lillian D. Wald, and Rev. Charles E. Jefferson of New York City, formed the League to Limit Armament to offset the agitation for preparation.[17] A few weeks later the Woman's Peace party was organized by Jane Addams and Carrie Chapman Catt to mobilize feminine sentiment. These and other peace groups kept up a steady reply to the preparedness propaganda.[18]

So long as the administration withstood the demand for increased armaments the peace forces felt reasonably secure. The President's desertion of the peace cause in the summer of 1915, however, caused the first real crisis in the progressive movement since 1912. Whether to follow Wilson and attempt to moderate his program, or to oppose him in what promised to be a doubtful battle—these were the difficult alternatives. For most progressives, however, there was only one answer: fight the President. For, as one pacifist warned, he was "sowing the seeds of militarism, raising up a military and naval caste." [19] Thus Wilson's preparedness appeal of November 4 was met by a thundering opposition. Bryan, who had already begun his peace campaign, now undertook a nation-wide appeal to persuade the people that Wilson was being duped by his enemies, the great business interests. Senator La Follette, too, entered the fight, charging that profiteers were the real promoters of preparedness.[20] And from every obscure corner of the country came angry demands, protests, pleas, and appeals. And even more meaningful to the politicians was the almost unanimous opposition of labor and farm organizations to the preparedness program.[21]

[17] "Organization Meeting of the American League to Limit Armament . . . December 18, 1914"; "Report of the Secretary . . . April 7, 1915," in the Papers of Oswald Garrison Villard, in Houghton Library, Harvard University.

[18] For the literature of the peace and antipreparedness movements see Essay on Sources, "The Preparedness and Peace Movements, 1914–17—General Studies; The Peace and Antipreparedness Crusades."

[19] O. G. Villard to Wilson, Oct. 30, 1915, Wilson Papers.

[20] R. M. La Follette, "Patriots," *La Follette's Magazine,* VII (Nov., 1915), 1.

[21] For example, see H. Q. Alexander, president of the National Farmers' Union, to Claude Kitchin, Nov. 3, 24, 1915, the Papers of Claude Kitchin, in the Library of the University of North Carolina; resolutions adopted by the North Carolina Farmers' Union, Nov. 18, 1915, *The New York Times,* Nov. 19, 1915; *American Socialist,* Dec. 4, 1915; Ohio Valley Trades and Labor As-

Antipreparedness sentiment at once focused upon the members of Congress, for the outcome of the controversy depended upon the success or failure of Bryan and his friends in wresting control of the legislative branch from the President. Appalled by Wilson's new departure, a group of from thirty to fifty Democratic radicals, most of them Southerners and Westerners, took counsel with one another during the summer and fall of 1915. The leaders of the group were Claude Kitchin, the new House majority leader [22] and farmer-lawyer from Scotland County, North Carolina, and Warren Worth Bailey, single taxer and publisher of the Johnstown, Pennsylvania, *Democrat*. With the tacit co-operation of the chairman of the House Military Affairs Committee, James Hay of Virginia, the antipreparedness leaders were able to pack and control that key body.[23]

When Congress assembled in December, 1915, Wilson made patriotism, preparedness, and a new shipping bill the keynotes of his Annual Message.[24] Having failed to budge Majority Leader Kitchin from his stubborn opposition, the President called the House and Senate minority leaders, James R. Mann of Illinois and Jacob H. Gallinger of New Hampshire, to the White House and asked for the opposition's aid. After beginning this energetic campaign, however, Wilson was drawn away from the developing controversy for several weeks by his marriage on December 18, 1915, to Mrs. Edith Bolling Galt of Washington. The consequence of his failure to press his measures at this time was that he soon lost control of the House of Representatives. Democratic members were apathetic, if not openly opposed, to the defense program.

Preparedness advocates were most alarmed, however, by the situation in the Military Affairs Committee. The leaders of this body had never got on well with Secretary Garrison, whom they thought dictatorial and responsive only to the military point of view. Now the

---

sembly to Wilson, Dec. 3, 1915, Wilson Papers; action of the United Mine Workers of America, Jan. 18, 1916, *The New York Times*, Jan. 19, 1916; Isaac R. Sherwood to W. W. Bailey, Nov. 5, 12, 1915, the Papers of Warren Worth Bailey, in the Library of Princeton University.

[22] Oscar W. Underwood, House majority leader from 1911 to 1915, was elected to the Senate in the latter year.

[23] The membership and activities of the antipreparedness radicals are fully revealed in the voluminous correspondence in the Kitchin and Bailey Papers and the Papers of William Jennings Bryan, in the Library of Congress, August through November, 1915.

[24] *The Public Papers, The New Democracy*, I, 406–428.

Committee were at positive loggerheads with Garrison over the most important feature of the administration's army plan, the Continental Army. The Army War College had emphatically asserted that because of constitutional limitations on federal control of the state forces, the National Guard could never be legally subjected to the control of the President and War Department.[25] Garrison reiterated this argument before the Committee, adding that any army plan that made the National Guard the core of the reserve force was not only futile but also dangerous, because it could provide no effective reserve force at all. The Committee members, however, were adamantly opposed to the idea of a national reserve force. The powerful National Guard lobby in Washington was active during the fight, to be sure, but its opposition to the Continental Army proposal was not the only reason for the Committee's opposition. A large, effective reserve army, under the absolute control of the War Department, seemed to the rural Democrats on the Committee the very symbol of uncontrolled militarism. Southerners, moreover, feared that a President hostile to their racial system might enlist Negroes in the volunteer reserve force. Chairman James Hay came forward, instead, with a plan to "federalize" the militia, that is, to give the War Department control over the enlistment, equipment, and training of the National Guard. The state forces, moreover, would be paid by the federal government. In spite of everything administration leaders could do, the Committee members insisted upon having their way.

This, therefore, was the stalemate that existed during the month following the President's second marriage. To the country at large he seemed helpless in face of the deadlock and, for the first time in his political career, ineffective. As friendly critics pointed out, he had abandoned his leadership of Congress at a critical juncture and had

---

[25] E.g., H. L. Scott to Charles M. de Bremond, Dec. 27, 1915, the Papers of Hugh L. Scott, in the Library of Congress; L. M. Garrison to Wilson, Jan. 12, 1916, Wilson Papers.

The Army War College and Garrison based their arguments in behalf of the Continental Army plan entirely on this assertion. The Committee members, on the other hand, declared that of course Congress had ample power to bring the state forces under federal control. In spite of the obvious necessity of clearing up this legal point, it was not until after the Continental Army plan had been abandoned and Secretary Garrison had resigned that Wilson sought to find an answer to this question. On February 25, 1916, Attorney General Thomas W. Gregory submitted a long memorandum, dated February 24, 1916, to the President. Gregory supported the Committee's assertion that the authority of Congress over the militia was practically unlimited.

left the business of creating opinion to a public bewildered by a multitude of discordant elements. "I cannot impress upon you too forcibly the importance of an appeal to the country at this time on the question of preparedness," Tumulty advised. ". . . Our all is staked upon a successful issue in this matter." [26] Stung by his critics and by Tumulty's warning, after returning from his honeymoon Wilson decided to carry the fight to the people. Opposition to preparedness was strongest in the rural areas of the South and Middle West; since Southern congressmen might support the administration out of party loyalty, Wilson decided to address his appeal to the East and Middle West.

Opening his tour in New York City on January 27, 1916, the President campaigned westward—through Pittsburgh, Cleveland, Chicago, Milwaukee, Des Moines, Kansas City, Topeka, and St. Louis. He explained and defended the Continental Army plan, and in a famous slip at St. Louis on February 3 he declared the United States should have "incomparably the greatest navy in the world." [27] He affirmed the necessity of defending the Western Hemisphere against hostile attack; he declared he could not defend the national honor without military power; he depicted the explosive and unpredictable European situation. Preparedness, he declared, was not a partisan cause, but a national necessity.[28]

Everywhere Wilson went he was welcomed by friendly editors and cheering throngs, a fact that deluded him into thinking he had changed the Midwestern mind. And he came back to Washington on February 4 and waited for the ground swell he thought would soon overwhelm Congressional opposition. It soon became evident, however, that the masses of farmers and workers in the Midwest were unconverted.[29]

[26] Tumulty to Wilson, Jan. 17, 1916, Wilson Papers.

[27] In the official printed version Wilson changed this phrase to read "incomparably the most adequate navy in the world." For criticisms of the St. Louis address, see New York *Journal of Commerce,* Feb. 4, 1916; Springfield *Republican,* Feb. 5, 1916; *The Nation,* CII (Feb. 10, 1916), 153.

[28] Wilson's addresses are printed in *The Public Papers, New Democracy,* II, 1–121.

[29] This, at least, was the opinion of competent observers. See Governor Arthur Capper, of Kansas, to O. G. Villard, Feb. 3, 1916, Villard Papers; H. E. Farnham to W. W. Bailey, Feb. 5, 1916, Bailey Papers; S. H. Smith to Bailey, Feb. 8, 1916, *ibid.*

As preparedness enthusiasm throughout the country was largely concentrated in the cities and towns, there was actually a large body of favorable opinion in the Middle West before Wilson began his tour. There can be no doubt that his speeches, which were delivered in the large cities of the region,

More important, it was obvious the President had failed to convince many leaders of opinion that the United States confronted any grave danger from abroad.

"I see no real change in the attitude of the Members since the President's Western tour," Claude Kitchin observed five days after Wilson returned to the capital.[30] Events soon proved the accuracy of Kitchin's surmise. By now the deadlock between Garrison and the House Military Affairs Committee was apparently hopeless, for Garrison had taken such advanced ground he could never compromise, while the Democratic congressmen were more than ever determined to scrap the Continental Army plan and to strengthen the National Guard. Convinced that the Committee's alternative was vicious, because it would prevent enactment of effective legislation, Garrison intimated he would resign if the President surrendered.

Even before he left on his Western tour, Wilson had given signs of weakening. On February 5, the day after his return, Chairman Hay advised him that the Democrats would never accept the Continental Army scheme; three days later he added that Garrison and the military spokesmen had thoroughly antagonized the Committee. In order to get any army bill at all, the President had to give in, abandon the Continental Army, and accept "federalization" of the National Guard. As he had no other choice, he surrendered to the Committee and allowed Garrison to resign on February 10. Immediately the tension between the Committee and the executive department vanished. Garrison left hurriedly for home, deeply aggrieved but still too loyal to his chief to vent his feelings.[31]

The appointment of Garrison's successor was another move calculated to heal the breach between the President and the Military Affairs Committee. He was Newton D. Baker, Mayor of Cleveland, who, until

stimulated middle- and upper-class support for preparedness. But it seems likely that Wilson failed to change rural antipreparedness sentiment. For one thing, the opposition of the rural members in Congress to the defense program did not diminish. For another, rural opposition, as revealed in farm journals and letters to congressmen, did not noticeably subside after Wilson's tour.

[30] Kitchin to Bryan, Feb. 9, 1916, Kitchin Papers; also W. W. Bailey to W. E. Ewer, Feb. 11, 1916, Bailey Papers.

[31] Only once in later years did Garrison say what he thought of Wilson. "I once heard a description which as nearly fits the case of President Wilson as any other I know," he wrote in 1929. "In describing someone it was said, 'He was a man of high ideals but no principles.'" Garrison to W. E. Brooks, Feb. 24, 1929, the Papers of William E. Brooks, in the Library of Congress.

within a month of his appointment on March 7, was outspokenly opposed to preparedness. Wilson had followed Baker's rise to a position of leadership among young, progressive Democrats with admiration and in 1913 had twice offered him the Secretaryship of the Interior. Baker came as Secretary of War because Wilson convinced him it was his duty to come, and the President thereafter had no more loyal or congenial friend in the Cabinet.

After the administration's acceptance of the Hay plan and Garrison's withdrawal, the Democratic leaders made steady progress in Congress. On March 23, 1916, the House, 402 to 2, adopted the Committee bill, which increased substantially the Regular Army and brought the National Guard under the control of the War Department. It was true, however, as Kitchin claimed, that the victory belonged to the antipreparedness group. They had waged what seemed in the beginning a hopeless battle against the combined force of the administration, the metropolitan press, and a part of the Republican minority. They had forced the President to abandon the heart of his military program, the Continental Army, and to sacrifice a Secretary of War who had won the affection of the military leaders and a reputation for courage and loyalty to principle. As Kitchin further pointed out, however, there still remained the danger that the Garrison plan would triumph in the Senate, where the Military Affairs Committee was dominated by large-army men.

The month following the adoption by the House of the Hay army bill was a time of severe crisis in German-American relations. Following the torpedoing of the French packet, *Sussex,* in the English Channel on March 24, the President announced that if the Germans did not thereafter adhere to the rules of cruiser warfare in their submarine operations the United States would sever diplomatic relations with the Imperial government. The preparedness leaders in the Senate, whose spokesman was George E. Chamberlain, chairman of the Military Affairs Committee, used the *Sussex* crisis to advance their cause. On April 18, the same day Wilson threatened to break relations with the German government, the Senate adopted a bill that embodied virtually the War College-Garrison program. The House bill had increased the Regular Army from 100,000 to 140,000 officers and men. In contrast, the Senate measure increased the regulars to 250,000, "federalized" the National Guard, provided $15 million for the construction of nitrate plants, and, most important, established a national volunteer reserve force—the Continental Army—of 261,000 men.

Thus the issue between the moderates and the preparedness advocates was frankly raised in the ensuing struggle between the two houses for control of the major aspects of the military bill. In this struggle Wilson displayed all his powers of leadership and mediation. He quickly spotted weaknesses in the Hay bill to "federalize" the National Guard and obtained their correction. He threw his support behind Secretary Baker's suggestion for the creation of a Council of National Defense. And in the struggle between the House and Senate he offered a compromise, in which the House's demand for a smaller standing army and the Senate's plan for a larger number of regiments would be reconciled. When the conferees adjourned without agreement on May 5, Wilson entered the controversy again, pleading with the House members to meet the Senate halfway.

Under steady presidential pressure the legislative deadlock was finally broken, and on May 13 the conferees agreed on a bill embodying mutual concessions. The measure [32] more than doubled the Regular Army, increasing it from an authorized peacetime strength of 5,029 officers and 100,000 men to 11,327 officers and 208,338 men. The Garrison plan for a large national reserve force was abandoned, but the National Guard was thoroughly integrated into the federal defense structure and increased to an authorized strength of 17,000 officers and 440,000 men within five years. In addition, the War Department was allowed to establish a number of volunteer summer training camps, patterned after the highly successful experimental camp at Plattsburg, New York. Finally, the War Department was authorized to construct and operate a nitrate plant, to cost not more than $20 million. Later legislation provided for a Council of National Defense.

Because the army bill constructed the first line of the nation's reserve upon the cornerstone of the National Guard, the extreme preparedness advocates denounced it as "a menace to public safety in that it purports to provide a military force of value" and does not.[33] With customary exaggeration, Roosevelt called it "one of the most iniquitous bits of legislation ever placed on the statute books," and the National

[32] Approved by the Senate on May 17 and by the House on May 20, 1916.
[33] Leonard Wood, "Memorandum with respect to legislation affecting the Militia," sent to E. M. House, Apr. 17, 1916, Wilson Papers.

Security League urged the President to veto the measure.[34] On the other hand, the progressive, antipreparedness leaders congratulated themselves that the country had been saved from the worst consequences of the preparedness hysteria and that the traditional American defensive structure had been preserved. As Warren Worth Bailey's newspaper claimed, they had forced the administration to accept "reasonable" preparedness.[35]

Meanwhile, the House and Senate Naval Affairs committees had been biding their time until the army issue was settled. Actually, there had been little controversy over naval expansion. The die-hard pacifists in the House in principle opposed increased naval appropriations; but they concentrated their energies on the army bill, which seemed to them more important. On May 18 the House Committee presented a bill that ignored the administration's request for approval of the five-year building program but provided more tonnage than Secretary Daniels had requested for the first year: five battle cruisers, four cruisers, ten destroyers, twenty submarines, and smaller vessels. The scrapping of the five-year program, the provision for battle cruisers instead of dreadnoughts, and the addition of an amendment authorizing the President to convene a naval disarmament conference at the end of the war all represented substantial achievements by the antipreparedness group. During the final debate in the House, on June 2, a Republican "big navy" amendment was narrowly defeated, 189 to 183, although the Democrats agreed to increase the number of submarines to fifty and almost to double the appropriations for the naval air force, from $2 million to $3½ million. The House on May 31 had approved a Senate bill to establish a government armor-plate factory.[36]

[34] Roosevelt to A. C. Wiprud, Dec. 21, 1916, Roosevelt Papers; Robert Bacon, president, National Security League, to Wilson, May 26, 1916, Wilson Papers. The military leaders, of course, regarded the bill as "a gold brick." For a detailed criticism by a member of the Army War College, see W. H. Johnston to H. L. Scott, May 26, 1916, Scott Papers.

[35] Johnstown *Democrat,* May 25, 1916.

[36] The passage of this bill was a personal triumph for old Senator "Pitchfork" Ben Tillman of South Carolina, who had been at war with the armor-plate manufacturers since the Spanish-American War. When Tillman brought his bill out in December, 1915, the manufacturers offered to reduce their prices substantially if the South Carolinian would abandon his measure. Tillman replied that they were "robbers." Then the manufacturers threatened to increase prices $200 a ton if the measure passed. This threat, however, backfired by arousing the entire country and expediting passage of the bill. See

The House navy bill, however, was wrecked by the complete triumph of the "big navy" forces in the Senate and by the battle of Jutland, which naval experts said demonstrated the superiority of the dreadnought over the faster and more lightly armored battle cruiser. Thus the Senate measure, passed on July 21, provided for the completion of the administration's program within three years, not five, and for the construction during the first year of four battleships, four battle cruisers, four cruisers, twenty destroyers, thirty submarines, and a number of lesser craft.

Up to this point the President had not interfered directly in the course of the legislation; now, however, he turned the full force of his personal and political pressure on the House leaders, to obtain acceptance of the astonishing Senate bill. The reasons for his sudden and decisive intervention are not hard to find. There was, first of all, the possibility of a war between Germany and the United States should the former triumph in Europe. In the second place, fear that Japan would emerge from the war expansionist and aggressive was another major cause for the Senate's action and the President's vigorous support of it.[37] But a more immediate cause was the fact that relations between Britain and the United States were becoming exceedingly strained at this time. Although the naval building program could have no immediate effect on foreign policy, Wilson was anxious to hasten the day when the American navy was larger than Britain's. "Let us build a navy bigger than hers and do what we please," he told Colonel House.

After considerable wrangling, the conferees voted on August 7 to disagree and refer the bills to their respective houses. The first break in the House ranks came the following day, when Chairman Lemuel P. Padgett of the House Committee conferred with Wilson and agreed to support the Senate bill. Then, on August 15, the House capitulated and accepted the important provisions of the Senate measure without altering a sentence. The antipreparedness leaders were heartsick. "The United States today becomes the most militaristic naval nation on earth," Kitchin shouted. "The forces on the other side are too great," Bailey lamented.[38]

Francis B. Simkins, *Pitchfork Ben Tillman* (Baton Rouge, La., 1944), pp. 512–513.

[37] *The New York Times,* July 18, 19, 1916. Outten J. Clinard, *Japan's Influence on American Naval Power, 1897–1917* (Berkeley, Calif., 1947), pp. 145–172, offers convincing evidence to support this statement.

[38] *The New York Times,* Aug. 16, 1916; W. W. Bailey to C. F. Dole, Aug. 8, 1916, Bailey Papers.

In the meantime, the administration also obtained the adoption of a much revised shipping bill as part of the general preparedness legislation. As early as May 24, 1915, the President had revived the defunct ship purchase bill, and all during the following summer McAdoo urged the proposal in administration circles and before the country. In his speeches after the *Lusitania* and *Arabic* crises, however, McAdoo placed increasing emphasis upon the need for a strong merchant marine as an indispensable adjunct to the navy. He began, moreover, to think in terms of comprehensive federal regulation of maritime rates and services, rather than merely of the purchase and operation of ships.[39]

By late October, 1915, McAdoo had drafted a new shipping bill, which furnished the basis for administration discussions during the following weeks. Then, on January 31, 1916, Chairman Alexander of the Merchant Marine Committee introduced the administration's measure in the House. Carefully phrased to meet the objections of the Democratic senators who had helped defeat the ship purchase bill a year before, the Alexander bill authorized the appointment of a United States Shipping Board, which might spend up to $50 million in the construction or purchase of merchant ships suitable for use as naval auxiliaries. The Board was empowered to operate shipping lines but might also lease or charter its vessels to private corporations. Finally, the agency was endowed with full power to regulate the rates and services of all vessels engaged in the interstate, coastwise, and foreign trade of the United States.

The Merchant Marine Association inveighed against this "socialistic scheme"; the shipping companies sent experts to testify against it before the House Committee; yet administration leaders made rapid headway in pushing the bill. Early in May, 1916, the Committee approved the Alexander bill, slightly revised,[40] and the House adopted it on May 20. There was no longer any real opposition to the proposal among Senate Democrats, only a general apathy and still a lingering

[39] See e.g., McAdoo's speech before the businessmen and commercial organizations of Indianapolis, Oct. 13, 1915, mimeographed copy in Wilson Papers; also speeches at St. Louis, Oct. 14, and Kansas City, Oct. 15, *The New York Times,* Oct. 15, 16, 1915.

[40] The Committee's major change stipulated that the shipping lines owned and operated by the Shipping Board should go out of business five years after the end of the European war and that all the Board's property, except vessels designed primarily as naval auxiliaries, should be sold.

fear that purchase of German vessels would involve the country in a serious dispute with the British government. When, in mid-July, the Senate Democrats finally consented to consider the measure, they amended it to prevent the Shipping Board from purchasing any ships under belligerent registry. As the presidential campaign was by now getting into full swing, debate in the Senate was desultory, with the Republican stalwarts, Warren G. Harding of Ohio and Jacob H. Gallinger of New Hampshire, leading the opposition. By a strict party vote the bill was adopted on August 18, 1916.

Although McAdoo complained that the shipping bill was "tremendously emasculated," the truth was the act Wilson signed on September 7 had been immensely strengthened by Congress. In the place of regulation of ocean rates and services by the overburdened Interstate Commerce Commission, which McAdoo's draft had contemplated, the House Committee had substituted thoroughgoing regulation by a powerful independent commission. Instead of McAdoo's ill-advised plan to purchase the German vessels, the Senate had insisted on a frank statutory avowal that the United States would be guilty of no such unneutral conduct. Thus what had begun in 1914 as a hastily conceived emergency measure had metamorphosed into one of the most important pieces of legislation of the Wilson era, for historians date the birth of the modern American merchant marine from the passage of this Shipping Act of 1916.

The great defense appropriations of 1916 entailed for that day enormous outlays and compelled Congress in an election year either to impose new taxes or to approve a bond issue. In short, the Democrats had to find large new revenues; and in their search for them they provoked a new discussion and gave a powerful impetus to the movement then being agitated for a progressive tax policy. In light of federal fiscal policy since 1916, one is tempted to believe the Revenue Act of that year marked another milestone in the progress toward a more democratic America: a dividing point between the old tax policy and the new.

The federal tax structure in 1914 was so constructed as to throw the major share of the tax burden on the lower and middle classes. Almost $300 million of the government's total revenues of $734,673,167, exclusive of postal receipts, came from customs receipts, which were paid by the mass of consumers. Another $300 million were paid by the rank and file in the form of taxes on tobacco, liquor, wine, and beer.

Individuals and corporations paid $71 million in income taxes, while the balance was derived from surplus postal receipts, the sale of public lands, and miscellaneous sources. The wealthy, obviously, enjoyed relative immunity from taxation.

If conservatives had had their way, the entire cost of the new armaments would have been met by a bond issue and by increased consumption taxes. Rejecting the suggestion of a bond issue, McAdoo presented in November, 1915, a comprehensive tax plan that threw the burden of paying for preparedness as much on the lower and middle classes as on the rich.[41] When Congress on December 17 extended the emergency war tax act of 1914 for another year, it seemed the administration still had firm control of fiscal policy.

McAdoo's proposal to place the heaviest burden of increased taxation on the lower and middle classes, however, aroused bitter comment and opposition from radicals and progressives, as well as from Democratic politicians with uneasy eyes on the coming campaign.[42] The Central Labor Union of Seattle, for example, suggested that since the capitalists sought to provoke a war to increase their own profits, Congress should instruct the War Department to seize all bank deposits and all security holdings worth more than $5,000.[43] More significant was the organization by a group of Eastern progressives, including John Dewey, Frederick C. Howe, and George L. Record, of the Association for an Equitable Federal Income Tax. Their executive secretary, Benjamin Marsh, undertook a speaking campaign in the Middle

[41] Specifically, McAdoo proposed (1) to retain the emergency war taxes voted in the autumn of 1914, which were mainly stamp and excise taxes; (2) to retain the duty on sugar, instead of allowing it to enter free in 1916, as the Underwood Act provided; (3) to reduce the income tax exemption from $4,000 to $3,000 for married persons and from $3,000 to $2,000 for single persons; (4) to begin application of the surtax on incomes at $10,000 or $15,000, instead of at $20,000; (5) to double the normal income tax of 1 per cent, but not to increase the surtax; and (6) to levy new taxes on gasoline, crude and refined oil, and automobile horsepower. McAdoo to Wilson, Nov. 23, 1915, Wilson Papers; *The New York Times*, Nov. 26, 1915.

[42] See, e.g., W. J. Bryan, "The President's Message Analyzed," *The Commoner*, Dec., 1915; "Who Will Pay?" *Harper's Weekly*, LXI (Dec. 18, 1915), 577; Edwin O. Wood, member of the Democratic National Committee for Michigan, to Tumulty, Dec. 1, 1915, Wilson Papers; R. B. Glenn to C. Kitchin, Dec. 30, 1915, Kitchin Papers.

[43] Resolution adopted c. Jan. 21, 1916, Wilson Papers. Local 5, Amalgamated Sheet Metal Workers' Alliance, Youngstown, Ohio, and Local 24, International Association of Machinists, Topeka, Kansas, adopted identical resolutions on January 13 and February 27, 1916.

West in January, 1916, and reported strong popular sentiment for increasing the maximum surtax to 20 or 30 per cent. Finally, on February 1 Representative Warren Worth Bailey came forward with a plan to meet the entire cost of preparedness by raising the maximum surtax to 50 per cent. "If the forces of big business are to plunge this country into a saturnalia of extravagance for war purposes in a time of peace," he declared on introducing his bill, "it is my notion that the forces of big business should put up the money." [44]

This ground swell had immediate impact on the Southern and Western radicals who controlled the House Ways and Means Committee and who agreed among themselves to force through a tax bill acceptable to the labor and farm spokesmen. In late January and early February of 1916, Chairman Kitchin was suddenly deluged with letters from Democratic congressmen, most of them representing rural or labor constituencies, warning they would not support the administration's tax program, even if a Democratic caucus thus ordered. Moreover, all demanded that the money for preparedness be raised by greatly increasing taxes on large incomes and by imposing new taxes on inheritances and the profits of munitions manufacturers. "The people of the United States are now paying annually $250,000,000 for the national defense," a Nebraskan wrote. "I think this is sufficient but if it is not let the surplus wealth that is claiming additional protection pay for it." [45] Kitchin of course replied that he agreed completely. To Bryan he confided that he was "persuaded to think that when the New York people are thoroughly convinced that the income tax will have to pay for the increase in the army and navy, . . . preparedness will not be so popular with them as it now is." [46]

It was not publicly apparent until July, 1916, but control of the Ways and Means Committee had been wrested from the administration for the first time since March 4, 1913. The radicals made one

[44] Johnstown *Democrat*, Feb. 2, 1916; also *ibid.*, Feb. 15, 1916, and *The Public*, XIX (Mar. 3, 1916), 194–195, for significant comment.

[45] Dan V. Stephens to Kitchin, Jan. 29, 1916, Kitchin Papers. See also the following letters to Kitchin, all in *ibid.*: R. L. Doughton, Jan. 25, 1916; Oscar Callaway, Jan. 26, 1916; Carl C. Van Dyke, Clyde H. Tavenner, Isaac R. Sherwood, W. L. Hensley, William Gordon, W. W. Bailey, Jan. 27, 1916; T. J. Steele, Jan. 28, 1916; W. W. Hastings, Jim McClintic, James H. Mays, James S. Davenport, William A. Ayres, Jan. 29, 1916; Carl Hayden, Jouett Shouse, William H. Murray, Jan. 31, 1916; Scott Ferris, D. S. Church, J. R. Connelly, Feb. 1, 1916.

[46] Kitchin to Bryan, Jan. 31, 1916, *ibid.*

concession, by voting to retain the one-cent duty on sugar. But the bill that the Committee presented to the House on July 1, 1916, was a far cry from McAdoo's and Wilson's proposals. It doubled the normal income tax, from 1 to 2 per cent, without lowering exemptions; raised the surtax on incomes over $40,000 to a maximum of 10 per cent, instead of the maximum of 6 per cent under the law of 1913; imposed a federal estate tax ranging from 1 to 5 per cent on estates over $50,000; levied a tax of from 1 to 8 per cent on the gross receipts of munitions manufacturers making a net profit of 10 per cent and over, and repealed the hated stamp tax sections of the war emergency tax law of 1914.[47] In all, Kitchin asserted, the bill would produce some $250 million in new revenues, enough to pay for the military and naval increases that Congress contemplated. Amid angry charges in the House that the South and West had combined in a gigantic raid on Northern wealth,[48] the House adopted the revenue bill on July 10.

Under the spur of progressives like George W. Norris and Robert M. La Follette, the Senate Finance Committee went even further than the House had gone in "soaking the rich," and the Senate bill finally adopted on September 6 and agreed to by the House represented a frank assessment against privileged wealth. In addition to the House provision which doubled the normal income tax, the Senate bill increased the surtax on incomes over $20,000 to a maximum of 13 per cent, which, with the normal tax of 2 per cent, set the maximum income tax at 15 per cent; levied a new tax on corporation capital, surplus, and undivided profits; increased the estate tax to a maximum of 10 per cent, and increased to 12½ per cent the tax on gross receipts of munitions industries.

What the passage of the revenue bill of 1916 signified was clear to both the friends and the enemies of preparedness, to both the progressives and the spokesmen for great property. Heretofore, the advocates of a progressive tax policy—the single taxers, the Socialists, and the labor and agrarian progressives—had been a minority, scourged and ridiculed by conservatives as purveyors of class prejudice and despoilers of the rich. Now for the first time in the saddle, these progressives used

[47] For this and the following analysis of the Senate amendments I am indebted to Sidney Ratner, *American Taxation* (New York, 1942), pp. 345–361.

[48] Martin Madden, Illinois Republican, for example, pointed out that four states—New York, Pennsylvania, Massachusetts, and Illinois—had paid $85 million in individual and corporation income taxes in 1915, while twelve Southern states combined had paid only $5,389,670.

the necessity for vastly increased revenues as the occasion for putting their advanced tax theories into effect. The new income and inheritance taxes constituted, for that day, a powerful equalitarian attack on great property, unrivaled even by Lloyd George's "Tax on Wealth" of 1909.

Nor did the progressives fail to derive satisfaction from the way in which they had seemingly turned the tables on the preparedness-big business element. "What has become of the dollar patriots?" Bailey taunted. "Where are the members of the Preparedness league and the Navy league? In the counting room hollering loud and long because they find that incomes must bear a portion of the burden they had hoped to unload upon the farmer and the steel worker." [49] This was the progressives' economic interpretation of the movement to make America strong enough to defend herself.

By the autumn of 1916 the administration's preparedness program was fairly well accomplished. Looking back over the enormous obstacles that the President had faced, both from pacifists and from ardent preparationists, it was clear his accomplishment was considerable indeed. It was a program designed, not to meet the immediate needs of diplomacy, but rather to afford some measure of security to the United States in a troubled postwar era. It did not satisfy the National Security League any more than it pleased the extreme pacifists. But opinion in the country as a whole agreed that the administration's program provided "reasonable" preparedness for the uncertain years ahead. Still doggedly noninterventionist, the rank and file were thinking in terms, not of preparedness for war, but of preparedness for peace.

[49] Johnstown *Democrat,* July 15, 1916.

CHAPTER 8

Devious Diplomacy, 1915-16

THE FAVORABLE settlement of the nation's most urgent controversies with Germany and Britain in the autumn of 1915 brought relief to a people distraught at the thought of active intervention. Yet the calm that settled upon the country with the exacting of the *Arabic* pledge was not shared by the few men who controlled the foreign policy of the United States. Obviously, the great majority of Americans wanted peace, yet the maintenance of peace depended upon German observance of the *Arabic* promise, which was beyond Wilson's power to control. Nor was a break with Britain an impossibility, although it seemed unlikely at the time.

With his usual perspicacity, Colonel House saw that the surest way to end the dilemma and create a situation subject to American direction was to inaugurate a movement for peace under President Wilson's leadership. His earlier efforts to persuade the Germans to agree to the *status quo ante* as a basis for peace talks having been rebuffed,[1] House was by the late summer of 1915 convinced that the triumph of unbridled German militarism in Europe would gravely imperil future American security. He concluded, moreover, that the only chance for peace lay in coming to firm agreement with the Allies and in cooperating with them in a drive for peace, based on the *status quo ante,* so powerful the Germans could not resist it.[2]

Although mediation had been much in House's thought since the

[1] See above, pp. 160–162.
[2] House to Edward Grey, Sept. 3, 1915, the Papers of Edward M. House, in the Library of Yale University. House later explained the objectives of his peace plan in a letter to George S. Viereck, Feb. 13, 1932, *ibid.,* written in connection with Viereck's *Strangest Friendship in History.*

failure of his first peace mission, it was probably Sir Edward Grey's suggestion that the United States intervene to bring the war to an end that prompted House's action soon afterward. During a brief conference in New York City on October 8 he first presented to Wilson a daring plan that had been taking shape in his mind: either to compel a peace settlement or else to bring the United States into the war on the Allied side. The President was startled but seemingly acquiesced by silence.[3] A few days later House received letters from Grey intimating that the Allies might be willing to consider a negotiated and reasonable peace if the United States were prepared to join a postwar League of Nations to prevent aggressive war in the future.[4]

House went at once to Washington where, with Grey's letters in hand, he and Wilson collaborated on a reply. The time might soon come, House advised Grey, when the United States should demand a peace conference upon the basis of the elimination of militarism and navalism. "What I want you to know is that whenever you consider the time propitious for this intervention I will propose it to the President." After conferring with the British government, House added, he would go to Berlin and tell the German leaders that the President intended to stop the war. He would not, however, tell the Germans of his prior understanding with the Allies. "If the Central Powers were still obdurate, it would probably [5] be necessary for us to join the Allies and force the issue." [6]

[3] Specifically, House proposed that he ask the Allies whether they would accept the President's mediation. He thought they would accept. If the Central Powers accepted also, all would be well. If the Central Powers refused, however, "we could then push our insistence to a point where diplomatic relations would first be broken off, and later the whole force of our Government . . . might be brought against them." The Diary of Edward M. House, in House Papers, Oct. 8, 1915.

[4] Grey to House, Sept. 22, 1915, two letters, House Papers; also Spring Rice to House, Oct. 15, 1915, *ibid.* "I cannot say which Governments would be prepared to accept such a proposal, but I am sure that the Government of the United States is the only Government that could make it with effect," Grey wrote. Perhaps the most significant part of Grey's communication, however, was his intimation that, although the Allies would like to see Alsace-Lorraine returned to France and the Dardanelles given to Russia, the British government might be willing to negotiate on a basis of the restoration of Belgium and the evacuation of France.

[5] The word "probably" was inserted by Wilson. "I do not want to make it inevitable quite, that we should take part to force terms on Germany, because the exact circumstances of such a crisis are impossible to determine," he wrote. Wilson to House, Oct. 18, 1915, the Ray Stannard Baker Collection, in the Library of Congress.

[6] House to Grey, Oct. 17, 1915, House Papers.

Because the ship that carried House's letter to England was delayed, it was not until November 9 that Grey replied, asking what House meant by "elimination of militarism and navalism" and whether House agreed that the peace of the world could be secured only by the United States' joining a League of Nations and guaranteeing the peace settlement. In relaying Grey's message to the President, House begged him to come out forthrightly behind Grey's proposal. "This is the part I think you are destined to play in this world tragedy," he urged, "and it is the noblest part that has ever come to a son of man. This country will follow you along such a path, no matter what the cost may be." [7] Wilson agreed, and House at once replied affirmatively to the Foreign Secretary.

In a long conference in New York City with Wilson on November 28, House again pressed his proposal for an Anglo-American *entente*. There was an irrepressible conflict between German autocracy and American democracy, he declared, and the United States could not permit a military autocracy to dominate the world. The President, moreover, should make these convictions known to the Allied leaders. Wilson agreed and suggested that House go to London to begin secret talks.[8] Two weeks later the momentous decision was made. House would go to London and Berlin to sound out the possibilities of peace on the basis of military and naval disarmament and a League of Nations to prevent aggression and maintain the "absolute" freedom of the seas. "If either party to the present war will let us say to the other that they are willing to discuss peace on such terms," the President's confidential instructions read, "it will clearly be our duty to use our utmost *moral* force to oblige the other to parley, and I do not see how they could stand in the opinion of the world if they refused." [9]

[7] House to Wilson, Nov. 10, 1915, the Woodrow Wilson Papers, in the Library of Congress.

[8] House Diary, Nov. 28, 1915. By now Wilson was convinced that Walter Page was thoroughly unreliable and totally ineffective, because of his partiality to the British cause. The President, moreover, had no confidence in the British Ambassador in Washington, Sir Cecil Spring Rice, that "highly excitable invalid," Wilson called him. Like his successor, Franklin D. Roosevelt, Wilson seemed obsessed with a desire to circumvent diplomatic channels and to establish direct, personal communication with the British leaders.

[9] Wilson to House, Dec. 24, 1915, Baker Collection; italics mine. Wilson's use of the term "moral force" did not necessarily imply a qualification of his statement. He meant, actually, diplomatic force, which in the then existing circumstances could have been a powerful weapon of coercion. Diplomatic force used strongly against Germany, for example, might have led to a rupture in relations and war.

In order to understand the reasons for the profoundly significant change in policy implied in Wilson's determination to intervene decisively for peace, it is necessary to review briefly the troubled state of German-American relations from October through December, 1915, during the time when Wilson and House agreed to embark upon the new course. Too often it has been assumed that the President simply decided upon a policy of intervention, diplomatic if possible, military if necessary, on general moral grounds. The fact was, however, that Wilson's and House's willingness to think boldly was conditioned by the knowledge that German-American relations, already extremely tense, might worsen at any moment to the point of an open rupture.

The giving of the *Arabic* pledge by the Germans had prevented a break in relations without effecting a comprehensive settlement of outstanding grievances and without convincing the Washington government that a friendly understanding was possible. To begin with, this, the fall of 1915, was the time when German agents in the United States and Mexico were most active and stimulated genuine alarm among the administration. As early as August 4 Wilson was convinced the country was "honeycombed with German intrigue and infested with German spies." As evidence of German espionage began to unfold on all sides,[10]

[10] The most important case that developed during the summer of 1915 involved the head of the powerful German secret-service organization in the United States, Franz Rintelen von Kleist, who came to America in April, 1915. News of Rintelen's activities came to Lansing in July. Investigation by American agents revealed that Rintelen was head of the German intriguers, had engaged in a number of schemes to stop the export of munitions to the Allies, and had intrigued with Villa and Huerta to provoke a war between the United States and Mexico. The Diary of Chandler P. Anderson, in the Library of Congress, July 22, 1915, summarizing report by Charles Warren, Assistant Attorney General.

Later and more comprehensive reports by United States secret-service agents established that Rintelen and the German military and naval attachés, Franz von Papen and Karl Boy-Ed, had spent at least $27 million before December, 1915, as follows: (1) $12 million to promote a Huerta-Villa counterrevolution against Carranza in Mexico; (2) $5 million for the Bridgeport Projectile Company, which the Germans bought in order to tie up Allied war orders; (3) $3 million for secret-service and detective work; (4) $3 million for lecturers, press bureaus, and foreign language publications; (5) $2½ million to supply German warships; and (6) $1½ million for miscellaneous expenses.

The reports of the United States agents were given to the press and were summarized in *The New York Times*, Dec. 5, 8, 1915, and the New York *World*, Dec. 8, 1915. See also Lansing to Wilson, Sept. 27, 1915, enclosing Page to Lansing, Sept. 25, 1915, Wilson Papers, for another interesting case. Attorney General Gregory reviewed the work of the German Embassy among Ameri-

Wilson grew indignant and threatened to send Bernstorff home.[11] The Department of Justice, heretofore almost criminally negligent, turned in full force on the German intriguers, while the Attorney General issued an unprecedented appeal for assistance to state authorities. The climax of the government's campaign came early in December, when Lansing demanded the recall of Von Papen and Boy-Ed, German military and naval attachés, for their proved complicity in plots against American neutrality. Soon afterward Bernstorff disavowed Rintelen, but he could not so easily repudiate his two attachés.

It was at this time, also, that Lansing began his diplomatic campaign to wrest from the Imperial government an apology and disavowal for the destruction of American lives on board the *Lusitania*. This was still the most rankling wound of all, and until it was healed cordial relations between the two governments were impossible. From the voluminous correspondence on the matter that passed among Wilson, Lansing, Bernstorff, and the German Foreign Office, it is clear the Washington administration were resolved to obtain full satisfaction or else to break diplomatic relations, and that the Foreign Office would surrender only if that were necessary to avoid a rupture.[12] During the first weeks of the negotiation, however, the Foreign Office stubbornly refused to concede the illegality of the destruction of the *Lusitania*. The result was that, at the very time Wilson and House were making

can organizations in a letter to Vance McCormick, Sept. 30, 1916, copy in House Papers.

George S. Viereck, who was a key figure in the German propaganda agency in New York City, gives the best description of how that organization functioned in *Spreading Germs of Hate* (New York, 1930), pp. 43–118. H. C. Peterson, *Propaganda for War* (Norman, Okla., 1939), pp. 134–158, is a brief account of German sabotage and propaganda activities.

[11] House Diary, Oct. 8, 1915. Bernstorff protested piously that he had absolutely no connection with the various intrigues. The fact was, however, that he knew everything about and was a key figure in them. See, for example, Foreign Office to Bernstorff, Jan. 13, 1916, "Bernstorff Wireless Messages—1916," in the Papers of Walter H. Page, in Houghton Library, Harvard University; Bernstorff to Foreign Office, Mar. 21, 1916, *ibid.;* Wolf von Igel to War Office, May 10, 1916, *ibid.;* Bernstorff to Foreign Office, Aug. 26, 1916, *ibid.*

Lansing, however, was never fooled by Bernstorff's protestations of innocence. See the Diary of Robert Lansing, in the Library of Congress, "Count von Bernstorff," entry in Notes, dated May, 1916.

[12] The documents covering the first phase of the negotiation are printed in *Papers Relating to the Foreign Relations of the United States, The Lansing Papers, 1914–1920* (2 vols., Washington, 1939–40), I, 488–497.

plans for the second peace mission, a break in relations with Germany seemed likely almost any day.

Finally a break between the United States and Austria impended over the sinking of the Italian liner *Ancona* in the Mediterranean on November 7, with the loss of twenty-seven lives, by a German submarine flying the Hapsburg ensign. Only a few days before Wilson and House made plans for their peace move, the State Department had dispatched a virtual ultimatum to Vienna. Although the Austrian government later yielded completely to the American demands for disavowal and reparation, it was not certain at the height of the crisis that the outcome would be a happy one.

Obviously, then, House's peace plan was not conceived in a vacuum, or even as a means of needlessly hastening American intervention. Wilson and House knew a break with Germany might become necessary if the *Lusitania* negotiations failed, and they realized it would be difficult to arouse popular approval for war over this somewhat stale issue. It is clear, therefore, that they hoped to avert such a break by compelling a reasonable peace settlement that would benefit all mankind. But if this effort failed because of German unreasonableness, then the President could appeal in the name of humanity for the support of the American people in a drive to end the war.

These thoughts were much in House's mind when he arrived in London on January 6, 1916. It seemed a propitious time to begin serious peace talks. Russia was wounded beyond hope of recovery, while the prospect of the Allies' breaking through the German lines in the West was at best remote. In fact, it seemed the situation would get worse, not better, for the Allies in the coming months of 1916.[13] During his two-weeks stay in London, before leaving for the Continent, House talked with every official of consequence in the government. Although he, Grey, and Balfour, head of the Admiralty, discussed only the major aspects of the President's plan and the British leaders did not make any commitments, House was so encouraged by the prospects for successful mediation that he begged Wilson not to break relations with Germany over the *Lusitania* issue, as that would wreck the entire project.

From London House went to Berlin where, from January 26 to 29, he conferred with the chief civilian leaders. As he had already led

[13] As Sir Edward Grey later pointed out in *Twenty-Five Years, 1892–1916* (2 vols., New York, 1925), II, 128–129.

Bernstorff to believe he was as friendly to Germany as to the Allies, House received a cordial welcome. To the Colonial Secretary he declared that the moderate elements in Britain and Germany could and should come to agreement. With the Imperial Chancellor and the Foreign Secretary, House pleaded movingly the cause of understanding and peace, pointing to the impending danger of a collapse of Western civilization and the futility of the war. Disclaiming any responsibility for the tragedy, Chancellor Bethmann-Hollweg agreed; but he made it clear Germany would entertain no peace offer that did not include indemnities from Britain and France and German control of Belgium and Poland.

By the end of his stay in Berlin, therefore, House was convinced neither side was yet ready to begin serious peace discussions. "Hell will break loose in Europe this spring and summer as never before," he advised the President; but he was certain Wilson could intervene after the summer campaigns were over.[14] This conviction was strengthened in Paris where, from February 2 to 8, House had a series of confidential talks with the French Premier and Foreign Minister, Aristide Briand and Jules Cambon. Grey had been reluctant to broach the subject of peace with the French government. Convinced of the urgency of a complete understanding with the French, House revealed the President's plan and on February 7 made an important agreement with Briand and Cambon. *"In the event the Allies are successful during the next few months,"* House related, *"I promised that the President would not intervene. In the event they were losing ground, I promised the President would intervene."* He declared, moreover, that the lower the fortunes of the Allies ebbed, the closer the United States would stand by them. Briand and Cambon, in turn, "agreed not to let the fortunes of the Allies recede beyond a point where our intervention could save them." [15]

In reporting this conference to the President, House for the only time in the writer's knowledge failed to convey a faithful account of what he did and said. Omitting any reference to his sweeping promise of American support for the Allies in his letter to Wilson, House merely reported: "It was finally understood that in the event the Allies had some notable victories during the spring and summer, you would

14 House to Wilson, Feb. 3, 1916, Wilson Papers.
15 House Diary, Feb. 7, 1916.

[not] [16] intervene; and in the event that the tide of war went against them or remained stationary, you would intervene." [17] The important point, of course, was House's sweeping assurances of American intervention under certain conditions and support under almost all conditions. These assurances led the French Cabinet to believe they could expect the military support of the United States if their prospects darkened. Yet House was probably thinking, as Wilson assuredly was, only in terms of diplomatic intervention. House later claimed Briand and Cambon misinterpreted and exaggerated his promises to them.[18] There is no evidence in his Diary or letters to Wilson, however, that he sought to make clear to the French leaders the important distinction in his mind between military intervention and diplomatic intervention.

In London again on February 9, House moved swiftly to bring Grey to some agreement. At a conference the following morning, the Foreign Secretary made it clear he preferred American military intervention to mediation, but he finally agreed that the President might demand that the war be ended and a peace conference be held.[19] Next came the more difficult task of winning the approval of the other Cabinet members. The decisive conference was held on February 14, with House, Grey, Balfour, Asquith, Lloyd George, and Lord Reading, the Chief Justice, present. House promised that Wilson would preside at the peace conference, and he wanted to know specifically when the President should issue his peace demand. The British conferees agreed that early fall would be the best time. Lloyd George insisted that the Allies and the United States come to agreement on terms before the conference was called, but House refused to make any such promise. What would Wilson do if the Allies insisted on terms he considered unjust?

[16] Professor Seymour, in *The Intimate Papers of Colonel House* (4 vols., Boston, 1926–28), II, 164, made this sentence read as follows: "It was finally understood that in the event the Allies had some notable victories during the spring and summer, you would not intervene. . . ." It seems reasonable to assume that House's omission of this important "not" in his letter to Wilson was an inadvertence.

[17] House to Wilson, Feb. 9, 1916, Wilson Papers.

[18] "The Memoirs of Colonel House," in the Papers of George Sylvester Viereck, in the Library of Yale University.

[19] "I argued the matter earnestly and convinced him," House wrote in his Diary Feb. 10, 1916, "that for the good of all it would be best for us to smooth over the Lusitania incident, and intervene by demanding a conference of the belligerents for the purpose of discussing peace terms. We finally agreed it was best for the President not to set any conditions whatever, but merely to demand that war cease, and a conference be held."

Asquith asked. "I replied that he would probably withdraw from the conference and leave them to their own devices." But what would Wilson do if the Germans insisted on unreasonable terms? "In these circumstances, I thought the President would throw the weight of the United States on the side of the Allies. In other words, he would throw the weight of the United States on the side of those wanting a just settlement—a settlement which would make another such war impossible." [20]

Three days after this epochal meeting, on February 17, Grey and House drafted a memorandum embodying the Anglo-French-American understanding.[21] Grey was now anxious that the President intervene quickly. "History will lay a grave charge against those of us who refuse to accept your proffered services at this time," he declared with obvious feeling.[22] House sailed from Falmouth on February 25, therefore, confident the day was not far distant when the President might perform the greatest service ever given man to render: to end the most destructive war in history and to lay the foundations of a secure, just, and lasting peace.

In the meantime, however, while House was in Europe, Wilson and Lansing had embarked upon an independent diplomatic campaign that nearly wrecked House's negotiations, threatened to draw the United States and Germany together against the Allies, and backfired in a most spectacular way in Congress. It was the controversy over armed ships, provoked by the administration's drive to disarm

[20] House Diary, Feb. 14, 1916. The writer believes that on this supremely important occasion House faithfully reflected the President's position. House also revealed the true purpose behind Wilson's plan of mediation, which was a purpose chiefly to bring peace to Europe, not to involve the United States in the war. To be sure, the risk of war with Germany was inherent in the plan, but that risk would be even more serious if the mediation effort failed. And Wilson undoubtedly believed that, once an armistice had been effectuated and a peace conference actually held, there was little chance the people of Europe would allow their governments to resume hostilities.

[21] Initialed by Grey on February 22, 1916, the memorandum began: "Colonel House told me that President Wilson was ready, on hearing from France and England that the moment was opportune, to propose that a Conference should be summoned to put an end to the war. Should the Allies accept this proposal, and should Germany refuse it, the United States would probably enter the war against Germany." The full text is printed in *Intimate Papers*, II, 201–202.

[22] House Diary, Feb. 17, 1916. Grey confessed, however, that the Cabinet would have to be guided by military judgment in deciding upon the best time for the President's mediation. *Ibid.*, Feb. 21, 1916.

Allied merchantmen. One of the most maladroit blunders in American diplomatic history, it revealed the immaturity and inherent confusion of the President's policies.

The immediate background of the episode was the nearly successful conclusion of the *Lusitania* negotiations and the generous guarantees the German government gave regarding submarine operations in the Mediterranean. All during January the *Lusitania* negotiations proceeded, the Imperial government refusing to admit the illegality of the sinking and insisting on arbitration, the United States just as stubbornly demanding an explicit admission of wrongdoing. Finally, on January 25 the President threatened to break diplomatic relations unless Germany gave in.

Then, moved by House's pleading to avoid a break, Wilson backed down and indicated he would accept a "handsome apology" without explicit disavowal. For their part, the Germans were ready to go to any length except to admit the illegality of the destruction of the *Lusitania*. The final German proposal, handed to Lansing on February 4, expressed regret at the loss of American lives, for which the Imperial government assumed liability and offered to pay indemnity. It was the maximum Germany could concede, Bethmann-Hollweg declared in an unprecedented direct appeal to the American people. "I cannot concede a humiliation of Germany and the German people, or the wrenching of the submarine weapon from our hands." [23]

And it was enough. As Lansing pointed out, the German concessions came so close to meeting the American demand that the Imperial government had surrendered in spirit if not in explicit language. Moreover, it was evident Congressional sentiment would never sanction a rupture of relations over a semantic disagreement. On February 11, therefore, Lansing, Vice-President Thomas R. Marshall, the chairman of the House and Senate Foreign Relations committees, and Senator Hoke Smith of Georgia answered Bethmann-Hollweg by assuring the German people the United States sought only honorable friendship.

In this manner was a severe crisis settled, or would have been settled had not the armed ship controversy arisen to revive old animosities and create new tensions. During the first months of the war, long before the submarine issue was raised, the State Department had issued regulations classifying defensively armed merchant ships as peaceful vessels. For almost a year the question of the status of armed ships was

[23] New York *World*, Feb. 9, 1916.

quiescent, mainly because the British Admiralty did not begin arming ships in the American trade until the late summer of 1915. The issue was first raised in September, 1915, when an armed British steamer entered the port of Norfolk and Lansing, for reasons that are not clear, suggested changing the regulations.[24] This case was settled when the

Harper's Weekly, October 2, 1915

So sorry!

ship's guns were removed. In the following months, however, the issue assumed larger proportions as the British and Italians began to arm even passenger liners.

[24] Lansing to Wilson, Sept. 12, 1915, *Lansing Papers,* I, 330–331. Lansing's position was revealed to the British Cabinet, whose members became much agitated lest the United States attempt to change international law during the progress of the war. A. J. Balfour to House, Sept. 12, 1915, House Papers; Horace Plunkett to House, Sept. 17, 1915, *ibid.* After reading the letters from Balfour and Plunkett, Wilson commented: "The matter of armed merchant-men is not so simple as Balfour would make it. It is hardly fair to ask Sub-marine commanders to give warning by summons if, when they approach as near as they must for that purpose they are to be fired upon. It is a question of many sides and is giving Lansing and me some perplexed moments." Wilson to House, Oct. 4, 1915, Baker Collection.

The matter came to a head when the *Persia,* an armed British liner, was torpedoed in the Mediterranean on December 30, 1915, and when armed Italian liners began to enter the port of New York. Lansing, whose sense of fairness sometimes outran his strategic thinking, laid the matter before the President on January 2, 1916. Since so-called defensively armed merchant ships could destroy submarines, and since many of them were under orders to attack submarines on sight, how could the United States expect submarines to surface and give warning before they attacked? Lansing asked. Moreover, should not armed merchant ships entering American ports be dealt with as warships? On the other hand, Lansing suggested a few days later, would it not be possible to settle the whole submarine question if the Allies agreed to disarm their merchant ships and the Germans, in turn, agreed to observe the rules of cruiser warfare in all submarine operations against merchant vessels?

Agreeing that Lansing's proposal was "reasonable, and thoroughly worth trying," Wilson authorized the Secretary of State to undertake a diplomatic campaign to obtain a revision of the rules. On January 18, 1916, therefore, Lansing issued to the Allied governments his proposal for a new *modus vivendi* to govern maritime warfare. Repeating the German argument that under modern conditions any armed merchant ship was offensively armed, Lansing warned the Allies that the United States was seriously considering treating armed merchantmen as auxiliary cruisers and suggested that all merchant ships be disarmed.

In London Lansing's *modus vivendi* caused dismay and confusion. Grey must have been sorely puzzled for, as he cabled Spring Rice on January 25, the American government had proposed nothing less than that "sinking of merchant vessels shall be the rule and not the exception." In short, the *modus vivendi* envisaged a change in international law, during the course of the war, that would profoundly benefit Germany. "It confronts us with a most serious situation," Grey added, "which must of course be considered in consultation with our Allies." [25] On the same day, Grey called Ambassador Page to the Foreign Office. "I have only once before seen Sir Edward so grave and disappointed," Page reported, "and that was when he informed me that the British had sent the German Government an ultimatum." [26] House, too, at

[25] Grey to Spring Rice, Jan. 25, 1916, handed to Lansing by Spring Rice, Jan. 27, 1916, enclosed in Lansing to Wilson, Jan. 27, 1916, Wilson Papers; also Grey to Spring Rice, Feb. 3, 1916, *ibid.*

[26] Page added: "Then he asked me for House's address because, as I gath-

once realized the disastrous consequences the *modus vivendi* was bound to have and on February 14 cabled Lansing that it was extremely urgent the proposal be held in abeyance.[27]

Grey's and House's alarm at the *modus vivendi* was well founded. Had the State Department insisted upon the proposed arrangement, the British would have faced the fatal choice of either allowing their vast merchant fleet to be sunk or defying the American government and running the risk of an Anglo-American rupture. Moreover, House's efforts looking toward the President's mediation would assuredly have been blasted. No one realized these facts better than the Germans, who must have been gleeful over this turn of events. On January 26 Lansing saw the Austrian Chargé, Baron Erich Zwiedinek, and told him confidentially about the proposal of January 18. Zwiedinek replied that the German and Austrian governments were contemplating issuing a declaration of unrestricted warfare against armed ships; he wondered if it would be wise to do this. Lansing replied that he thought the sooner it were done the better the situation would be.[28]

This, then, was the involved background of the armed ship controversy that exploded soon afterward. Taking Lansing at his word, the German government on February 10, 1916, announced that its submarines would soon receive orders, to go into effect February 29, to attack armed merchant ships without warning.[29] For several days

---

ered, he had talked with him at my table so frankly and freely about the relations of our two Governments that he thought he ought to inform House that he [did not] then know that this proposal would come. He spoke as one speaks of a great calamity. He said that he would not mention the subject in his speech in the House of Commons to-morrow because the announcement that such a proposal had been made by the United States would cause a storm that would drive every other subject out of the mind of the House and of the country." *Paper Relating to the Foreign Relations of the United States, 1916, Supplement* (Washington, 1929), p. 151.

[27] House to Lansing, Feb. 14, 1916, *Lansing Papers*, I, 342. Sir Horace Plunkett presented the British view forcibly in talks with House on February 12, 13, and 14, 1916. The Diary of Horace Plunkett, microfilm copy in possession of Herbert Brayer, Evanston, Ill., Feb. 12–14, 1916.

[28] The Desk Diary of Robert Lansing, in the Library of Congress, Jan. 26, 1916; "Memorandum by the Secretary of State . . . February 9, 1916," *Lansing Papers*, I, 341. Zwiedinek of course at once cabled this information to Vienna and Berlin, except that he reported Lansing had said he would "welcome" the Austro-German declaration of unrestricted submarine warfare against armed merchant ships.

[29] Gerard to Secretary of State, Feb. 10, 1916, *Foreign Relations, 1916, Supplement,* p. 163; memorandum of the German government dated Feb. 8,

American newspapers predicted the State Department would approve the new decree and warn Americans against traveling on armed ships. Then, on February 15, Lansing startled the country by telling reporters that although the Department believed the interests of humanity would best be served by the disarming of merchant ships, none the less, should the Allies reject the *modus vivendi* the United States would not insist upon a change in the conventional rules. Nor would the United States warn its citizens against traveling on ships armed defensively. Moreover, on February 17 Lansing called Bernstorff to the Department and informed him that, in view of the new submarine policy, the American government could not accept the *Lusitania* note of February 16.

By this startling reversal the administration set off a new dispute with Germany and an explosion in Congress. Although Wilson and Lansing nowhere set in writing the explicit reasons for their abrupt change of policy, those reasons can easily be inferred from other evidence and from the circumstances. In the first place, Wilson and Lansing had blundered in proposing the *modus vivendi* because they were desperately trying to avoid another showdown with Germany over the submarine issue.[30] Wilson later admitted he had made a serious mistake. Secondly, insistence upon the disarming of merchant ships would have driven a deep wedge between the United States and Great Britain and would have wrecked Wilson's mediation plan. Wilson obviously did not consider these consequences when he allowed Lansing to launch his bolt on January 18; but Grey and House made them ominously apparent. Thirdly, the President executed his sudden change of policy in order to restore his standing among the Allies as neutral mediator. It was no mere coincidence the British leaders consented to the possibility of Wilson's mediation on the same day the President abandoned the ill-fated *modus vivendi*.

Although the reasons for the reversal were sound, the administration's action had tragic consequences in Congress and the country at

1916, *ibid.,* pp. 163–166. The Austrian government followed suit on February 10, 1916.

[30] House recorded in his Diary, Mar. 7, 1916: "Spring-Rice told me what Lansing said to the Italian Ambassador, an indiscretion of which I am sorry Lansing was guilty. He told him that his purpose in proposing the disarming of Allied merchantmen was to please Germany and get a favorable settlement of the Lusitania controversy. This is exactly what Lansing and the President have been charged with."

large. Completely ignorant of the President's peace move and of the necessity for abandoning the *modus vivendi,* Congressional leaders began for the first time to suspect Wilson was maneuvering to involve the country in the war. Troubled and perplexed, Senate Majority Leader John W. Kern, Chairman William J. Stone of the Senate Foreign Relations Committee, and Chairman Hal D. Flood of the House Foreign Affairs Committee went to the White House on February 21, 1916. The Congressional leaders wanted to know what would happen if a submarine without warning sank an armed ship upon which Americans were traveling. Wilson replied that he would hold Germany to strict account and that he would not compel the Allies to disarm their merchantmen. At this Senator Stone, heretofore Wilson's most loyal and admiring friend in the upper house, lost his temper. Banging his fist on the table, he shouted: "Mr. President, would you draw a shutter over my eyes and my intellect? You have no right to ask me to follow such a course. It may mean war for my country." [31]

News of the President's position was at once taken back to Congress. "Flood told me today," a Texan wrote, "that Stone & Kern (& he also) were afraid of an immediate break, & the two former thought the President was almost determined on war." [32] At almost the same time the Imperial Foreign Secretary announced publicly that Germany would not recede from her new position. The result of the simultaneous declarations was to provoke an unprecedented panic in Congress on February 23. Veteran congressmen said that not for many years had they seen a situation so dramatic and sensational. The Democratic members of the House Foreign Affairs Committee met and agreed unanimously to demand prompt action on a resolution already offered by Representative Jeff: McLemore of Texas, warning Americans against traveling on armed belligerent ships. Although they

[31] W. J. Stone to Wilson, Feb. 24, 1916, Wilson Papers, repeats the gist of the conversation. The quotation is from *The New York Times,* Feb. 24, 1916. Senator Thomas P. Gore told the Senate on March 2 that he "had it on good authority" that Wilson had said war with Germany might not necessarily be undesirable, as American intervention might operate to bring the war to a speedy conclusion. Charles C. Tansill, *America Goes to War* (Boston, 1938), pp. 465–466, uses Gore's statement (saying Gore got his information from Stone) to reinforce the dubious thesis that Wilson was at this point seeking to promote full-scale American intervention. Yet Wilson, Stone, and Flood all denied emphatically that the President had in any way intimated he desired American intervention. *The New York Times,* Mar. 3, 1916.

[32] J. L. Slayden to O. G. Villard, Feb. 23, 1916, the Papers of Oswald Garrison Villard, in Houghton Library, Harvard University.

strongly favored the resolution, Speaker Clark and Majority Leader Kitchin pleaded with their colleagues to take no action until they had consulted with the President. Senator Stone, also, worked diligently to prevent the impending revolt in the House.

Confronted with an uprising that threatened to wrest control of foreign policy from his hands, the President struck back at his critics in Congress. In an open letter to Stone, Wilson declared that of course he would do his utmost to keep the country out of war. Even so, he could not consent to the abridgment of the rights of American citizens, and to bow to the German threat against armed ships would be a "deliberate abdication of our hitherto proud position as spokesmen, even amidst the turmoil of war, for the law and the right." Once accept a single abatement of the right and "the whole fine fabric of international law might crumble under our hands piece by piece." [33]

The hysteria rapidly subsided after the publication of Wilson's letter. At nine in the morning of February 25 the Democratic leaders in the House, Clark, Kitchin, and Flood, visited the President to inform him of sentiment in Congress. The McLemore resolution would carry two to one, the Speaker announced, if members were allowed to vote on it. He intended to stand by his announced policy, Wilson replied, in spite of Congressional resolutions. But what if an armed ship were torpedoed with the loss of American lives? the congressmen asked. He would break relations with the Central Powers, the President declared. What then? He had been told this might lead to war, Wilson replied. What would be the effect of American intervention? one of the congressmen asked. American participation might have the effect of bringing the war to an end sooner than would otherwise be the case, Wilson countered. But why should any man think he wanted war? he added. His policies were the policies of peace, not of war. "In

[33] Wilson to Stone, Feb. 24, 1916, printed in Ray S. Baker and William E. Dodd (eds.), *The Public Papers of Woodrow Wilson* (6 vols., New York, 1925–27), *The New Democracy*, II, 122–124.

During the early evening of February 24 Tumulty wrote to Wilson suggesting he write an identic letter to Chairmen Flood and Stone. This was necessary, Tumulty added, because he had talked with Speaker Clark, Senator Key Pittman, and Representative T. W. Sims, who had all warned that action on the McLemore resolution could not be delayed much longer. Tumulty went on to suggest what the President should say in the letter, and the phrases "the whole fabric of international law" and "What we are contending for in this matter is of the very essence of the things that have made America a sovereign nation" were Tumulty's. Tumulty to Wilson, Feb. 24, 1916, Wilson Papers.

God's name," he exclaimed, "could any one have done more than I to show a desire for peace?" [34]

Meanwhile, the McLemore resolution, warning Americans against traveling on armed belligerent ships, was hanging like a sword over Wilson's head, while Senator Thomas P. Gore of Oklahoma introduced a similar resolution of warning in the upper house on February 25. It was an intolerable situation, for so long as these resolutions hung fire no one knew who controlled the foreign policy of the United States. With Burleson in command and brandishing the patronage stick, administration leaders worked desperately to bring the Democratic members into line. On February 29, when he was certain of a favorable vote, the President demanded that the Rules Committee allow the House to vote on the McLemore resolution. Newspapers and journals of opinion rushed to the President's defense, one of them de-

[34] This was the celebrated "Sunrise Conference." The above is based upon full accounts of the conference printed in *The New York Times,* Feb. 26 and Mar. 3, 1916.

The time has come to clear away the misunderstanding about this important event created by Professors Arnett and Tansill. As Ray S. Baker, *Woodrow Wilson: Life and Letters* (8 vols., Garden City, N.Y., 1927–39), VI, 169, points out, the date of the conference was February 25, 1916, not February 22, as Tansill asserts. The meeting was no secret and was reported in some detail by the newspapers on the following day, February 26. Moreover, there is not a shred of reliable evidence that the President in any way intimated he *desired* American participation in the war. Kitchin's memorandum is, therefore, entirely untrustworthy. Tansill points out that at the time he wrote his memorandum Kitchin was suffering from a severe stroke. Tansill asserts that Kitchin was mistaken as to the date of the conference and admits that Kitchin's memory might have been affected by the stroke. Yet Professor Tansill proceeds to quote Kitchin's memorandum, in order to prove his own impossible thesis that Wilson was actually maneuvering to get the country into the war.

It is remarkable that in his correspondence at the time, Kitchin never once mentioned the President's alleged request. One thing, at least, is certain: if Wilson had been moving to get a war resolution from Congress he would not have divulged his plans to his bitter critics, Clark and Kitchin.

Five years after this meeting, Kitchin wrote an account for the journalist, Gilson Gardner, that placed the date of the conference in early April, 1916. Kitchin also recalled that Wilson had declared the time had come to put the United States in the war and that Wilson desired Congressional co-operation in achieving this objective. Gilson Gardner, "Why We Delayed Entering the War," *McNaught's Monthly,* III (June, 1925), 171–173.

Alex M. Arnett, *Claude Kitchin and the Wilson War Policies* (Boston, 1937), pp. 183–192, accepts Kitchin's version of the affair. C. C. Tansill, *America Goes to War,* pp. 467, 485–486, disagrees with Kitchin and Arnett as to the date of the conference; but Tansill quotes with seeming approval Kitchin's statement that Wilson requested support for American intervention.

claring, "Whoever defends these resolutions defends German lawlessness against American rights and American honor." [35] The New York *World,* moreover, published a series of documents, which were widely reprinted, revealing that the German-American Alliance had been conducting a powerful lobby to apply pressure on congressmen in behalf of a foreign policy partial to the "Fatherland." [36]

So overwhelming, in fact, was the apparent popular and editorial support for the President that the wonder was his opposition did not collapse entirely. The Senate, where Wilson had strong support among Eastern Republicans like Lodge, voted first, on March 3, to table the Gore resolution.[37] After more than a week's delay, during which time Bryan rushed to the capital to bolster his discouraged followers, the House came to the showdown. On March 7 ninety-three Republicans joined with most of the Democrats in an emphatic vote, 276 to 142, to stand by the President.[38] Wilson's support came chiefly from the Atlantic states and the South. In contrast, the Middle West recorded a majority against Wilson, with the delegations from Iowa, Nebraska, Minnesota, and Wisconsin solidly arrayed.

In the meantime, the German government refused to rescind its warfare against armed merchantmen, claiming it had in no manner violated the *Arabic* pledge, as was true. The Foreign Office, moreover, assured the State Department on February 28 that no armed liner would be sunk "unless such armament is proved." None the less, Lansing pressed for a break and urged Wilson to accuse the Imperial government of violating its pledges. The President, however, apparently refused to force a break over a dubious point and after the tabling of the Gore and McLemore resolutions simply waited to see what events would bring.

[35] New York *World,* Mar. 3, 1916; also *The New York Times,* Mar. 7, 1916, and *Outlook,* CXII (Mar. 8, 1916), 545–546.

[36] New York *World,* Mar. 7, 1916.

[37] By a last-minute maneuver Gore reversed his resolution, which originally warned Americans against traveling on armed belligerent ships, to read that the destruction of American lives on such ships would constitute a cause for war. In this form the resolution was tabled sixty-eight to fourteen, although the parliamentary situation was so confused many senators did not know what they were voting for. *The New York Times,* Mar. 4, 1916.

[38] The vote for and against tabling the resolution was as follows: in favor of tabling, 182 Democrats, 93 Republicans, 1 Progressive; against tabling, 33 Democrats, 102 Republicans, 5 Progressives, 1 Independent, and 1 Socialist. *Ibid.,* Mar. 8, 1916.

The opportunity to force a final showdown with Germany over all aspects of the submarine question soon came, with the torpedoing without warning of the unarmed French Channel steamer *Sussex* on March 24, with eighty casualties. Lansing was ready to break relations at once, but Wilson moved with customary deliberateness. After first denying a submarine had attacked the *Sussex*, on April 10 Von Jagow admitted that a U-boat commander had sunk what he thought was a warship in the English Channel on March 24, at the same spot where the *Sussex* had been hit.

For days the President fought an agonizing struggle for the right course to follow. Pressed by his wife, Lansing, and House either to break relations immediately or else to issue an ultimatum,[39] he held firm against warlike moves and drafted a note that left wide room for future negotiation. In the end, however, Wilson gave in and followed the counsel of his close advisers. The note that he drafted on April 16 and sent to Berlin two days later was an unequivocal denunciation of the ruthless German campaign against all shipping, whether belligerent or neutral, armed or unarmed. The United States had waited with extraordinary patience; it was now painfully evident that the use of submarines against merchant ships was "utterly incompatible with the principles of humanity, the long-established and incontrovertible rights of neutrals, and the sacred immunities of non-combatants." Unless the Imperial government abandoned its relentless warfare against merchant and passenger ships, therefore, the United States had no alternative but to sever relations with the German Empire. The following day, April 19, 1916, Wilson went before a joint session and reiterated his ultimatum.[40]

Published in the German press on April 22–23, Wilson's note caused a wave of hot anger to sweep over the German people, most of whom now believed the President was seeking to wrest from their government's hands the one weapon that could bring the war to a speedy and victorious conclusion. "We can no longer retreat," declared a Berlin

[39] Lansing drafted a note denouncing Germany's "brutal," "inhuman," and "lawless" submarine warfare, which Wilson rejected on the ground that it was tantamount to a declaration of war. See Lansing's "Draft Instructions . . ." and "Suggested Insertion . . .," *Lansing Papers*, I, 540–543; House Diary, Apr. 11, 1916, gives an account of House's and Mrs. Wilson's talks with the President.

[40] Lansing to Gerard, Apr. 18, 1916, *Foreign Relations, 1916, Supplement,* pp. 232–234; *The New York Times,* Apr. 20, 1916.

newspaper, "but rather must use the freedom which the enemy has given us to conduct unlimited submarine warfare, with consideration for no one." [41] The moderate editors were angry, too, but they continued to urge calmness and to deprecate the idea of war with the United States.

Wilson's ultimatum also sharpened the struggle over submarine policy then going on between the military and naval leaders and the civilian heads of government in Germany. Since the beginning of the year, the heads of the War and Navy departments had been pressing hard for unrestricted submarine warfare, even at the cost of war with the United States.[42] Arguing that such policy would inevitably bring America into the war, Chancellor von Bethmann-Hollweg had steadfastly resisted this strong pressure and had brought the Emperor to his side.[43] One concession, however, had been made to the navy, that hereafter all belligerent merchant ships in the war zone, whether armed or unarmed, should be sunk without warning.[44] Thinking the *Sussex* was either a troopship or a merchantman, and acting under the new orders, the commander of the U-29 had torpedoed the *Sussex*.

Wilson's demands, therefore, compelled the German rulers to calculate whether American friendship was worth an abandonment, not only of the campaign against armed ships, but also of the unrestricted campaign against belligerent merchantmen in the war zone. Bethmann-Hollweg and the Foreign Office were still desperately anxious to avert war. In spite of the mounting pressure applied by his military and naval chieftains, on May 1 the Emperor announced his submission to the President's demands, even if that meant abandoning submarine activity altogether in the war zone.[45]

---

[41] *Täglische Rundschau,* morning ed., Apr. 23, 1916; also *Morgenpost* (Berlin), Apr. 23, 1916; *Berliner Lokal-Anzeiger,* morning ed., Apr. 23, 1916; *Germania* (Berlin), Apr. 23, 1916; *Vossische Zeitung* (Berlin), morning ed., Apr. 23, 1916; *Frankfurter Zeitung,* 2d morning ed., Apr. 23, 1916; *Kölnische Zeitung,* 2d morning ed., Apr. 23, 1916.

[42] "Report . . . of Imperial Chancellor v. Bethmann-Hollweg," Jan. 4, 1916; Chief of Admiralty Staff, Von Holtzendorff, to Bethmann-Hollweg, Jan. 7, 1916; Von Tirpitz to Bethmann-Hollweg, Feb. 13, 1916; Chief of General Staff, Von Falkenhayn, to Bethmann-Hollweg, Feb. 13, 1916, all printed in *Official German Documents Relating to the World War* (2 vols., New York, 1923), II, 1116–1130.

[43] Bethmann-Hollweg to Von Jagow, Mar. 5, 1916, *ibid.,* pp. 1139–1142.

[44] Admiralty Order of Mar. 13, 1916, cited in Tansill, *America Goes to War,* p. 491.

[45] Arno Spindler, *La Guerre Sous-Marine* (René Jouan, trans., 3 vols., Paris,

Dated May 4, the German reply admitted that U-boat commanders had recently been waging unrestricted warfare against belligerent merchant ships in the war zone. But it conceded Wilson's minimum demand by announcing that hereafter submarines would observe the rules of visit and search before sinking merchant vessels, both within and outside the war zone. The note, however, was truculent, almost insolent, in tone and ended with the threat that if the United States did not compel the British to observe international law, "the German Government would then be facing a new situation in which it must reserve itself complete liberty of decision." German editors agreed their government had gone the extreme limit, and that it was now incumbent upon the United States to bring Britain to book.[46]

In America reaction to the German reply was sharply divided. A few bellicose editors suggested rejecting it altogether,[47] while many moderate journals resented its accusatory tone. However, the rank and file, especially in the Middle West and South and among the German-Americans, hailed the German note with unalloyed relief as a victory for the United States that precluded even the possibility of a war they desperately wanted to avoid. As the President shared this desire for peace, he, too, regarded the German reply as a welcome surrender to his long-standing demand. When Lansing tried to warn him that the note had all the appearances of a " 'gold brick' swindle, with a decidedly insolent tone," he at first ignored the admonition and drafted a reply expressing gratification and accepting the German promises. Wilson finally eliminated the paragraph expressing gratification, however. His note, sent to Berlin May 8, simply accepted the German concessions, warned that friendly relations would depend upon a scrupulous observance of them, and declared the United States could not

---

1933–35), III, 191–197, is the best account of the German deliberations during the *Sussex* crisis. The Emperor still believed the navy was not strong enough to institute an effective blockade. Only two months before he had declared that the U-boat forces "were insufficient to overcome England; that as a matter of fact England could not be overcome." Bethmann-Hollweg to Von Jagow, Mar. 5, 1916, *Official German Documents*, II, 1142.

[46] E.g., *Kölnische Zeitung,* evening ed., May 5, 1916; *Frankfurter Zeitung,* evening ed., May 5, 1916; *Vossische Zeitung* (Berlin), evening ed., May 5, 1916.

[47] The New York *Tribune,* quoted in New York *World,* May 6, 1916, for example, declared the President had no choice left but to sever relations immediately. See also Providence *Evening Journal,* Louisville *Courier-Journal,* Louisville *Times,* Atlanta *Journal,* Philadelphia *Record,* Philadelphia *Evening Bulletin,* all cited in New York *World,* May 6, 1916.

accept the conditions upon which the German concessions had been made.[48]

The passing of this great crisis marked a major turning point in American attitudes and policies toward the war. As the months passed and no incident occurred to mar German-American relations, American opinion toward Germany softened perceptibly. This changing attitude was reflected on all sides—in the press and in the comments of public leaders. It was reflected even more significantly, however, in the consequent hardening of American attitudes toward the British and the nearly disastrous worsening of official Anglo-American relations that occurred during the spring and summer of 1916.

A hardening of popular attitudes toward Great Britain was inevitable after the *Sussex* settlement focused attention on alleged British wrongdoing. Thus, no sooner had the *Sussex* notes been exchanged than there arose demands for stern action, now against the British. This was, however, only the beginning, for events following hard upon the *Sussex* settlement provoked hostility against the British government and widened the gulf between the two countries. First came the Irish Rebellion of April 24, 1916, which the British authorities suppressed so ruthlessly that even Anglophiles in America were shocked.[49] Next occurred the trial and execution of the leaders of the Rebellion, including the Irish nationalist, Sir Roger Casement, who had come from Germany to lead the revolt. The Senate of the United States formally petitioned the British government to spare the Irish prisoners, but the appeal merely exacerbated mutual bitterness. As the best American journal of opinion put it, "The Dublin executions have done more to drive America back to isolation than any other event since the war began." [50] Finally, as the British intensified further their economic warfare, the movement in the United States for outright retaliation grew stronger than at any time since the beginning of the war.

The worsening of official Anglo-American relations was, if anything, even more evident than the change in popular attitudes. Certainly it had more serious consequences, for the President's heart so hardened against the British that before the year had ended he regarded the

[48] Secretary of State to Gerard, May 8, 1916, *Foreign Relations, 1916, Supplement*, p. 263.

[49] For a moving protest by a shocked Anglophile, see William Dean Howells to the Editor, May 6, 1916, New York *Evening Post*, May 8, 1916.

[50] *New Republic*, VII (July 29, 1916), 321–322.

Allies with suspicion, almost contempt, and was contemplating the possibility of a sympathetic alliance with Germany.[51]

This momentous change in Wilson's attitude had many causes, but the most important was probably Sir Edward Grey's refusal to allow the President to set the machinery of mediation in motion. The House-Grey memorandum of February 22, 1916, to be sure, had made it plain that the final decision rested with the British Cabinet. But Grey had given House rather definite verbal assurances that Wilson's mediation would be welcomed in the late summer or early autumn. During April and months following, House pleaded with Grey to consent to mediation on the basis of the memorandum of February 22. House warned explicitly that dire consequences would follow an Allied rejection, but each time Grey evaded the request. Emboldened by the failure of the German attack on the French fortress of Verdun and the apparent success of the great British offensive beginning July 1, 1916, the Allies grew more and more confident of their ability to defeat Germany on the battlefield.[52] Moreover, it was evident that Grey sincerely doubted the President's ability to bring the United States into the war if the proposed peace conference should fail. In late August, therefore, Sir Edward had to come out flatly and tell House a peace conference could not yet be held.[53]

As it became evident that the British and French leaders would allow the President's mediation only if their hopes of victory were shattered beyond recall, the attitude of Wilson and House became increasingly recriminatory, even hostile. Wilson made it plain that

[51] See below, pp. 252–253, 255–257.

[52] As Grey pointed out in a memorandum for the Cabinet in the autumn of 1916, "Nothing but the defeat of Germany can make a satisfactory end to this war and secure future peace." However, he added, if an absolute victory could not be won, then Wilson's mediation would be desirable. Grey, *Twenty-Five Years*, II, 131–133. The British military leaders were confident they could deliver a decisive blow against the German lines in 1916. Wilson's mediation, therefore, would not be considered until the success or failure of this impending British offensive was demonstrated.

[53] For the important correspondence between House and Grey see House to Grey, Apr. 7, May 10, 11, 19, 23, 27, June 8, July 15, 1916; Grey to House, Apr. 7, 8, May 12, 29, June 28, Aug. 28, 1916, all in House Papers.

Looking back over these events, Grey concluded that the Germans had made a fatal mistake in not joining with the President in a drive for a reasonable peace. He also acknowledged that the Allies, by rejecting Wilson's leadership, had missed a great opportunity to save the Western community from the dire consequences of a prolongation of the war. Grey, *Twenty-Five Years*, II, 135–137.

Britain would have to either consent to mediation or else expect stern efforts by the United States to protect its maritime rights. Later he resolved to cut loose from the Allies altogether and to issue his own peace demand at the right time. For his part, House began to criticize Allied "selfishness" and "ingratitude"; to tell himself, and probably the President also, that the trouble was the Allies did not want a reasonable settlement; and even to advise Wilson that he might have to appeal directly to the British and French peoples, over the heads of their governments.

The really dangerous tension in official Anglo-American relations came, however, when the British tightened their economic warfare and moved directly and indirectly to bring all neutral trade and shipping under their control. When the British and French seized and examined parcels in the American mails, for example, Lansing objected in language that betrayed the administration's growing anger. "The Government of the United States . . . can no longer tolerate the wrongs which citizens of the United States have suffered and continue to suffer through these methods," the note concluded. "To submit to a lawless practice of this character would open the door to repeated violations of international law by the belligerent powers." [54] The mails dispute was never settled and continued to rankle. But the event that had spectacular consequences was the British government's attempt to extend its economic warfare directly to the United States and Latin America—by the publication on July 19, 1916, of a "blacklist" of 87 American and some 350 Latin American firms, with whom British subjects were forbidden to deal in any way.[55]

To Wilson, the publication of the "blacklist" came as the culmination of a series of British indignities. "I am seriously considering asking Congress to authorize me to prohibit loans and restrict exportations to the Allies," he advised House. ". . . Polk [Counselor of the State Department] and I are compounding a very sharp note. I may feel obliged to make it as sharp and final as the one to Germany on the

[54] Lansing to Spring Rice and Jusserand, May 24, 1916, *Foreign Relations, 1916, Supplement,* pp. 604–608.

[55] British spokesmen correctly claimed that the "blacklist" was a lawful attempt to forbid British subjects to give aid to the enemy. On the other hand, American officials asserted that the practical effect of the measure was to put the proscribed firms entirely out of business, because British shipping would be denied them and because the balance of American and other neutral firms would refuse to do business with them, for fear of being put on the "blacklist" themselves. See *The New York Times,* July 19, 20, 22, 24, 1916; New York *World,* July 21, 23, 1916.

submarines." Publicly the President declared that the "blacklist" had "got on his nerves"; privately he called the British leaders "poor boobs." [56] Although the note of protest that Wilson and Frank L. Polk, Counselor of the State Department, sent to London on July 26 was not the ultimatum Wilson had threatened, it was ominous in tone and harsh in language, forecasting grave consequences if the British government persisted in their attacks on American commerce.[57]

That the President's wrath was mounting was evidenced in a way that threatened to bring the United States and Britain to a parting of the ways. At the beginning of the "blacklist" dispute, Acting Secretary of State Polk had warned the British Ambassador that Wilson was considering retaliatory measures. And when the British refused to withdraw the "blacklist" and the Foreign Office failed to reply promptly to the American note of July 26,[58] Wilson moved swiftly to obtain from Congress a means of redress.[59] An amendment to the Shipping Act of September 7 empowered the President to refuse clearance to any vessel refusing to carry the freight of a blacklisted American citizen. More important, however, were amendments to the Revenue Act adopted the following day, which authorized the President to deny clearance and port facilities to ships of any nation that discriminated unfairly against American commerce, and to use the armed forces to enforce these provisions.

There was, of course, a vast difference between enacting such legislation and using it, but the significant fact was that the administration had taken leadership in providing retaliatory recourses which, if used, might deal the Allied cause a death blow. Indeed, friends of the Allies were shocked by the hardening of Wilson's attitude and by the concomitant severity with which the British were being dealt. Lansing sensed the danger that the President's resentment would lead him to retaliation and shuddered at the prospect of his government's aligning itself on the German side.[60]

[56] Wilson to House, July 23, 1916, Baker Collection; *The New York Times,* July 25, 1916; Wilson to House, July 27, 1916, Baker Collection.

[57] Polk to Page, July 26, 1916, *Foreign Relations, 1916, Supplement,* pp. 421–422.

[58] The British reply was not sent until October 12, 1916. *Ibid.,* pp. 461–465.

[59] The fact that Wilson took the initiative in obtaining retaliatory legislation is evidenced in the Diary of Frank L. Polk in the Library of Yale University, July 26, 1916; Lansing to Wilson, Aug. 26, 1916, the Papers of Albert S. Burleson, in the Library of Congress; Lansing Desk Diary, Aug. 29, 30, 31, Sept. 6, 7, 8, 1916.

[60] "The President's Attitude Toward Great Britain and Its Dangers," Lansing Diary, Sept., 1916.

Wilson's change of attitude was a crushing blow, however, to Walter Page, who came to Washington in August, 1916, to have full-dress conferences, he thought, on the British situation. Nothing better illustrated the changed atmosphere in Washington than the reception accorded this distinguished champion of Anglo-American friendship. From August 17 to September 25 Page had five conferences with Lansing; but Lansing was mindful of Wilson's hostility to Page and would talk of nothing but complaints against the British government. "I have tried in vain to inform the Secretary of the larger view of the subject," Page recorded in his Diary; "he changes the topic of conversation and discusses some technicality or some 'case.' " [61] Wilson invited the Ambassador to lunch the day after he arrived and on August 29, but on both occasions other guests were present and Wilson refused to talk about the war. On September 22, five weeks after he had arrived in the United States, Page finally obtained a private interview with the President. What Wilson told him only deepened Page's despair. "The P[resident] said to me that when the war began he and all the men he met were in hearty sympathy with the Allies; but that now the sentiment toward England had greatly changed. He saw no one who was not vexed and irritated at the arbitrary English course." [62]

To such a state had Anglo-American relations come, therefore, by the autumn of 1916. The favorable settlement of the submarine controversy had practically eliminated the German-American tension and focused American resentment on the British maritime system. This resentment had hardened into bitterness and near hostility as a result of the rejection of Wilson's offer of mediation, the ruthless suppression of the Irish Rebellion, and the intensification of Britain's economic warfare. The fact that the nation was in the throes of a presidential campaign prevented Wilson either from using his new retaliatory powers or from launching an independent peace campaign. But he stood ready, if sustained by the people, to embark upon a bold policy, portentous for the United States and the world—a policy of genuinely neutral mediation.

[61] The Diary of Walter H. Page, in Houghton Library, Harvard University, n.d.

[62] Ibid., n.d. For an extended discussion see Burton J. Hendrick, The Life and Letters of Walter H. Page (3 vols., Garden City, N.Y., 1924–26), II, 148–188.

CHAPTER 9

Progressivism and Peace:
The Campaign of 1916

NOT SINCE 1910 had the American political scene seemed so confused as at the beginning of 1916, when both major parties began to lay plans for the coming presidential election. The Republicans were slowly recovering from the great rupture of four years before. Theodore Roosevelt was now back in the G.O.P. in all but name, but no one could predict whether the great body of Progressives would follow their erstwhile leader. Nor could any man forecast the policies the Republican party might unite upon, for Republicans were, if anything, more divided than their opponents on the great issues of the day.

The Democrats, too, were rent by factionalism and conflict over policies. The President's preparedness program had antagonized a large body of progressives and rural voters, and there were rumors of an impending revolt of the pacifist element, under Champ Clark's leadership.[1] More important, Bryan was in a rebellious mood, angered by Wilson's stand on preparedness and the armed ship issue, and threatening to disrupt the party if the President made further warlike moves. "I have been amazed at the slush he [Wilson] has been pouring out upon the West," Bryan wrote at the time of Wilson's preparedness tour. ". . . It is disturbing to see our party's chances of success de-

[1] *The New York Times,* Jan. 26, 1916; especially Chicago *Herald,* Feb. 28, 1916. Clark, however, hotly denied these charges. See Clark to Wilson, Mar. 10, 1916, the Woodrow Wilson Papers, in the Library of Congress.

stroyed and the country's peace menaced by one in whom we had such great hope. If I find that his purpose is to drag this nation into this war I may feel it my duty to oppose his nomination." [2]

As it turned out, however, these were momentary alarms that quickly vanished once the *Sussex* crisis and the controversies over the defense bills were settled. All Democrats knew they could win only under Wilson's leadership and that revolt would merely insure a Republican victory. Looking at the election returns of 1912, moreover, Wilson and his party leaders realized they could convert the Democratic minority of 1912 into a majority in 1916 only if they won over a large number of former Progressives.

But how could these Progressives be lured into the Democratic camp? The answer was so obvious most commentators took it for granted. The administration would have to convince Progressives that the Democratic party was an acceptable vehicle of reform of the kind they wanted; that it had, once and for all, cast off the doctrines of *laissez-faire* and state rights that had heretofore shackled it. Thus far Wilson had either thwarted or failed to support the advanced progressive objectives, like rural credits and child labor legislation, woman suffrage, and other economic and social legislation. Could he now reverse himself and sponsor such dynamic measures of domestic reform?

Those observers who predicted the President would adhere stubbornly to New Freedom concepts did not well understand Woodrow Wilson. He had broad political principles, to be sure; but he was no inflexible dogmatist on methods or details. As he thought the Democratic party offered the only hope of constructive, progressive change, he believed his party's most important task was to stay in power. Nowhere did he come out and say that his desire to maintain the Democrats in power was responsible for the commitment he made to advanced progressivism in 1916. Yet he became almost a new political creature, and under his leadership a Democratic Congress enacted the

[2] Bryan to Josephus Daniels, Feb. 4, 1916, the Papers of Josephus Daniels, in the Library of Congress. See also Bryan to Claude Kitchin, c. Feb. 5, 1916, the Papers of Claude Kitchin, in the Library of the University of North Carolina; Bryan to Burleson, Mar. 8, 1916, the Papers of Albert S. Burleson, in the Library of Congress; David Lawrence, in New York *Evening Post*, Feb. 15, 1916; the Diary of Edward M. House, in the Papers of Edward M. House, in the Library of Yale University, Mar. 7, 1916, in which House recorded Wilson's fear that Bryan would bolt.

most sweeping and significant progressive legislation in the history of the country up to that time.

The first public sign of the new departure was Wilson's nomination, on January 28, of Louis D. Brandeis to the Supreme Court.[3] It was an open defiance of and a personal affront to the masters of capital as well as to conservative Republicans like Taft. Nor was the significance of the appointment lost upon rejoicing progressives and labor leaders. "The appointment . . . tends to restore faith in President Wilson," the single-tax oracle declared,[4] while Senator La Follette gladly acknowledged the people's debt to the President for a courageous act.[5] As the forces of privilege mustered all their resources to prevent Brandeis' confirmation, and as the President took up the gage, publicly defending the champion of social justice and throwing the whole force of the administration behind the nominee, the battle became a test of strength between conservatives and progressives. After a grueling struggle the administration won on June 1.[6] "The confirmation of Mr. Brandeis is an important mile-stone in the progress of the republic," one progressive asserted. "For the first time within my knowledge the vested interests have gone out to defeat an important nomination, and after using every possible source have been soundly beaten." [7]

A second major test of the President's attitude involved the much controverted rural credits bill, which he had blocked in 1914 and 1915 and which seemed certain to become an important issue in the impending campaign.[8] The sponsors of the Hollis-Bulkley bill, Senator Henry F. Hollis and Representative A. F. Lever, decided to make one last appeal to Wilson to support the provision for federal underwriting

[3] Attorney General Thomas W. Gregory strongly urged Brandeis' nomination, as did certain independent progressive leaders.

[4] *The Public,* XIX (Feb. 4, 1916), 97.

[5] R. M. La Follette, "Brandeis," *La Follette's Magazine,* VIII (Feb., 1916), 1–2; also Amos Pinchot to Norman Hapgood, c. Jan. 29, 1916, Wilson Papers; several hundred letters of approval from civic and labor leaders in Box 522, File VI, *ibid.;* "A Secret!" *Harper's Weekly,* LXII (Feb. 12, 1916), 145; *Collier's,* LVI (Feb. 26, 1916), 14; Springfield *Republican,* Apr. 4, 1916.

[6] There is a splendid account of this battle in Alpheus T. Mason, *Brandeis: A Free Man's Life* (New York, 1946), pp. 465–508.

[7] H. F. Hollis to E. F. McClennen, June 7, 1916, the Papers of Louis D. Brandeis, in the Law School Library of the University of Louisville.

[8] As the secretary of the American Rural Credits Association, Frank G. Odell, warned on January 9, 1916: "The support of the farmers, which would be engaged by rural credit legislation, is necessary to the Democratic Party in the Middle West." *The New York Times,* Jan. 10, 1916.

of the proposed system. They were willing, Lever told Wilson and Secretary Houston at a White House conference in late January, 1916, to reduce the amount of federal farm bonds the government might have to buy to $250,000 for each of the proposed twelve federal farm loan banks. "I have only one criticism of Lever's proposition," the President replied, "and that is that he is too modest in the amount." Then and there it was agreed the government should establish and operate the farm loan banks and provide an initial capital of $500,000 for each of them.

From that day on, the rural credits bill had the full support of the administration. Denounced by radicals because it did not go far enough, castigated by conservatives as a dangerous socialistic measure and as "class legislation, using the public resources to do for some what is not done for others," it none the less passed the Senate on May 4 and the House on May 15 almost unanimously and became law on July 17.[9] Thus the Democratic campaigners had ample opportunity to appear as friends of the farmer in the presidential campaign of this year.

The great social justice movement also came to its first legislative culmination, on the national level, in this year of the new progressive dispensation, but not before the President virtually bludgeoned his party leaders into allowing the necessary measures to pass.[10] Then suddenly the log jam was broken. Under administration pressure, the Kern-McGillicuddy bill, a model workmen's compensation measure for federal employees drafted by the American Association for Labor Legislation, was resurrected and passed by Congress on August 19 and quickly signed. Even more astonishing was the manner in which Wilson forced the passage of the Keating-Owen child labor bill. This measure, the special project of the National Child Labor Committee, passed the House on February 2, with only a few dissenting votes from Southern textile states. Then the bill languished in the Senate, where

[9] Only a handful of urban votes were cast against the bill. The vote in the Senate was 58 to 5, in the House, 295 to 10.

[10] Stymied time and again by the administration's refusal to support their measures, the leaders of this important segment of independent opinion were growing restive by the spring of 1916. John B. Andrews to L. D. Brandeis, May 17, June 1, 1916, Brandeis Papers; A. O. Lovejoy to C. Kitchin, June 3, 1916, Kitchin Papers. Their suspicion that the administration was not sincere in its professions of support seemed borne out when Wilson and Congressional leaders agreed, on March 24, 1916, on a legislative schedule that made no provision for the social justice bills. *The New York Times*, Mar. 25, 1916.

it would have died had not political exigencies demanded decisive presidential action. Before July 17 Wilson had said not a word in support of the bill. On July 17 the Democratic liaison with the social workers warned the President that the independent progressives considered the Keating-Owen bill a test of the administration's progressivism and that the Democrats might stand or fall on this issue. The following day, July 18, Wilson went to the Capitol, pleaded with the Democratic Senate leaders to allow the measure to come to a vote, and warned that the fortunes of their party depended upon prompt and favorable action. After much grumbling, the obstructive Southerners gave in and the measure was adopted on August 8 and signed by the President on September 1, "with real emotion," he said.

Nor was this all, though it represented perhaps the high peak of Wilsonian progressivism.[11] The movement to give the Filipinos a larger measure of autonomy, perhaps independence, the product of years of anti-imperialistic, progressive agitation, also came to fruition in 1916. Wilson had early endorsed the bill sponsored by Representative William A. Jones of Virginia to give self-government at once and full independence within a short time to the Philippines. Then, under pressure from Republicans, Catholics, and the War Department, the President had reversed himself on the question of independence and had helped to shape a new Jones bill drafted by the Bureau of Insular Affairs, which gave legislative autonomy and a larger measure of administrative control to the Filipinos, but reserved final sovereignty to the United States and made no definite promises about independence.

---

[11] The child labor law forbade the shipment in interstate commerce of goods manufactured in whole or in part by children under fourteen, of products of mines and quarries involving the labor of children under sixteen, and of any products manufactured by children under sixteen employed more than eight hours a day. Many Southerners opposed the measure out of the conviction, until recently shared by Wilson, that the bill represented an unconstitutional invasion of the police power of the states. The National Association of Manufacturers also opposed the bill, not because they favored child labor, but because they realized the bill was merely the beginning of a new federal regulation under the commerce cause, as the spokesman in Washington of the N.A.M. wrote, "of any commodity produced in whole or part by the labor of men or women who work more than eight hours, receive less than a minimum wage, or have not certain educational qualifications." James A. Emery to W. H. Taft, Apr. 4, 1916, the Papers of William Howard Taft, in the Library of Congress.

In 1918 the Supreme Court, in Hammer v. Dagenhart, 274 U.S., 251, declared this child labor law unconstitutional. The Court declared that the purpose of the law was not to regulate commerce, but to regulate the labor of children, which fell solely within the competence of the states.

This revised Jones bill passed the House on October 14, 1914, but Republicans easily blocked it in the Senate during the hectic short session of 1914–15. The measure could not be delayed for long, however. In complete control of the Senate, the anti-imperialists on February 4, 1916, adopted the Jones bill with the so-called Clarke amendment, promising independence to the Filipinos by March 4, 1921. The country expected an automatic approval by the House. But the Catholic hierarchy in the United States, fearful that an independent Philippines might confiscate church property,[12] brought enormous pressure to bear upon the Catholic membership of the House against the Clarke amendment.[13] On May 1, therefore, thirty Catholic Democrats joined with the Republicans and defeated the amendment, and the bill as passed and signed by Wilson lacked any definite promise of independence, although it did greatly enlarge the liberties of the Philippine peoples.

Finally, as if to make his new program complete and his bid for support all inclusive, Wilson capitulated also to the mounting demands of business organizations for a tariff commission,[14] antidumping legislation,[15] and legislation allowing Americans engaged in the export

[12] The Catholic position was ably and candidly set forth by the representatives of the Philippine hierarchy in Washington, in W. N. Kinkaid to Wilson, Feb. 11, 1916, Wilson Papers.

[13] William H. Taft, who had been on intimate terms with American Catholic leaders since the time when he was Governor General of the Philippines, was a key figure in marshaling Catholic opposition to the Clarke amendment. For his negotiations with Cardinals Gibbons and O'Connell, see Taft to J. Cardinal Gibbons, Jan. 11, 16, 1916, and Gibbons to Taft, Jan. 12, 1916, all in Taft Papers; also The New York Times, Apr. 27, 28, 1916; New York World, Apr. 29, 1916.

[14] As late as August 27, 1915, Wilson had steadfastly opposed the establishment of a tariff commission, which Roosevelt and the Progressives had advocated in 1912. But the demands of the business groups were so overwhelming that Wilson finally gave in and on January 24, 1916, came out in favor of a strong, independent, and nonpartisan commission, which would allegedly work to remove the tariff issue from politics. Wilson to C. Kitchin, Jan. 24, 26, 1916, printed in The New York Times, Jan. 27, 1916. Because it represented such a radical departure from traditional Democratic policies, Kitchin refused to sponsor the tariff commission bill in the House. Leadership in putting the bill through fell, therefore, to Representative Henry T. Rainey of Illinois. The measure was incorporated as a part of the Revenue Act of 1916.

[15] Especially alarmed were American chemical and dye manufacturers, who feared the German chemical trust would resume its destructive competition once the war had ended. On January 4, 1916, Secretary Redfield presented an antidumping measure (Redfield to Wilson, Jan. 4, 1916, Wilson Papers) that McAdoo roundly condemned as a Republican device (W. G. McAdoo, "Confi-

trade to combine.[16] In making these concessions to the business community, Wilson in effect reversed the historic Democratic policy [17] and put the government at the service of American businessmen.[18] There was no reason why he should not have done this, to be sure, but the point was he had espoused the very program of co-operation between business and government that Theodore Roosevelt had proposed in 1912 and that he, Wilson, had then strongly condemned. A few Democratic leaders, who prized the old Democratic tariff principles, rebelled and uttered futile protests, but most Democrats followed the President.

The significance of the astonishing metamorphosis in Democratic policies that occurred during the summer of 1916 was apparent to all observers. Regardless of the motivation behind Wilson's commitment to advanced doctrines, the fact was the Democratic Congressional majority had, by the fall of 1916, enacted almost every important plank in the Progressive platform of 1912. Wilson, therefore, could affirm that Democrats were also Progressives, and Democratic cam-

dential Memorandum for the President," Jan. 14, 1916, *ibid.*). Soon afterward a representative of the dye manufacturers conferred with the President and urged the importance of sizable tariff protection for the infant dye industry (Andrew C. Imbrie, "Memorandum of talk with President Wilson, March 8th, 1916," the Ray Stannard Baker Collection, in the Library of Congress), and this was the instrumentality finally agreed upon and included in the Revenue Act of September, 1916.

[16] Wilson and the administration strongly supported the Webb bill to amend the antitrust laws so as to allow manufacturers engaged in the export trade to combine for purposes of selling abroad. The bill was not passed, however, until 1918.

[17] That the President had gone over to the protectionist principle was publicly evidenced when he wrote the president of the Illinois Manufacturers' Association: "It ought to be possible by such [nonpartisan] means to make the question of duties merely a question of progress and development, a question of adapting means to ends, of facilitating and helping business and employing to the utmost the resources of the country in a vast development of our business and enterprise." Wilson to S. M. Hastings, July 28, 1916, Wilson Papers.

[18] Wilson proposed, among other things, to use the resources of the government to gather information and statistics, to help businessmen find new markets abroad, and to assist trade associations in standardizing products and eliminating cut-throat competition. He outlined this program in an address before the United States Chamber of Commerce, February 10, 1916, *The New York Times*, Feb. 11, 1916; see also L. Ames Brown, "Preparedness for Peace, an Authorized Statement of President Wilson's Plans," *Collier's*, LVIII (Sept. 16, 1916), 12–13, and Wilson to Edward N. Hurley, May 12, 1916, printed in Ray S. Baker and William E. Dodd (eds.), *The Public Papers of Woodrow Wilson* (6 vols., New York, 1925–27), *The New Democracy*, II, 167–168.

paigners could espouse the cause of social justice with mounting fervor. Whether this acceptance of the New Nationalism signified a fundamental change in Democratic philosophy, or whether it was executed solely for expediency's sake, no man could tell. In any event, on the surface, at least, progressivism had come momentarily to fruition and had found acceptance by one of the major parties. And the future of American politics would be profoundly altered by this fact.[19]

While the Democrats were writing into legislation the nationalistic, progressive program of 1916, their opponents were floundering in a sea of confusion and conflicting counsels. For months Theodore Roosevelt had waged a strenuous campaign for strong action against Mexico and Germany; and when Elihu Root and Henry Cabot Lodge took up the theme in important political speeches in February and March, it seemed almost certain the Republicans would make Wilson's Mexican policy, his failure to protest the violation of Belgium, and his weak and futile defense of American rights on the seas their chief points of attack during the presidential campaign.[20]

Or so it seemed at the beginning of the preconvention campaign. But Republican leaders like Taft protested that the G.O.P. was heading straight for disaster if it nominated Roosevelt on a war platform. A series of startling developments soon demonstrated, moreover, that the Eastern interventionists did not speak for the Republican rank and file, even of their own section. The action of a majority of the Republican representatives and of an almost solid Midwestern contingent in voting to warn American citizens off armed merchant ships was the first sign that the Republican masses, especially in the Midwest, valued peace more highly than a heroic assertion of technical rights. The defeat of Robert Bacon, an avowed interventionist, for the Republican senatorial nomination in New York by William M. Calder, who had the support of the German-Americans and the peace element, signified that interventionism could not command a majority among Republicans even in Root's and Roosevelt's own state. More important, however, was the success of Henry Ford, a pacifist leader of dubious wis-

[19] For incisive comments on the triumph of the New Nationalism in the Democratic party, see *New Republic,* VII (June 24, 1916), 185–187; VIII (Sept. 2, 9, 1916), 103–104, 128–129; also *Collier's,* LVIII (Sept. 16, 1916), 14.

[20] Root spoke before the New York Republican state convention in New York City on February 15, 1916, Lodge before the Republican Club of Lynn, Massachusetts, on March 16, 1916. Their speeches are printed in *The New York Times,* Feb. 16, 1916, and the Boston *Evening Transcript,* Mar. 17, 1916.

dom, in the Republican presidential primaries in Michigan and Nebraska, despite the fact that he was not a candidate and had tried to take his name off the ballots in these states. Obviously, Midwestern Republican leaders were using the Ford candidacy as a warning to the national leaders. Finally, German-American spokesmen gave early notice they would enter the presidential campaign and bitterly oppose any interventionist candidate. As they were for the most part Republicans, the significance of their admonition was not lost upon the men who controlled the G.O.P.

After minor booms for Root and former Governor Myron T. Herrick of Ohio had fizzled, the Republican preconvention contest settled into a test of strength between Roosevelt and Charles Evans Hughes, Associate Justice of the Supreme Court. The party managers liked Hughes little better than Roosevelt, but he was their best hope of heading off the alleged destroyer of the party. Outwardly, at least, Hughes bore many resemblances to Wilson. Like the President, he had integrity, independence, great power of leadership, and, above all, intellectual depth. Hughes had come first into public notice in 1905, when he conducted investigations of the New York utilities ring and the great insurance companies. His methods were so relentless and his disclosures were so startling that at once he was catapulted into leadership of the progressive wing of the Republican party in New York. Elected Governor in 1906 and 1908, Hughes, like Wilson a few years later, electrified the country by his defiance of the bosses and his magnificent battles for reform legislation. He might have been elected President in 1908, but he spurned Theodore Roosevelt's overtures. Appointed to the Supreme Court in 1910 by President Taft, Hughes by 1916 had won a place of leadership among the liberal minority of that tribunal. In 1912 he flatly refused to accept the Republican presidential nomination, but four years later the draft was so strong that he could not refuse duty's command.[21]

For his part, Theodore Roosevelt worked strenuously for the nomination and apparently thought his chances were good,[22] but the bosses knew better. They went to the national convention at Chicago on June 8 to prevent Roosevelt's triumph, even if that meant nominating the

[21] This paragraph is a brief summary of Merlo J. Pusey, *Charles Evans Hughes* (2 vols., New York, 1951), I, 132–324.

[22] So did the professional odds makers. Roosevelt was the favorite in the betting in St. Louis on June 1, when his supporters offered two to one odds in his favor. *The New York Times,* June 2, 1916.

independent and progressive Hughes. The leaders of the nearly defunct Progressive party also gathered in Chicago at the same time.
Die-hard Progressives insisted that their rump convention nominate
Roosevelt and make a hopeless campaign, rather than surrender
abjectly to the enemy, the Old Guard. Most Progressives did not know
it, but Roosevelt was using them to bludgeon the Republicans into
nominating him. The strategy, of course, failed, and Hughes was
nominated easily on June 10. Having failed to win a single important
concession from the Republican managers, the rebellious Progressives
proceeded in sheer anger and desperation to nominate Roosevelt anyway. Roosevelt declined the dubious honor at once and suggested that
the Progressives and Republicans unite behind Henry Cabot Lodge—
one of the "staunchest fighters for different measures of economic
reform in the direction of justice," Roosevelt said. Two weeks later the
Progressive National Committee followed their leader's instructions
and disbanded the party that had been launched with such hope and
enthusiasm in 1912.[23]

The nomination of Hughes on a platform that carefully avoided
any denunciation of hyphenism and the extreme German-American
element and that called for "a straight and honest" neutrality was,
therefore, an implicit repudiation of the Rooseveltian interventionists.[24] As Roosevelt wrote soon after the convention, "the country
wasn't in a heroic mood." The selection of Hughes was also a signal
victory for the German-American element of the party, for, whether
he liked it or not, Hughes had become the German-American candidate.

Meanwhile, Wilson, House, and other Democratic leaders had been

[23] George E. Mowry, *Theodore Roosevelt and the Progressive Movement*
(Madison, Wis., 1946), pp. 345–360. A minority of the Progressives, led by
John M. Parker, Matthew Hale, and Bainbridge Colby, held a new Progressive
convention in Indianapolis in early August, repudiated Roosevelt, and came out
for Wilson. As will be shown, they were an important factor in accomplishing
Wilson's re-election in November.

[24] The Republican platform, among other things, demanded protection of
American rights, "by land and sea," but also called for an "honest neutrality."
It condemned the administration's interference in Mexico and blamed it for
much of the alleged chaos prevailing in that country. On the preparedness issue,
the Republicans equivocated by simply demanding "adequate" land and naval
forces. Finally, they reaffirmed their allegiance to the principle of tariff protection, condemned the Democrats for attempting to abandon the Philippines, and
pledged themselves to support effective rural credits and federal child labor
legislation. *Republican Campaign Text-Book* (New York, 1916), pp. 48–52.

laying their own plans for the coming campaign. The party machinery was reorganized and the erratic and ineffective national chairman, William F. McCombs, was eased out and replaced by the young and progressive Vance C. McCormick of Pennsylvania. After the happy settlement of the armed ship and *Sussex* crises the President was once again in undisputed control of party policies. In consultation with party leaders,[25] he wrote the Democratic platform, which contained an open bid for Progressive support in the form of a plank approving an advanced program of social legislation, promised a neutral foreign policy, endorsed reasonable preparedness, commended the cause of woman suffrage to the states, and denounced groups that placed the interests of foreign countries above the interests of the United States. Finally, the platform committed the party to support entrance by the United States into a postwar League of Nations pledged to enforce peace by collective security measures against aggressors.[26]

When delegates began to assemble for the national convention in St. Louis on June 11, the Democratic situation seemed so firmly under presidential control that the vanguard of party leaders on the scene expected a dull affair. Irritated by the Republicans' claim to a monopoly on patriotism, the President sent instructions that "Americanism" should be the keynote of the convention and that frequent demonstrations should attest to Democratic loyalty to the flag. When former Governor Martin H. Glynn of New York gave the keynote address at the opening session on June 14, however, he failed to evoke more than dutiful enthusiasm for the President, preparedness, and 100 per cent Americanism. Glynn then moved on to the war and American

[25] Senators W. J. Stone, Henry F. Hollis, F. M. Simmons, O. W. Underwood, and T. J. Walsh all submitted suggestions for the platform. These suggestions were sent to Wilson by Burleson on June 7, 1916, and are in the Wilson Papers.

[26] In fact, Wilson had already personally committed the country to this project in a significant address at Washington on May 27 before the League to Enforce Peace, a nonpartisan organization formed in 1915 to propagate the League plan. It is interesting that in preparing this address, which alleged America's willingness to depart from its historic policy of isolation, Wilson consulted only Colonel House and Secretary Lansing. In spite of his failure to confer with Democratic Congressional leaders on the matter, the Democrats willingly accepted a plank embodying the far-reaching proposal. It was a significant commentary on Wilson's mastery over the party leaders. The League to Enforce Peace speech is printed in *The Public Papers, New Democracy*, II, 184–188. The Democratic platform of 1916 is printed in *The Democratic Text Book, 1916* (New York, 1916), pp. 3–26, and in many other contemporary sources.

neutrality, invoking historical parallels to prove that Wilson's diplomacy of note writing had good precedent in the American past. But this would be a dull recital, he averred; and he was about to pass over that portion of his address when the immense crowd were on their feet, shouting, "No! No! Go on!" This was an unexpected development, but Glynn sensed the electrical quality of the situation and at once launched into his historical exposition. As he cited one case after another in which the United States had refused under provocation to go to war, the mighty throng would chant, "What did we do? What did we do?" And Glynn would roar back, "We didn't go to war, we didn't go to war!" On and on he went, while the convention indulged in one frenzied demonstration after another. It was as if the delegates had just discovered that pacifism, jeered at and derided, was the cornerstone upon which American foreign policy had been built.

Events of the following day gave even more spectacular evidence of the passion for peace that consumed the delegates and deafened their ears to any other appeals. The permanent chairman, Senator Ollie M. James of Kentucky, was a veteran of many campaigns with a sharp understanding of crowd psychology. He appealed stirringly to the delegates' desire for peace, and with the famous peroration, "Without orphaning a single American child, without widowing a single American mother, without firing a single gun or shedding a drop of blood, he [Wilson] wrung from the most militant spirit that ever brooded over a battlefield the concession of American demands and American rights," James provoked a nearly riotous demonstration that lasted twenty-one minutes.

At the night session of June 15 the cries for Bryan grew so loud that The Commoner had to speak. Cast out of party councils and castigated by the Democratic press, Bryan had even been refused election as a delegate from Nebraska and had come to the convention as a reporter.[27] He it was who became the hero of the convention, when he urged the delegates to renominate Wilson and thanked God the country had a President who did not want war. A few hours later Wilson was named by one mighty acclamation, and the convention adjourned the following day after adopting the platform.[28]

The meaning of the peace demonstration at St. Louis was unmistak-

---

[27] Bryan's letters to the newspapers from the convention are printed in *The Commoner*, June, 1916.

[28] *The New York Times*, June 16, 17, 1916.

ably clear to Wilson and his campaign managers. Irresistibly they were drawn into the ground swell for peace, and, as will be shown, the Democratic campaign that followed became in many respects a prolonged demonstration for peace. But while the managers in both camps were busy constructing their organizations and raising their funds, another development occurred that had a profound impact on the course of the contest. It was the near occurrence of a general railroad strike and the President's method of averting it.

Storm clouds had gathered on the horizon in early spring, when the presidents of the four railroad brotherhoods presented demands for an eight-hour day, with no reduction in wages, and time and a half for overtime work. On June 15 the railroad managers rejected these demands, although they offered to submit them to arbitration, and a weary conference broke up. When the United States Board of Mediation failed to bring agreement and 94 per cent of the nation's 400,000 engineers, firemen, conductors, and trainmen approved a general strike call, Wilson decided the time for decisive action had come. On August 13 he invited the brotherhood chiefs and the railroad managers to the White House and reminded them of the catastrophic consequences of a general strike—suffering, even starvation, in the great cities, disruption of the nation's economic life, and a setting back of the preparedness effort. The following morning the contending parties presented their cases, and Wilson appealed solemnly for compromise in the national interest. When both sides refused to budge he then and there resolved to impose his own settlement. The workers' demand for the eight-hour day was right, he declared; but they must abandon their demand for punitive overtime pay, and a federal commission should be appointed to study the entire railroad labor problem.[29]

The brotherhood chiefs accepted the President's proposal on August 18, but the managers had rejected it the day before. At once Wilson summoned the presidents of the great railroad systems to the White House and set Congressional leaders at work on legislation to be rushed through if his last-ditch efforts failed. Thirty-one railroad presidents appeared at the White House on August 18, but they were unmoved by the President's pleading.[30] Then Wilson issued a public

<hr />

[29] *Ibid.*, Aug. 14, 15, 16, 17, 1916. Wilson's solution was embodied in "Proposal. R. R. Conference," memorandum prepared by Wilson c. Aug. 16–17, 1916, Wilson Papers.

[30] *The New York Times,* Aug. 19, 1916. There were indications that some of the railroad presidents welcomed the prospect of a general strike, which they

appeal for support and summoned twelve more railroad presidents to Washington. To the railroad executives assembled and sweating in 100 degrees of heat in the East Room on August 21, Wilson appealed in the name of humanity that they accept his compromise. When they refused he exclaimed bitterly, "I pray God to forgive you, I never can," and left the room.[31]

Further futile negotiations between executives and union leaders only highlighted the hopelessness of the deadlock. On August 27 the brotherhood local chairman left Washington with orders to call a nation-wide strike on September 4. The railroad presidents' committee gave Wilson their final refusal to accept his plan. Wilson went to the Capitol, where he was closeted with Senate Democratic leaders during the afternoon of August 28, and before a joint session the following day he outlined legislation to prevent a strike and guarantee that the country would never again be threatened by such a catastrophe.[32] More important for the long future, however, was his sweeping endorsement of the eight-hour day, as a cause so vital to the health and happiness of the people that its fate could not be arbitrated.

The next few days were extraordinarily hectic. For a while it seemed Congress might refuse to act and, thinking he had failed, the President called fifteen thousand national guardsmen from the Mexican border to preserve order. Meanwhile, however, Chairman William C. Adamson of the House Interstate Commerce Committee and Majority Leader Kitchin drafted a bill imposing the eight-hour day, beginning

---

were sure they could break and which they thought would destroy the brotherhoods. "President Ripley of the Santa Fe road believes that if a violent strike should occur, it can be broken in thirty days," wrote the publisher of the reactionary Los Angeles *Times*. "In that case the organized railroad men would be the losers by a tremendous majority, and the outcome would be the ultimate non-unionizing of the railway service." Harrison Gray Otis to H. L. Scott, Aug. 24, 1916, the Papers of Hugh L. Scott, in the Library of Congress; also *The New York Times*, Aug. 29, 1916.

[31] *Ibid.*, Aug. 22, 1916; C. W. Eliot to J. P. Tumulty, Sept. 11, 1916; Wilson to Tumulty, c. Sept. 21, 1916, Wilson Papers.

[32] Wilson proposed (1) the eight-hour day for railroad workers engaged in interstate commerce, which, in the absence of punitive overtime, meant ten hours' pay for eight hours' work; (2) compulsory suspension of railroad strikes pending investigation by a federal commission; (3) that the Interstate Commerce Commission be enlarged and directed to study the cost of the eight-hour day, with a view to allowing the railroads to increase rates; and (4) that the President be authorized to compel railroad officials and workers to operate trains for military purposes. His address is printed in *The Public Papers, New Democracy*, II, 267–274.

January 1, 1917, and providing for a commission to study the railroad problem. As it was the only measure that could be passed quickly, it was approved August 31 by Wilson, Burleson, and the Congressional leaders. The House approved the following day, 239 to 56; and after a day of acrimonious debate the Senate accepted the bill on September 2 and the President signed it in his private car in the Union Station the next morning, just before he left for Hodgenville, Kentucky, for an address at Lincoln's birthplace.[33]

Passage of the Adamson Act prevented the railroad strike, to be sure, but it also injected a new issue, which Hughes gladly seized upon to bolster his sagging campaign. For it was now plain that he was not doing well. He had entered the contest with the respect and admiration of most independent and many Democratic journals. The four leading independent organs of opinion, the *New Republic,* the *Nation, The New York Times,* and the New York *Evening Post,* stood predisposed to support him. But his acceptance speech at Carnegie Hall on July 31 had been a bitter disappointment, reflecting mainly the advice of Henry Lane Wilson on the Mexican question.[34] Soon afterward Hughes had set out on a long tour of the Middle West and Far West, and everywhere he spoke he made votes for Wilson by his petty criticisms and failure to offer any constructive alternatives.[35] The great

[33] *The New York Times,* Sept. 2, 3, 4, 1916. There is a dénouement to this story that should not be overlooked. The railroad managers refused to accept the Adamson settlement and immediately instituted proceedings to test the act's constitutionality. When the railroads refused to abide by the law after January 1, 1917, the brotherhoods, on March 15, issued a general strike order. As the nation was on the verge of war with Germany, Wilson and the Council of National Defense appealed to both sides to remember that the country was already in dire peril. On March 17 the brotherhoods postponed the strike forty-eight hours; and the following day, after German submarines sank three American ships, the railroad managers gave in and conceded the eight-hour day. Then, on March 19, the Supreme Court, in a five-to-four decision, upheld the constitutionality of the Adamson Act. This important decision, rendered in Wilson *v.* New, 243 U.S., 332, affirmed that Congress' control over transportation facilities operating in interstate commerce was absolute.

[34] It was a significant commentary on Hughes' campaign that he should have chosen the discredited former Ambassador as his chief adviser on Mexico. See H. L. Wilson to Taft, June 23, 1916, Taft Papers; H. L. Wilson, "Memorandum on Mexico," undated, sent to Hughes, copy in *ibid.; The New York Times,* July 23, 28, 1916. For comment on Hughes' acceptance speech see Denver *Post,* Aug. 1, 1916; *The New York Times,* Aug. 1, 1916; Springfield *Republican,* Aug. 1, 1916; New York *Evening Post,* Aug. 1, 1916; New York *World,* Aug. 1, 1916; *New Republic,* VIII (Aug. 5, 1916), 4–5.

[35] See, for example, his speeches at Detroit, Aug. 7, in New York *Evening*

Eastern journals, which had hailed Hughes' candidacy with real enthusiasm, were baffled and searched about for an explanation, for, as one editor put it, "No other candidate for President within the memory of living man ever ran downhill so rapidly." [36]

The triumph of the brotherhoods in the epochal struggle for the eight-hour day, however, breathed life into the corpse of the Hughes campaign. For one thing, it aroused the business community to frantic anger and overwhelming support of the Republican ticket and sent a cold chill down the spines of the Democratic managers. For another, Hughes finally had an issue and launched a vigorous attack on Wilson for betraying the cause of arbitration and knuckling under to the rail-road workers—"the most shameful proceeding," he said, "that has come to my attention since I have observed public life." [37]

For his part, Wilson stayed at his post until the threat of a railroad strike was past. He made a few short speeches in the capital, important only as portents of the course he would later follow; and he wrote a long letter to Representative Lever, reviewing the agricultural legisla-tion of his administration.[38] His first important pronouncement, how-ever, he saved for his acceptance speech at Shadow Lawn, New Jersey, his temporary summer home, on September 2. It was more a scholarly summary of recent Democratic achievements than a rousing campaign address.[39] Then, on September 23, the President began a series of hard-hitting speeches that got his campaign into high gear and left his opponents dazed. Instead of apologizing for the Adamson Act, he

---

Post, Aug. 8, 1916; at Chicago, Aug. 8, in *The New York Times*, Aug. 9, 1916; at St. Paul, Aug. 9, *ibid.*, Aug. 10, 1916; at Fargo, N.D., Aug. 10, *ibid.*, Aug. 11, 1916; at Butte, Mont., Aug. 12, *ibid.*, Aug. 13, 1916.

[36] New York *World*, Aug. 17, 1916; for similar comments see *The New York Times*, Aug. 17, Sept. 8, 1916; *Independent*, LXXXVII (Aug. 28, 1916), 289–290; *The Nation*, CIII (Sept. 14, 1916), 251; Oswald G. Villard to William L. Phelps, July 21, 1916, the Papers of Oswald Garrison Villard, in Houghton Library, Harvard University.

Although Merlo J. Pusey, Hughes' biographer, makes out the best possible case for his subject, he nowhere answers the baffling question of why Hughes failed to wage a positive, constructive type of campaign. Nor, it might be added, is Mr. Pusey fair to Wilson, whom he accuses of using the peace issue at a time when the President knew war with Germany was likely. Pusey, *Hughes*, II, 356–357. The evidence Mr. Pusey uses to substantiate this charge is totally unreliable.

[37] C. E. Hughes to Taft, Sept. 16, 1916, Taft Papers.

[38] *The New York Times*, July 5, 14, 1916; the letter to Lever is printed in *The Public Papers, New Democracy*, II, 260–263.

[39] Printed in *ibid.*, pp. 275–291.

boldly defended it and the principle of the eight-hour day. In October he campaigned into the Middle West, defending his Mexican policy, reiterating the blessings his administration had brought the farmers, and in general magnifying his and the Democratic party's devotion to the great cause of progressive reform.[40]

Wilson's bold championship of labor's supreme objective and of the cause of social justice stood out in vivid contrast to the equivocation of the Republican platform and Hughes' evasive declarations. The result, therefore, was such a division on domestic issues as the country had not seen since 1896. The left wing of the progressive movement, including many Socialists and most single taxers, did not like Wilson's advocacy of preparedness and of measures calculated to appease the business community, but they never once seemed to doubt they had no alternative but to support the President.[41] Even more astonishing, however, was the way in which independent progressives—the social workers, sociologists, and articulate intellectuals—moved en masse into the Wilson camp. To name them is to name practically the entire leadership of the advanced wing of the progressive movement in the United States.[42] If this did not suffice to prove that the Democratic party was being transformed and re-created, then the wholesale movement of the former leaders of the Progressive party into the Democracy must have convinced the most cynical observer. One by one, the men and women who had gone into the Roosevelt party in 1912 to fight for principles and social regeneration, rather than to follow a hero, came out for Wilson—Jane Addams of Illinois, Francis J. Heney of California, John M. Parker of Louisiana, Edgar C. Snyder, chairman of the state committee in Washington, Bainbridge Colby of New York, Victor Mur-

[40] Addresses at Chicago, Oct. 4, 1916, *The New York Times,* Oct. 5, 1916; at Omaha, Oct. 5, 1916, printed in *The Public Papers, New Democracy,* II, 344–355; at Indianapolis, Oct. 12, 1916, *ibid.,* pp. 356–363; at Cincinnati, Oct. 26, 1916, *ibid.,* pp. 376–382; at Buffalo, Nov. 1, 1916, New York *World,* Nov. 2, 1916.

[41] On this point, see the significant articles: Victor S. Yarros, "Hughes, Wilson and the Radicals," *The Public,* XIX (June 16, 1916), 559–560, and Louis F. Post, "A Campaign Talk to Old Friends," *ibid.,* XIX (Oct. 20–27, 1916), 992–995, 1016–1019.

[42] A partial list would include William Kent, Norman Hapgood, Francis J. Heney, Frederic C. Howe, E. W. Scripps, A. J. McKelway; a host of journalists, including John Reed, Ray S. Baker, Lincoln Steffens, Ida M. Tarbell, Irvin S. Cobb, Walter Lippmann, Herbert Croly, and George Creel; Ben B. Lindsey, Jane Addams, Lillian D. Wald, David Lubin, Amos Pinchot, John Dewey, Max Eastman, Washington Gladden, and Bishop Francis J. McConnell of the Methodist Episcopal Church.

dock of Kansas, Edward P. Costigan of Colorado, Matthew Hale of Massachusetts, acting chairman of the national committee, and many others. Finally, a week before the election, eleven out of the nineteen members of the Progressive platform committee at the Chicago convention joined in a public appeal for Wilson, on the ground that the Democrats had redeemed the Progressive promises of 1912.

Obviously, Wilson's strategy of building a new coalition and drawing large accessions to his party had succeeded brilliantly. But there were other and as important additions to Democratic strength. The railway brotherhoods, the American Federation of Labor, and other organized labor groups were profoundly grateful to the administration and abandoned all pretense of neutrality during the campaign.[43] So vigorous was their support of the Democratic ticket, in fact, that at least two Old Guard bosses demanded that Hughes drop the eight-hour issue at once.[44] There were also many signs that Wilson's appeal for farm support was paying large dividends. The distinguished farm editor, Herbert Quick, traveled with the Federal Farm Loan Board through the Middle West in September and noted that everywhere the Board went Republican farmers were going in droves into the Wilson ranks. The Non-Partisan League, which was spreading like wildfire in the region, came out officially for Wilson because of the adoption of the rural credits act. Everywhere, in practically every state of the Middle West, farm groups endorsed Wilson.

Finally, the accession to the Democratic ranks of practically all independent newspapers and periodicals completed the great progressive coalition and added powerful support to Wilson's candidacy. "I shall vote not for the Wilson who has uttered a few too many noble sentiments," one independent declared, "but for the Wilson who is evolving under experience and is remaking his philosophy in the light of it, for the Wilson who is temporarily at least creating, out of the reactionary, parochial fragments of the Democracy, the only party which at this moment is national in scope, liberal in purpose, and

[43] Statements of Samuel Gompers, Andrew Furuseth, *et al.,* in *Wilson and Labor* (Democratic National Committee, 1916); Samuel Gompers *et al.,* "To the Officers of All Organized Labor," Oct. 14, 1916, copy in Wilson Papers; appeal of the presidents of the four brotherhoods, *The New York Times,* Oct. 27, 1916; *Locomotive Firemen's and Engineers' Magazine,* Nov., 1916; Samuel Gompers, "On Which Side Are You?" *American Federationist,* XXIII (Nov., 1916), 1067–1068.

[44] W. Murray Crane to Taft, Sept. 5, 1916, Taft Papers; David Baird to Taft, Oct. 7, 1916, *ibid.*

effective in action." [45] Herbert Croly confessed that he would vote for Wilson because the President had reconstructed the Democratic party into a responsible instrument of progressive nationalism, but that a few years before he would not have believed such a miracle was possible.[46] Thus the *New Republic, The New York Times,* the New York *Evening Post,* the *Nation, Pearson's Magazine,* the Scripps newspapers, and other leaders of independent opinion came out, some of them reluctantly, for Wilson as the hope of the country.

It is clear, therefore, that the campaign witnessed an almost perfect alignment of progressives and conservatives into two opposing camps and that the issue of further advancement toward a dynamic social welfare democracy drew large numbers to Wilson's side. But to interpret the campaign solely within this framework would be to miss the most important phenomenon of the contest: the fusion of the peace cause with the ideal of progressive democracy that the President and his campaigners effected.

As he was profoundly impressed by the mounting manifestations of the deep peace longings of the people, and particularly by the developments at St. Louis, Wilson must have deliberately decided to make a direct appeal to what was obviously an overwhelming popular sentiment. Nor was he motivated by considerations of expediency alone. By September his efforts to co-operate with the Allies in ending the war had failed, and he was growing suspicious of British motives and was persuaded neither side should win. Thus his metamorphosis from the firm defender of American rights on the seas to a leading champion of nonintervention was facilitated by developments both at home and abroad.

In an address at Shadow Lawn on September 30, the President first sounded the new keynote of his campaign. He brought his audience to their feet by charging that the Republicans were a war party and that Hughes' election must mean intervention in Mexico and the European war.[47] It was as if he had finally found the one great issue, and time and again he expounded this theme, in the Midwest and in the East, until it became the staccato note of his addresses. Moreover, by implication he promised to keep the United States out of war if the

[45] Walter Lippmann, "The Case for Wilson," *New Republic,* VIII (Oct. 14, 1916), 263–264.
[46] Herbert Croly, "The Two Parties in 1916," *ibid.,* Oct. 21, 1916, pp. 286–291.
[47] New York *World,* Oct. 1, 1916.

people sustained him. "I am not expecting this country to get into war," he declared at Shadow Lawn on October 21, for example. "I know that the way in which we have preserved peace is objected to, and that certain gentlemen say that they would have taken some other way that would inevitably have resulted in war, but I am not expecting this country to get into war, partly because I am not expecting those gentlemen to have a chance to make a mess of it." [48] Or again, ten days later he wrote for publication in Western newspapers the following letter: "Thank you warmly for your letter of October twenty-third. The reason you give for supporting me touches me very deeply, that you should feel when you see 'the boys and mother' together in your home circle that I have preserved the peace and happiness of the home. Such a feeling on the part of my fellow-citizens is a sufficient reward for everything that I have done." [49]

Wilson, moreover, shared with the people his great vision of a post-war community of nations co-operating to maintain the peace. There were times when he warned that the day might come when America must fight for the right. But he made it clear he was talking about the future, after the war, when the United States would use its strength in concert with other nations to prevent aggression. That was what he meant in his Cincinnati address of October 26, when he declared, "the business of neutrality is over." [50]

As the Republican interventionists, led by Theodore Roosevelt, took up Wilson's peace challenge and increased the ferocity of their attacks on his alleged failure to defend American rights on the seas, the President indignantly denounced them for dragging questions of foreign policy into the campaign in a partisan way. The Democratic campaign committee and orators, however, were elated by Roosevelt's blasts and used the peace issue for all it was worth. They knew the slogan, "He kept us out of war," [51] had vast potentialities, and when

[48] *The Public Papers, New Democracy,* II, 371–372.

[49] Wilson to J. W. Wasson, Velva, N.D., Oct. 31, 1916, Wilson Papers.

[50] In this same address Wilson also denounced those persons who said the United States should now be at war. "Have you ever heard what started the present war?" he asked. "If you have, I wish you would publish it, because nobody else has, so far as I can gather. Nothing in particular started it, but everything in general." *The Public Papers, New Democracy,* II, 381.

[51] Robert W. Woolley, publicity director for the Democratic National Committee in 1916, claims that he and Richard L. Metcalfe, his assistant, invented the phrase, "With honor, he has kept us out of war," and that it was used in all official literature. Woolley admitted, however, that the shorter "He kept us out of war" was used thousands of times by Democratic campaigners. Woolley

Wilson sounded the peace note on September 30 they were delighted and urged him on. So overwhelming was the popular response in the Midwest to Wilson's speech that Senator Thomas J. Walsh, in charge of Midwestern headquarters in Chicago, at once sent instructions to an army of orators in the region to adopt the peace issue as their main theme. Thus it was that "He kept us out of war" became the battle cry of peace that was thundered over the plains.

To lead the Democratic peace campaigners in the Middle and Far West the great apostle himself, Bryan, was chosen. No longer a pariah, up and down the West he went, carrying the good news of peace and progressivism to countless throngs. "Bryan's speeches at Pueblo last night and Colorado Springs tonight were masterpieces in argument and power," the former Governor of Colorado wrote.[52] Democratic leaders in Wisconsin reported that The Commoner had never been so well received in their state.[53]

It was in the millions of pamphlets and thousands of newspaper advertisements they published, however, that the campaign committee attained the maximum effectiveness. No matter what the subject of the written appeal happened to be, the peace issue was highlighted. Thus, a pamphlet entitled *Woodrow Wilson and Social Justice* concluded: "More than all, our country is at peace in a world at war," while an essay devoted to the child labor law reminded mothers that Wilson had saved their children from mines, mills, and sweatshops, as he had "saved their sons and their husbands from unrighteous battlefields!" [54] The climax of this propaganda came just before the election, when the Wilson Business Men's League on November 4 published the following advertisement in leading newspapers:

---

to R. S. Baker, Nov. 21, 1928, Baker Collection. Vance C. McCormick, Democratic national chairman in 1916, could not later remember who invented the slogan, although he well recalled how effectively it was used. R. S. Baker, interview with Vance C. McCormick, July 15, 1928, *ibid.* In so far as the present writer knows, Wilson never used the phrase.

[52] Alva Adams to T. J. Walsh, Oct. 13, 1916, the Papers of Thomas J. Walsh, in the Library of Congress.

[53] Joseph Martin to T. J. Walsh, Oct. 27, 1916, the Papers of William Jennings Bryan, in the Library of Congress.

[54] *Children's Emancipation Day* (Democratic National Committee, 1916); also *"Yes" or "No!" Mr. Hughes?, Ten Reasons for Voting for Wilson, by Dr. Irving Fisher, "Complete Accord with Roosevelt," Wilson and Labor, War Menace Masked by Republican Policy, The Wilson Volunteers, Wilson Workers' Manual,* all issued by the Democratic National Committee, 1916.

You Are Working—*Not Fighting!*
Alive and Happy;—*Not Cannon Fodder!*
Wilson and Peace with Honor?
or
Hughes with Roosevelt and War?

Roosevelt says we should hang our heads in shame because we are not at *war* with Germany in behalf of Belgium! Roosevelt says that following the sinking of the Lusitania he would have foregone diplomacy and seized every ship in our ports flying the German Flag. That would have meant *war!*

Hughes Says He and Roosevelt are in Complete Accord!

. . . . .

The Lesson is Plain:
If You Want WAR, vote for HUGHES!
If You Want Peace with Honor
VOTE FOR WILSON!

While the Democrats were pressing a united and powerful campaign, Hughes and his managers fumbled from one issue to another, confused and continually embarrassed by feuds within their ranks. The Democrats kept pounding away, demanding that Hughes tell what he would have done. At Louisville on October 12 the former Justice finally shot back that he would have broken relations with Germany after the sinking of the *Lusitania,* although he said the tragedy would never have occurred if the Germans had believed Wilson meant what he had said about "strict accountability." Even more embarrassing to the Republicans than the Democratic gadflies, however, was Theodore Roosevelt, who barnstormed the country, denouncing the President for cowardly weakness abroad. Indeed, Roosevelt was a virtual millstone around Hughes' neck, for the hapless candidate was drawn into approving Roosevelt's declarations, which enabled the Democrats to charge that Hughes also harbored warlike designs.[55] Bernstorff was not far wrong when he wrote the Foreign Office, "If Hughes is defeated he has Roosevelt to thank for it." [56]

[55] When Roosevelt made one of his usual addresses at Lewiston, Maine, Hughes telegraphed him from Kansas: "I heartily congratulate you on your speech at Lewiston, and warmly appreciate your effective support." *Outlook,* CXIV (Sept. 13, 1916), 63. For the way in which the Democrats used this incident, see *"Complete Accord with Roosevelt."*

[56] Oct. 19, 1916, "Bernstorff Wireless Messages—1916," in the Papers of Walter H. Page, in Houghton Library, Harvard University.

Hughes' difficulties with the peace issue, his failure to attract wide independent and Progressive support, and Roosevelt's bellicose speeches were serious encumbrances to the Republican cause, to be sure, but in the showdown it was the bitter factionalism within the party that caused its undoing. For one thing, the Old Guard resented Hughes' approval of Roosevelt and the appointment of former Progressives to positions of leadership in the campaign organization. For another, in certain Western states the old-line bosses were more interested in preventing the Progressives from capturing the party than they were in electing Hughes. This was the situation, for example, in California, through which Hughes campaigned in August. The former Progressives were preparing to move back into the Republican party and to nominate Governor Hiram Johnson for the Senate on the G.O.P. ticket. From the day he entered the seething California campaign, Hughes went from one blunder to another. He allowed himself to be surrounded and his itinerary to be determined by the Old Guard leaders, who had declared open war on the Progressives. He followed the Republican state chairman across a picket line in San Francisco. Finally, he unwittingly failed to confer with Governor Johnson, when the two men were in a Long Beach hotel at the same time.

As if to compound Republican difficulties, Hughes was also embarrassed by the open support of organized German-American groups and practically the entire German-language press. It was a difficult situation, and Hughes tried to play both ends against the middle. On the one hand, he talked boldly of "straight Americanism" and applauded Roosevelt; on the other he conferred with the most extreme pro-German spokesmen in the country—the leaders of the German-financed American Independence Conference [57]—and satisfied them he would pursue a policy of true neutrality.[58] Apparently to prove his sincerity, at Philadelphia on October 9 Hughes affirmed that he would take strong action against the British if he were elected. Unhappily for the luckless Hughes, the Democratic National Committee bought or stole the records of the American Independence Conference and published the details of the German- and Irish-American plot to defeat

[57] They were Jeremiah A. O'Leary, Carl E. Schmidt, Will R. McDonald, Frank Seiberlich, Jaspar T. Darling, St. John Gaffney, Joseph Frey, Victor Ridder, and Daniel F. Cohalan.

[58] The meeting took place around the middle of September, probably in New York City.

Kirby in the New York *World*

Berlin's candidate

Wilson and of Hughes' negotiations with the leaders of that movement.[59]

The Democratic managers tried just as shamelessly to curry favor with the so-called hyphen vote,[60] but Wilson personally refused to

[59] The documents were printed in *The New York Times,* Oct. 23, 24, 25, 1916; New York *World,* Oct. 24, 25, 1916.

[60] For details of these negotiations see Kent E. Keller to N. Hapgood, Sept. 16, 1916, Wilson Papers; William J. Stone to J. P. Tumulty, Sept. 25, 1916,

engage in any such negotiations. Indeed, when the blatant president of the American Truth Society, Jeremiah A. O'Leary, tried to compel the President to state his views, Wilson shot back: "I would feel deeply mortified to have you or anybody like you vote for me. Since you have access to many disloyal Americans and I have not, I will ask you to convey this message to them." [61] It was a telling blow that many voters remembered when the details of Hughes' conference with O'Leary and his brethren were later published.

In their effort to turn out what many of them sincerely thought was a disgraceful administration, the Republicans thundered and volleyed on Mexico, made a vain bid for women's votes in the Western states, accused Wilson and Bryan of adding a postcript to the first *Lusitania* note, telling the German government they did not mean what they had just said, and charged that Southerners in control of Congress were plundering the wealth of the North and Middle West to pay for preparedness. Finally, the Republicans organized vast whispering campaigns against the President, accusing him of all kinds of irregularities, but especially of numerous infidelities to his first wife.

In spite of all the din and confusion, however, two issues—peace and progressivism—stood out above all the rest, and nothing the Republicans could do diverted attention from them. Even so, it seemed at first that the new Democratic-Progressive coalition had failed to convert the normal Democratic minority into a majority. Outside the South, the majority of farmers, businessmen, and professional people normally voted Republican. The great mass of laborers and minority groups were in that day politically illiterate and leaderless. In 1912 Taft and Roosevelt combined had received 1,311,484 more votes than Wilson; perhaps it was unreasonable to think Wilson could overcome such a preponderance against his party.

Early returns on Tuesday evening, November 7, revealed that Hughes had made almost a clean sweep of the East, except for Ohio and possibly New Hampshire, and the Democratic spokesman, the

---

ibid.; The New York Times, Oct. 11, 12, 13, 14, 1916; also *"Complete Accord with Roosevelt,"* the most extraordinary document issued by the Democratic National Committee during the campaign. It accused Hughes of sympathizing with England and of desiring a war with the beloved Fatherland. "Such a bloody war," it declared, "would help crush a nation, millions of whose sons and daughters dwell in our land and love our flag; and help destroy a people who lead in art, poetry, music, philosophy, and science" and "drain our veins in order that Germany might bleed the more."

[61] Wilson to O'Leary, Sept. 29, 1916, *The New York Times,* Sept. 30, 1916.

New York *World,* conceded defeat. Wilson went to bed at ten that evening and slept soundly in the knowledge that he could soon turn his thoughts to matters less pressing than affairs of state. But the Democratic managers kept their eyes on the West and refused to concede, and as one Western state after another recorded its vote for Wilson

(Courtesy, *Knickerbocker News*).

The suspense which followed the November, 1916, election depicted by a cartoonist for the Albany, N. Y., Knickerbocker Press.

the margin between the two candidates narrowed. In Delaware, New Hampshire, Minnesota, New Mexico, North Dakota, and California the contest was so close a handful of votes either way would have turned the tide. Wilson won all these doubtful states except Delaware and Minnesota, which went to Hughes by pluralities of 1,258 and 392, respectively. With a total of 277 electoral votes, Wilson had a majority of twenty-three in the Electoral College.[62] He received in all 9,129,606 votes, as against 8,538,221 for Hughes—a gain for the President of nearly three million votes over 1912. It was the best possible evidence that the progressive-peace issue had succeeded in drawing together a new coalition. The congressional and senatorial contests had been so close, however, that the Democratic majority in the Senate was reduced to eight, while control of the House of Representatives would rest with a handful of Progressives and Independents.[63]

After the ballots in the hotly contested states had been recounted, analysts tried to discover the factors that had enabled Wilson to win. A close examination of the returns yielded many surprises and portents. To begin with, the vaunted German-American bloc had been so riddled by the Democratic peace appeal and Roosevelt's campaign blasts that the so-called hyphen vote almost vanished.[64] The labor vote, while not yet solidly organized, went largely to Wilson and was a factor in his success in New Hampshire, Ohio, Washington, and California. In the Middle and Far Western states the women's vote went disproportionately to Wilson.[65] Moreover, Socialists deserted their party by the

[62] Wilson carried all the Southern states, including Maryland, Kentucky, Missouri, and Oklahoma, plus New Hampshire, Ohio, Kansas, Nebraska, North Dakota, Montana, Wyoming, Colorado, New Mexico, Arizona, Utah, Nevada, Idaho, Washington, and California.

[63] The Sixty-Fifth Congress would contain, in the House, 213 Democrats, 217 Republicans, 2 Progressives, 1 Prohibitionist, 1 Socialist, and 1 Independent; in the Senate, 54 Democrats and 42 Republicans.

[64] The German-American vote went largely to Hughes in Oregon, Minnesota, and Illinois, and was apparently important in the Republican success in the first two states. On the other hand, in Maryland the German-Americans voted largely for Wilson and probably swung the state to him. Hamilton County, Ohio (Cincinnati), an important German-American center, returned a twelve thousand plurality for Hughes. On the other hand, Taft carried the county by 18,374 in 1908 and the combined Taft-Roosevelt vote exceeded Wilson's vote by 16,036 in 1912. With its large German-American population, Ohio gave Wilson a plurality of 89,503 in 1916, although Taft carried the state by 69,591 in 1908 and Taft and Roosevelt together in 1912 polled a vote that exceeded Wilson's by 83,341. In the six "German" wards of St. Louis, Hughes gained only two-tenths of one per cent over the combined Republican-Progressive percentage of the total vote four years before. Hughes gained 12,480 votes in twelve "German" counties in Wisconsin, but Wilson carried the most important of them, Milwaukee County, by seven thousand, although not another Democrat received a majority in the county. This note is based upon the excellent analysis in *The New York Times,* Nov. 12, 1916.

[65] Democratic and Republican leaders in Kansas estimated, for example, that

hundreds of thousands—the Socialist vote declined from 901,873 in 1912 to 585,113 in 1916—and it is a safe assumption that all the seceders went to Wilson. They, too, could claim a large share in determining the result.[66]

So much for the voting behavior of the several important groups. As for the issues, all observers agreed the key factor in Democratic success was Wilson's and his party's promise of continued peace, prosperity, and progressive democracy.[67] These were the issues that won a majority of the women, a large minority of the Socialists, and a large enough number of former Progressives to put Wilson across.[68]

What the election portended for the long future of American politics would in large measure depend upon the administration's success in holding the new coalition together, and this in turn might depend upon a redemption of the Democratic promises to keep the country out of war. The election's immediate significance, however, was apparent to all observers and especially to the President. "It is the South and West united," a distinguished historian wrote; "the farmers, small business men and perhaps a large sprinkle of Union labor against the larger industrial, transportation and commercial interests." [69] It was, indeed, the South and West united again in an emphatic mandate for progressivism and peace.[70] In short, Wilson had consummated the

---

70,000 women Republicans in the state, out of a total of 625,000 voters, voted for Wilson on the peace issue; it was estimated, moreover, that 90,000 out of 155,000 registered women voted for Wilson in Washington, where his plurality was only 16,594; and that women also helped carry California, Idaho, Utah, and Arizona for the President. These estimates were made by local politicians and newspaper correspondents. See *The New York Times,* Nov. 12, 1916.

[66] The Socialist losses were heaviest in the key states. Expressed in percentages, the losses were as follows: Ohio, 58 per cent; Pennsylvania, 50 per cent; Illinois, 50 per cent; California, 62 per cent; New York, 27 per cent; Washington, 47 per cent. In California the Socialist presidential vote in 1916 declined fifty thousand from the high point of 1912.

[67] William Allen White was the only contemporary observer who thought the peace issue was not important. He believed Midwestern and Western Progressives supported Wilson solely on the ground that the administration was committed to further progressive reforms. William A. White, "Who Killed Cock Robin?" *Collier's,* LVIII (Dec. 16, 1916), 5–6, 26–27.

[68] It was estimated that 20 per cent of the former Progressives voted for Wilson in 1916, but this was a national average and the percentage was much higher in the West.

[69] William E. Dodd to E. M. House, Nov. 10, 1916, House Papers.

[70] There were special reasons, which did not generally operate in the West, to account for Hughes' victory in the East and in the central Midwestern states of Illinois, Indiana, Minnesota, Wisconsin, and Iowa.

union of most of the agricultural states, which Bryan had narrowly failed to do in 1896, and had added to the Democratic column two Eastern states and a large portion of the social justice element, who had heretofore followed Roosevelt.

No war clouds darkened the horizon. No convulsion threatened domestic tranquillity. To Democrats and progressives it was a time full of joy and hope for another four years of peace and an intensification of the drive for social justice.[71] The poet Witter Bynner expressed this feeling:

> The morning-sun arose, the evening star:
> America renewed her light all day
> And stood serene at evening, and from far
> Freedom was visible with lifted ray . . .
> Wilson!—humanity once more is true—
> The light that shone on Lincoln shines on you.[72]

Hughes carried Minnesota and Wisconsin, normally heavily Republican states, by greatly reduced Republican majorities, which fact was testimony to the power of the progressive-peace appeal. In Illinois and Iowa the reunion of the Republican party had resulted in a shift of control to former Progressives or progressive Republicans. Reunion had been accomplished in Indiana under Old Guard auspices, but without recrimination or bitterness. Thus Republican losses, by defection of former Progressives to Wilson, were small in these two states.

In Illinois, Indiana, and the Eastern states, moreover, other factors contributed to Hughes' success. Firstly, the Democratic city machines, especially in Boston, Chicago, and New York City, either knifed the national ticket or else made only halfhearted campaigns. Secondly, the Negro vote went almost solidly to Hughes. Thirdly, a part of the Catholic hierarchy and many priests and Catholic journals entered the campaign against Wilson. Catholics were particularly aroused against the President's Mexican policy. The opposition of the Catholic Church had its most profound impact upon the Irish-Americans, who were already angry because Wilson had refused to intervene in behalf of the Irish during the Rebellion of the preceding April and May. They left the Democratic party in droves, and Wilson did not carry a single state in which they were an important factor.

[71] For significant comments on the meaning of the election, see the New York *World*, Nov. 9, 1916; R. M. La Follette, "Jingoism Rebuked," *La Follette's Magazine*, VIII (Nov., 1916), 1; W. J. Bryan, "The Election of 1916," *The Commoner*, Nov., 1916; *The New York Times*, Nov. 10, 1916; *New Republic*, IX (Nov. 11, 1916), 31–32; *The Public*, XIX (Nov. 17, 1916), 1092–1093.

[72] "Wilson," printed in *The Public*, XIX. (Nov. 24, 1916), 1121.

CHAPTER 10

From Peace Without Victory to War

WHILE Wilson, the Democratic campaigners, and a large segment of the American people displayed their deep desire for peace during the autumn of 1916, events in Europe were conspiring to make continued American neutrality difficult, if not impossible. After the failure of the German Verdun offensive in the spring and of the Allied Somme offensive in the summer and fall, both sides resolved to use their most desperate weapons to break the deadlock and end the awful slaughter.

For Great Britain, this decision involved an intensification of economic warfare, which would inevitably exacerbate Anglo-American tension. Thus, instead of yielding to American pressure on the "blacklist," the British extended their warfare against suspected American firms. "We have the rawest kind of cases all over the world," the Counselor of the State Department complained, "where British officials have threatened and browbeaten American merchants." [1] The British, moreover, devised a new scheme to obtain control of all neutral shipping: the so-called bunkering agreement, by which the neutral shipowner submitted to the regulations of the British Admiralty in return for the privilege of buying British coal in various ports of the world.[2]

---

[1] F. L. Polk to Irwin Laughlin, Dec. 8, 1916, the Papers of Frank L. Polk, in the Library of Yale University.

[2] When a neutral shipowner entered into this agreement, he promised to keep the British Admiralty informed of the names of all his vessels, not to charter ships to any person or country not approved by British authorities, not to trade with any country at war with Great Britain, to co-operate closely with British authorities in operations with Holland and Scandinavia, and to carry no goods

When the British trade representative in the United States, Sir Richard Crawford, frankly admitted the purpose of the bunkering agreement, the issue became to the American government even more serious than the "blacklist" dispute.

It is no exaggeration to say that official Anglo-American relations reached the point of highest tension during the critical period from November, 1916, through the following January. This was true, not only because of the tightening of British economic controls, but also because of the British refusal to co-operate in the German and American peace drives. It is perhaps conjectural to say the two countries were heading toward a break in relations, yet such a catastrophe was not impossible. On November 24, for example, Wilson asked Colonel House to tell Sir Edward Grey that Americans "were growing more and more impatient with the intolerable conditions of neutrality, their feeling as hot against Great Britain as it was at first against Germany and likely to grow hotter still against an indefinite continuation of the war." [3] "I hate to feel that the two great democratic countries are drifting apart," Polk wrote, "but . . . I cannot persuade myself that the fault is entirely ours, or even half ours." [4] Nor was all the exasperation on the American side. British nerves were on edge and British resentment at American efforts to enforce the rules of neutrality was noticeably increasing.[5]

---

consigned "to order." There is a copy of the bunkering agreement in *Papers Relating to the Foreign Relations of the United States, 1916, Supplement* (Washington, 1929), pp. 458–459.

[3] Wilson to House, Nov. 24, 1916, the Ray Stannard Baker Collection, in the Library of Congress.

[4] F. L. Polk to W. H. Page, Nov. 23, 1916, Polk Papers. "Confidentially," Polk wrote a short time later, "what I am afraid of is that Congress will get on to this [blacklist] abuse, call for a Congressional investigation of the way the blacklist is being administered, and then the lid will be off. . . . I have become a most violent believer in a large army and navy, because I see that we are fast arriving at a station, if we have not already reached it, where everyone hates us and we have got to be in a position to protect ourselves and ask no favors." Polk to Irwin Laughlin, Dec. 8, 1916, *ibid.* See also Polk to W. H. Page, Sept. 29, 1916, and to F. R. Coudert, Oct. 6, 1916, *ibid.*

[5] Lansing relates the story of an extraordinary interview on January 18, 1917, with the British Ambassador, Sir Cecil Spring Rice, which illustrated the possibility of difficulties on other issues. The British Admiralty had placed a gun crew on a certain merchant vessel, which caused the State Department to protest and warn that such vessels would be regarded as warships. Spring Rice inquired if the protest were authentic. Lansing replied that it was. Spring Rice's "face twitched, his eyes blazed, and his hands clenched until the knuckles showed white." The two men stood facing each other about three feet apart.

At the same time, events on the seas and developments in the German government pointed to the grave danger that Germany would burst the bonds of the *Sussex* pledge and use her submarines in such a way as to imperil good relations with the United States. For one thing, a series of borderline U-boat sinkings during October and November raised the question whether the German government had not in fact already violated its pledges. There were a number of questionable sinkings, but the two important cases involved the British merchant ship *Marina,* sunk without warning October 28, and the British liner *Arabia,* torpedoed without warning November 6, 1916.[6] Wilson was not willing to raise a serious issue over doubtful cases at this time because he planned to begin a peace campaign immediately after the election. Even within the limits of the *Sussex* pledge, however, the submarine campaign was being tremendously stepped up. German submarines, raiders, and mines sank on an average about 350,000 tons a month from October, 1916, through January, 1917, as compared with 185,800 tons sunk in August, 1915, 191,600 tons in April, 1916, and 230,400 in September of the same year. During the eight months that the Germans honored the *Sussex* pledge, from June, 1916, to February, 1917, their submarines and raiders accounted for an over-all total of 2,099,523 tons.[7]

The intensified submarine operations during the fall and early winter of 1916–17 had a profound impact upon the British, making them all the more determined to intensify their own economic warfare.[8] But so long as the Germans remained reasonably within the bounds of the *Sussex* pledge, the Washington government would offer

---

The Ambassador leaned forward and "fairly hissed," "If you follow this course, sir, of doing nothing while helpless people are murdered or put in open boats three hundred miles from land, and at the same time of stopping our vessels from defending themselves, you will be held personally responsible, yes, you and the President will be personally responsible." "Memorandum of an Interview with the British Ambassador, Thursday, January 18, 1917," the Diary of Robert Lansing, in the Library of Congress.

[6] Robert Lansing, "Memorandum. Vessels Sunk by German and Austrian Submarines, November 13, 1916," the Woodrow Wilson Papers, in the Library of Congress, and two memoranda by Lansing, entitled "Marina Case" and "Arabia Case," sent to the President Dec. 8, 1916, and in *ibid.*

[7] These figures are taken from the tables in R. H. Gibson and Maurice Prendergast, *The German Submarine War, 1914–1918* (New York, 1931), pp. 380–381.

[8] For a discussion of the impact of this warfare on the British economy before February, 1917, see *Official German Documents Relating to the World War* (2 vols., New York, 1923), II, 702–705.

no objections. Of serious consequence to the United States, however, were the increasing evidences that the Germans contemplated inaugurating unrestricted submarine warfare at an early date. The question entered an acute stage of discussion at a conference of all civilian and military chieftains at Pless Castle on August 31, 1916. The naval leaders pressed for immediate resumption of all-out, ruthless warfare, but Hindenburg and Ludendorff, the new masters of the army, agreed with Chancellor Bethmann-Hollweg that the military situation was too unpromising to invite the certain intervention of the United States. Rumors of an impending all-out submarine campaign were alternately affirmed and denied by American representatives in Berlin, but the possibility hung like a sword over the President's head.

This, therefore, was the uncertain and dangerous situation confronting Wilson during the last weeks of the presidential campaign and immediately afterward. The two giants in Europe were obviously preparing for a desperate bid for victory, which would inevitably abridge further American neutral rights. To preserve neutrality in the face of such assaults would be nearly impossible at best. Yet that was obviously what the American people wanted the President to do. Even more, they apparently preferred to abandon their rights on the seas rather than go to war to defend them, and Wilson was so impressed by the peace manifestations that his will to maintain his submarine policy was profoundly shaken. "I do not believe the American people would wish to go to war no matter how many Americans were lost at sea," he told House and Vance McCormick. He was sorry this was true, but it was his firm opinion.[9]

The only course of peace and safety for the United States, was, therefore—so the President thought—to bring the war to an end. Yet the House-Grey understanding was dead, and British spokesmen, aware of the possibilities of an American mediation attempt, publicly announced that anyone who talked of peace was a friend of Germany.[10] As the wisest British journalist warned, the mere suggestion of peace would make the British people "wild with fury." If Wilson

[9] The Diary of Edward M. House, in the Papers of Edward M. House, in the Library of Yale University, Nov. 2, 1916.

[10] Lloyd George, for example, on September 28 warned that Britain would "tolerate" no mediation by the United States and was determined to fight until "Prussian military despotism is broken beyond repair." *The New York Times,* Sept. 29, 1916. For the background of Lloyd George's statement see the Diary of Chandler P. Anderson, in the Library of Congress, Sept. 15, 1916.

could expect nothing but hostility to peace in British circles, then where could he turn? Obviously, there was no alternative left but to seek peace through diplomatic co-operation with the German government.

Since the happy settlement of the *Sussex* crisis, Colonel House had dangled the lure of Wilson's mediation before Bernstorff's eyes, and in turn the Ambassador had excited the hopes of his government. At first disdainful of the President's help, by autumn Bethmann-Hollweg and the Foreign Office had concluded that Wilson's mediation on terms favorable to Germany was the only hope of forestalling a resumption of unrestricted submarine operations. The Imperial Chancellor, therefore, began urgently to request that Wilson take an early initiative for peace.[11] And Bernstorff and Gerard made it abundantly plain what the consequences of the failure of the peace campaign would be.

In a pacific mood, the President welcomed the German overtures as the first ray of hope since the collapse of the House-Grey talks. Bernstorff talked with him around October 14 and made the following revealing report: "Wilson gave his remarks a particular weight through referring to the fact that the leaders of the opposition, Roosevelt, Lodge, *et al.*, wanted war with Germany, a desire which he could not understand. He stated that he had but the one wish, to remain neutral and to help bring the war to an end, since in his opinion a decision could not be reached by force of arms." [12] As soon as his re-election was beyond doubt, the President summoned House to Washington and on November 14 told him that, in order to avert the necessity of American intervention, he planned to demand that the war be ended. House protested that such a move would be highly prejudicial to the Allies. The following morning Wilson announced he had made up his mind to move for peace. But what if Germany agreed to a reasonable settlement and the Allies refused? House asked. In that case would not the United States drift into a sympathetic alliance with Germany? Might not France and Britain declare war on

[11] Bethmann-Hollweg to Bernstorff, Sept. 25, Oct. 9, 1916, *Official German Documents,* II, 984–986, 986–987.   At the same time, Gerard left Berlin for Washington with Jagow's and Bethmann's request that he ask the President to move quickly for peace, in order to prevent resumption of ruthless submarine warfare. James W. Gerard, *My First Eighty-Three Years in America* (Garden City, N.Y., 1951), pp. 241–243.

[12] Bernstorff to Foreign Office, received Oct. 14, 1916, *Official German Documents,* II, 988.

the United States? If the Allies wanted war, Wilson replied, he would not shrink from it.[13]

The event that caused Wilson to pause was not House's opposition or the threat of a break with Great Britain, which he did not take seriously. It was the deportation by the German government of some 300,000 Belgians for forced labor in the Reich. This act, which the Germans justified on the ground of desperate necessity, provoked a wave of indignation in the United States that exceeded initial American anger at the violation of Belgian neutrality. At first Wilson thought he had no right to protest, but the rising popular wrath soon caused him to change his mind.

Even so, pressure from Germany and at home for daring presidential leadership in the peace movement was also heavy, and Wilson set to work on his note soon after his conference with House of November 14–15. By November 25 he had completed the first draft and read it to House on November 26. As the President for the first time since 1914 unburdened his most secret thoughts on the war and America's relation to it, the note was a document of extraordinary importance.[14] He described the futility of the war and its baneful effects on civilization. Declaring that the causes of the war were obscure, he went on to point out that the position of neutrals was becoming intolerable, not only because of the conduct of the belligerents, but also because neutrals still did not know what the war was about.[15] Future American

---

[13] "He [Wilson] thought they would not dare resort to this and if they did, they could do this country no serious hurt. I disagreed with him again. I thought Great Britain might conceivably destroy our fleet and land troops from Japan in sufficient numbers to hold certain parts of the United States. He replied they might get a good distance but would have to stop somewhere, to which I agreed." House Diary, Nov. 15, 1916.

[14] The original is in the Wilson Papers. R. S. Baker, *Woodrow Wilson: Life and Letters* (8 vols., Garden City, N.Y., 1927–39), VI, 381–386, reprints it in full.

[15] "And yet *the reasons for this upheaval of the world remain obscure, and* the objects which would, if attained, satisfy the one group of belligerents or the other have never been definitely avowed. *As it is not known what motives led to the war's sudden outbreak so it is not known, the* The world can still only conjecture what definitive results, what actual exchange of guarantees, what political readjustments or changes, what stage or degree of military success even, would bring it to an end. If any other nation now neutral should be drawn in, it would know only that it was *forced* drawn in by some force it could not resist, because it had been hurt and saw no remedy but to risk still greater, it might be even irreparable, injury, in order to make the weight in the one scale or the other decisive; and even as a participant it would not know

policy would depend upon the objectives for which the respective alliances were fighting, yet leaders on both sides had avowed the same objectives. He was clearly within his rights, therefore, in urging the belligerents to define their objectives, and to do this at an early conference.

Because the proposed note reflected a cool, neutral detachment, House did not like it and prophesied it would have dire consequences for Anglo-American relations. He urged delay, but Wilson was apparently unmoved. Lansing, too, was gravely troubled. "Suppose . . . Germany listens to the President and the Allies decline to do so, what will be our situation?" he asked. "How can we turn then to the Allies? This is causing me the gravest concern." [16] Wilson agreed to delay action, but not for long; and when House tried to divert him by reviving the House-Grey understanding, Wilson answered flatly: "We cannot go back to those old plans. We must shape new ones." [17]

One of the new plans involved calling a halt to the partial financing of the Allied war effort by American bankers. The British were near the point of exhausting the securities they could use as collateral for loans, while their dependence upon American food, raw materials, and munitions was increasing daily. J. P. Morgan & Company proposed to solve the difficulty by taking the unsecured and renewable short-term bills of the British and French treasuries. A majority of the Federal Reserve Board, however, decided the time to call a halt had come, lest the American economy become too dependent upon the war trade. Their spokesman, W. P. G. Harding, conferred with Lansing on No-

how far the scales must tip before the end would come or what was being weighed in the balance!" The words italicized were crossed out by Wilson in his original draft.

[16] The Diary of Robert Lansing, in the Library of Congress, Dec. 3, 1916. Lansing further outlined the danger in a letter to Wilson on December 10, 1916 (Wilson Papers):

"I think, among other questions, we should consider these: Unless the answers of *both* parties are made in the right spirit, will there be any other course than to declare in favor of the one most acceptable and abandon a neutrality which is becoming more and more difficult? But suppose that the unacceptable answer comes from the belligerents whom we could least afford to see defeated on account of our own national interest and on account of the future domination of the principles of liberty and democracy in the world—then what? Would we not be forced into an even worse state than that in which we are now? . . . Can we avoid the logic of our declarations? And if we act in accordance with that logic, would it not be a calamity for the nation and for all mankind?"

[17] Wilson to House, Dec. 8, 1916, Baker Collection.

vember 20 and with Wilson on November 25 and proposed that the Board caution American bankers against accepting the short-term Treasury notes. Wilson, however, wanted a strong warning and was pleased when the Board, on November 27, advised bankers that it did not "regard it in the interest of the country at this time that they invest in foreign Treasury bills of this character." Although Wall Street grumbled and threatened to buy the Treasury notes anyway, the British discreetly decided not to issue them.

While Wilson was debating with Lansing and House the wisdom of launching his peace bolt, the civilian and military leaders of Germany agreed that events had finally created a situation favorable to a peace move. Poor harvests in the United States and Britain and the ravages of the submarines would make the British susceptible, while the spectacular success of the German campaign in Rumania had stabilized the military situation. Bethmann-Hollweg and Hindenburg reached accord on peace terms by November 7, and when Wilson did not act during November the Germans grew restive. Bucharest fell on December 6; two days later Hindenburg and the Emperor allowed Bethmann-Hollweg to launch an independent peace campaign. If it failed, unrestricted submarine warfare should be inaugurated in January, 1917.

On December 12, therefore, the Chancellor announced to an excited Reichstag that the Imperial government was ready to join with its enemies to end the war.[18] He said nothing about the German terms, which, if they had been disclosed, would have shocked the world. They included, in the East, establishment of the Kingdom of Poland and German annexation of the Baltic provinces of Courland and Lithuania; in the West, "guarantees in Belgium" or the annexation of Liége and "corresponding areas," annexation of Luxemburg and the French territories of Briey and Longwy, which contained great iron deposits, strategic boundary adjustments in Alsace-Lorraine, and indemnities; overseas, the return of German colonies, except Kiaochow, the Carolines, and the Marianas, and acquisition of all or part of the Belgian Congo.[19]

[18] For his speech, see *The New York Times*, Dec. 13, 1916. The German peace note is printed in *Foreign Relations, 1916, Supplement*, p. 90.

[19] These were the terms agreed upon by the Emperor, Hindenburg, and Bethmann-Hollweg. See *Official German Documents*, II, 1059–1062, 1064. For an excellent discussion see Hans W. Gatzke, *Germany's Drive to the West* (Baltimore, 1950), pp. 139–144.

On December 5 the American Chargé in Berlin, Joseph C. Grew, had told Bethmann-Hollweg, "What the President now most earnestly desires is practical cooperation on part of German authorities in bringing about a favorable opportunity for early and affirmative action." [20] On the day he announced Germany's willingness to negotiate, the Chancellor dispatched an earnest appeal to Wilson: "It is my sincere hope that this formal and solemn offer to enter immediately into peace negotiations . . . will coincide with the wishes of the President of the United States." [21] At first Wilson was depressed because he thought the Germans had acted hastily. Within a week, however, he was writing—and without any knowledge of the German terms—"We are just now . . . holding our breath for fear the overtures of the Central Powers with regard to peace will meet with a rebuff instead of an acceptance." [22] Even Lansing admitted the Germans might sincerely desire peace and that, in any event, they had put the Allies in a difficult position.[23]

On the day the German offer was announced, December 12, Wilson, House, and Lansing were debating the President's proposed peace message. Wilson at once revised his draft, which he submitted to Lansing on December 17. Lansing thought the revision "far superior, . . . much more forceful and convincing" than the original draft had been. Actually, the note as sent to all belligerents on December 18 had been vastly weakened by the force of House's and Lansing's advice and of recent circumstances. The warning that the future policies of the United States would depend upon a frank avowal by the belligerents of their war objectives was absent. Also eliminated was the President's virtual demand for a conference to discuss peace terms. In brief, the

[20] Quoted in Bernstorff to House, Dec. 12, 1916, House Papers.

[21] Grew to Secretary of State, Dec. 12, 1916, *Foreign Relations, 1916, Supplement,* p. 87.

[22] Wilson to P. A. Stovall, Dec. 19, 1916, Wilson Papers.

[23] Robert Lansing, "The German Proposal to Enter on Peace Negotiations," Dec. 14, 1916, *ibid.*

The Allies wasted no time in replying to the German offer. On December 15 the Russian Czar and Duma unanimously rejected the offer to negotiate, and four days later Lloyd George, the new British Prime Minister, gave answer for Britain and France. The Allies, Lloyd George declared, would be putting their heads into a noose, with Germany holding the end of the rope, if they agreed to enter a peace conference without knowing the German terms. The Prime Minister, however, left large loopholes for future negotiations. *The New York Times,* Dec. 16, 20, 1916. The official Allied reply was sent to the German government on December 30, 1916. *Ibid.,* Dec. 31, 1916.

note of December 18 simply called upon the belligerents to define the objectives for which they were fighting.[24]

American reaction to Wilson's appeal, which was published on December 20, accurately reflected the commentator's attitude toward the war. The defenders of Germany, the peace element, and the great mass of noninterventionists hailed it as the beginning of the end of the war.[25] In contrast, American champions of the Allied cause denounced Wilson for playing Germany's game and approving Germany's attempt to impose a dictated peace settlement.[26] Many German editors naturally interpreted Wilson's move as co-operation with their own government, while a large segment of the English and French press were in a state of virtual frenzy.

Unperturbed by the violence of his critics at home and abroad, the President now proceeded to carry his peace campaign beyond the level of suggestion to direct negotiation with the German government. His negotiations were based upon the hope that the Germans, at least, would agree to the kind of reasonable peace he contemplated. The unhappy truth was, however, that the German leaders now had no intention of allowing Wilson to participate in the peace discussions. They would be glad to use him to force the Allies to negotiate directly with the German government, but their plans left small scope for the play of Wilsonian idealism, and they still suspected that Wilson was pro-British.

In order to head off any "meddling" by Wilson in the peace negotiations, the German Foreign Office answered the President's request for a definition of objectives by evading his query and suggesting the

[24] The note is printed in *Foreign Relations, 1916, Supplement,* pp. 97–99.

[25] There could be no doubt that an overwhelming majority of American newspapers, periodicals, and public spokesmen approved the move. For samples of this dominant opinion see the statements of Congressional leaders in *The New York Times,* Dec. 21, 1916; New York *World,* Dec. 21, 22, 1916; Herbert Croly to E. M. House, Dec. 26, 1916, House Papers; *New Republic,* IX (Dec. 30, 1916), 228–231; W. J. Bryan in *The Commoner,* Jan., 1917; *New Yorker Staats-Zeitung,* Dec. 21, 1916; *New Yorker Herold,* Dec. 21, 1916.

[26] E.g., H. C. Lodge to T. Roosevelt, Dec. 21, 1916, the Papers of Theodore Roosevelt, in the Library of Congress; T. Roosevelt to G. W. Perkins, Jan. 11, 1917, *ibid.;* T. Roosevelt, statement in *The New York Times,* Jan. 4, 1917; George Burton Adams to the Editor, Dec. 24, 1916, *ibid.,* Dec. 26, 1916; Rev. Dr. William T. Manning, cited in *ibid.;* Frank J. Mather, Jr., to the Editor, Dec. 24, 1916, *The Nation,* CIII (Dec. 28, 1916), 607; Rev. Newell Dwight Hillis *et al.,* "To the Christians of America," *The New York Times,* Jan. 1, 1917.

speedy assembling of a conference of the belligerents only. After the peace conference had accomplished its task, then the German government stood ready to co-operate with the United States in preventing future wars. Gravely disappointed by the Imperial government's refusal frankly to state its terms, House and Bernstorff at once began personal negotiations that they hoped would draw the Chancellor and the President into sympathetic co-operation.

On December 29 Bernstorff informed his government that House had invited him to take part in "absolutely confidential" negotiations. The President was not concerned with territorial adjustments, the Ambassador continued, but was anxious to obtain guarantees for the future. In reply, Secretary Zimmermann sent specific and important instructions. Germany positively did not desire American participation in the actual peace negotiations. However, Bernstorff might say Germany stood ready to sign an arbitration treaty with the United States and to join with it in establishing a League of Nations and setting general disarmament under way after the war. Moreover, Germany's terms were moderate and did not include the annexation of Belgium. On the other hand, Zimmermann concluded, only quick and decisive action by the President could forestall a resumption of unrestricted U-boat warfare.

On January 15 Bernstorff transmitted to House Zimmermann's assurances for the future and his offer to sign a treaty of arbitration. Bernstorff's message, House declared in astonishment, was the most important pronouncement he had received from any belligerent government since the war began. "In my opinion," he advised Wilson, "the best interests of the Allies and ourselves would be met by taking Germany at her word and concluding peace as speedily as possible." And if Bernstorff had expressed his government's views correctly, he added, Wilson would be justified in forcing the Allies to consider peace negotiations.[27]

House's enthusiasm was soon dampened, however, when Bernstorff finally admitted that his government did not want the President's presence at the peace conference and that the German assurances applied only to the future, after the peace treaty had been signed. In short, while the Imperial government would be delighted to use Wilson to force the Allies to go to the peace table, at a time when the military situation greatly favored Germany, there would be no room at that

[27] House to Wilson, Jan. 18, 1917, Wilson Papers.

table for the President of the United States! The disclosure of this important fact caused Wilson to lay his cards on the table. Germany could have peace, he declared, if she were ready to state her terms frankly, propose a reasonable settlement, and confide in him. "It occurs to me that it would be well for you to see Bernstorff," Wilson wrote House, ". . . and tell him this is the time to accomplish something, if they really and truly want peace. . . . Feelings, exasperations are neither here nor there. Do they want me to help? I am entitled to know because I genuinely want to help and have now put myself in a position to help without favour to either side." [28]

In other words, Wilson was not deceived by the evasive German promise to join a League of Nations and co-operate in a general disarmament—after the peace treaty had been signed. The first task was to build a righteous peace, and the Germans had to give him frank assurances that this was the kind of peace they desired. If they could give such assurances, however, then he would gladly join hands with them in compelling the Allies [29] to accept a settlement including, by and large, the *status quo ante,* disarmament, and the establishment of a new concert of power. Such a settlement did not offer victory to Germany. It offered only the promise of the friendship of the United States and a secure, peaceful, and prosperous future. Unfortunately for mankind, time had already run out on the House-Bernstorff negotiations. The men who governed Germany preferred victory, with annexations and indemnities, because they were confident they could win such a victory. The military and naval leaders, who had taken control out of the Chancellor's hands, had decided on January 8 to launch the all-out submarine campaign on February 1.

House did not know the secret, and Bernstorff kept it from him until the last moment.[30] Meanwhile, was there any chance the Allies would abandon their hope of victory and join with the United States

[28] Wilson to House, Jan. 24, 1917, Baker Collection.

[29] As will soon be shown, if Wilson had obtained such assurances from the German government at this time, the Allies would probably have consented to a negotiated settlement under Wilson's direction. But if the Allies had refused to mediate on this basis, Wilson would almost certainly have used strong diplomatic pressure to force them to the peace table.

[30] Bethmann-Hollweg informed Bernstorff of the decision on January 16, 1917. *Official German Documents,* II, 1017–1019. It should be added that Bernstorff urged his government to delay taking the fateful step until Wilson had had a chance to complete his peace plans. Bernstorff to Foreign Office, Jan. 19, 1917, *ibid.,* p. 1021.

and Germany in peace negotiations? To find an answer to this question, House had also been conducting secret talks with the Allied representatives, particularly with Sir William Wiseman, chief of British Intelligence in the United States. A few hours after Bernstorff made his remarkable pronouncement on January 15 about Germany's willingness to co-operate in peace plans, House told Wiseman Germany was willing to negotiate on liberal terms. Five days later House advised Wiseman that his government should agree immediately to enter a peace conference, as this alone would prevent Germany from inaugurating a submarine campaign that might soon bring Great Britain to her knees. On January 26, therefore, Wiseman gave to House his government's reply. After telling House what he already suspected, that he was in direct communication with the British Cabinet, Wiseman declared that Great Britain was ready to begin peace discussions, provided the Germans were willing to negotiate on a reasonable basis.[31]

In the meantime, however, the peace talks on the public level had collapsed. On December 30 the Allied governments with one voice indignantly rejected the German proposal of a peace conference. The German government replied in a note to the neutral powers on January 10, accusing the Allies of prolonging the war for conquest and answering the Allied aspersions. Two days later the Allied powers made formal answer to Wilson's request of December 18. Without specifying their objectives, they made it plain they intended to exact huge reparations from the Central Powers and to destroy German power in Europe.

In order to clarify the American position in the light of these developments, to strengthen House's hand, and to appeal directly to the peoples of the countries at war,[32] Wilson decided to lay frankly before the world his concept of a peace settlement the United States would be willing to support in a League of Nations. Preliminary discussions with House on January 3 and 11 and a reading of the provocative suggestions outlined in the *New Republic*[33] helped to crystallize his

[31] House to Wilson, Jan. 20, 26, 1917, Wilson Papers. The British already knew of the German decision to launch unrestricted submarine warfare, and it is possible this was an important factor in their willingness to talk of peace.

[32] "The real people I was speaking to was neither the Senate nor foreign governments, as you will realize, but the *people* of the countries now at war." Wilson to J. P. Gavit, Jan. 29, 1917, *ibid.*

[33] In "Peace Without Victory," IX (Dec. 23, 1916), 201–202, "The Note as Americanism," IX (Dec. 30, 1916), 228–231, and "Beneath the Outcry," IX (Dec. 30, 1916), 231–232, the editors of the *New Republic* called for a

thought. By January 16 he had completed the address and discussed it with Lansing and Senator Stone; and on January 22, after the message had been secretly telegraphed to the American embassies, he delivered it before the Senate.

Wilson began by asserting the right of the United States to claim a share in laying the broad foundations of a lasting peace. While his government would have no voice in determining the specific details of settlement, he continued, the world should know what kind of arrangement the American people would help to guarantee. It must be a "peace without victory," without humiliation, for only a "peace among equals" could last. It must be a peace based upon the principle of the equality of all nations, upon the right of peoples now under alien domination to govern themselves, and upon the freedom of the seas and an end to huge armies. These were "American principles, American policies," approved by forward-looking men everywhere. "I would fain believe," the President concluded, "that I am speaking for the silent mass of mankind everywhere who have as yet had no place or opportunity to speak their real hearts out concerning the death and ruin they see to have come already upon the persons and the homes they hold most dear." [34]

It was a clarion call to the Old World to shake off war's stupor before European civilization was destroyed, and many men of good will in all the Western nations were intoxicated by the President's vision of a postwar order founded upon the principle of Christian love, rather than upon the precepts of *Realpolitik*. But was it possible that the millennium could be conceived during such a war and given birth during a conference of mortal men? No one could answer this question, but the reaction of liberal groups among the Allied nations and in the British press seemed to offer hope that mankind was indeed ready to meet the President's challenge.[35] In any event, Wilson had high hopes

___

negotiated peace, based upon the *status quo ante,* and warned that the American people would not support a dictated settlement of the old imperialistic kind, involving annexations, indemnities, and attempts to construct a new imperialistic balance of power.

[34] Ray S. Baker and William E. Dodd (eds.), *The Public Papers of Woodrow Wilson* (6 vols., New York, 1925–27), *The New Democracy,* II, 407–414.

[35] On January 26 the 89 Socialist members of the French Chamber of Deputies hailed Wilson's speech as "the charter of the civilized universe," while on the same day the British trades unions endorsed the League of Nations proposal. *The New York Times,* Jan. 27, 1917. Even the Russian Foreign Office affirmed its approval of the President's "broad humanitarian principles." *Ibid.*

and noble expectations. "I have said what everybody has been longing for but has thought impossible," he declared. "Now it appears to be possible." [36]

Noble expressions, however, emphasize the tragic and abiding fact of history: that a wide gulf separates the ideal from the attainable. No one could sneer at Wilson's vision without abandoning his hope for the eventual redemption of human society. But to believe that his address embodied a practical solution would make cynics out of dreamers. Thus Wilson's effort had a tragic and ironic, as well as a noble, quality. He affirmed the necessity of a negotiated peace, a "peace without victory," and declared that no other kind of peace could last. In the next breath he depicted a settlement that could be imposed only when Germany's military power was broken and the Allies could dictate the terms. [37] And if this came to pass, the possibility of a reasonable and just peace, of a "peace without victory," was slight indeed.

On January 31 the German government finally gave its answer to Wilson's request for the terms upon which it would have been willing to negotiate. The German terms included territorial adjustments in the East, "which would protect Germany and Poland against Russia, strategically and economically"; additional colonies; the return of French territory occupied by Germany, but "under reservations concerning the establishment of strategic and economic boundaries, as well as financial compensation"; the restoration of Belgium, but "under certain guarantees assuring Germany's safety, which would have to be reached by negotiations with the Belgian Government"; indemnification of German corporations and individuals injured by the war; and freedom of the seas. [38]

Bernstorff delivered this message at the same time he gave Germany's answer to the President's demand for a peace of justice and understanding. After February 1, the Imperial government announced,

---

[36] *Ibid.,* Jan. 23, 1917.

[37] For example, Wilson declared that governments derive their just powers from the consent of the governed and that peoples under alien domination should be given "inviolable security of life, of worship, and of industrial and social development"—in other words, complete autonomy, if not independence. This was also what the Allies had promised to give the subject peoples of Germany and Austria-Hungary. Certainly Germany and Austria would not have negotiated for the dissolution of their empires. Nor would the British, for that matter. It should be pointed out again, moreover, that the kind of peace the German leaders thought they could obtain was a far cry from a "peace without victory" among equals.

[38] *Official German Documents,* II, 1048–1050.

submarines would sink without warning all ships, belligerent and neutral, found in a zone around Great Britain, France, and Italy, and in the eastern Mediterranean. The German Admiralty, however, would allow one American passenger ship to sail between New York and Falmouth weekly, provided the ship were painted with red and white stripes and carried no contraband. The decision had been made deliberately, "in the certain consciousness that the commencement of an unrestricted U-boat warfare would inevitably be followed by war with America." [39]

Thus it happened that the President found himself in the dilemma he had tried so desperately to avoid. Had the Germans declared unrestricted submarine warfare only against armed merchantmen, or even against all belligerent shipping, he might well have acquiesced and allowed the two giants to fight it out. But the Germans had quite deliberately promised to sink on sight all American ships found in the broad war zones, because destruction of neutral shipping was as much essential to their plan as was destruction of Allied shipping. Moreover, the strategists in the German Admiralty were confident they could bring England to her knees before American manpower and resources could be brought effectively to bear upon the conflict. "By entering into the war," the chief of the Admiralty predicted, "the United States Government will give up by a single move the sources of that commercial prosperity which has given it the towering political prominence which it now occupies. It stands face to face with the Japanese peril; it can neither inflict material damage upon us, nor can it be of material benefit to our enemies. . . . I guarantee that for its part the U-boat war will lead to victory." [40]

Could Wilson view this wholesale assault upon American commerce with his customary philosophic detachment? He was indignant and bitterly disappointed, but not belligerent. Indeed, he was so persuaded that mankind's salvation depended upon a negotiated peace that he hesitated even to break diplomatic relations with Germany, as that might be the prelude to full-scale American participation. He revealed his mental agony during a two-hour conference with Lansing on the evening of January 31. Obsessed with the fear that American interven-

[39] From the "Report of the Second Subcommittee of the Committee of Inquiry," June 18, 1920, *ibid.*, I, 150.

[40] Chief of the Admiralty Staff Admiral von Holtzendorff to Chief of the General Staff General Field Marshal von Hindenburg, Dec. 22, 1916, *ibid.*, II, 1269–1270.

tion would hasten the disintegration of "white" civilization, he wondered whether America could perform her duty only by bearing the German insult. None the less, he asked Lansing to prepare the note announcing severance of relations with the German Empire. The following morning Colonel House arrived at the White House. He believed an immediate break was necessary, and Wilson and Lansing agreed. Thus the decision was already made when the President presented Lansing's draft to the Cabinet on February 2 and discussed it with Democratic senators soon afterward.[41]

Even so, Wilson had not changed his opinion that the war should end without victory, and he continued to hope that somehow he would not have to drink the bitter cup. This hope he expressed movingly in his address to a joint session of Congress on February 3 announcing the break in relations he had just effected. The message was no such condemnation of German "barbarism" as Lansing had advised him to deliver, nor was it a stirring appeal to the American people to prepare for inevitable war. "We do not desire any hostile conflict with the Imperial German Government," Wilson declared. "We are the sincere friends of the German people and earnestly desire to remain at peace with the Government which speaks for them. We shall not believe that they are hostile to us unless and until we are obliged to believe it." [42]

During the remainder of February the President and probably a large majority of people continued to hope for peace, while circumstances were developing that would soon force the nation to make a decision. Army leaders who suggested rapid preparation for war were abruptly told to mind their own business, but slowly and quietly the government laid its plans. The naval appropriations bill, then under discussion in the House, was immediately amended to provide increased construction and to empower the President to seize shipyards and munitions factories in the event of war or national emergency. The War College was set to work on a conscription bill. Even so, the administration acted as if war would not occur and precautions would suffice.[43]

[41] "Memorandum on the Severance of Diplomatic Relations with Germany," Lansing Diary, Feb. 4, 1917; Josephus Daniels to Wilson, Feb. 2, 1917, Wilson Papers, summarizing Wilson's views; *The New York Times*, Feb. 3, 1917.

[42] *The Public Papers, The New Democracy*, II, 422–426. The note announcing severance of relations was Lansing to Bernstorff, Feb. 3, 1917, *Papers Relating to the Foreign Relations of the United States, 1917, Supplement* 1 (Washington, 1931), pp. 106–108.

[43] Especially in so far as army preparations were concerned. The army bill

Thus it turned out that the three weeks following the break in relations were a time of waiting, wasted in the false hope that no overt act by the German government would compel abandonment of neutrality. As the days of waiting ripened into weeks, the deep peace longing of the people revived and the pacifist leaders had full opportunity to get a nation-wide campaign under way. New committees to keep the country out of war were hastily organized, while all the old ones, like the American Union Against Militarism, leaped into action.[44] As in 1915 and at the height of the *Sussex* crisis, monster rallies in the great cities demanded that Americans stay out of the war zone. Bryan made a fervent, last-ditch campaign. In their desperate search for any alternative to war, the peace groups demanded embargoes, a war referendum, or a general strike if war occurred. At the other extreme, the interventionists redoubled their propaganda, calling for a bold and heroic defense of American rights.[45] But before March 1, at least, they still represented only a small Eastern minority, and their appeals roused no response among the rank and file of the people.

Still, the German campaign of sea terror was obviously succeeding in one of its main objectives, the frightening of neutral shipping from the seas. When the administration on February 7 refused to use battleships to convoy ships through the war zone, the International Mercantile Marine Company of New York canceled the sailing of its passenger ships, the *Saint Louis* and *Saint Paul*. As more and more ships stayed at their berths and goods began to pile up on wharves and in warehouses, the demand for the arming and protection of American

---

passed by the House on February 22, 1917, for example, appropriated only a normal $250 million for the coming fiscal year. As the Chief of Staff wrote, "The President does not want us to do anything which will give Germany an idea that we are getting ready for war, so we are not allowed to ask for any money or to get ready in a serious way, until the soft pedal is taken off." H. L. Scott to D. Hunter Scott, Feb. 15, 1917, the Papers of Hugh L. Scott, in the Library of Congress.

[44] For a comprehensive description of all the peace organizations and their activities, see the New York *World,* Mar. 4, 1917.

[45] American Rights Committee, appeal to the American people for a declaration of war, *The New York Times,* Feb. 12, 1917; American Rights Committee, "A CALL TO AMERICANS to assure the President that he will receive *The United Support of the American People* in taking effective action to UPHOLD AMERICAN RIGHTS and DEFEND THE NATIONAL HONOR," *ibid.,* Feb. 26, 1917. For the activities of the Committee see George H. Putnam to John G. Hibben, Feb. 2, 1917, the Papers of John Grier Hibben, in the Library of Princeton University; R. G. Monroe to J. G. Hibben, Feb. 21, 1917, *ibid.;* Paul D. Cravath to J. G. Hibben, Feb. 21, 1917, *ibid.*

ships grew on all sides. Discussion of the subject within the administration began on February 6 and continued through February 23. At Cabinet meetings on February 6 and 13 the President declared that, while ships might arm for defense, he would not ask Congress for

Kirby in the New York *World*

Nailing It There

authority to arm them. Continuing their demand that the government protect its sea-borne commerce, Houston, Lane, and McAdoo provoked a crisis in the Cabinet on February 23. Wilson bitterly reproached the champions of belligerency for appealing to the code duello and asserted that the country was not willing to run the risk of war.

Two events coming immediately on the heels of the Cabinet session of February 23 caused Wilson to change his mind. First, the Republican leaders in the Senate agreed on that day to filibuster the important appropriations bills, in order to force Wilson to call the next Congress into special session.[46] Secondly, on February 25 the President received a message from London so shocking as to end all doubts of German intentions. It was a dispatch from Page, transmitting a message from the German Foreign Secretary, Zimmermann, to the German Minister in Mexico City. In the event Germany and the United States went to war, the message read, the Minister should propose to the Mexican government an alliance by which Mexico would enter the war against the United States and receive in return "the lost territory in Texas, New Mexico, and Arizona." Moreover, President Carranza should be asked to invite Japan to join the coalition.[47]

The day after the receipt in Washington of the Zimmermann note Wilson went before a joint session to ask Congress for authority, first, to arm American merchant ships, and second, to "employ any other instrumentalities or methods that may be necessary and adequate to protect our ships and our people in their legitimate and peaceful pursuits on the seas." It was not, however, a warlike speech. Wilson did not mention the Zimmermann note; he admitted that the "overt act" had not been committed, and he voiced a fervent desire for continued peace.[48] Except for a few interventionist newspapers, which protested that Wilson would not defend American commerce in any event,[49] the press of the country overwhelmingly endorsed the President's request.[50]

[46] *The New York Times,* Feb. 24, 1917; New York *World,* Feb. 24, 1917. "I have also come to the conclusion that we must force an extra session," Lodge wrote to Theodore Roosevelt, February 27, 1917 (Roosevelt Papers). "Although I have not much faith in Congress we should be safer with Congress here than we would be with Wilson alone for nine months."

[47] Page to Secretary of State, Feb. 24, 1917, *Foreign Relations, 1917, Supplement 1,* pp. 147–148. The Zimmermann note had been sent to Bernstorff on January 19, with instructions that he relay it to Minister von Eckhardt in Mexico City. The British had intercepted the message and were able to decipher it because they had Bernstorff's code. For an exciting account of this episode see Burton J. Hendrick, *The Life and Letters of Walter H. Page* (3 vols., Garden City, N. Y., 1924–26), III, 331–348.

[48] *The Public Papers, New Democracy,* II, 428–432.

[49] New York *Sun,* Feb. 27, 1917; Boston *Herald,* Feb. 27, 1917; Boston *Advertiser,* Feb. 27, 1917.

[50] There is a comprehensive survey of press opinion in *The New York Times,* Feb. 27, 1917. Even the spokesmen of the peace element approved the idea of armed neutrality, as they saw in it a possible alternative to full-fledged war.

Indeed, there was little opposition in either house of Congress to giving the President authority simply to arm merchantmen. Extreme noninterventionists like La Follette would vote against such a bill, to be sure, but they were not prepared to block it by desperate obstruction. The entire controversy that developed revolved, therefore, around Wilson's additional request for broad authority to use "any other instrumentalities or methods" to protect American lives and commerce. Senate Republican leaders like Lodge did not object to giving the President authority to wage limited war, but they were determined that Congress should be in session. The extreme anti-interventionists in the Senate, however, so strongly opposed giving Wilson virtual blanket authority that they would fight an armed ship bill with such a provision to the point of a filibuster. When this fact became apparent, the Republican leaders quickly abandoned their own plans for a filibuster to force a special session and let the noninterventionists carry the burden of opposition and receive the opprobrium.

That the President would encounter bitter opposition was evident from the beginning. In spite of heavy administration pressure, the House Foreign Affairs Committee refused to empower the President to use "other instrumentalities or methods" and would only approve a bill authorizing the arming of merchant ships.[51] Just at the moment, therefore, when it appeared neither house would grant the virtual war-making authority he desired, the President gave the Zimmermann note to the Associated Press, which published it on March 1. The bolt struck so suddenly that Congress and the country were stunned and confused. Could this fantastic news be true, or was the note, as George Sylvester Viereck, the leading Germanophile, claimed, "unquestionably a brazen forgery planted by British agents"?[52] Most doubts were dis-

---

Professor Carlton J. H. Hayes of Columbia University first made the proposal, which was soon taken up by peace groups all over the country, for armed neutrality instead of war. See C. J. H. Hayes, "Memorandum on Constructive Action if Confronted by Alternative of War," sent by House to Wilson, Feb. 8, 1917, Wilson Papers; C. J. H. Hayes, "Which? War Without a Purpose? Or Armed Neutrality with a Purpose?" *The Survey,* XXXVII (Feb. 10, 1917), 535–538; New York *Evening Post,* Feb. 10, 1917; *The Nation,* CIV (Feb. 15, 1917), 178–179; Paul U. Kellogg, "The Fighting Issues," *The Survey,* XXXVII (Feb. 17, 1917), 572–577.

[51] The House bill also prohibited the insuring by the War Risk Bureau of ships carrying munitions. A. S. Burleson, penciled note to Wilson, c. Feb. 27, 1917, the Papers of Albert S. Burleson, in the Library of Congress; Wilson to Burleson, c. Feb. 27, 1917, *ibid.; The New York Times,* Feb. 28, Mar. 1, 1917.

[52] G. S. Viereck to A. S. Burleson, Mar. 1, 1917, Burleson Papers.

pelled at once [53] when Wilson, in reply to a pointed inquiry by the Foreign Relations Committee, affirmed the note's authenticity.[54]

American incredulity now burst into anger that swept the country. Not since August, 1914, had the people been so aroused or so convinced of the hostile intentions of the German government. The House of Representatives quickly passed the armed ship bill on March 1, 403 to 13, but without giving the President broad authority.[55] In the Senate, however, administration leaders pressed a bill empowering the President to wage an undeclared naval war; and the Republican leaders were willing to agree, since the important appropriation bills could not be passed before March 5 and Wilson would have to call a special session in any event. But a group of eleven or twelve die-hard noninterventionists, including Senators La Follette and George W. Norris, refused to abdicate the warmaking power to the Chief Executive and insisted on talking the bill to death.[56] The newspapers fiercely denounced the "dastardly moral treason" of these alleged "descendants of Benedict Arnold," but it remained for Wilson to coin the phrase to

[53] Not all, however. The defenders of Germany continued to charge that the note was a piece of British humbuggery, until Zimmermann himself admitted on March 3, 1917, that he had sent the note, pointing out that Eckhardt had been instructed to suggest an alliance to the Mexican government only in the event the United States declared war on Germany. Official statement, Mar. 3, 1917, *The New York Times*, Mar. 4, 1917. Zimmermann further defended himself in a speech before the Reichstag on March 29, 1917, *ibid.*, Mar. 31, 1917.

[54] *Ibid.*, Mar. 2, 1917; H. C. Lodge to T. Roosevelt, Mar. 2, 1917, Roosevelt Papers.

[55] The House also prohibited the War Risk Bureau from insuring ships carrying munitions. *The New York Times*, Mar. 2, 1917. The anti-interventionists in the House had also tried to add an amendment forbidding any armed merchant ship from carrying munitions. This, the so-called Cooper amendment, received 125 votes. For significant comment see *New Republic*, X (Mar. 24, 1917), 218–219.

[56] The senators who prevented passage of the armed ship bill objected to giving extraordinary authority to the President and protection to ships carrying munitions. They charged that Wilson had brought the bill forward near the end of the session and then had sprung the Zimmermann note solely to stampede the country and coerce Congress into giving him dictatorial power. And, they argued, if the armed ship bill were vital to the country's safety, then Wilson could easily call Congress into special session and obtain passage of the measure in a short time.

Most of the so-called filibusterers later issued statements defending their action and claiming there had been no real filibuster. See R. M. La Follette, "The Armed Ship Bill Meant War," *La Follette's Magazine*, IX (Mar., 1917), 1–4; W. J. Stone to the Editor, March 4, 1917, New York *World*, Mar. 5, 1917; statements by Senators Vardaman, O'Gorman, Kenyon, Cummins, and Lane, March 6, 1917, in *The New York Times*, Mar. 7, 1917.

fit the crime. Immediately after the Senate adjourned he indignantly declared: "A little group of willful men, representing no opinion but their own, have rendered the great Government of the United States helpless and contemptible." [57]

Thus the Sixty-Fourth Congress passed out of existence amid a display of bad temper on all sides and the country entered upon a month of increasing tension. After obtaining opinions from Lansing and Attorney General Gregory that arming merchant ships would not contravene the piracy statute of 1819, and after discussing the implications of such action with his naval advisers,[58] the President on March 9 announced he would forthwith put guns and naval crews on merchant ships and called Congress into special session for April 16. Soon afterward the work of arming the ships was begun and the crews were ordered to fire on any submarine that approached within striking range or acted suspiciously.

By this time, also, public opinion had reached a point of near alarm, and for the first time since the outbreak of the war the interventionists found a sympathetic audience. On March 18 submarines sank without warning and with heavy loss of life three American merchant vessels, the *City of Memphis, Illinois,* and *Vigilancia.* It was the "overt act" for which the President had been waiting, and Theodore Roosevelt issued a call for war, the echoes of which reverberated over the country, from New York to the plains of Kansas.[59] At this moment of

[57] *Ibid.,* Mar. 5, 1917.

[58] There is a group of documents in the Papers of Josephus Daniels, in the Library of Congress, relating to the armed ship question. The most important are Daniels to Wilson, Mar. 9, 1917, two letters; memorandum by Commander F. H. Schofield for the Secretary of the Navy, dated Mar. 9, 1917; an undated memorandum entitled "Rules for the Conduct of American Merchant Vessels"; draft of a proclamation announcing the arming of American merchant ships; and a memorandum in Daniels' handwriting of a conversation with P. A. S. Franklin, president of the International Mercantile Company.

[59] Roosevelt's statement is printed in *The New York Times,* Mar. 20, 1917. The Union League of New York demanded adoption of a war declaration on March 20. The following day the New York *World* seconded the demand. On March 22 a mass meeting of twelve thousand persons at Madison Square Garden cheered for Roosevelt and war. On March 23 a group of prominent Socialists, including William English Walling, Charles Edward Russell, Upton Sinclair, and William J. Ghent, condemned the antiwar resolution adopted by the Socialist National Executive Committee. On March 24 Governor Arthur Capper of Kansas, heretofore an antipreparedness and antiwar leader, declared the United States had to resist the "murderous assaults" of the German government. *The New York Times,* Mar. 21, 23, 24, 25, 1917; New York *World,* Mar. 21, 1917.

mounting tension occurred the first Russian Revolution, with the overthrow of the autocratic Czarist government and the establishment of a constitutional monarchy. To Americans who had tried to convince themselves the Allies were fighting for democracy, the news from Petrograd ended all doubt as to the issues of the war. The fear of Russian despotism and future aggression, which all along had been the greatest single handicap to Allied spokesmen in the United States, was at once swept away.

It was also the hour of supreme crisis for the peace forces. If anything, their appeals during the last critical days were more fervent than before.[60] On the extreme left wing, the Socialist leader, Eugene V. Debs, demanded a general strike if Rockefeller, Morgan, and the rest of the Wall Street crowd succeeded in their insidious war campaign. The more moderate peace spokesmen continued to petition the President and to hope for a miracle. As for the great mass of citizenry, not during the height of the *Lusitania* and *Sussex* crises had there been such an outpouring of peace sentiment. The public opinion of a great nation during a period of crisis and stimulated hysteria cannot be measured with any precision, for the great mass of people have no means of expressing their sentiments, while spokesmen for organized groups are necessarily minorities. From such evidence as is available, however, one might hazard the guess that even as late as April 1, 1917, the majority of people were still firmly for peace.[61]

The week from about March 12 to 20 was also the time of Wilson's Gethsemane, when events on the seas compelled him to a reluctant decision for war. During the early part of this week of spiritual agony

[60] Committee for Democratic Control (Amos Pinchot, R. S. Bourne, Max Eastman, Winthrop D. Lane), "Do the People Want War?" *New Republic*, X (Mar. 3, 1917), 145; Emergency Peace Federation, "Mothers, Daughters and Wives of Men," *The New York Times*, Mar. 29, 1917; American Union Against Militarism, "To the People of New York," *ibid.;* W. J. Bryan, "To the Members of the U.S. Senate and House of Representatives," Mar. 28, 1917, the Papers of Thomas J. Walsh, in the Library of Congress.

[61] Evidence supporting this generalization abounds in the papers of Claude Kitchin, W. J. Bryan, Library of Congress, Warren Worth Bailey, George W. Norris, Thomas J. Walsh, Robert M. La Follette, Oswald G. Villard, and other such public leaders. The present writer knows how deceptive such evidence can be. Yet one cannot read through the thousands of letters, telegrams, and petitions from people in all walks of life and all sections of the country without being profoundly impressed by the depth of the popular desire for peace and the positive hostility to a war resolution in response to the German submarine challenge.

he remained secluded in the White House. From all sides he was bombarded with advice and pleadings for peace and for war. From Page came an appeal to bolster the credit of the British government, lest the whole system of international exchange collapse.[62] For the first time came reports that the Allies were in a desperate military situation, that Allied morale was cracking, and that only American intervention could turn the tide. Finally, it was obvious the German campaign against sea-borne commerce was succeeding even beyond the expectations of the most ardent champions of the submarine. Nearly 600,000 tons of Allied and neutral shipping were sunk during March, 1917, and the toll reached nearly 900,000 tons the following month.

In spite of these appeals and warnings, the President still hesitated. On March 19, the day after the sinking of the three American ships, he conferred with Lansing and told him he opposed immediate action. The following afternoon Wilson called the Cabinet to consider the crisis and advise him on the course he should follow. McAdoo, Houston, Redfield, and Baker urged an immediate declaration of war. Lansing agreed, pointing out the ideological issues and the importance of speedy American aid to the Allies. Wilson replied that he did not see how he could speak of a war for democracy in addressing Congress. Secretary Wilson and Attorney General Gregory concurred with Lansing; his eyes filled with tears, Daniels admitted there was no other course. And so all of them declared. "The solemnity of the occasion as one after another spoke was increasingly impressive and showed in every man's face as he rose from the council table and prepared to leave the room." [63]

The President gave his advisers no sign of his decision, but the next day he called Congress into special session for April 2, "to receive a communication concerning grave matters of national policy." Moreover, his action during the ten days that followed left no doubt that he had resolved to ask for a war resolution. On March 24, for example, he ordered the withdrawal of American diplomatic and relief officials

[62] In an urgent telegram to Lansing on March 5, 1917, Page warned that the British government had absolutely reached the end of the resources it could use to obtain credit in the United States. If the United States government did not supply the credit or guarantee a large Allied loan, Page added, the great war trade would come to an end. *Papers Relating to the Foreign Relations of the United States, 1917, Supplement 2* (2 vols., Washington, 1932), I, 516–518.

[63] "Memorandum of the Cabinet Meeting, 2:30–5 P.M. Tuesday, March 20, 1917," Lansing Diary.

from Belgium. On the same day he authorized Daniels to begin conversations with the British Admiralty for the co-ordination of the naval
operations of the two countries. On March 25 and 26 he called the
National Guard of the Eastern, Midwestern, and Far Western states
into the federal service, and on March 25 he increased the enlisted
strength of the navy to the statutory limit of 87,000.

Meanwhile, Wilson had begun writing his war message. Gethsemane
was over; the decision was made. But the road ahead pointed straight
to Golgotha, and in his turmoil he could find no sleep at night. Colonel
House came to Washington on March 27 and tried to calm his spirit,
but the anguish would not leave him and on April 1 he sent for Frank
Cobb, editor of the New York *World,* and unburdened his soul.

He said he couldn't see any alternative, that he had tried every way he knew
to avoid war [Cobb later recalled]. . . . He said war would overturn the
world we had known; that so long as we remained out there was a preponderance of neutrality, but that if we joined with the Allies the world would be
off the peace basis and onto a war basis. . . . He had the whole panorama
in his mind. He went on to say that so far as he knew he had considered
every loophole of escape and as fast as they were discovered Germany deliberately blocked them with some new outrage.

Then he began to talk about the consequences to the United States. He
had no illusions about the fashion in which we were likely to fight the
war. . . .

"Once lead this people into war," he said, "and they'll forget there ever
was such a thing as tolerance. To fight you must be brutal and ruthless, and
the spirit of ruthless brutality will enter into the very fibre of our national
life, infecting Congress, the courts, the policeman on the beat, the man in the
street." . . .

He thought the Constitution would not survive it; that free speech and the
right of assembly would go. He said a nation couldn't put its strength into
a war and keep its head level; it had never been done.

"If there is any alternative, for God's sake, let's take it," he exclaimed.[64]

At no time during this critical period did the President recognize the
necessity for American intervention on idealistic grounds or because
such intervention was necessary to protect the security of the United
States. Indeed, had he been a free agent he would probably have
adhered to the course of armed neutrality he had embarked upon on

[64] Quoted in Baker, *Wilson,* VI, 490, 506–507.

March 9.[65] Much of his despair stemmed from the fact that events beyond his control were impelling the nation blindly into a war it did not want. In brief, the country had now arrived at the situation Wilson had described so vividly in the first draft of his peace note of December 18, 1916: "If any other nation now neutral should be drawn in, it would know only that it was drawn in by some force it could not resist, because it had been hurt and saw no remedy but to risk still greater, it might be even irreparable, injury, in order to make the weight in the one scale or the other decisive; and even as a participant it would not know how far the scales must tip before the end would come or what was being weighed in the balance!" [66]

What forces and events impelled a divided nation and a distraught President and Congress to do the thing they had fought so desperately to avoid?

The progressives, pacifists, and Socialists gave an answer in 1917 that was reiterated by the Nye Committee in 1934 and 1935. To these observers, the causes for American intervention were mainly economic and psychological. That was what Senator George W. Norris meant by his assertion, made during his speech against the war resolution, that the Senate would stamp the dollar mark on the American flag if it approved a declaration of belligerency. Before the United States entered the war American bankers had lent $2,145 million to the Allied governments for war purposes. The economic masters of the United States had invested the savings of the American people in an Allied victory—a cause they could not now afford to abandon. Moreover—so the progressive-pacifist argument ran—by April, 1917, American pros-

[65] During the last days of March, Wilson received four letters of great significance, from J. P. Gavit, Senator Joseph I. France of Maryland, Matthew Hale, and Senator Gilbert M. Hitchcock of Nebraska, all of them urging him to adhere to armed neutrality and a course of limited participation as the only sensible method of defending American rights on the seas and avoiding entanglement in the peace plans of the Allies. Gavit to Wilson, Mar. 25, 1917; France to Wilson, Mar. 28, 1917; Hale to Wilson, Mar. 28, 1917; Hitchcock to Wilson, Mar. 29, 1917, all in Wilson Papers. In his reply to Hale, Mar. 31, 1917, *ibid.*, Wilson declared he would be inclined to adhere to armed neutrality, but that such a course was no longer feasible. "To defend our rights upon the seas, we must fight submarines," he explained. ". . . Germany has intimated that she would regard the only sort of warfare that is possible against her submarines as an act of war and would treat any persons who fell into her hands from the ships that attacked her submarines as beyond the pale of law. Apparently, to make even the measures of defense legitimate we must obtain the status of belligerents."

[66] Baker, *Wilson,* VI, 382.

perity had become so dependent upon a continuation of the war trade that the country went to war also to protect it.[67] Munitions-makers, who sought a new market for their products, added their voices to the rising clamor for war. Finally, propagandists, voluntary and hired, had misled Americans into believing that the Allies were fighting for democracy and that Germany's triumph would spell the doom of Western civilization. These and other forces more subtle had caused the administration to pursue an unneutral course from the beginning— to enforce the rules against Germany, but not against Britain—and had compelled Germany to adopt desperate measures in 1917.

At the other extreme, Walter Lippmann, in a series of articles in the *New Republic* published in 1916–17 and later in *U.S. Foreign Policy: Shield of the Republic*,[68] developed the thesis that the United States had followed a deliberate policy of unneutrality, had accepted British transgressions of international law and stood firm against German transgressions, because the American people condemned the objectives for which Germany was fighting. When German success seemed imminent, Lippmann continued, the United States had gone to war to preserve the supremacy of the Atlantic Community in Europe and to protect its vital stake in a peaceful and orderly world.

What is the truth? Does it lie somewhere in between these extremes? The events, forces, and developments from 1914 to 1917 were too complex to permit any simple generalizations on the causes of American intervention. There is no evidence that bankers or munitions-makers influenced the decision for war. On the contrary, because it furnished deadly ammunition to the progressives and pacifists, the support that bankers and munitions-makers gave the preparedness and intervention movements was a great obstacle to the success of those movements. The power of the propagandists has been vastly overrated, and it is doubtful if they played a major role.[69] Although Lansing and occasionally House shared Lippmann's views, they had only an incidental influence on Wilson.

[67] The foreign trade of the United States with the Allied countries increased from $824,860,237 in 1914, to $1,991,747,493 in 1915, to $3,214,480,547 in 1916.

[68] The passage in *U.S. Foreign Policy: Shield of the Republic* (Boston, 1943) is pp. 33–39; see also Walter Lippmann to Wilson, Mar. 11, 1917, Wilson Papers, enclosing "Memorandum" on the reasons for the American determination to resist the German bid for domination of Europe.

[69] See above, pp. 145–148.

In the final analysis, American policy was determined by the President and public opinion, which had a great, if unconscious, influence upon him. It was Wilson who decided to accept the British maritime system in the first instance, who set the American government against unrestricted use of the submarine, and who made the final decision for war instead of a continuance of armed neutrality.

Before the summer of 1916 the President's policies, on the whole, constituted a differential neutrality, favorable to the Allies. This was true because Wilson accepted the British sea measures and resisted the German, a course that seemed necessary in the light of a number of factors: German unfriendliness, as manifested by the network of intrigue and conspiracies against American neutrality, the invasion of Belgium and the deliberate killing of civilians on the high seas, and the fact that there seemed to be a hope for a reasonable settlement by working with Britain and France.

The policy of differential neutrality was, therefore, grounded upon Wilson's personal assessment of the situation, which in turn was determined by his moralistic judgment of events. When he became convinced the Allied governments did not want a reasonable peace, he began to change differential neutrality into impartiality. Moreover, he began to shift his personal moral condemnation from Germany to Great Britain. And in the process he came to the firm conviction that neither side was fighting for worthy objectives and that the hope of the world lay in a negotiated settlement and a future concert of all the powers.

These were the concepts paramount in Wilson's mind toward the end of 1916 and in early 1917. So long as the German government paid lip service, at least, to the *Sussex* pledge he would have pursued his neutral course relentlessly. Or, if the German leaders had at any time desired a genuinely reasonable settlement and evidenced a willingness to help build a peaceful and orderly postwar world, they would have found a friend in the White House eager to join with them in accomplishing these high goals.

Given the circumstances existing at the beginning of 1917, therefore, the Germans had three alternatives, which were carefully considered by them. Firstly, they could have accepted Wilson's leadership in the peace campaign, which would also have involved abandoning their hopes for winning on the fields of battle the ambitious program they had set for themselves. Secondly, they could have rejected Wilson's mediation and continued their "legal," although devastating, submarine campaign in the hope of obtaining a draw. Or, thirdly, they could run the risks involved in American intervention by launching an overwhelming submarine campaign against all commerce. They took the third alternative because their strategists told them it would bring complete victory and a chance to establish German domination in Europe, if not in the world.[70]

The German decision to gamble on all-out victory or complete ruin, therefore, alone compelled Wilson to break diplomatic relations, to adopt a policy of armed neutrality, and finally to ask for a declaration of war—because American ships were being sunk and American citizens were being killed on the high seas, and because armed neutrality seemed no longer possible. Considerations of America's alleged economic stake in an Allied victory did not influence Wilson's thought during the critical weeks from February 1 to April 2, 1917. Nor did considerations of the national interest, or of the great ideological issues at stake in the conflict.

In response to the President's call Congress assembled on the appointed day, April 2, and with the help of the independents the Democrats organized the House and elected Champ Clark Speaker again. At eight-thirty in the evening Wilson went before the joint session and read his message before the expectant throng. He reviewed the recent German warfare against commerce, which he termed "warfare against mankind." He declared that armed neutrality was no longer feasible and that there was no choice but to admit that the recent course of the Imperial German government was war against the United States. After enumerating the steps necessary to put the country on a war footing, Wilson abruptly turned to a discussion of the issues and objectives for which the nation would fight. The American people now knew the Imperial government, like all autocracies, was a natural foe of liberty. Therefore, "The world must be made safe for democracy. Its peace must be planted upon the tested foundations of political liberty." And then, with one great peroration, which has gone ringing down the years, the long ordeal of neutrality was over:

It is a distressing and oppressive duty, Gentlemen of the Congress, which I have performed in thus addressing you. There are, it may be, many months

[70] The sanest and most convincing opinion on German motivation yet written was offered by the majority of the Reichstag's committee of inquiry in its report dated June 18, 1920, *Official German Documents,* I, 128–150.

of fiery trial and sacrifice ahead of us. It is a fearful thing to lead this great peaceful people into war, into the most terrible and disastrous of all wars, civilization itself seeming to be in the balance. But the right is more precious than peace, and we shall fight for the things which we have always carried nearest our hearts,—for democracy, for the right of those who submit to authority to have a voice in their own Governments, for the rights and liberties of small nations, for a universal dominion of right by such a concert of free peoples as shall bring peace and safety to all nations and make the world itself at last free. To such a task we can dedicate our lives and our fortunes, everything that we are and everything that we have, with the pride of those who know that the day has come when America is privileged to spend her blood and her might for the principles that gave her birth and happiness and the peace which she has treasured. God helping her, she can do no other.[71]

From the halls of Congress the deafening thunder of applause reverberated round the world. Men in the trenches took hope, and the Allied peoples thanked God their cause was not lost. Even Wilson's bitterest critics, Lodge, Root, and Roosevelt, admitted the President had epitomized their own thoughts. But for Wilson it was not a day of triumph but of sadness and, one is tempted to believe, of doubt and soul searching. Tumulty recalled a scene in the White House after Wilson returned from the Capitol, when the President broke down and sobbed like a child.[72] The story is probably fictional, but it conveys poetic truth.

In spite of the opposition in both houses of men like Claude Kitchin, George W. Norris, and Robert M. La Follette, the war resolution was quickly passed. On April 4 the Senate adopted the resolution, 82 to 6; at 3:12 A.M. on April 6 the House concurred, 373 to 50; and at 1:18 the following afternoon Wilson signed the resolution. Minutes later the news was sent by telegraph and wireless around the world. A new epoch in the history of the United States had begun.

[71] *The Public Papers, War and Peace*, I, 6–16.
[72] J. P. Tumulty, *Woodrow Wilson As I Know Him* (Garden City, N.Y., 1921), p. 259.

Essay on Sources

PREFACE

The following essay does not include all works and sources on American history for the period 1910–1917. Even if it were susceptible of compilation, such a list would more than fill the present volume and would be a source of confusion rather than of help to students. The writer, however, has endeavored to include all significant and relevant works and sources and to arrange them in an orderly and purposeful manner.

Thus, the first seven sections include the general sources—manuscripts, newspapers, periodicals, published writings and memoirs, and the like—that relate in a broad way to the politics, personalities, and diplomacy of the period. In contrast, the last sections are arranged roughly to follow the chapters of the book and include monographs, articles, and other works that bear specifically upon the subjects under which they are listed.

Finally, the author has attempted to avoid repeating in this bibliography the references that he lists in the footnotes. It has not been possible to avoid such repetition entirely; generally, however, the footnotes cite letters, diaries, and newspaper and periodical articles and editorials, while the bibliographical essay attempts to survey works and sources in a more general and comprehensive manner.

MANUSCRIPTS

The Wilson Administration

Of greatest importance for the period from 1912 to 1917 are the Papers of Woodrow Wilson in the Library of Congress, which are excellently arranged and, in spite of their huge volume, easily used. They are open to advanced students by permission of Mrs. Woodrow Wilson. An important supplement to the Wilson Papers is the Ray Stannard Baker Collection, Library of Congress, which Baker gathered while writing the President's authorized biography. The Baker Collection contains correspondence not available in the

Wilson Papers, transcripts of interviews with and memoranda by many of the leaders of the period, and a large collection of articles on Wilson. For certain fields, particularly the diplomacy of the neutrality period, the Papers and massive Diary of Edward M. House, Yale University Library, rival the Wilson Papers in significance.

The papers of most of the chief figures of the Wilson administration are available and together constitute a fairly complete documentation of the period. They include the Papers of William Jennings Bryan in the Library of Congress and the National Archives; the Papers, Diary, and Desk Diary of Robert Lansing, Library of Congress; the Papers, Diary, and Desk Diary of Josephus Daniels, Library of Congress, a collection as large as the Wilson Papers; and the Papers of Albert S. Burleson, Library of Congress. The Papers of David F. Houston, Houghton Library, Harvard University, are fragmentary and should be supplemented by the Department of Agriculture Papers in the National Archives, which contain Houston's letter-books. The Papers of William B. Wilson are in the Pennsylvania Historical Society, Philadelphia, and should be used with the Department of Labor's file in the National Archives. The Papers of Lindley M. Garrison, Princeton University Library, are extremely disappointing; for Garrison's correspondence one has to go to the Wilson Papers and the War Department Papers in the National Archives. The Papers of Newton D. Baker, Wilson's other Secretary of War, have just come to the Library of Congress. The Papers of William G. McAdoo, in the Library of Congress, will not be opened until around 1960. The Papers of Joseph P. Tumulty, in the possession of the family in Washington, are valuable for the light they shed on patronage policies. Most of Tumulty's important letters are in the Wilson Papers.

Among administration officials of the second rank, the papers of the following are most important: Frank L. Polk, Diary and Papers, Yale University Library; Chandler P. Anderson, Diary and Papers, Library of Congress; Franklin D. Roosevelt, Roosevelt Library, Hyde Park; Louis F. Post, Library of Congress; Francis Burton Harrison, Library of Congress; Charles S. Hamlin, Diary and Scrapbooks, Library of Congress; Robert W. Woolley, Library of Congress; and John Purroy Mitchel, Library of Congress.

The Papers of Walter H. Page, Houghton Library, Harvard University, include not only Page's voluminous letters and intimate Diary but also the London Embassy files for the period 1913–18. The Diary of Joseph C. Grew, Houghton Library, sheds much light on German developments, 1913–17. The Papers of John Lind, Minnesota Historical Society, St. Paul, bear chiefly on Mexico during the period 1913–17.

Of the papers of military leaders during the prewar period, the Papers of Hugh L. Scott, Tasker H. Bliss, Leonard Wood, and John J. Pershing, all in the Library of Congress, are the most important. The Wood Papers are tightly sealed, but the Scott Papers are indispensable for a study of Mexican-American relations during this period.

The Senate

Of great value for a study of Democratic policies in the Senate and of public opinion in various sections are the Papers of John Sharp Williams, Library of Congress; Thomas J. Walsh, Library of Congress; Furnifold M. Simmons, Duke University Library; Francis J. Newlands, Yale University Library; John H. Bankhead, Alabama Department of Archives, Montgomery; Benjamin R. Tillman, University of South Carolina Library; Gilbert M. Hitchcock, Library of Congress; Thomas R. Marshall, Indiana Historical Society, Indianapolis; Lee S. Overman, University of North Carolina Library; and Paul O. Husting, State Historical Society of Wisconsin, Madison.

Republican insurgency, the revolt of 1910–12, progressive Republican reaction to Wilsonian reform, and Midwestern public opinion are revealed in enormous detail in the papers of the leading insurgent senators: Miles Poindexter, Alderman Library, University of Virginia; Jonathan P. Dolliver, State Historical Society of Iowa, Iowa City; Albert J. Beveridge, Library of Congress; Moses Clapp and Knute Nelson, Minnesota Historical Society, St. Paul; Albert B. Cummins, Historical Memorial and Art Department of Iowa, Des Moines; Joseph H. Bristow, Kansas Historical Society, Topeka; John D. Works, Stanford University Library and University of California Library; George W. Norris, Library of Congress; William E. Borah, Library of Congress; and Robert M. La Follette, in the possession of Miss Fola La Follette, Washington.

Conservative Republican policies in the Senate are amply revealed in the Papers of Henry Cabot Lodge, Massachusetts Historical Society, Boston; of Elihu Root, Library of Congress; and of Philander C. Knox, Library of Congress. The Lodge Papers are temporarily closed. The Root Papers are somewhat disappointing, but the Diary of Chandler P. Anderson, Library of Congress, records many intimate conversations with the distinguished New Yorker.

The House of Representatives

The papers of most of the House Democratic leaders during the Wilson period are now available. The Papers of Oscar W. Underwood, Alabama Department of Archives, Montgomery, and of Hal D. Flood, Library of Congress, are disappointing; but the Papers of Carter Glass, Alderman Library, University of Virginia, and of Claude Kitchin, University of North Carolina Library, are immensely rich.

The papers of two independent congressmen, William Kent, Yale University Library, and Warren Worth Bailey, Princeton University Library, contain important materials on progressive politics, conservation, the Japanese question, and the preparedness and peace movements. For reaction in the upper Middle West to Wilson's policies and the war see the Papers of Charles A. Lindbergh, Minnesota Historical Society, and of Nils P. Haugen, State Historical Society of Wisconsin. The Papers of Richmond P. Hobson, Library of Congress, are loaded with materials on the prohibition crusade.

Republican Leaders

Most important in this group are the Papers of Theodore Roosevelt and of William Howard Taft, both in the Library of Congress. Both collections are enormous and contain voluminous materials on all phases of public affairs.

Significant for a study of progressive Republican opinion and politics are the Papers of William Allen White, Library of Congress; Herbert S. Hadley, University of Missouri Library; Gifford Pinchot, Library of Congress; Chester H. Rowell, University of California Library; Frank O. Lowden, University of Chicago Library; and Charles J. Bonaparte, Library of Congress.

For conservative and middle-of-the-road Republican politics see the Papers of Henry L. Stimson, Yale University Library; Charles Evans Hughes, Library of Congress; Nicholas Murray Butler, Columbia University Library; Charles G. Dawes, Northwestern University Library; and Joseph B. Foraker, Library of Congress and Historical and Philosophical Society of Ohio, Cincinnati.

Editors and Newspapermen

One of the most important manuscript collections in the field of recent American history is the Papers of Oswald Garrison Villard, Houghton Library, Harvard University. The Papers of Lincoln Steffens, now in the University of California Library, shed much light on radical thought and on Mexican relations. The Papers of Henry Watterson, Library of Congress, are thin for the period of 1910–17, but the Papers of Albert Shaw, New York Public Library, are rewarding, as are the Papers of Ray Stannard Baker and of Charles E. Russell, both in the Library of Congress.

Miscellaneous

For the social justice, labor, Negro rights, and peace movements, see the Papers of Andrew Carnegie, of Alexander J. McKelway, of Ben B. Lindsey, of George Foster Peabody, of Booker T. Washington, and of Amos Pinchot, all in the Library of Congress; of Samuel Gompers, American Federation of Labor Archives, Washington; of Jane Addams, Swarthmore College Library; and of Edward P. Costigan, University of Colorado Library.

One of the great collections in recent American history is the Papers of

Louis D. Brandeis, Law School Library, University of Louisville, which is especially important for a study of the origins of the Federal Reserve Act, the Clayton Act, the Federal Trade Commission Act, and of progressive politics during the Wilson era.

The Papers of Charles W. Eliot, Harvard College Archives, are valuable for a study of pro-Allied opinion in the United States. The Papers of John Grier Hibben, Princeton University Library, shed some light on the intervention movement, 1915–17, and on the presidential campaign of 1916.

Business opinion may be consulted in the Papers of Henry Lee Higginson, Houghton Library, Harvard University, and of Daniel A. Tompkins, University of North Carolina Library and the Library of Congress. Finally, the Papers of Richard Olney, Library of Congress, are valuable for conservative Democratic opinion; the Papers of Henry White, Library of Congress, contain correspondence by leading Republicans; and the Papers of Moreton Frewen, Library of Congress, include important letters from Frewen's friends in the United States and Great Britain.

PUBLISHED LETTERS AND WRITINGS

Most useful to the student of this period are the published writings of Wilson, Theodore Roosevelt, and Edward M. House. Ray S. Baker and William E. Dodd (eds.), *The Public Papers of Woodrow Wilson* (6 vols., New York, 1925–27), is carefully edited and fairly complete for the period after 1912. There is no edition of Wilson's letters. Charles Seymour (ed.), *The Intimate Papers of Colonel House* (4 vols., Boston 1926–28), is masterfully edited. Elting E. Morison and John M. Blum (eds.), *The Letters of Theodore Roosevelt* (8 vols., Cambridge, Mass., 1951–54), is one of the great sources for the period 1901–19. *The Works of Theodore Roosevelt* (20 vols., National Ed., New York, 1926) reprints Roosevelt's important speeches during the period 1910–17. Henry Cabot Lodge (ed.), *Selections from the Correspondence of Theodore Roosevelt and Henry Cabot Lodge, 1884–1918* (2 vols., New York, 1925), is not always reliable. For the period after 1900 the student can consult the Lodge file in the Roosevelt Papers.

Burton J. Hendrick, *The Life and Letters of Walter H. Page* (3 vols., Garden City, N.Y., 1924–26), prints some of Page's best letters. The first two volumes are filled with errors, with large portions of the original text often omitted. The third volume, which includes Page's letters to Wilson, is on the whole carefully edited.

The following are also useful: Anne W. Lane and Louise H. Wall (eds.), *The Letters of Franklin K. Lane, Personal and Political* (Boston, 1922); Stephen Gwynn (ed.), *The Letters and Friendships of Sir Cecil Spring Rice*

(2 vols., Boston, 1929); Allan Nevins (ed.), *The Letters and Journal of Brand Whitlock* (2 vols., New York, 1936); Worthington C. Ford (ed.), *Letters of Henry Adams, 1892–1918* (Boston, 1938); Arthur B. Darling (ed.), *The Public Papers of Francis G. Newlands* (2 vols., Boston, 1932); Ella Winter and Granville Hicks (eds.), *The Letters of Lincoln Steffens* (2 vols., New York, 1938); Constance Gardner (ed.), *Some Letters of Augustus Peabody Gardner* (Boston, 1920); and Walter Johnson (ed.), *Selected Letters of William Allen White, 1899–1943* (New York, 1947).

NEWSPAPERS

The New York Times and the New York *World* were easily the two best newspapers in the United States from 1910 to 1917. The *Times'* reporting of news was better than the *World's,* but the *World* excelled in editorials, cartoons, special features, and the reporting of political news.

Along with the *World,* which was the editorial spokesman of the Wilson administration, a number of other progressive newspapers carried the Democratic-progressive banner from 1910 to 1917. They included the *Springfield Republican,* which Wilson read avidly, the Raleigh *News and Observer,* the Baltimore *Sun,* the St. Louis *Post-Dispatch,* the Milwaukee *Journal,* and the San Francisco *Bulletin.*

The pre-eminent spokesmen of Wall Street and Old Guard Republicanism were the New York *Sun* and *Evening Sun.* Harrison Gray Otis' Los Angeles *Times,* however, rivaled the New York *Sun* as the leading champion of reactionary policies.

In a special class were the Hearst newspapers. Although nominally a Democrat, William R. Hearst was lukewarm in his support of Wilson's domestic program, and during the neutrality period he was so violently anti-British as to be almost pro-German. The leading Hearst newspapers during the prewar years were the New York *American* and Chicago *American.*

Other newspapers noteworthy for their editorials and features were the Chicago *Daily Tribune,* Des Moines *Register,* Topeka *Capital,* Louisville *Courier-Journal,* Boston *Advertiser,* Minneapolis *Tribune,* Kansas City *Star,* New York *Herald,* New York *Tribune,* Charlotte *Daily Observer,* and Dallas *Morning News.*

The chief editorial spokesmen of militant Negro opinion were *The Crisis* (New York, 1910–   ), edited by William E. B. DuBois, the Boston *Guardian,* edited by William Monroe Trotter, the New York *Age,* and the Pittsburgh *Courier.* For radical American opinion the New York *Call,* the *Appeal to Reason* (Girard, Kan., 1895–   ), *Pearson's Magazine* (New York, 1899–1925), *International Socialist Review* (Chicago, 1900–18), and *The Masses* (New York, 1911–17) are most useful.

PERIODICALS

General

The magazines in this group often published articles and editorials of contemporary significance, although they were not primarily journals of opinion. Among the more important were the *Review of Reviews* (New York, 1890–1937), *Collier's* (New York, 1888–), *Cosmopolitan* (New York, 1886–1925), *Everybody's Magazine* (New York, 1899–1929), *American Magazine* (New York, 1876–), *Metropolitan* (New York, 1911–24), *Munsey's Magazine* (New York, 1889–1929), *The Independent* (New York, 1848–1928), *Saturday Evening Post* (Philadelphia, 1821–), *World's Work* (New York, 1900–32), *McClure's Magazine* (New York, 1893–1929), and *Literary Digest* (New York, 1890–1937), useful for its summaries of press opinion.

Political Journals

Easily the most significant periodical in this group was the *New Republic* (New York, 1914–), which was the pre-eminent spokesman of advanced progressive and internationalist thought. *The Nation* (New York, 1865–) generally expressed nineteenth-century liberal opinions. Under the editorship of Norman Hapgood, *Harper's Weekly* (New York, 1857–1916) was a spokesman of the Wilson administration. The *Outlook* (New York, 1870–1935) was Roosevelt's chief editorial mouthpiece and a leader in the preparedness movement. *La Follette's Magazine* (Madison, Wis., 1909–29) was the Wisconsin senator's personal outlet, while *The Commoner* (Lincoln, Neb., 1901–23) was Bryan's. George Harvey's *North American Review* (Boston and New York, 1815–1940) was the leading conservative periodical. *Capper's Weekly* (Topeka, Kan., 1875–) is useful for Midwestern farm opinion.

The Religious Press

As the religious periodicals often expressed social and economic opinions and printed articles of significance, the student of this period cannot well ignore them. Most advanced socially were the Congregational, Baptist, Methodist, and Episcopal organs. For the Congregationalists see the *Congregationalist and Christian World* (Boston, 1816–1934); for the Baptists, the *Watchman-Examiner* (New York, 1819–) and *The Standard* (Chicago, 1853–1920); for the Methodists, the *Christian Advocate* (Nashville, 1832–1940) and *Christian Advocate* (New York, 1826–); for the Episcopalians, *The Churchman* (New York, 1845–) and *The Living Church* (Milwaukee, 1878–). The Presbyterian journals generally followed a conservative editorial policy. See *The Presbyterian* (Philadelphia, 1831–) and *Christian*

Observer (Louisville, 1813–   ). Although the Lutheran periodicals usually ignored political and social issues, during the period of neutrality they were militantly pro-German. For two leading Lutheran papers see *The Lutheran* (Lebanon, Penna., 1896–1919) and *Lutheran Church Work and Observer* (Philadelphia, 1908–19).

The Catholic press is especially important for a study of the Mexican and Philippine questions. All Catholic newspapers were opposed to administration policies in these fields, but most outspoken were *The Extension Magazine* (Chicago, 1906–   ) and the Jesuit organ, *America* (New York, 1909–   ).

The Agricultural Press

The rural press is an indispensable source for opinion on all administration policies, but particularly on rural credits, the Underwood tariff, and preparedness. The following are most important: *Progressive Farmer* (Raleigh and Birmingham, 1886–   ), *Wisconsin Farmer* (Madison, Wis., 1881–1929), *Wallace's Farmer* (Des Moines, 1874–   ), *Nebraska Farm Journal* (Omaha, 1897–1924), *Capper's Farmer* (Topeka, 1893–   ), and *Dakota Farmer* (Aberdeen, S.D., 1881–   ). For radical Midwestern farm opinion see the organs of the Farmer's Non-Partisan League, *The Farmer's Open Forum,* later *United Farmers' Forum* (Washington, 1915–21) and the *Non-Partisan Leader,* later *National Leader* (Minneapolis and Fargo, 1915–23).

Banking Journals

Banking journals are useful for their views on the Federal Reserve bill, antitrust legislation, the appointment of the Federal Reserve Board, and financial policies toward the belligerents. The following provide a cross-section of banking opinion: *Bankers' Magazine* (New York, 1846–   ), *Commercial and Financial Chronicle* (New York, 1865–   ), *Financial Age* (New York, 1900–   ), *Magazine of Wall Street* (New York, 1907–   ), *Wall Street Journal* (New York, 1889–   ), *Southern Banker* (Atlanta, 1904–   ), *Texas Bankers' Record* (Austin, 1911–   ), *Bankers' Monthly* (Chicago, 1883–   ), *Northwestern Banker* (Des Moines, 1895–   ), and *Kansas Banker* (Topeka, 1910–   ).

Commercial and Industrial Journals

The commercial and industrial magazines also provide one of the best sources of specific class and interest points of view. Thus the *Manufacturers' Record* (Baltimore, 1882–   ) spoke for the Southern textile interests, *American Industries* (New York, 1902–31) for the National Association of Manufacturers, *Iron Age* (New York, 1859–   ) for the American Iron and Steel Institute, *Commercial Bulletin* (Boston, 1859–   ) and *News Bureau*

(Boston, 1887–) for the Boston commercial interests, *Commercial America* (Philadelphia, 1904–), for the commercial interests of the Middle states, *Annalist* (New York, 1913–40) and *Journal of Commerce and Commercial* (New York, 1827–) for the New York commercial interests, and *Commercial West* (Minneapolis, 1901–) for the commercial and banking interests of the Midwest.

The Labor Press

Easily the commanding voices in this field were the *American Federationist* (Washington, 1894–) and the *American Federation of Labor Weekly News Letter* (Washington, 1911–). Both are indispensable sources. The *Coast Seamen's Journal* (San Francisco, 1887–1937) should be used in connection with the passage of the Seamen's Act of 1915. The *United Mine Workers' Journal* (Indianapolis, 1891–) is especially important for a study of the Colorado Coal Strike of 1913–14.

British Journals of Opinion

The following British periodicals are included in this section because of their significant observations on domestic politics in the United States, Mexican-American relations, and the United States and the European war: *The Nation* (London, 1907–31), *The Outlook* (London, 1898–1928), *The Spectator* (London, 1828–), *The Economist* (London, 1843–), *The Fortnightly Review* (London, 1865–), *The Statist* (London, 1878–), *The Saturday Review* (London, 1855–1938), and *The Nineteenth Century* (London, 1877–).

GENERAL MEMOIRS

The autobiographical material for the period 1910–17 is immensely rich. Among the leaders of the administration, Bryan, Houston, Lansing, Daniels, McAdoo, Tumulty, House, Marshall, Clark, and Redfield have written memoirs. Mary B. Bryan (ed.), *The Memoirs of William Jennings Bryan* (Philadelphia, 1925), is honest for Bryan's motivation. David F. Houston, *Eight Years with Wilson's Cabinet, 1913–1920* (2 vols., Garden City, N.Y., 1926), is generally reliable. Robert Lansing, *The War Memoirs of Robert Lansing* (Indianapolis, 1935), must be supplemented by the Lansing Diary in the Library of Congress. Josephus Daniels, *The Wilson Era* (2 vols., Chapel Hill, N.C., 1944–46), must be used with great caution. William G. McAdoo, *Crowded Years* (Boston, 1931), goes to 1917 and reveals, among other things, McAdoo's high regard for himself. Joseph P. Tumulty, *Woodrow Wilson As I Know Him* (Garden City, N.Y., 1921), is not reliable.

Tumulty's versions of Wilson's conversations are often semifictional. George S. Viereck, Transcripts of conversations with Edward M. House, unpublished MS entitled "The Memoirs of Colonel House," in the George Sylvester Viereck Papers, Yale University Library, is revealing but demands critical scrutiny. William C. Redfield, *With Congress and Cabinet* (Garden City, N.Y., 1924), is undistinguished. A reading of Champ Clark, *My Quarter Century of American Politics* (2 vols., New York, 1920), and Thomas R. Marshall, *Recollections of Thomas R. Marshall* (Indianapolis, 1925), makes one grateful neither was indulged his wish to become President. William F. McCombs, *Making Woodrow Wilson President* (New York, 1921, is the bitter memoir of a man who fell from Wilson's grace. For the personal politics of the administration see also Daniel C. Roper, *Fifty Years of Public Life* (Durham, N.C., 1941); Cordell Hull, *The Memoirs of Cordell Hull* (2 vols., New York, 1948); Frederic C. Howe, *Confessions of a Reformer* (New York, 1925); and Henry Morgenthau, Sr., *All in a Life-Time* (Garden City, N.Y., 1922).

Excellent for the insurgent revolt, progressive Republican politics, and the coming of the First World War are George W. Norris, *Fighting Liberal* (New York, 1945); William Allen White, *The Autobiography of William Allen White* (New York, 1946); Harold L. Ickes, *Autobiography of a Curmudgeon* (New York, 1943); Gifford Pinchot, *Breaking New Ground* (New York, 1947); Owen Wister, *Roosevelt: The Story of a Friendship* (New York, 1930); and Donald Richberg, *Tents of the Mighty* (New York, 1930). Henry L. Stimson, *On Active Service in Peace and War* (New York, 1948); Nicholas Murray Butler, *Across the Busy Years* (2 vols., New York, 1939–40); and James E. Watson, *As I Knew Them* (Indianapolis, 1936), are valuable sources for the Republican politics of the era.

Intimate and revealing accounts of the politics and personalities of the Wilson period are presented in the following autobiographies of editors and reporters: Lincoln Steffens, *Autobiography of Lincoln Steffens* (New York, 1931); Oswald Garrison Villard, *Fighting Years, Memoirs of a Liberal Editor* (New York, 1939); Ray S. Baker, *American Chronicle* (New York, 1945); George Creel, *Rebel at Large* (New York, 1947); Oscar K. Davis, *Released for Publication* (Boston, 1925); Arthur W. Dunn, *From Harrison to Harding* (2 vols., New York, 1922); J. Frederick Essary, *Covering Washington* (Boston, 1927); H. H. Kohlsaat, *From McKinley to Harding* (New York, 1923); Henry L. Stoddard, *As I Knew Them* (New York, 1927); and Henry Watterson, *"Marse Henry"* (2 vols., New York, 1919).

Also important are Samuel Gompers, *Seventy Years of Life and Labor* (2 vols., New York, 1925); Hugh L. Scott, *Some Memories of a Soldier* (New York, 1928); and Thomas W. Lamont, *Across World Frontiers* (New York, 1951).

BIOGRAPHIES

Theodore Roosevelt, the Insurgent Revolt, and Republican Politics, 1910–17

Although Henry F. Pringle does not take Roosevelt seriously enough, his *Theodore Roosevelt, A Biography* (New York, 1931), is still the best study of the man. Much better for the period 1909–19, however, is George E. Mowry, *Theodore Roosevelt and the Progressive Movement* (Madison, Wis., 1946). Russell Buchanan, "Theodore Roosevelt and American Neutrality, 1914–1917," *American Historical Review*, XLIII (July, 1938), 775–790, is also useful.

The two best biographies relating to the insurgent revolt and progressive Republican politics are Walter Johnson, *William Allen White's America* (New York, 1946), and Claude Bowers, *Beveridge and the Progressive Era* (Boston, 1932). The literature on the regular Republican leaders is unusually rich. Merlo J. Pusey, *Charles Evans Hughes* (2 vols., New York, 1951), is marred only by lack of critical judgment. Philip C. Jessup, *Elihu Root* (2 vols., New York, 1938), is the authorized biography, but Richard W. Leopold's forthcoming study of Root is not only briefer but also more critical. Henry F. Pringle, *The Life and Times of William Howard Taft* (2 vols., New York, 1939), is practically definitive, but lacks a critical quality, while Nathaniel W. Stephenson, *Nelson W. Aldrich* (New York, 1930), is helpful for the background and writing of the Federal Reserve bill.

Woodrow Wilson, the Administration, and the Democratic Party, 1910–17

The most nearly complete biography of Wilson is Ray S. Baker's authorized *Woodrow Wilson: Life and Letters* (8 vols., Garden City, N.Y., 1927–39). The first four volumes, which carry the biography to August, 1914, are uncritical and often ignore the important historical processes. Volumes V and VI, which cover the neutrality period, were written during the disillusionment over American participation in the war and reflect the temper of the time in which they were written. The best one-volume biography of Wilson is Herbert C. F. Bell, *Woodrow Wilson and the People* (Garden City, N.Y., 1945), although David Lawrence, *The True Story of Woodrow Wilson* (New York, 1924); James Kerney, *The Political Education of Woodrow Wilson* (New York, 1926); Robert E. Annin, *Woodrow Wilson: A Character Study* (New York, 1924); and William B. Hale, *Woodrow Wilson: The Story of His Life* (Garden City, N.Y., 1912), have a special value because they were written by contemporaries.

Scholarly and historical works on Wilson are few. Laura S. Turnbull, *Woodrow Wilson, A Selected Bibliography* (Princeton, N.J., 1948), is a useful guide. Arthur S. Link, *Wilson: The Road to the White House* (Princeton, N.J., 1947), is the first volume of a new multi-volume biography. Harley Notter, *The Origins of the Foreign Policy of Woodrow Wilson* (Baltimore, 1937), is thorough but based on published sources. William Diamond, *The Economic Thought of Woodrow Wilson* (Baltimore, 1943), is good for the period before 1913 but weak on the presidential years.

Scholarly biographies of leaders in the Wilson administration and the Democratic party are also scarce. For House the best work is still Seymour, *The Intimate Papers of Colonel House,* previously cited, which of course is not strictly a biography. Arthur D. H. Smith, *Mr. House of Texas* (New York, 1940), and George Sylvester Viereck, *The Strangest Friendship in History* (New York, 1932), were written with House's collaboration and exaggerate his influence. There is no biography of Lansing. Paxton Hibben and C. H. Grattan, *The Peerless Leader* (New York, 1929); M. R. Werner, *Bryan* (New York, 1929); Wayne C. Williams, *William Jennings Bryan* (New York, 1936); and J. C. Long, *Bryan, the Great Commoner* (New York, 1928), are either overly critical or else worshipful.

One of the best biographies for the period is Alpheus T. Mason, *Brandeis, A Free Man's Life* (New York, 1946). John M. Blum, *Joe Tumulty and the Wilson Era* (Boston, 1951), is also excellent. For other administration and party leaders see Mary Synon, *McAdoo* (Indianapolis, 1924); Rixey Smith and Norman Beasley, *Carter Glass, A Biography* (New York, 1939); George C. Osborn, *John Sharp Williams* (Baton Rouge, La., 1943); Francis B. Simkins, *Pitchfork Ben Tillman* (Baton Rouge, La., 1944); John L. Heaton, *Cobb of the World* (New York, 1924); Frederick Palmer, *Newton D. Baker: America at War* (2 vols., New York, 1931); and F. Palmer, *Bliss, Peacemaker* (New York, 1934).

Miscellaneous

Disparate but excellent biographies relevant to the period are Allan Nevins, *Henry White, Thirty Years of American Diplomacy* (New York, 1930); Hermann Hagedorn, *Leonard Wood, A Biography* (2 vols., New York, 1931); Willis F. Johnson, *George Harvey, "A Passionate Patriot"* (Boston, 1929); Ferdinand Lundberg, *Imperial Hearst, a Social Biography* (New York, 1936); Ray Ginger, *The Bending Cross: A Biography of Eugene Victor Debs* (New Brunswick, N.J., 1949); and C. Vann Woodward, *Tom Watson: Agrarian Rebel* (New York, 1938).

GENERAL WORKS

The only general works that treat this period specifically are Frederick L. Paxson, *The Pre-War Years, 1913–1917* (Boston, 1936), and Mark Sullivan, *Our Times, The United States, 1900–1925* (6 vols., New York, 1926–35), V. Of great value for its analysis of economic institutions and social and economic legislation is Harold U. Faulkner, *The Decline of Laissez-Faire, 1897–1917* (New York, 1951). The best general account of the progressive movement is still Harold U. Faulkner, *The Quest for Social Justice, 1898– 1914* (New York, 1931), but no student of this period should overlook Russell B. Nye, *Midwestern Progressive Politics* (East Lansing, Mich., 1951), or Eric F. Goldman, *Rendezvous with Destiny* (New York, 1952), a history of the American reform movement since 1865. Sidney Ratner, *American Taxation* (New York, 1942), is another invaluable study.

FROM THE NEW FREEDOM TO THE NEW NATIONALISM, 1910–17

The Years of Revolt, 1910–12

The culmination of the progressive movement evoked the writing of many commentaries on the changing political order. The following are selected samples of this literature: Herbert Croly, *The Promise of American Life* (New York, 1909) and *Progressive Democracy* (New York, 1914); Thomas N. Carver, *Essays in Social Justice* (Cambridge, Mass., 1915); Allan L. Benson, *Our Dishonest Constitution* (New York, 1914); Nicholas M. Butler, *Why Should We Change Our Form of Government?* (New York, 1912); and Elihu Root, *Experiments in Government and the Essentials of the Constitution* (Princeton, N.J., 1913).

The best secondary sources on the insurgent revolt and the campaign of 1912 are Mowry and Link, cited above, and Kenneth W. Hechler, *Insurgency: Personalities and Politics of the Taft Era* (New York, 1940). See also the biographies and memoirs of the leaders involved, cited above, to which should be added chapters from Robert M. La Follette, *La Follette's Autobiography* (Madison, Wis., 1913).

The best sources for the conventions and platforms of 1912 are the newspapers and the official party publications. W. J. Bryan, *A Tale of Two Conventions* (New York, 1912), is a day-by-day account of the Republican and Democratic conventions. A. S. Link (ed.), "A Letter from One of Wilson's Managers," *American Historical Review,* L (July, 1945), 768–775, presents an inside view of the Democratic convention.

Wilson's and Roosevelt's important speeches during the campaign of 1912 may be found in Woodrow Wilson, *The New Freedom* (Garden City, N.Y., 1913), *The Public Papers of Woodrow Wilson,* and the *Works of Theodore Roosevelt.*

The Underwood Tariff

The best source for contemporary opinion on the tariff question is House Ways and Means Committee, *Tariff Schedules, Hearings . . . ,* 62d Cong., 3d sess. (7 vols., Washington, 1913). An excellent contemporary comment is Frank W. Taussig, *Some Aspects of the Tariff Question* (Cambridge, Mass., 1915).

The activities of the various tariff lobbies in 1913 were fully revealed and analyzed in Senate Judiciary Committee, *Maintenance of Lobby to Influence Legislation, Hearings* . . . , 63d Cong., 1st sess. (4 vols., Washington, 1913).

The great source for Congressional debates on the tariff and all other legislation for the period 1911 to 1917 is *Congressional Record,* 62d Cong., 1st sess.–64th Cong., 2d sess. (Washington, 1911–17).

The Federal Reserve Act

The Federal Reserve Act had a long background of public discussion and agitation over the shape that banking reform should assume. Discussions of the movement for a new banking and currency system and significant accounts of the writing of the Federal Reserve Act may be found in the following general works by some leaders of the era: H. Parker Willis, *The Federal Reserve System* (New York, 1923); J. Laurence Laughlin, *The Federal Reserve Act, Its Origins and Problems* (New York, 1933); Paul M. Warburg, *Essays on Banking Reform in the United States* (New York, 1914); and *The Federal Reserve System, Its Origin and Growth* (2 vols., New York, 1930).

The revelations of the Pujo Committee during the early months of 1913 dramatized the extent of the concentration of banking credits in the United States and set off a widespread demand for legislation to destroy the "Money Trust." For the report of the Pujo Committee see *Report of Committee Appointed Pursuant to H.R. 429 and 504* . . . , 62d Cong., 3d sess. (Washington, 1913). Louis D. Brandeis summarized the testimony taken by the Pujo Committee in *Other People's Money and How the Bankers Use It* (New York, 1914).

A violent tempest in a teapot raged in 1926 and 1927 over the authorship of the Federal Reserve Act. Professor Seymour's assertion, made in the *Intimate Papers of Colonel House,* I, 160, that House was the "unseen guardian" of the Federal Reserve bill so infuriated Carter Glass that he wrote *An Adventure in Constructive Finance* (Garden City, N.Y., 1927) to prove that House and Samuel Untermyer, counsel for the Pujo Committee, had nothing to do with the measure. Untermyer shot back at Glass in *Who Is Entitled to the Credit for the Federal Reserve Act? An Answer to Senator Carter Glass* (New York, 1927). Glass' rejoinder, "Vapor vs. the Record," a manuscript in the Carter Glass Papers, was apparently never published.

The best sources on the writing and passage of the Federal Reserve bill are Willis, *The Federal Reserve System;* Glass, *An Adventure in Constructive Finance,* and Robert L. Owen, *The Federal Reserve Act* (New York, 1919).

For opinions on the bill see House Banking and Currency Committee,

Banking and Currency Reform. Hearings before Subcommittee . . . , 62d Cong., 3d sess. (13 parts, Washington, 1913), and Senate Banking and Currency Committee, *Hearings on H.R. 7837 (S. 2639)* . . . , 63d Cong., 1st sess. (3 vols., Washington, 1913). Academy of Political Science, *Banking and Currency in the United States* (New York, 1913), includes criticisms and defenses of the Federal Reserve bill by leading bankers and administration spokesmen.

The best works on the development of Federal Reserve policies are Willis, cited above, and Seymour E. Harris, *Twenty Years of Federal Reserve Policy* (2 vols., Cambridge, Mass., 1933).

Antitrust Legislation

For a general discussion of the background and adoption of the antitrust legislation of the Wilson administration, the following are useful: John D. Clark, *The Federal Trust Policy* (Baltimore, 1931); Henry R. Seager and C. A. Gulick, Jr., *Trust and Corporation Problems* (New York, 1929); and Oswald W. Knauth, *The Policy of the United States Towards Industrial Monopoly* (New York, 1914).

Progressive opinion on a policy toward big business diverged sharply from 1910 through 1914. The main body of Democrats, who advocated destruction of the great combinations, found an eloquent spokesman in Louis D. Brandeis, whose articles on the trust question were reprinted in *Business—A Profession* (Boston, 1914). Wilson's views in 1912 are set forth in *The New Freedom,* previously cited. The Progressive program for acceptance and federal regulation of the great corporations was most explicitly set forth in Charles R. Van Hise, *Concentration and Control: A Solution of the Trust Problem in the United States* (New York, 1912).

All shades of opinion on the question, however, were most completely set forth in American Academy of Political and Social Science, *Industrial Competition and Combination* (Philadelphia, 1912); House Judiciary Committee, *Trust Legislation, Hearings,* 63d Cong., 2d sess. (4 vols., Washington, 1914); and Senate Interstate Commerce Committee, *Hearings on Bills Relating to Trust Legislation,* 63d Cong., 2d sess. (2 vols., Washington, 1914).

The Rural Credits Act

The background of the Federal Farm Loan Act of 1916 is briefly discussed in Theodore Saloutos and John D. Hicks, *Agricultural Discontent in the Middle West, 1900–1939* (Madison, Wis., 1951). More detailed are James B. Morman, *The Principles of Rural Credits* (New York, 1915), and Edna D. Bullock, *Agricultural Credit* (New York, 1915).

The conservative argument that a federal rural credits system would constitute special privilege for a favored class may be found in Myron T.

Herrick and R. Ingalls, *Rural Credits* (New York, 1914). All phases of current opinion may be conveniently found in House Banking and Currency Committee, *Rural Credits, Hearings Before Subcommittee* . . . , 63d Cong., 2d sess. (Washington, 1914), and Senate Banking and Currency Committee, *Rural Credits, Joint Hearings Before Subcommittees on Banking and Currency of Senate and House of Representatives,* 63d Cong., 2d sess. (2 vols., Washington, 1914).

The Seamen's Bill

The campaign for the passage of the Furuseth seamen's bill can be followed in the *Coast Seamen's Journal, La Follette's Magazine, The Survey* (New York, 1897–1932), and the *American Labor Legislation Review* (New York, 1911–   ). A wide range of opinion for and against the bill may be found in House Merchant Marine and Fisheries Committee, *Seamen's Bill, Hearings on S. 136* . . . , 63d Cong., 2d sess. (2 parts, Washington, 1914), and Senate Commerce Committee, *Seamen's Bill, Hearings on S. 136* . . . , 63d Cong., 2d sess. (Washington, 1914).

The Child Labor Act

The passage of the Child Labor Act in 1916 marked the first culmination of a movement already a decade old. For background and related discussions see Elizabeth Brandeis, "Labor Legislation," in J. R. Commons *et al., History of Labor in the United States* (4 vols., New York, 1918–35), III; Elizabeth H. Davidson, *Child Labor Legislation in the Southern Textile States* (Chapel Hill, N.C., 1939); Miriam E. Loughran, *The Historical Development of Child-Labor Legislation in the United States* (Washington, 1921); and C. G. Bowers, *Beveridge and the Progressive Era,* cited above.

The best sources for contemporary opinion on the measure are House Labor Committee, *Child-Labor Bill, Hearings on H.R. 12292* . . . , 63d Cong., 2d sess. (Washington, 1914); House Labor Committee, *Child-Labor Bill, Hearings on H.R. 8234* . . . , 64th Cong., 1st sess. (Washington, 1916); and Senate Interstate Commerce Committee, *Interstate Commerce in Products of Child Labor, Hearings on H.R. 8234* . . . , 64th Cong., 1st sess. (2 parts, Washington, 1916).

The Burnett Immigration Bills of 1915 and 1917

Samuel Gompers, "Immigration Legislation Effected," *American Federationist,* XXIV (Mar., 1917), 189–195, reviews the long struggle for restriction. House Immigration and Naturalization Committee, *Restriction of Immigration, Hearings* . . . , 63d Cong., 2d sess. (3 parts, Washington, 1913–14), and House Immigration and Naturalization Committee, *Hear-*

ings . . . , 64th Cong., 1st sess. (Washington, 1916), are the best sources for contemporary opinion.

The Negro, 1910–17

Negro reaction to administration policies, especially segregation, can best be followed in *The Crisis* and other Negro newspapers. William E. B. DuBois, *Dusk of Dawn* (New York, 1940), and Alexander Walters, *My Life and Work* (New York, 1917), are two memoirs by Negro leaders during the Wilson period. The following contemporary accounts of the segregation of Negroes in the federal departments are excellent: Belle Case La Follette, "Color Line to Date," *La Follette's Weekly*, VI (Jan. 24, 1914), 6–7; O. G. Villard, "The President and the Segregation at Washington," *North American Review*, CXCVIII (Dec., 1913), 800–807; McGregor (A. J. McKelway), "Segregation in the Departments," *Harper's Weekly*, LIX (Dec. 26, 1914), 620–621.

THE UNITED STATES, THE CARIBBEAN, AND LATIN AMERICA, 1910–17

General

The best summaries are Samuel F. Bemis, *The Latin American Policy of the United States* (New York, 1943), and Wilfred H. Callcott, *The Caribbean Policy of the United States, 1890–1920* (Baltimore, 1942). Less detailed treatments are Dexter Perkins, *The United States and the Caribbean* (Cambridge, Mass., 1947), and Julius W. Pratt, *America's Colonial Experiment* (New York, 1950). Selig Adler, "Bryan and Wilsonian Carribean Penetration," *Hispanic American Historical Review*, XX (May, 1940), 198–226, is the only detailed study of this subject.

As for contemporary materials, the richest published sources for a study of Taft's and Wilson's Latin American and Caribbean policies are the *Papers Relating to the Foreign Relations of the United States, 1910–1917* (8 vols., Washington, 1915, 1918–20, 1922, 1924–26). These volumes are so incomplete, however, that the student must go to the State Department Papers in the National Archives for the full record.

Special Studies

Isaac J. Cox, *Nicaragua and the United States, 1909–1927* (Boston, 1927), is fairly complete, although not based upon archival materials. The standard history of Santo Domingo, Sumner Welles, *Naboth's Vineyard, the Dominican Republic, 1844–1924* (New York, 1928), has a critical account of the American occupation. A wealth of information on the occupations of Santo Domingo and Haiti may be found in Senate Select Committee, *Inquiry into*

Occupation and Administration of Haiti and Santo Domingo, 67th Cong., 1st and 2d sess. (2 vols., Washington, 1922). Detailed accounts of the American occupation of Haiti may be found also in Raymond L. Buell, *The American Occupation of Haiti* (New York, 1929); Arthur C. Millspaugh, *Haiti Under American Control, 1915–1930* (Boston, 1931); and Emily G. Balch (ed.), *Occupied Haiti* (New York, 1927). The only general work on Colombian-American relations is J. Fred Rippy, *The Capitalists and Colombia* (New York, 1931). For Cuban-American relations during the Wilson period see Russell H. Fitzgibbon, *Cuba and the United States, 1900–1935* (Menasha, Wis., 1935), and Leland H. Jenks, *Our Cuban Colony: A Study in Sugar* (New York, 1928). Charles C. Tansill, *The Purchase of the Danish West Indies* (Baltimore, 1932), is definitive.

THE UNITED STATES AND THE FAR EAST, 1910–17

General Works

Several general works offer excellent guides in studying this area of American foreign relations: A. Whitney Griswold, *The Far Eastern Policy of the United States* (New York, 1938); Edwin O. Reischauer, *The United States and Japan* (Cambridge, Mass., 1950); and John K. Fairbank, *The United States and China* (Cambridge, Mass., 1948). Roy H. Akagi, *Japanese Foreign Relations, 1542–1936* (Tokyo, 1936), is the only survey in English by a Japanese scholar.

The California Controversy of 1913

General treatments are Carey McWilliams, *Prejudice: Japanese-Americans* (Boston, 1944); Yamato Ichihashi, *Japanese in the United States* (Stanford, Calif., 1932); Toyokichi Iyenaga and Kenoske Sato, *Japan and the California Problem* (New York, 1921); and Sidney L. Gulick, *The American Japanese Problem: A Study of the Racial Relations of East and West* (New York, 1914). A contemporary report of unusual significance is H. A. Millis, *The Japanese Problem in the United States, an Investigation for the Commission on Relations with Japan Appointed by the Federal Council of the Churches of Christ in America* (New York, 1915).

The Crisis over the Twenty-One Demands

Stanley K. Hornbeck, *Contemporary Politics in the Far East* (New York, 1916), is an excellent contemporary discussion. Paul S. Reinsch, *An American Diplomat in China* (New York, 1922), is the memoir of the American Minister at Peking during the crisis. Tien-yi Li, *Woodrow Wilson's China Policy, 1913–1917* (New York, 1952), is an excellent discussion. For the documents in the Japanese-Chinese negotiations of 1915 see Carnegie Endowment for

International Peace, *The Sino-Japanese Negotiations of 1915* (Washington, 1921).

The United States and the Philippines

The Wilson administration sponsored legislation and pursued policies that greatly enlarged the self-government of the Filipino peoples. Wilson's Governor General, Francis B. Harrison, tells the story in *The Corner-Stone of Philippine Independence: A Narrative of Seven Years* (New York, 1922), as does Manuel L. Quezon, *The Good Fight* (New York, 1946). Highly critical of Wilson's policies was W. Cameron Forbes in *The Philippine Islands* (2 vols., Boston, 1928).

THE UNITED STATES AND MEXICO, 1910–17

Official and Manuscript Sources

The most important published official sources are the volumes in the *Foreign Relations* series, cited on p. 299. The sections on Mexico in these volumes, however, are so incomplete that the student must work through the Mexican files in the State Department Papers to understand the formation of policies. There are, moreover, many important documents, not elsewhere available, in the Wilson and Frank L. Polk Papers.

The relation between American oil and railroad promoters and the Madero Revolution was revealed in Senate Foreign Relations Committee, *Revolutions in Mexico* . . . , 62d Cong., 3d sess. (Washington, 1913). Senate Foreign Relations Committee, *Investigation of Mexican Affairs* . . . , 66th Cong., 2d sess. (2 vols., Washington, 1920), was an effort to discredit Wilson's Mexican policy but contains much useful data.

General Works on the Mexican Revolution

There is no authoritative history of the Mexican Revolution in any language. Charles C. Cumberland, *The Mexican Revolution, Genesis Under Madero* (Austin, Tex., 1952), is excellent for the first phase of the Revolution. Ernest H. Gruening, *Mexico and Its Heritage* (New York, 1928), and Frank Tannenbaum, *The Mexican Agrarian Revolution* (New York, 1929), are two general works by American scholars. Miguel Alessio Robles, *Histórica Política de la Revolución* (Mexico City, 1946), is the only good Mexican work on the subject.

Contemporary Accounts, Critiques, and Documents of the Revolution, 1913–17

Edith L. O'Shaughnessy, *Diplomatic Days* (New York, 1917) and *A Diplomat's Wife in Mexico* (New York, 1916), are editions of the letters of the wife of the American Chargé in Mexico City from 1912 to 1914. Important defenses of Huerta are Rafael de Zayas Enríquez, *The Case of Mexico and the Policy of President Wilson* (New York, 1914), and Manuel Calero, *Un Decinio de Política Mexicana* (New York, 1920). For an eloquent defense of the Revolution, however, see Luis Cabrera, *The Mexican Situation from a Mexican Point of View* (Washington, 1913 [?]).

John Reed, *Insurgent Mexico* (New York, 1914), and Casper Whitney, *What's the Matter with Mexico?* (New York, 1916), are reports by journalists friendly to the Revolution. The following are samples of anti-Revolutionary propaganda: Edward I. Bell, *The Political Shame of Mexico* (New York, 1914); Randolph W. Smith, *Benighted Mexico* (New York, 1916); and Thomas E. Gibson, *Mexico Under Carranza* (Garden City, N. Y., 1919).

American Catholics and Mexico

Catholic comment on the Revolution and Wilson's policies may be followed in the newspapers and magazines cited above. Francis C. Kelley, *The Book of Red and Yellow, Being a Story of Blood and a Yellow Streak* (Chicago, 1915), was a severe condemnation of Wilson's allegedly cowardly policies. *Blood-Drenched Altars* (Milwaukee, 1935) is Father Kelley's autobiographical account. Dr. A. Paganel [Carlo de Fornaro], *What the Catholic Church Has Done to Mexico* (Mexico City, 1916), was a Constitutionalist reply to Catholic charges.

The United States and Mexico, 1913–17

J. Fred Rippy, *The United States and Mexico* (New York, 1931), is now superseded by Howard F. Cline, *The United States and Mexico* (Cambridge, Mass., 1953). There is a wealth of information on Wilson's policy toward Huerta in George M. Stephenson, *John Lind of Minnesota* (Minneapolis, 1935). Stuart A. MacCorkle, *American Policy of Recognition Towards Mexico* (Baltimore, 1933), is helpful for the period 1913–17.

Contemporary observations on Wilson's Mexican policy are usually critical. Henry Lane Wilson, *Diplomatic Episodes in Mexico, Belgium and Chile* (Garden City, N.Y., 1927), is hardly objective. Francisco Bulnes, *The Whole Truth About Mexico, President Wilson's Responsibility* (New York, 1916), and Manuel Calero, *The Mexican Policy of President Wilson As It Appears to a Mexican* (New York, 1916), are condemnations of Wilsonian intervention. Henry Morris, *Our Mexican Muddle* (Chicago, 1916), is a thoroughgoing denunciation by an American observer.

The British and Mexico

Edward Grey, *Twenty-Five Years, 1892–1916* (2 vols., New York, 1925), and B. J. Hendrick, *The Life and Letters of Walter H. Page,* help to explain

Britain's Mexican policy. John A. Spender, *Weetman Pearson, First Viscount Cowdray, 1856–1927* (London, 1930), is also useful. The best sources of British opinion, however, are the British journals of comment, cited on p. 291, which, until the war in Europe began, made the most penetrating and permanently valuable observations on Wilson's policy that we have.

AMERICAN NEUTRALITY, 1914–17, GENERAL

Official American Sources and Manuscripts

Papers Relating to the Foreign Relations of the United States, Supplements, 1914–1917 (6 vols., Washington, 1928–29, 1931–32), the great storehouses of materials relating to American neutrality, are magnificently edited and complete for all important issues. *Papers Relating to the Foreign Relations of the United States, The Lansing Papers* (2 vols., Washington, 1939–40), and Carlton Savage (ed.), *Policy of the United States Toward Maritime Commerce in War, 1776–1918* (2 vols., Washington, 1934–36), are also absolutely indispensable. Special Senate Committee, *Hearings Before the Special Committee Investigating the Munitions Industry,* 74th Cong., 2d sess. (40 parts, Washington, 1937), reprints much of the important correspondence of bankers and administration leaders bearing on the question of loans to the belligerents.

The Wilson, House, Page, Bryan, Lansing, Daniels, Polk, and McAdoo Papers all contain documents relating to the manifold aspects of the problems of neutrality that cannot be found elsewhere.

General Works

It has now been more than thirty-five years since the United States entered the First World War; most of the important documents bearing upon that event have been available to scholars at least since 1941. Even so, we still do not have a general study that can be recommended to students as comprehensive and dispassionate.

Ray S. Baker, *Woodrow Wilson: Life and Letters,* V–VI; Harley Notter, *The Origins of the Foreign Policy of Woodrow Wilson,* and Newton D. Baker, *Why We Went to War* (New York, 1936), are useful. Among the general studies, however, Charles Seymour's *American Diplomacy during the World War* (Baltimore, 1934) and *American Neutrality, 1914–1917* (New Haven, Conn., 1935), remain the most balanced discussions of the subject. One of the most perceptive commentaries has not yet been published—Edward H. Buehrig, "Our First European Intervention: 1917" (MS in possession of the author). C. Harley Grattan, *Why We Fought* (New York, 1929), and Walter Millis, *Road to War: America, 1914–1917* (Boston, 1935), are vividly written journalistic studies that often ignore the important issues. Alex M. Arnett,

Claude Kitchin and the Wilson War Policies (Boston, 1937), is reliable only for Congressional opinions on preparedness and the question of intervention. Alice M. Morrissey, *The American Defense of Neutral Rights, 1914–1917* (Cambridge, Mass., 1939), is legalistic and unrealistic.

Because of their impact upon subsequent historical writing, Edwin M. Borchard and W. P. Lage, *Neutrality for the United States* (New Haven, Conn., 1937), and Charles C. Tansill, *America Goes to War* (Boston, 1938), deserve special notice. Professor Borchard was imbued with a sense of mission to expose Wilson's duplicity and to prove that a truly neutral conduct would have kept the United States out of the war. Professor Tansill's volume is based upon enormous research but is marred by a deep anti-British tension and by Tansill's willingness to use doubtful evidence to bolster a weak case.

Bibliographical Aids

Bernadotte E. Schmitt, "American Neutrality, 1914–1917," *Journal of Modern History,* VIII (June, 1936), 200–211, and D. F. Fleming, "Our Entry into the World War in 1917: the Revised Version," *Journal of Politics,* II (Feb., 1940), 75–86, are older commentaries. Richard W. Leopold, "The Problem of American Intervention, 1917: An Historical Retrospect," *World Politics,* II (Apr., 1950), 405–425, is a comprehensive survey of the literature.

ANGLO-AMERICAN RELATIONS, 1914–17

General

In addition to the general works cited above, the following are useful supplementary monographs by American scholars: Malbone W. Graham, *The Controversy between the United States and the Allied Governments, Respecting Neutral Rights and Commerce during the Period of American Neutrality, 1914–1917* (Austin, Tex., 1923); Richard W. Van Alstyne, "The Policy of the United States Regarding the Declaration of London, at the Outbreak of the Great War," *Journal of Modern History,* VII (Dec., 1935), 434–447; Thomas A. Bailey, "The United States and the Blacklist during the Great War," *Journal of Modern History,* VI (Mar., 1934), 14–35; Joseph V. Fuller, "The Genesis of the Munitions Traffic," *Journal of Modern History,* VI (Sept., 1934), 280–293; R. W. Van Alstyne, "Private American Loans to the Allies, 1914–1916," *Pacific Historical Review,* II (June, 1933), 180–193; T. A. Bailey, "World War Analogues of the *Trent* Affair," *American Historical Review,* XXXVIII (Jan., 1933), 286–290; J. C. Crighton, "*The Wilhelmina:* An Adventure in the Assertion and Exercise of American Trading Rights during the World War," *American Journal of International Law,* XXXIV (Jan., 1940), 74–88.

Contemporary American Comment

One of the most influential contemporary comments on the British maritime system was Edwin J. Clapp, *Economic Aspects of the War* (New Haven, Conn., 1915), which was highly critical of British measures. Some Americans, however, well recognized that British victory and the preservation of British sea power in the North Atlantic were essential to the security of the United States. For samples of such views see Roland G. Usher, *The Challenge of the Future* (Boston, 1916), and George Louis Beer, "America's Part Among Nations," *New Republic,* V (Nov. 20, 1915), 62–64. The most perspicacious articles in this vein, however, were a series by Walter Lippmann in the *New Republic,* published from February, 1916, to April, 1917.

British Newspapers and Periodicals

Armin Rappaport, *The British Press and Wilsonian Neutrality* (Stanford, Calif., 1951), is an excellent summary. British newspapers and journals of opinion commented freely and often caustically on Wilson's neutral policies. Among the daily press, the London *Chronicle,* London *Observer,* London *Daily Telegraph,* Manchester *Guardian,* London *Times, Westminster Gazette,* and London *Pall Mall Gazette* were generally friendly to the United States, while the London *Clarion,* London *Daily Express,* London *Daily Mail,* London *Daily News and Leader,* London *Morning Post,* and Glasgow *Herald* were usually highly critical of American policies. For a list of the significant British journals of comment see p. 291.

Letters, Memoirs, and Biographies of British Leaders

Stephen Gwynn (ed.), *The Letters and Friendships of Sir Cecil Spring Rice* (2 vols., Boston, 1929), is important, but more useful for British opinion are Herbert H. Asquith, *Memories and Reflections, 1852–1927* (2 vols., Boston, 1928); Arthur J. Balfour, *Retrospect: An Unfinished Biography* (Boston, 1930); Winston S. Churchill, *The World Crisis* (4 vols. in 5, New York, 1923–29); Edward Grey, *Twenty-Five Years, 1892–1916,* cited above; David Lloyd George, *War Memoirs of David Lloyd George* (6 vols., Boston, 1933–37); and Henry W. Steed, *Through Thirty Years, 1892–1922* (Garden City, N.Y., 1924).

Also helpful in understanding British policies are Blanche E. C. Dugdale, *Arthur James Balfour* (2 vols., London, 1936); Herbert A. L. Fisher, *James Bryce* (2 vols., New York, 1927); and George M. Trevelyan, *Grey of Fallodon* (Boston, 1937).

FRANCO-AMERICAN RELATIONS, 1914–17

Most of the general works cited under "American Neutrality, 1914–17, General" advert to the relations between the United States and France.

T. Bentley Mott, *Myron T. Herrick, Friend of France* (Garden City, N.Y., 1929), and William G. Sharp, *War Memoirs of William Graves Sharp* (London, 1931), are the biography and memoir of the two American Ambassadors in Paris from 1914 to 1917. Georges E. B. Clemenceau, *In the Evening of My Thought* (Charles M. Thompson and John Heard, Jr., trans., 2 vols., Boston, 1929), is the only autobiography of an important French statesman. André P. G. A. Tardieu, *France and America* (Boston, 1927), is also useful.

GERMAN-AMERICAN RELATIONS, 1914–17

General

The general sources and works cited under "American Neutrality, 1914–17, General" are of course especially pertinent here. In this connection, see also James W. Gerard, *My Four Years in Germany* (New York, 1917), *Face to Face with Kaiserism* (New York, 1918), and *My First Eighty-Three Years in America* (Garden City, N.Y., 1951); Hugh Gibson, *A Journal from Our Legation in Belgium* (Garden City, N.Y., 1917), and Joseph C. Grew, *Turbulent Era, A Diplomatic Record of Forty Years, 1904–1945* (Walter Johnson, ed., 2 vols., Boston, 1952).

Johann H. von Bernstorff, *My Three Years in America* (New York, 1920) and *Memoirs* (New York, 1936), and Constantin Dumba, *Memoirs of a Diplomat* (Ian F. D. Morrow, trans., Boston, 1932), should be used with care.

William H. Skaggs, *German Conspiracies in America* (London, 1915), is somewhat exaggerated, but Franz Rintelen von Kleist, *The Dark Invader* (London, 1933), is the story of German intrigues in the United States by the chief German agent.

American Comment on Germany—General

For sympathtic analyses of and comment on the German war effort and objectives by Americans see E. F. Henderson, *Germany's Fighting Machine* (Indianapolis, 1914); John W. Burgess, *The European War of 1914* (Chicago, 1915); George S. Fullerton, *Germany of Today* (Indianapolis, 1915); Max Eastman, *Understanding Germany* (New York, 1916); and Albert J. Beveridge, *What Is Back of the War?* (Indianapolis, 1915).

In contrast to these Americans who viewed the German cause sympathetically, other American observers asserted that Germany had begun the war in order to achieve hegemony in the world and condemned the Prussian military class as a dire menace to liberty everywhere. In this vein see James M. Beck, *The Evidence in the Case* (New York, 1914); J. M. Beck, *The War and Humanity* (New York, 1916); Frederick W. Whitridge, *One*

American's Opinion of the European War (New York, 1914); John Jay Chapman, *Deutschland Über Alles, or Germany Speaks* (New York, 1914); Oswald G. Villard, *Germany Embattled* (New York, 1915); William Roscoe Thayer, *Germany vs. Civilization* (Boston, 1916); and A. D. McLaren, *Germanism from Within* (New York, 1916).

German Atrocities

The report of the Bryce Commission, *Report of the Committee on Alleged German Outrages,* was published in full in *The New York Times* and other American newspapers on May 13, 1915. For other such contemporary indictments against the German government see, e.g., Joseph Bédier, *Les Crimes Allemands d'après Témoignages Allemands* (Paris, 1916); J. H. Morgan, *German Atrocities* (New York, 1916); and James M. Beck, *The Case of Edith Cavell* (New York, 1916).

There is considerable doubt, however, that these atrocity charges significantly affected American public opinion. This was true primarily because American reporters with the German armies in Belgium and northern France unanimously repudiated the accusations. See, e.g., Roger Lewis *et al.,* in New York *World* and other newspapers, Sept. 7, 1914; John T. McCutcheon, in New York *World,* Sept. 19, 1914; Arno Dosch, "Louvain the Lost," *World's Work,* XXVIII (Oct., 1914), A–H; Irvin S. Cobb, "Being a Guest of the German Kaiser," *Saturday Evening Post,* CLXXXVII (Oct. 24, 1914), 14–15, 48–50; Arthur Sweetser, "With the German Army In Its Dash toward Paris," *Outlook,* CIX (Jan. 27, 1915), 186–190.

The Submarine Controversy, 1915–17

The most authoritative work on German submarine operations before February, 1917, is Arno Spindler, *La Guerre Sous-Marine* (René Jouan, trans., 3 vols., Paris, 1933–35), but the following are also useful: Albert Gayer, "Summary of German Submarine Operations in the Various Theaters of War from 1914 to 1918," *Proceedings of the United States Naval Institute,* LI (1926), 621–659; and Maurice Prendergast and R. H. Gibson, *The German Submarine War, 1914–1918* (New York, 1931).

All available data on the sinking of the *Lusitania* are brought together in Thomas A. Bailey, "The Sinking of the *Lusitania,*" *American Historical Review,* XLI (Oct., 1935), 54–73, and "German Documents Relating to the 'Lusitania,' " *Journal of Modern History,* VIII (Sept., 1936), 320–337.

German Sources

The Archives of the German Foreign Office for the period 1914–18 are now available on microfilm in the National Archives. Except for data on German intrigues in the United States and Mexico, however, the record of

German diplomacy toward the United States is fully revealed in *Official German Documents Relating to the World War* (2 vols., New York, 1923). *Die Grosse Politik der Europäischen Kabinette, 1871–1914* (40 vols. in 54, Berlin, 1922–27) goes only through the outbreak of the war.

An excellent source for a study of German policies is the memoirs of the leaders of the government and the armed forces: Theobald von Bethmann-Hollweg, William II, Matthias Erzberger, Erich Georg von Falkenhayn, Karl Helfferich, Paul von Hindenburg, Erich Ludendorff, and Alfred von Tirpitz. The best source for German opinion on the developing tension between Germany and the United States, however, is the German press, which was enlightened and subjected only to slight censorship. Among the Liberal newspapers the *Berliner Tageblatt,* which often spoke for the Foreign Office, the *Kölnische Zeitung,* and the *Frankfurter Zeitung,* were the leaders. *Vorwärts* of Berlin spoke for the Social Democrats and consistently championed peace with America. The *Lokal-Anzeiger* (Berlin) was an organ of the government, while the *Vossische Zeitung* (Berlin) was another moderate spokesman. *Deutsche Tageszeitung* and *Täglische Rundschau,* both of Berlin, were organs of the Conservative party and mouthpieces of the military and naval leaders. The spokesman of Rhenish Catholic opinion was the *Kölnische Volkszeitung.*

AMERICAN PUBLIC OPINION ON THE WAR, 1914–17

There is no comprehensive study of this important subject, but Robert E. Osgood, *Ideals and Self-Interest in America's Foreign Relations* (Chicago, 1953), analyzes the thought of an important segment of American leadership, while Ralph O. Nafziger, "The American Press and Public Opinion During the World War 1914 to April 1917," unpublished Ph.D. thesis, University of Wisconsin Library, is also helpful.

The following specialized studies contribute toward understanding the great diversity of American attitudes: Edwin Costrell, *How Maine Viewed the War, 1914–1917* (Orono, Me., 1940); Cedric C. Cummins, *Indiana Public Opinion and the World War, 1914–1917* (Indianapolis, 1945); John C. Crighton, *Missouri and the World War, 1914–1917* (Columbia, Mo., 1947); Joseph Rappaport, "Jewish Immigrants and World War I: A Study of American Yiddish Press Reactions," unpublished Ph.D. thesis, Columbia University Library; Ray A. Billington, "The Origins of Middle Western Isolationism," *Political Science Quarterly,* LX (Mar., 1945), 44–64; and Harold C. Syrett, "The Business Press and American Neutrality, 1914–1917," *Mississippi Valley Historical Review,* XXXII (Sept., 1945), 215–230.

Although they are fragmentary and inconclusive, several contemporary surveys by Americans offer insight: Samuel H. Church, *The American Verdict on the War* (Baltimore, 1915); J. M. Baldwin, *American Neutrality* (New York, 1916); and Joseph H. Choate *et al., Sixty American Opinions on the War* (London, 1915). The keenest analyses of American opinion, however, were made by British observers, most of whom never deluded themselves into believing the American people wanted to enter the war. Three documents of extraordinary importance are Gilbert Parker, *Memorandum on the Attitude of the American Press* (London, 1914); G. Parker, *Report of the Opinion of the Universities and Colleges in America upon the War* (London, n.d.); and Horace Plunkett, *Memorandum on the Anglo-American Situation, Printed for the use of the Cabinet* (London, 1916).

Representative American Comment on the War

American comment on all phases of the difficulties with Germany is cited on pp. 306–307. American comment on the British conduct of the war is listed on pp. 304–305. For general German-American comment, see p. 310.

In addition, George Harvey, "Europe at Armageddon," *North American Review,* CC (Sept., 1914), 321–332, and the Pastoral Letter of the Bishops of the Methodist Episcopal Church, May 12, 1915, printed in New York *Christian Advocate,* XC (May 20, 1915), 677, were balanced commentaries on the causes of the war.

For representative interventionist or quasi-interventionist sentiment see William Dean Howells, "Why?" *North American Review,* CCI (May, 1915), 676–682; George Harvey, "The German Attitude," *North American Review,* CCII (Oct., 1915), 481–488; American Rights Committee, *A Memorial to the President of the United States* (New York, 1915); Josiah Royce, *The Duties of Americans in the Present War* (Boston, 1916); and William T. Manning, *The Present Crisis in Our National Life* (New York, 1916).

GERMAN- AND IRISH-AMERICANS AND THE WAR

General

Carl Wittke, *German-Americans and the World War* (Columbus, Ohio, 1936), and Clifton J. Child, *The German-Americans in Politics, 1914–1917* (Madison, Wis., 1939), provide a fairly complete picture. Alden Jamison, "The Irish Question and American Diplomacy, 1895–1921," unpublished Ph.D. thesis, Harvard University Library, is excellent.

German-American Periodicals and Newspapers

The Fatherland (New York, 1914–33), *The Vital Issue,* later *Issues and Events* (New York, 1914–18), and *The Open Court* (Chicago, 1887–1936) were the leading German-American periodicals. Among the many German-language newspapers, the following were most influential: New York

Deutsches Morgen-Journal, New York *Staats-Zeitung,* Chicago *Abendpost,* Chicago *Illinois Staats-Zeitung,* St. Louis *Westliche Post,* Milwaukee *Germania,* and Cincinnati *Freie Presse.*

German-American Comment and Propaganda

Gustavus Ohlinger, *Their True Faith and Allegiance* (New York, 1916), is a compilation of utterances by German-American leaders. The following are samples of German-American appeals for sympathy for the Fatherland: Edmund von Mach, *What Germany Wants* (Boston, 1914); Kuno Francke, *A German-American's Confession of Faith* (New York, 1915); Roland Hugins, *Germany Misjudged* (Chicago, 1916); S. I. Stefan, *Neutrality?* (Chicago, 1916); Charles F. Aked and Walter Rauschenbusch, "Private Profit and the Nation's Honor," Chicago *Standard,* LXII (July 31, 1915), 1486–1487.

Irish-Americans and the War

The best source for Irish-American efforts to obtain an arms embargo and acquiescence in the German submarine campaign is the Hearst press and the several Irish-American periodicals, New York *Irish World,* New York *Gaelic American,* and Los Angeles *Irish Review.* Typical of Irish-American tracts are J. K. McGuire's *The King, the Kaiser, and Irish Freedom* (New York, 1915) and *What Could Germany Do for Ireland?* (New York, 1916).

For samples of the propaganda of the most vociferous Irish-American organization, the American Truth Society, see J. A. O'Leary, *Why Woodrow Wilson Should be Defeated and a Republican Congress Elected* (New York, 1916), and *A Statement Issued by the American Truth Society in defense of its President against an unjust attack made upon him by the President of the United States* (New York, 1916).

PROPAGANDA AND AMERICAN OPINION ON THE WAR

General Surveys

All of the studies of propaganda exaggerate its role in shaping American opinions on the war. H. C. Peterson, *Propaganda for War* (Norman, Okla., 1939), is the best of the general works. J. D. Squires, *British Propaganda at Home and in the United States from 1914–1917* (Cambridge, Mass., 1935), analyzes the content of British propaganda. Arthur Willert, *Road to Safety: A Study in Anglo-American Relations* (London, 1952), is a revealing study by the former Washington correspondent for the Northcliffe Press. George Sylvester Viereck, *Spreading Germs of Hate* (New York, 1931), is especially good for the operations of the German propaganda machine in the United States.

How the belligerents utilized propaganda as a weapon of war is well presented in J. M. Read, *Atrocity Propaganda, 1914–1919* (New Haven, Conn., 1941); Georges Demartial, *La Guerre de 1914: Comment On Mobilisa les Consciences* (Paris, 1922); Harold D. Lasswell, *Propaganda Technique in the World War* (New York, 1927); and Arthur Ponsonby, *Falsehood in War-Time* (New York, 1928).

British Propaganda

From 1914 to 1917 the American periodical press printed hundreds of statements and appeals by British leaders. Good examples of books in this category are Ramsay Muir, *Britain's Case Against Germany* (New York, 1914), and Douglas Sladen, *The Real "Truth About Germany"* (New York, 1914).

For the student who wishes to go thoroughly into this subject, there is a practically complete listing of British propaganda books and articles in Hermann Wanderscheck, *Bibliographie zur englischen Propaganda im Weltkrieg* (Stuttgart, 1935).

German Propaganda

American magazines and newspapers printed hundreds of articles, statements, and appeals by various German leaders during the period 1914–17. For representative books and pamphlets see Adolph von Baeyer *et al., To the Civilized World* (n.p., n.d.); *How the Franco-German Conflict Could Have Been Avoided* (Berlin, 1914); Notable Germans, *The Truth About Germany* (New York [?], 1914); Hugo Münsterberg, *The War and America* (New York, 1914); Bernhard Dernburg, *The Case of Belgium in the Light of Official Reports Found in the Secret Archives of the Belgian Government* . . . (New York, 1915 [?]); H. Münsterberg, *The Peace and America* (New York, 1915); and Alexander Fuehr, *The Neutrality of Belgium* (New York, 1915).

THE PREPAREDNESS AND PEACE MOVEMENTS, 1914–17

General Studies

The best general surveys of the preparedness and peace movements are William H. Harbaugh, "Wilson, Roosevelt, and American Interventionism, 1914–1917," unpublished Ph.D. thesis in Northwestern University Library, and R. E. Osgood, *Ideals and Self-Interest in America's Foreign Relations,* cited above. William W. Tinsley, "The American Preparedness Movement, 1913–1916," unpublished Ph.D. thesis in the Stanford University Library, is useful for the literature of preparedness.

Hermann Hagedorn's *The Bugle That Woke America* (New York, 1940) and *Leonard Wood, A Biography,* cited above, and Elting E. Morison, *Admiral Sims and the Modern American Navy* (Boston, 1942), are excellent on the most aggressive preparedness elements.

The only general studies of the peace movement are Merle Curti, *The American Peace Crusade* (Durham, N.C., 1929); M. Curti, *Bryan and World Peace* (Northampton, Mass., 1931), and Jane Addams, *Peace and Bread in Time of War* (New York, 1922).

In a special category is Ruhl J. Bartlett, *The League to Enforce Peace* (Chapel Hill, N.C., 1944), an excellent study of the most important internationalist organization in the United States during the neutrality period.

Preparedness Periodicals

Leaders in the preparedness movement were the periodicals published by the military and naval societies and by the armed services. The *Seven Seas Magazine* (New York, 1915–16) and *Sea Power* (Washington, 1916–21, 1935–) were organs of the Navy League. Spokesmen for the military branch included the *Army and Navy Magazine* (Washington, 1893–), *Army and Navy Journal* (New York, 1863–), and *Infantry Journal* (Washington, 1904–). In addition, a number of general periodicals, including *Outlook, Everybody's Magazine,* and *New Republic,* were active in the preparedness agitation.

The Literature of Preparedness

The following books illustrate the propaganda of the preparedness movement and often reflect the conviction that a conflict between the United States and Germany was almost inevitable: Hudson Maxim, *Defenseless America* (New York, 1915); Frederick L. Huidekoper, *The Military Unpreparedness of the United States* (New York, 1915); Howard D. Wheeler, *Are We Ready?* (Boston, 1915); Theodore Roosevelt, *Fear God and Take Your Own Part* (New York, 1916); John B. Walker, *America Fallen!* (New York, 1916); Owen Wister, *The Pentecost of Calamity* (New York, 1915); Julius W. Muller, *The Invasion of America* (New York, 1916); Cleveland Moffett, *The Conquest of America* (New York, 1916); Porter E. Browne, *Scars and Stripes* (New York, 1917).

The Peace and Antipreparedness Crusades

The best contemporary sources for these movements are *The Survey, The Nation,* the New York *Evening Post,* the Johnstown (Penna.) *Democrat,* Bryan's *Commoner,* the Chicago *Public,* and *La Follette's Magazine.* For accounts of the peace movement and its objectives, see Jane Addams *et al., Women at The Hague* (New York, 1915), and Randolph S. Bourne (ed.),

Towards an Enduring Peace (New York, 1916), an elaboration of various current peace proposals.

The campaign against preparedness was an outgrowth of the peace movement and closely related to it. Among the contemporary arguments against preparedness, the following are representative: Allen L. Benson, *Inviting America to War* (New York, 1916); William I. Hull, *Preparedness: The American versus Military Programme* (New York, 1916); Oswald G. Villard, *Preparedness* (Washington, 1915); Charles E. Jefferson, *Christianity and International Peace* (New York, 1915) and *What the War Is Teaching* (New York, 1916); Washington Gladden, *The Forks of the Road* (New York, 1916); John Haynes Holmes, *New Wars for Old* (New York, 1916); and Frederick C. Howe, *Why War?* (New York, 1916).

The Army Bills of 1916–17

The whole range of public and professional opinion on the army bills of 1916 and 1917 may be consulted in House Military Affairs Committee, *Army Appropriation Bill, 1917, Hearings* . . . , 64th Cong., 1st sess. (Washington, 1916); Senate Military Affairs Committee, *Preparedness for National Defense* . . . , 64th Cong., 1st sess. (Washington, 1916); House Military Affairs Committee, *Army Appropriation Bill, 1918, Hearings* . . . , 64th Cong., 2d sess. (Washington, 1917), and Senate Military Affairs Committee, *Universal Military Training, Hearings* . . . , 64th Cong., 2d sess. (Washington, 1917).

The Naval and Shipping Bills of 1916

Important background of this legislation is discussed in Outten J. Clinard, *Japan's Influence on American Naval Power, 1897–1917* (Berkeley, Calif., 1947). Storehouses of information and opinion on these measures are House Naval Affairs Committee, *Hearings on Estimates Submitted by Secretary of Navy, 1916,* 64th Cong., 1st sess. (3 vols., Washington, 1916), and Senate Commerce Committee, *Creating Shipping Board, Naval Auxiliary, and Merchant Marine, Hearings* . . . , 64th Cong., 1st sess. (Washington, 1916).

Index

Abbott, Lawrence F., 175–176
ABC mediation, 104, 126–127
Adams, Herbert Baxter, 8
Adamson, William C., a Democratic leader in the House, 35; helps prepare antitrust legislation, 68; opposes Federal Trade Commission idea, 72; and writing and adoption of Adamson Act, 236–237
Adamson Act, 235–237, 238–239
Addams, Jane, 16, 182, 239
Aguascalientes Convention, 130–131
Albert, Heinrich, 167
Aldrich, Nelson W., 3, 5, 44
Aldrich Plan, 44–45, 47
Alexander, Joshua W., 191
American Anti-Boycott Association, 74
American Association for Labor Legislation, 54, 226
American Bankers' Association, 50–51
American Federation of Labor, see Labor
American League to Limit Armament, 182
American Rights Committee, 176, 269
American Telephone & Telegraph Company antitrust settlement, 76
American Union Against Militarism, pleads against war with Mexico, 142; agitates against war with Germany, 269

Ancona affair, 202
Anderson, Chandler P., 155, 162–163
Antipreparedness movement, origins and motivation, 180–181; organization of, 181–182; champions in House of Representatives, 183; victory in controversy over Army Reorganization Act, 189
Antitrust legislation, discussion and formulation of original Wilsonian program, 66–69; controversy over, 69–70; adoption of Clayton Act, 70, 72–73; writing and adoption of Federal Trade Commission Act, 71–72
Arabia case, 254
Arabic case, 168–169
Armed neutrality, 271–272, 277–278
Armed ship controversy of 1916, 205–214
Armed ship controversy of 1917, 269–274
Armenian, 168
Arms embargo, 167
Army League of the United States, 177
Army Reorganization Act of 1916, Army War College proposal, 179–180; controversy over, 180–186; adoption of House bill, 187; Senate bill, 187–188; adoption and terms of final measure, 188; opinions of, 188–189

Army War College, prepares army reorganization bill, 179–180; prepares conscription bill, 268

Arredondo, Eliseo, 137, 138

Ashurst, Henry F., 35

Asquith, Herbert H., 204–205

Association for an Equitable Income Tax, 193

Bacon, Robert, 230

Bagehot, Walter, 8

Bailey, Warren Worth, a leader of antipreparedness group, 183; comments on Army Act, 189; laments passage of naval bill, 190; proposes huge increases in income tax, 194; praises Revenue Act of 1916, 196

Baker, Newton D., appointed Secretary of War, 28, 187; orders withdrawal of Punitive Expedition, 144; proposes establishment of Council of National Defense, 188; urges war resolution, 276

Baker, Ray S., 239

Balfour, Arthur J., and House's peace plan, 202, 204; and armed ship question, 207

Ballinger, Richard A. and the Ballinger Affair, 3–4, 5

Banco Nacional of Santo Domingo, 97–98

Bankhead, John H., 35

Beer, William C., 97

Belmont, August, 12

Bernstorff, Johann von, and House's first peace mission, 160–161; presents protest against sale of munitions, 163; disavows Rintelen, 201; connection with intriguers, 201; comments on Roosevelt and campaign of 1916, 244; excites German hopes of peace, 256; reports Wilson's comments on Roosevelt and Lodge, 256; secret negotiations with House, 262–263; urges postponement of unrestricted submarine warfare, 263

Bethmann-Hollweg, Theobald von, and the *Arabic* crisis, 168–169; discusses peace with House, 203; on *Lusitania* negotiations, 206; resists pressure for unrestricted submarine warfare, 216, 255; desires

Wilson's mediation, 256; issues peace offer to enemies, 259; appeals for Wilson's support, 260; loses control of foreign policy, 263

Beveridge, Albert J., 5

"Blacklist" dispute, 220–221, 252

Bobo, Rosalvo, 101

Bonillas, Ignacio, 143

Bordas, Valdés José, 98

Boyd, Captain, 141

Boy-Ed, Karl, 200–201

Brandeis, Louis D., Wilson's chief adviser in 1912, 20–21; not appointed to Cabinet in 1913, 28, 30–31; and framing of Federal Reserve bill, 48; helps prepare railroad securities bill, 68; evolving new antitrust solution, 69; and writing of Federal Trade Commission Act, 71–72; disappointed over failure of Federal Trade Commission, 74; comments on results of election of 1914, 78; nomination to Supreme Court, 225

Breitung, Edward N., 155

Briand, Aristide, 203, 204

Brown, E. N., 108

Bryan, William Jennings, dominant in Democratic party, 1908–1910, 2; and need for new leadership, 2–7; and elections of 1910, 7; and Baltimore convention, 12–13; sketch of as Secretary of State, 26–27; and income tax of 1913, 39; and writing of Federal Reserve bill, 45–50; and adoption of seamen's bill of 1915, 63; urges abolition of "rule of reason," 67; dynamics of foreign policy, 81–82; negotiates conciliation treaties, 82; and dispute with Japan, 84–87; and crisis over Twenty-One Demands, 87–90; and Panama Canal tolls dispute, 91; origins and motivation of Latin American and Caribbean policies, 93–94, 103–104; Nicaraguan policy, 94–97; Dominican policy, 97–99; Haitian policy, 99–102; negotiates treaty of reparation with Colombia, 104–105; and relations with Huerta government of Mexico, 1913–1914, 107–128; and ABC mediation,

126; and Villa's revolt, 129; supports Villa government, 131; refuses to sanction Catholic demands for repeal of Reform Laws, 135; bans war loans as unneutral, 151; implicitly revokes ban, 152; on ship purchase bill, 153; and the British food blockade, 159; and peace talks in 1914, 160–161; pleads against strong stand in Thrasher case, 163; seeks to find peaceful solution in *Lusitania* negotiations, 166; resigns, 166; sets out on peace campaign, 167; leader in antipreparedness, 182; threatens to bolt party, 223–224; hero of St. Louis convention, 234; and campaign of 1916, 243; makes last-ditch campaign for peace, 269

Bryce, James, 91, 147–148

Bryce *Report*, 147–148

Bulkley, Robert J., 57–59

Bunkering agreement, 252–253

Burleson, Albert S., patronage policies as Postmaster General, 29; segregates Negro workers, 64–65; uses patronage in tolls dispute, 92; protests *Lusitania* postscript, 166; uses patronage to defeat McLemore Resolution, 213

Burnett immigration bills of 1915 and 1917, *see* Immigration legislation

Bynner, Witter, 251

Cabrera, Luis, 121, 143

Calder, William M., 230

California alien land act of 1913, 84–87

Cambon, Jules, 203–204

Cannon, Joseph G., 3

Caperton, W. B., 102

Capper, Arthur, 274

Carden, Sir Lionel, 116–117, 120

Caribbean policy of the United States, 1910–1917, *see* Latin American Policy of the United States, 1910–1917

Carothers, George C., 128, 129

Carranza, Venustiano, begins revolt against Huerta, 109; establishes provisional government, 120; refuses to allow Wilson to control Constitutionalist movement, 120–

121; condemns American occupation of Vera Cruz, 125–126; occupies Mexico City, 128; and Villa's revolt, 128–129; concurs in plan for new government for Mexico, 129–130; declares war on Villa's government, 131; broadens program and crushes Villa, 131; repudiates Wilson's right to intervene in Mexico, 133–134; wins recognition by United States and Latin America, 135; alarmed by entry of Punitive Expedition, 137; demands withdrawal of Punitive Expedition, 138–139; rejects Scott-Obregón agreement, 140; threatens war against United States, 140; suggests direct negotiations, 143; and Joint High Commission, 143; establishes constitutional government and is recognized *de jure* by United States, 144; and the Zimmermann "note," 271

Carrizal incident, 141–142

Casement, Sir Roger, 218

Casey, John J., 70

Catt, Carrie Chapman, 182

Chadwick, French E., 146

Chamberlain, George E., 187

Child Labor Act of 1916, origins, 59; passage of, 226–227; significance, 227

China and the United States, American withdrawal from Six-Power Consortium, 82–84; American recognition of Republic of China, 84; and crisis over Twenty-One Demands, 87–90

Chinda, Viscount, 86, 89

City of Memphis, 274

Clark, Champ, a new Democratic leader, 7; biographical sketch, 11; and the Democratic pre-convention campaign of 1910–1912, 11–12; and Baltimore convention, 12–13; opposes Wilson in tolls dispute, 92; and armed ship controversy of 1916, 212; threatened revolt of, 223; elected Speaker in 1917, 281

Clarke amendment, 228

Clayton, Henry D., 35, 68

Clayton Act of 1914, writing of, 67–68; controversy over, 69; passage by House, 70; weakening of in Senate, 72–73. For adoption of labor provisions *see* Labor

Cleveland Automatic Machine Company, 168

Cobb, Frank, comments on segregation, 66; talk with Wilson, 277

Cobb, Irvin S., 239

Colby, Bainbridge, 232, 239

Colombia and the United States, 104–105

Columbus Raid, 136

Committee to Defend America by Aiding the Allies, 177

Conciliation treaties, 82

Constitutionalist movement in Mexico, *see* Mexican Revolution

Consumers' League, 54

Continental Army, Army War College proposal, 179–180; opposed by House Military Affairs Committee, 184, 186; defeat of, 188

Convention on Safety at Sea, 62–63

"Cooling-off" treaties, 82

Cooper amendment, 273

Costigan, Edward P., 240

Cotton, the cotton crisis of 1914, 149–150; cotton crisis of 1915, 169–170; Anglo-American agreement on, 171–172

Coudert, Frederic R., 176

Council of National Defense, 188

Covington, James H., 68

Cowdray, Lord (S. Weetman Pearson), 116–117

Crawford, Sir Richard, 171–172, 253

Creel, George, 239

Croly, Herbert, contribution to development of progressive thought, 18–19; comments on Wilson's concept of progressivism, 78–79; supports Wilson in 1916, 239, 240

Cuba and the United States, 103

Culberson, Charles A., 73

Cummins, Albert B., 41, 73

Dacia affair, 155–156

Daniels, Josephus, sketch of as Secretary of the Navy, 28–29; and controversy over general leasing bill, 30; on conditions in navy, 177; and formulation of naval preparedness program, 179; urges war resolution, 276; begins talks with British Admiralty, 277

Dartiguenave, Sudre, 102

Davies, Joseph E., 74–75

Debs, Eugene V., and campaign of 1912, 16–17; popular vote in 1912, 22; demands general strike in event of war, 275

Declaration of London, 153–154

Del Valle, Reginaldo F., 112

Democratic party, victory in elections of 1910, 6–7; preconvention campaign of 1910–1912, 8–13; Baltimore convention, 12–13; election of 1912, 22–24; patronage policies of Wilson administration, 29; leadership in Congress in 1913, 35; approves A.F. of L.'s legislative demands, 55; suffers reversal in elections of 1914, 78; situation in early 1916, 223–224; platform of 1916, 233; St. Louis convention, 233–235; campaign of 1916, 237–247; election of 1916, 247–251

Depression of 1913–1915, 75

Dewey, John, 193, 239

Díaz, Adolfo, 94, 96

Díaz, Félix, 112

Díaz, Porfirio, 107

Dolliver, Jonathan P., 5

Dominican Republic and the United States, 1913–1917, 97–99

Douglas, Charles A., 96

Du Bois, William E. B., 63

Dumba, Constantin, 167

Eagle, Joe H., 50

Eastman, Max, 239

Einstein, Lewis, 26

Elections of 1910, 1912, 1914, and 1916, *see* Democratic party and Republican party

Eliot, Charles W., 148, 174

Estrada, Juan J., 94

Evans, Mrs. Glendower, 60

Evening Post, New York, 237, 241

Falaba case, 162–164

Fall, Albert B., 42, 124–125

Farnham, Roger L., 100

Farnham Plan, 100

Federal Farm Loan Act of 1916, efforts of agrarian leaders to establish rural credits system blocked by Wilson administration, 56–59; passage of Act, 225–226

Federal Reserve Act of 1913, 43–53

Federal Reserve Board, controversy over appointment, 76–78; calls halt to extension of short-term credits to Allies, 258–259

Federal Trade Commission, purpose of, 74; failure to realize ambitions of its sponsors, 74–75

Federal Trade Commission Act of 1914, Roosevelt proposes and Wilson condemns during campaign of 1912, 16, 21; "weak" trade commission bill, 68; writing of "strong" trade commission bill and approval by Wilson, 71–72; passage of measure, 72

Fiske, Bradley A., 86

Fletcher, Duncan U., 57

Fletcher, Henry P., 144

Flinn, William, 16

Flood, Hal D., and *Lusitania* crisis, 166; assures Germany of American friendship, 206; and armed ship controversy of 1916, 211–212

Ford, Henry, 76, 230–231

Fort, John Franklin, 101

France, Joseph I., 278

Frick, Henry C., 76

Frye note, 169

Fuller, Paul, goes on secret mission to Mexico, 129–130; views on war, 175–176

Furuseth, Andrew, early campaign for seamen's bill, 61–62; denounces London Convention on Safety at Sea, 62; and passage of Seamen's Act, 62–63

Gallinger, Jacob H., 183, 192

Galt, Edith Bolling, 183

Gamboa, Federico, repudiates Wilson's right to intervene in Mexico, 114–115; candidate for Mexican presidency, 116

Gardner, Augustus P., 177

Gardner, Gilson, 213

Garrison, Lindley M., sketch of as Secretary of War, 28; favors strong action against Japan, 87; protests *Lusitania* postscript, 166; and

formulation of army preparedness program, 179–180; at loggerheads with House committee over army bill, 183–184, 186; resigns, 186; opinion of Wilson, 186

Gavit, J. P., 278

George, Henry, 1

Gerard, James W., 256

German-American Alliance, 214

German-Americans, and senatorial contest in New York, 230; and Republican preconvention campaign of 1916, 231; win victory in nomination of Hughes, 232; and campaign of 1916, 245–247; vote in election of 1916, 249

Germany, food situation in, 159; war objectives in 1915, 162; German anger over export of munitions to Allies, 167–168; German reaction to *Sussex* ultimatum, 215–216; internal struggle over submarine policy, 216; intensifies submarine campaign, 254; discussions of unrestricted submarine warfare, 255; deportation of Belgian laborers, 257; leaders decide upon peace campaign and, that failing, unrestricted submarine warfare, 259; war objectives in December 1916, 259; peace offer, 259–260, 264; decision for unrestricted submarine warfare, 263; reveals peace terms to Wilson, 266; announces unrestricted submarine warfare, 266–267; success of submarine campaign, 276. *See also* Germany and the United States

Germany and the United States, Bryan anxious to prevent German control of Haiti, 100; Germany supports United States in Mexico, 119; Germany foments trouble between United States and Mexico, 133–134; Wilson anxious to avoid war with Mexico because of trouble with Germany, 137; German propaganda during First World War and American opinion, 145–148; Germany challenges British blockade with submarines, 156–159; rejects Wilson's mediation, 160–162; the Thrasher case, 162–164; German protests over American sale of munitions to Allies, 163; sinking of *Lusitania* and subsequent crisis, 164–167; revelation of German propaganda in United States, 167; sinking of *Arabic* leads to first German submarine pledge, 168–169; growth of anti-German sentiment in United States, 174–177; German intrigues in Mexico and United States, 200–201; negotiations to settle *Lusitania* affair, 201, 206, 210; discussions over armed ships, 205–209; Germany issues proclamation against armed ships, 209–210; controversy over armed ships, 210–214; *Sussex* crisis and settlement, 215–218; intensified submarine campaign raises new cases, 254; and possibilities of Wilson's mediation, 255–257; Germany rejects Wilson's offer of mediation and friendship, 261–266; unrestricted submarine warfare causes break in relations, 266–268; the Zimmermann "note," 271; causes for war between, 278–281

Ghent, William J., 274

Giddings, Franklin H., 176

Gladden, Washington, 239

Glass, Carter, and writing of Federal Reserve bill, 45–50; and rural credits legislation, 58

Glynn, Martin H., 233–234

Godkin, Lawrence, 176

Gómez, Félix G., 141

Gompers, Samuel, president of A.F. of L., demands exemption of labor unions from prosecution under antitrust laws, 56, 69, 73; calls Clayton Act "Magna Carta" of labor, 73–74; supports Wilson in 1916, 240

Gonzáles, Pablo, 130–131

Gore, Thomas P., 211–214

Gore Resolution, 213–214

Gray, George, 143

Great Britain, British war objectives in 1915, 155, 198; interdicts all commerce with Germany, 160; inability to pay for war purchases in United States, 172; intensifies economic warfare, 252–253; and German peace offer, 260, 264. *See also* Great Britain and the United States

Great Britain and the United States, dispute over Panama Canal tolls, 90–93; British government supports Huerta, 116; Wilson contemplates strong protest to British government, 117–118; Wilson forces British government to abandon Huerta, 119–120; British propaganda during First World War and American opinion, 145–148; Anglo-American difficulties and negotiations over neutral trading rights, 154–155; *Dacia* controversy, 155–156; British food blockade, 157; cotton crisis of 1915, 169–172; negotiation of Anglo-French loan of 1915, 172–173; worsening of Anglo-American relations, 218–220; mails dispute, 220; "blacklist" dispute, 220–221; new antagonisms drive two nations further apart, 252–253; potential controversy over mediation, 255–257; restriction of American credit to Britain, 258–259; Anglo-American negotiations looking toward mediation, 263–264

Gregory, Thomas W., appointed Attorney General, 28; and controversy over general leasing bill, 30; submits memorandum on army bill of 1916, 184; reviews work of German Embassy, 200–201; issues appeal for help against German intriguers, 201; urges appointment of Brandeis to Supreme Court, 225; on legality of arming merchant ships, 274; urges war resolution, 276

Grew, Joseph C., 260

Grey, Sir Edward, denies "deal" with Wilson over Panama Canal tolls and Mexico, 92; denies that Cowdray controls Mexican policy of British government, 116; agrees to abandon support of Huerta, 119–120; protests ship purchase bill and American unneutrality, 153, 156; anxious to come to understanding with Wilson, 155; welcomes peace talks, 161; and House's peace mission of 1915, 162; suggests American mediation, 198–199; confers with House, 202–203, 204–205; understanding with House, 205; shocked by Lansing's *modus vivendi,* 208; refuses to allow Wilson's mediation, 219

Gronna, Asle J., 42

Guiterrez, Eulalio, 131

Haiti and the United States, 1913–1916, 99–102, 104

Hale, Edward J., 26

Hale, Matthew, 232, 240, 278

Hale, William Bayard, 112, 120–121

Hapgood, Norman, 31, 175, 239

Harding, Warren G., 192

Harding, W. P. G., 171, 258

Harmon, Judson, 7

Harvey, George, 9, 10, 56, 175

Hay, James, 183, 186

Hayes, Carlton J. H., 271–272

"He kept us out of war," 242–243

Hearst, William Randolph, supports Clark, 11; agitates for war with Mexico, 125

Hearst newspapers, 132

Heney, Francis J., 239

Henry, Robert L., 49–50

Hepburn, A. Barton, 51

Herrick, Myron T., 231

Hindenburg, Paul von, 255, 259

Hitchcock, Gilbert M., opposes Federal Reserve bill, 51–52; urges armed neutrality instead of war, 278

Hollis, Henry F., Democratic leader in Senate, 35; and controversy over rural credits bill, 57–59; and passage of rural credits bill, 225–226; and Democratic platform of 1916, 233

House, Edward M., and Democratic preconvention campaign of 1912, 12; personal relations with Wilson, 26; helps Wilson select Cabinet, 25, 26, 30–31; and appointment of Federal Reserve Board, 76–77; opinion on causes of First World War, 146; first mediation effort, 1914–1915, 160–162; formulates

plan to end war, 197–201; second peace mission, 202–205; understanding with Grey, 205; urges Lansing to hold *modus vivendi* in abeyance, 208–209; urges strong stand in *Sussex* crisis, 215; urges Grey to allow mediation, 219; suspicious of British motives, 219–220; Wilson consults on League speech, 233; excites Bernstorff's hopes of mediation, 256; warns Wilson of dangers of mediation, 256–258; and Wilson's peace note, 260; secret negotiations with Bernstorff and Wiseman, 262–264; urges severance of relations with Germany, 268; tries to calm Wilson, 277

House-Grey understanding (the "Gentlemen's Agreement"), 205

Houston, David F., sketch of as Secretary of Agriculture, 30; comments on Underwood tariff, 43; opposes rural credits bill, 57–58; and passage of rural credits bill, 226; urges arming of merchant ships, 270; urges war resolution, 276

Howe, Frederick C., 193, 239

Howland, Charles P., 176

Huerta, Victoriano, deposes Madero and seizes power in Mexico, 107–108; Wilson offers mediation to, 112–113; repudiates Wilson's right to intervene, 113–115; establishes military dictatorship, 116–117; again refuses to retire, 119; grows in strength, 122; refuses to salute American flag during Tampico affair, 122–123; and ABC mediation, 126–127; abdicates, 128; and German intrigues, 200

Hughes, Charles Evans, and presidential nomination in 1908, 3; biographical sketch, 231; nomination for President, 232; failure of campaign appeals, 237–238; denounces Adamson Act, 238; embarrassments in campaign, 244–245; confers with German-Americans, 245–246; and election of 1916, 247–251

Hughes, William, 35

Hull, Cordell, 38, 39–40

Hurley, Edward N., 74, 75

Illinois, 274
Immigration legislation, movement for immigration restriction, 60; Wilson vetoes Burnett bill of 1915, 60–61; passage of Burnett bill in 1917 over Wilson's veto, 61
Income tax of 1913, 38–40; income tax of 1916, 192–196
International Harvester Company, 77
International Mercantile Company, 269
Irish-Americans and campaign and election of 1916, 245–247, 251
Irish Rebellion, 218

Jagow, Gottlieb von, 162, 166, 211, 215
James, Ollie M., 29, 234
Japan and the United States, crisis over California alien land act of 1913, 84–87; crisis over Twenty-One Demands, 87–90; difficulties over Mexico, 91
Jarvis, Samuel M., 97
Jefferson, Charles E., 182
Jiménez, Juan Y., 99
Johnson, Hiram W., elected Governor of California, 6; Progressive vice-presidential candidate, 16; and crisis over California alien land act, 85–86; and campaign of 1916 in California, 245
Joint Board of Army and Navy, 86–87
Joint Neutrality Board, opinion on purchase of belligerent merchant ships, 150; opinion in Thrasher case, 163
Jones Act of 1916, 227–228
Jones, Thomas D., 77
Jones, Wesley L., 52
Jones, William A., 227

Kato, Baron, 87–89
Keating, Edward, 70
Keating-Owen child labor bill, 226–227
Kelley, Rev. Francis C., 135
Kent, William, 30, 85, 239
Kern, John W., 211
Kern-McGillicuddy bill, 226

Kitchin, Claude, leader of antipreparedness group, 183; comments on results of Wilson's tour, 186; claims victory for anti-preparedness group in army bill controversy, 187; denounces naval bill, 190; and writing of Revenue Act of 1916, 194–195; and armed ship controversy of 1916, 212–213; and "Sunrise Conference," 213; refuses to support tariff commission, 228; helps draft Adamson bill, 236; opposes war resolution, 282
Kleist, Franz Rintelen von, 200
Knapp, Harry S., 99
Knox, Philander C., and Six-Power Consortium, 83; and Nicaragua, 94, 96; on non-recognition of Huerta, 108

Labor, W. B. Wilson and development of Labor Department, 31; A.F. of L.'s unsuccessful campaign to win immunity for labor unions from application of antitrust laws, 55–56, 69–70, 73–74; attitude of organized labor toward immigration restriction, 60; passage of Seamen's Act, 61–63; labor legislation of 1916, 226–227; passage of Adamson Act, 235–237; A.F. of L. and campaign of 1916, 240; and election of 1916, 249
La Follette, Robert M., insurgent Republican leader, 13–14; and income tax of 1913, 39; and tariff lobby investigation, 41; denounces Federal Reserve Act, 55; sponsors seamen's bill, 61–63; denounces preparedness advocates, 182; and Revenue Act of 1916, 195; on Brandeis' nomination to Supreme Court, 225; opposes armed ship bill, 272–273; opposes war resolution, 282
Lane, Franklin K., sketch of as Secretary of Interior, 29–30; serves on Joint High Commission, 143; urges arming of merchant ships, 270
Lansing, Robert, sketch of as Secretary of State, 27; comments on Wilson's mental processes, 32–33; forces Haitians to sign treaty, 102;

on causes of Mexican Revolution, 127; convinced Germany desires war between United States and Mexico, 133–135; negotiates protocol for entry of Punitive Expedition into Mexico, 136–137; warns Carranza of danger of war, 141; and "strict accountability" note, 159–160; argues for strong protest in Thrasher case, 163; impact of *Lusitania* sinking on, 165; protests *Lusitania* postscript, 166; views on war, 175; investigates German intrigues, 200–201; begins *Lusitania* negotiations, 201; negotiations for disarming of merchant ships, 205–209; assures Germany of American friendship, 206; reverses position on armed ships, 210; his indiscretion, 210; and *Sussex* crisis and settlement, 215–218; protests British seizure of mails, 220; fears Wilson will retaliate against Britain, 221; refuses to discuss Anglo-American relations with Page, 222; Wilson consults on League speech, 233; unpleasant interview with Spring Rice, 253; warns Wilson of dangers of mediation, 258; on German peace offer, 260; and Wilson's peace note, 260; discusses "Peace without Victory" speech, 265; and decision to break relations with Germany, 267–268; affirms legality of arming ships, 274; urges war resolution, 276

Latin American policy of the United States, 1910–1917, origins and general aspects, 93–94, 103–104, 109; Nicaragua and United States, 94–97; Dominican Republic a n d United States, 97–99; Haiti and United States, 99–102; United States and major Latin American powers, 104; Colombian treaty, 104–105; Pan-American Pact, 105–106; limitations of, 106; relations between United States and Mexico, 1913–1914, 107–128; background and significance of Wilson's Mobile address, 117–118; United States and Mexican civil war, 128–133; United States recognizes Carranza

government, 133–135; sending of Punitive Expedition nearly provokes war between United States and Mexico, 136–142; Mexican-American Joint High Commission, 143; withdrawal of Punitive Expedition and *de jure* recognition of Carranza government by United States, 143–144

League of Nations, 233

League to Enforce Peace, 233

Lever, A. F., 225–226, 238

Lewis, David J., 70

Lind, John, goes to Mexico City as confidential agent, 113; presents Wilson's proposals to H u e r t a government, 114; is convinced British government supports Huerta, 116; urges Wilson t o depose Huerta by force, 122; dismissed as adviser on Mexico, 129

Lindsey, Ben B., 239

Lippitt, Henry F., 42

Lippmann, Walter, 239, 240, 279

Lloyd George, David, tax bill of 1909, 196; peace talks with House, 204; warns against mediation effort, 255; answers German peace offer, 260

Lloyd, Henry Demarest, 1

Loans, war, Bryan's ban, 151; revocation of ban, 152; negotiation of Anglo-French loan of 1915, 172–173; subsequent loans, 173; restriction of American credits, 258–259; and American intervention, 278–279

Lodge, Henry Cabot, leads fight against ratification of Colombian treaty, 105; urges strong action against Mexico, 124–125; opposes ship purchase bill, 153; supports Wilson in armed ship controversy, 214; attacks Wilson's foreign policy, 230; on necessity for special session, 271, 272; commends Wilson's war message, 282

Long, Boaz W., 99, 100

Lubin, David, 239

Ludendorff, Erich F. W., 255

Lusitania case and negotiations, 164–167, 201, 206, 210

Lusitania postscript episode, 166, 247

McAdoo, William G., leader in Wilson's preconvention campaign, 10; sketch of as Secretary of Treasury, 27; and framing of Federal Reserve bill, 46–48; and appointment of Federal Reserve Board, 76–77; acts in war crisis, 149; and cotton crisis of 1914, 149; and ships purchase bill, 152–153; urges Wilson to approve Anglo-French loan, 172; pushes revised shipping bill, 191–192; presents tax bill to pay for preparedness, 193; opposes anti-dumping measure, 228–229; urges arming of merchant ships, 270; urges war resolution, 276

McCombs, William F., 10, 25, 233

McConnell, Francis J., 239

McCormick, Vance C., 233, 243, 255

McKelway, A. J., 239

McLemore Resolution, 211–214

McReynolds, James C., sketch of as Attorney General, 28; new solution for trust problem, 76

Madden, Martin, 195

Madero, Francisco I., 107

Mails dispute, 220

Mann, James R., 183

Marina case, 254

Marsh, Benjamin, 193

Marshall, Thomas R., 206

Martin, Thomas S., 35, 166

Mayo, Henry T., and Tampico affair, 122

Mazatlán incident, 141

Mexican-American Joint High Commission, 143

Mexican Revolution, beginnings under Madero and counterrevolution by Huerta, 107–108; beginnings and early progress of Constitutionalist movement, 109, 120; triumph of Constitutionalists, 127–128; great schism in Revolution, 1914–1915, 128–131; triumph of Carranza, 131–135; adoption of Constitution of 1917 and establishment of *de jure* government, 144

Mexico and the United States, 1910–1917, United States and Huerta regime, 107–128; Tampico affair and occupation of Vera Cruz, 122–125; ABC mediation, 126–127; triumph of the Revolution, 127–128; United States supports Villa in civil war, 129–131; Pan-American conferences on Mexico, 133–135; Santa Ysabel massacre, 136; Columbus raid, 136; formation and sending of Punitive Expedition, 136–138; development of war situation, 138; Scott-Obregón conferences, 138–139; Glen Springs, Texas, raid, 140; Carrizal incident leads to verge of war, 141–142; Mexican-American Joint High Commission, 143; withdrawal of Punitive Expedition and *de jure* recognition of Carranza government by United States, 143–144; German agents try to stir trouble between, 200; Mexican-American relations as an issue in campaign of 1916, 230, 232, 237, 239, 246, 251

Mitchel, John Purroy, 52

Mobile Address, Wilson's, 117–118

Moore, John Bassett, on seamen's bill, 62; prevents Wilson from sending insulting note to London, 117–118

Morey, Lewis S., 141–142

Morgan, House of, withdraws from thirty directorships, 67–68; and French loan of 1914, 151; and French commercial credit, 152; negotiates Anglo-French loan of 1915, 173; attempts to extend short-term credit to British, 258–259

Morgan, J. Pierpont, Jr., 76

Morgan, J. Pierpont, Sr., 12

Morrison, Frank, 73

Mott, John R., 143

Munitions-makers and American intervention, 279

Murdock, Victor, 239–240

Murphy, Charles F., 13

Nation, disappointed by Hughes campaign, 237; supports Wilson in 1916, 241

National Association for the Advancement of Colored People, 54, 65

National Association of Manufacturers, 227

National Child Labor Committee, and advanced progressivism, 54; sponsors child labor bill in 1914, 59; sponsors child labor bill in 1916, 226–227

National City Bank of New York, and Dominican finances, 98; and Haiti, 100; and war loans, 152

National Farmers' Union, 54

National Guard, Wilson calls to Mexican border, 140; Army War College proposes to scrap, 179–180; controversy over, 184, 186; provision for control in House army bill, 187; provisions for expansion and federal control of in Army Act of 1916, 188; called by President in railroad strike crisis, 236; called into federal service, 277

National Monetary Commission, 44

National Security League, formation, 177; issues manifesto, 178; urges Wilson to veto Army Act, 188–189

Naval Appropriations Act of 1916, General Board proposes program of expansion, 179; House bill, 189; Senate bill, 190; Wilson wins adoption of Senate bill as final measure, 190

Navy League of the United States, 177–178, 179, 180

Negroes, Wilson's promises to in 1912, 63–64; segregation in federal departments under Wilson, 64–66; Negroes protest segregation, 65

New Freedom, see Wilson, Woodrow

New Haven Railroad antitrust case, 76

New Nationalism, see Roosevelt, Theodore

New Republic, disappointed by Hughes' campaign, 237; supports Wilson in 1916, 241; influences Wilson's views on peace settlement, 264–265

New York Times, The, disappointed by Hughes' campaign, 237; supports Wilson in 1916, 241

New York World, exposes intrigue behind appointment of J. M. Sullivan as Minister to Santo Domingo, 97; publishes revelations of German propaganda, 167; pub-lishes documents on German-American Alliance, 214; comments on Hughes' campaign, 238; concedes Republican victory in 1916, 247–248; demands war resolution, 274

Newlands, Francis G., 68

Nicaragua and the United States, 1909–1917, 94, 96–97, 103–104, 109

Non-Partisan League, 54, 240

Norris, George W., and income tax of 1913, 39; vote on Federal Reserve bill, 52; and Revenue Act of 1916, 195; opposes armed ship bill, 273; speech against war resolution, 278; votes against war resolution, 282

Obregón, Álvaro, 130–131, 139–140

O'Gorman, James A., 51–52, 92–93

Okuma, Count, 87, 89

O'Leary, Jeremiah A., 247

Orduna, 168

Oreste, Michel, 99

O'Shaughnessy, Nelson, 113

Outlook, 177

Overman, Lee S., 42

Owen, Robert L., Democratic leader in Senate, 35; and writing of Federal Reserve bill, 47–49; supports measure for control of stock exchanges, 70–71

Padgett, Lemuel, 190

Page, Walter H., leader in Wilson's preconvention campaign, 10; Panama Canal tolls dispute, 91; comments on House's mediation efforts, 161; on issues of the war, 174; Wilson's opinion of, 199; on Grey's dismay over Lansing's modus vivendi, 208–209; dismayed by anti-British sentiment in administration, 222; transmits Zimmermann "note," 271; appeals for credit for British government, 276

Panama Canal tolls dispute, 90–93

Pan-American Pact, 105–106

Pani, Alberto J., 143

Papen, Franz von, 200–201

Parker, Alton B., 12

Parker, John M., 232, 239

Parral incident, 138

Payne-Aldrich tariff of 1909, 3, 38, 40
Peabody, George Foster, 182
Peace issue in campaign of 1916, 241–244, 249–250
"Peace without Victory" speech, 264–266
Pearson's Magazine, 241
Perkins, George C., 52
Pershing, John J., 137, 141
Persia case, 208
Philippine Islands, 227–228
Pinchot, Amos, 239
Pinchot, Gifford, and the Ballinger affair, 3; and Roosevelt-Taft estrangement, 5; and controversy over general leasing bill, 30
Pittman, Key, 212
Plunkett, Sir Horace, 161, 209
Poindexter, Miles, 52
Polk, Frank L., and "blacklist" dispute, 220–221, 252; comments on Anglo-American tension, 253
Pollock, Sir Frederick, 148
Pomerene, Atlee, 35
Preparedness movement, beginnings, 177; literature of, 178; becomes crusade, 178–179; General Board's program, 179; War College's program, 179–180; opposition develops, 180–182; antipreparedness group controls House, 183; controversy in House over army bill, 183–184, 186; sectional alignment, 185–186; Wilson's preparedness tour, 185; adoption and provisions of Army Reorganization Act, 187–188; writing and adoption of Naval Appropriations Act, 189–190; adoption of Shipping Act, 191–192; paying for preparedness, 192–196
Progressive movement, origins, 1–2; and Republican party, 1901–1909, 2; divergence in ideology and movement, 1909–1912, 18–22; advanced segment of, 1913–1915, 54–55; Wilson's refusal to yield to advanced program, 54–66; Wilson accepts advanced program for regulation of business, 66–72; Wilson announces consummation of program, 79–80; and foreign policy and preparedness, 180–181; and culmination of democratic tax program, 192–196; Wilson adopts advanced progressive program, 224–230; progressives support Wilson in 1916, 239–241
Progressive party, organized, 16; platform in 1912, 16; election of 1912, 22–24; last effort during election of 1914, 78; Roosevelt disbands in 1916, 232; many leaders of party support Wilson in 1916, 239–240; significance of vote in election of 1916, 250
Propaganda and the First World War, 145–148, 279
Punitive Expedition, formation, 136; sent into Mexico, 137; strength of, 137; threatened by Carranza, 140; withdrawn, 144
Pusey, Merlo J., 238
Putnam, George Haven, 176

Quick, Herbert, 240

Ragsdale, J. Willard, 49
Railroad brotherhoods, and strike crisis of 1916, 235–237; and strike crisis of 1917, 237; and campaign of 1916, 240
Railroad securities bill, 68, 70
Rainey, Henry T., 228
Rauschenbusch, Walter, 146
Rayburn, Sam, 68
Reading, Lord, 204
Record, George L., 16, 193
Redfield, William C., sketch of as Secretary of Commerce, 31; states purpose of Federal Trade Commission, 74; suggests anti-dumping measure, 228; urges war resolution, 276
Reed, James A., and income tax of 1913, 39; opposes Federal Reserve bill, 51–52; comments on weakening of Clayton bill, 72
Reed, John, 239
Reid, Ogden, 176
Reinsch, Paul S., 89
Republican party, background of disruption of, 3–6; disruption of, 1911–1912, 13–16; election of 1912, 22–24; resurgence during

election of 1914, 78; situation in early 1916, 223; preconvention campaign of 1916, 230–231; Chicago convention of 1916, 231–232; platform of 1916, 232; campaign of 1916, 237–247; election of 1916, 247–251

Revenue Act of 1916, 192–196

Reynolds, George M., 51

Robinson, Joseph T., 35

Roman Catholic Church, campaign for intervention in Mexico, 132; resents recognition of Carranza, 135; desires repeal of Reform Laws, 135; opposes independence for Philippines, 227–228; Catholics and election of 1916, 251

Roosevelt, Theodore, contribution to progressive movement, 1901–1909, 2–3; estrangement from Taft, 5–6; enunciates New Nationalism during campaign of 1910, 6; unsuccessful bid for Republican presidential nomination in 1912, 14–15; organizes Progressive party, 16; development of New Nationalism, 18–20; and campaign and election of 1912, 20–24; on results of election of 1914, 78; condemns conciliation treaties, 82; and Colombian treaty, 104–105; opens campaign for intervention in Mexico, 132; for war during Lusitania crisis, 164; views on war, 175; denounces Wilson's failure to protest violation of Belgian neutrality, 175; characterizes Wilson's diplomacy, 176; assumes leadership of preparedness agitation, 177; denounces Army Reorganization Act, 188; campaigns for Republican nomination in 1916, 231–232; embarrasses Hughes, 244–245; issues call for war, 274; commends Wilson's war message, 282

Root, Elihu, contribution to Federal Reserve bill, 52–53; heartsick at thought of war with Mexico, 125; views on First World War, 146, 175; opposes ship purchase bill, 153; opinion on Lusitania sinking, 165; attacks Wilson's foreign policy, 230; boom for President in 1916, 231; commends Wilson's war message, 282

Rublee, George L., and writing of Federal Trade Commission bill, 71–72; disappointed over failure of Federal Trade Commission, 74–75; Senate refuses to confirm nomination as trade commissioner, 74

"Rule of Reason," 67, 71

Rural credits, see Federal Farm Loan Act of 1916

Russell, Charles Edward, 274

Russell, William W., 26, 98–99

Russian Revolution, 275

Ryan, Thomas Fortune, 12

Sam, Vilbrun G., 101–102

Scott, Hugh L., 129, 135, 139, 140, 140–141, 269

Scripps, E. W., 239, 241

Seamen's Act of 1915, 61–63

Segregation, see Negroes

Seymour, Charles, 204

Shaw, Anna Howard, 22

Sherwood, Isaac R., 70

Ship purchase bill of 1914–1915, 152-153

Shipping Act of 1916, 191–192

Simmons, Furnifold M., Democratic leader in Senate, 35; and politics of Underwood tariff bill in Senate, 39–42

Sims, T. W., 212

Sinclair, Upton, 274

Six-Power Consortium, origins, 82–83; American withdrawal from, 83–84

Slayden, James L., 105

Smith, Charles C., 101

Smith, Hoke, 206

Smith, James, Jr., 10

Snyder, Edgar C., 239

Socialist party, and campaign of 1912, 16–17; election of 1912, 22; and campaign of 1916, 239, 249–250; and war resolution, 274, 275

Southern agrarians, revolt against Federal Reserve bill, 48–50; plans for destruction of oligarchical economic structure, 70–71

Speyer, James, 108, 160–161

Spring Rice, Sir Cecil, British

Ambassador to United States, 161; negotiates cotton agreement, 171; Wilson's opinion of, 199; and Lansing's indiscretion, 210; unpleasant interview with Lansing, 253

Steffens, Lincoln, 239

Sterling, Thomas, 52

Stevens, Raymond B., 71–72

Stimson, Henry L., 176

Stone, William J., Democratic leader in Senate, 35; wavers in support of Wilson's Mexican policy, 136; assures G e r m a n y of American friendship, 206; and armed ship controversy of 1916, 211–212; and Democratic platform of 1916, 233; discusses "Peace without Victory" speech, 265

Submarine controversy, see Germany and the United States and Germany

Sullivan, James M., 97–98

Sullivan, Roger, 13

Sullivan, Timothy, 98

"Sunrise Conference," 212–213

Sussex crisis and settlement, 215–218

Taft, William Howard, and beginning of disruption of Republican party, 3–4; attacks insurgents, 4–5; becomes estranged from Roosevelt, 5–6; defeats Roosevelt for presidential nomination in 1912, 14–15; and campaign of 1912, 17; vote in election of 1912, 22–24; vetoes bill to exempt labor from prosecution under antitrust law, 55–56; comments on Wilson's signing of Sundry Civil Act, 56; vetoes seamen's bill in 1913, 62; refuses to recognize Huerta, 108; condemns Wilson's Mexican policy, 125; helps defeat Clarke amendment, 228; and the preconvention campaign of 1916, 230

Tampico affair, 122–123

Tansill, Charles C., 211, 213

Tarbell, Ida M., 239

Tariff Commission of 1916, 228

Thrasher case, 162–164

Théodore, Davilmar, 101

Tillman, Ben, 189

Tolls dispute, 90–93

Trotter, William Monroe, 63, 66

Tumulty, Joseph P., sketch of as Secretary to President, 31–32; protests Lusitania postscript, 166; urges Wilson to appeal to country on preparedness, 185; and the armed ship controversy of 1916, 212

Twenty-One D e m a n d s, Japanese-American crisis over, 87–90

Tyrrell, Sir William, 91, 119

Underwood, Oscar W., campaign for Democratic presidential nomination in 1912, 12; and Baltimore convention, 13; leader in House, 35; and writing of Underwood tariff bill, 36–40; opposes Wilson in tolls dispute, 92; elected to Senate, 183; and Democratic platform of 1916, 233

Underwood Tariff Act of 1913, 35–43

Union League of New York, 274

United States Chamber of Commerce, 71

United States Shipping Board, 191

United States Steel Corporation, 76

Untermyer, Samuel, and writing of Federal Reserve bill, 47; criticizes Clayton bill, 69; supports measure for control of stock exchanges, 70–71

Vardaman, James K., 39

Vera Cruz affair, occupation by United States, 123; Wilson's motivation, 123–124; Latin American and European reactions, 124; American reaction, 124–125

Viereck, George Sylvester, 272

Vigilancia, 274

Villa, Francisco, opposes Carranza during Vera Cruz crisis, 126; schemes to control Mexico and begins war against Carranza, 128–129; concurs in American plan for new government for Mexico, 129–130; joins forces with Zapata and seizes control at Aguascalientes convention, 130–131; defeated by Obregón, 131; offers to make peace with Carranza, 133–134; massacres Americans at Santa Ysabel, 136;

executes raid on Columbus, New Mexico, 136; escapes capture by Punitive Expedition, 137; raids Glen Springs, Texas, 140; and German intrigues, 200

Villard, Oswald Garrison, advises Wilson on race problem, 64; protests segregation, 65; denounces Germany, 148; active in peace and antipreparedness movements, 182

Wade, Festus J., 51
Wald, Lillian D., 182, 239
Walling, William English, 274
Walsh, Thomas J., Democratic leader in Senate, 35; and politics of Underwood tariff bill, 40–41; and Democratic platform of 1916, 233; and peace issue in 1916, 243
War Risk Insurance Bureau, 150–151, 272, 273
Warburg, Paul M., and framing of Aldrich Plan, 44; and framing of Federal Reserve bill, 46; controversy over appointment to Federal Reserve Board, 77
Ward, Lester F., 1
Washington, Booker T., 65
Webb, E. Y., 69–70
Weeks, John W., 52
West, Andrew F., 9
West, Duval, 132–133
Wexler, Sol, 51
White, Edward D., 67
White, William Allen, 5, 18, 250
Wilhelmina case, 157
William II, Emperor, orders abandonment of unrestricted submarine warfare, 169; and *Sussex* crisis, 216–217; agrees to peace campaign and, that failing, to approve unrestricted submarine warfare, 259
Williams, John Sharp, comments on Wilson, 32; urges abolition of "rule of reason," 67; on anti-British sentiment in South, 170
Willis, H. Parker, 45–46, 52
Wilson, Henry Lane, advises recognition of Huerta, 108; role in Huerta coup, 111–112; dismissed as Ambassador to Mexico, 113; Hughes' chief adviser on Mexico, 237
Wilson, William B., as Secretary of

Labor, 31; sponsors seamen's bill in 1912, 61–62; urges war resolution, 267
Wilson, Woodrow, new Democratic leader, 7; biographical sketch, 8; as president of Princeton University, 8–9; nominated and elected Governor of New Jersey, 9–10; and reform movement in New Jersey, 10; campaigns for presidential nomination, 10–11; near failure of campaign, 12; nomination for presidency, 13; enunciates New Freedom, 20–22; election, 22–24; maps legislative program and appoints Cabinet, 25–33; sketch of in early 1913, 32–33; inaugural, 33–34; his system of presidential leadership, 34–35; and writing and adoption of Underwood tariff bill, 35–43; and writing and adoption of Federal Reserve bill, 45–52; relations with advanced wing of progressive movement, 54–55; opposes exempting labor from prosecution under antitrust law, 56, 69–70, 73; opposes plan to establish federal rural credits system, 56–59; refuses to support child labor bill, 59; opposes women's suffrage, 59–60; vetoes Burnett immigration bills of 1915 and 1917, 60–61; and passage of Seamen's Act, 61–63; and Negro question, 63–64; and segregation controversy, 64–66; formulates New Freedom program for business, 66–69; abandons New Freedom program for business control and adopts Rooseveltian solution, 70–72; loses interest in Clayton bill, 72; purpose of antitrust program, 74; campaign to win friendship of business community, 75–76; appointment of Federal Reserve Board raises controversy, 76–78; disheartened by congressional election of 1914, 78–79; announces consummation of progressive program, 79; character of Wilson's progressivism, 79–80; dynamics of Wilson's foreign policy, 81–82; and dispute with Japan over California alien land act of 1913, 84–87; and

crisis over Twenty-One Demands, 87–90; and Panama Canal tolls dispute, 90–93; origins, formulation, and motivation of his Latin American and Caribbean policies, 93–94, 103–104; Nicaraguan policy, 94–97; Dominican policy, 97–99; Haitian policy, 99–102; relations with Huerta government of Mexico, 1913–1914, 107–128; early attempts to control Constitutionalist movement are rebuffed, 120–121; revokes arms embargo against Mexico, 121–122; and Tampico Affair, 122–123; orders occupation of Vera Cruz, 123–124; and ABC mediation, 126–128; turns against Carranza and supports Villa, 129–131; plans intervention in Mexico, 132–133; resents Catholic interference, 135–136; prepares for war with Mexico, 137–142; refuses to go to war with Mexico, 142–143; orders withdrawal of Punitive Expedition, 144; issues proclamation of neutrality, 148; urges adoption of measures to meet war crisis, 150–151; and question of war loans, 151–152; futile struggle for ship purchase bill, 152–153; replies to German submarine challenge, 159–160; attempts to obtain British-German agreement on blockade and submarines, 160; first efforts at mediation, 160–162; attempts to formulate policy toward submarines in Thrasher case, 162–164; during *Lusitania* crisis, 165–166; negotiations with German government, 166–167; obtains satisfaction in *Arabic* case, 168–169; and cotton crisis of 1915, 170–171; deprecates preparedness talk, 177–178; takes up preparedness, 179; presents preparedness program to country, 180; loses control of House, 183; campaigns for preparedness through East and Midwest, 185; accepts House army plan, 186; contributions to Army Reorganization Act, 188; supports Senate naval bill, 190; concurs in House's plan to end war through mediation, 198–199; opinion of Page and Spring Rice, 199; alarmed by German intrigues in Mexico and United States, 200–201; purpose of his proposed mediation, 205; and discussion over armed ships, 205–209; reverses position on armed ships, 210; and controversy over armed ships, 210–214; and *Sussex* crisis and settlement, 215–218; hardening of attitude toward British, 218–220; obtains retaliatory power from Congress, 220–221; confers with Page, 222; adopts advanced progressivism, 224–225; names Brandeis to Supreme Court, 225; supports rural credits bill, 225–226; supports workmen's compensation bill, 226; forces passage of child labor bill, 226–227; supports measures to aid business, 228–229; plans for campaign of 1916, 232–233; renominated by St. Louis convention, 234; and railroad strike crisis, 235–237; assumes leadership of progressives during campaign of 1916, 238–241; takes leadership of peace forces, 241–242; and election of 1916, 247–251; angered by British maritime practices, 253; unwilling to raise submarine issue during campaign, 254; determines to end war to avoid American intervention, 255–257; reads draft of peace note, 257–258; spurns Anglo-American co-operation for peace, 258; urges tightening credit to Allies, 259; impressed by German peace offer, 260; issues peace appeal, 260–261; negotiates directly with German and British governments, 261–264; voices American peace objectives in "Peace without Victory" speech, 264–266; breaks relations with Germany, 266–268; continues to hope for peace, 268; refuses to sanction arming of merchant ships, 269–270; receives Zimmermann message, asks Congress for authority to arm merchant ships, 271; publishes Zimmermann "note," 272; denounces opponents of armed ship bill, 273–274; arms merchant ships, 274; makes reluctant decision for war, 275–276; calls Congress into special session and begins war preparations, 276–277; talk with Frank Cobb, 277; his despair, 277–278; an analysis of his policies toward belligerents, 280; delivers war message and signs war resolution, 281–282

Wiseman, Sir William, 264
Wister, Owen, 176
Women's Peace party, 182
Woolley, Robert W., 241–242
Works, John D., 52
World War, First, American reaction to, 145, 174–177; German and British propaganda in United States, 145–148; early economic impact on American economy, 149–150; administration measures to meet war crisis, 150–151; military situation in January 1916, 202; causes for American entry into, 278–281

Zamor, Charles and Oreste, 99–101
Zapata, Emiliano, 130–131
Zaragoza, Morelos, 122
Zelaya, José Santos, 94, 96
Zimmermann, Alfred, sends instructions during peace negotiations, 262; message to Minister in Mexico, 271; admits authenticity of message, 273
Zimmermann "note," 271–273
Zwiedinek, Erich, 209

Set in Intertype Baskerville
Format by D. F. Bradley
Manufactured by The Haddon Craftsmen, Inc.
Published by HARPER & BROTHERS, *New York*